SUPER **50** BOWL

CELEBRATING FIFTY YEARS

50

SUPER BOWL

OF AMERICA'S GREATEST GAME

BETHANY BRADSHER

JKR VENTURES, LLC

FOREWORD BY DWIGHT CLARK

JKR Ventures titles are available at quantity discounts when purchased in bulk for client gifts, sales promotions, and premiums. Special editions, including books with corporate logos, customized covers, and letters from the company printed in the front matter can be created in large quantities for special uses.

For details and discount information contact Jerrold Jenkins at jrj@bookpublishing.com or call 231-883-5365.

Published by
JKR Ventures, LLC
Traverse City, MI
www.SuperBowl50Book.com

Second Printing: October 2015
Publisher's Cataloging-in-Publication Data
Bradsher, Bethany.

Super Bowl 50 : celebrating fifty years of America's greatest game / Bethany Bradsher. – Traverse City, MI : JKR Ventures, LLC, 2015.

p. ; cm.

ISBN13: 978-0-9860850-0-0 (hardcover)
978-0-9860850-1-7 (softcover)

1. Super Bowl—History. 2. Football—United States—History. I. Title.

GV956.2.S8 B73 2015
796.332648—dc23   2015937816

"THE SPIRIT, THE WILL TO WIN, AND THE WILL TO EXCEL ARE THE THINGS THAT ENDURE. THESE QUALITIES ARE SO MUCH MORE IMPORTANT THAN THE EVENTS THAT OCCUR."

Vince Lombardi

CONTENTS

FOREWORD

The game of football gave me plenty of unforgettable moments over the years, and some of the ones I cherish the most happened at the Super Bowl. In my third season with the San Francisco 49ers, we won Super Bowl XVI, my teammates and I won a second ring three years later in Super Bowl XIX, and I was privileged to be part of the team's front office for three more Super Bowl victories between 1989 and 1995.

Each of those big games was special, but just as memorable for me was the path to the first Super Bowl. The Cowboys were heavy favorites going into the NFC Championship Game, and they were leading by six with less than a minute remaining when I leaped up to snag a high, short pass from Joe Montana that the world now knows as "the Catch." Before that play, the 49ers were just another team aiming for glory, but the Catch kicked off an era of excellence that made us the Super Bowl dynasty team of the 1980s.

It was a thrilling time to live and play by the Bay. Montana could engineer a comeback drive like no one ever had, and as one of his favorite receivers, I got to lend my own fireworks to the development of a legendary team. In my eight years with the team, there was always that winning attitude — that firm belief that we could make it to the Super Bowl over and over.

The Super Bowl gets bigger and flashier every year, and everyone associated with the 49ers is thrilled that our city gets to host the game's biggest milestone so far — Super Bowl 50 at Levi's Stadium. The 49ers brought so much Super Bowl glory to our city decades ago, and with the golden anniversary, we can recapture some of that excitement, even as we work to claim another Lombardi Trophy for the 49ers organization.

From the big plays that changed the course of the game to the legendary players and coaches, the Super Bowl has been the source of some amazing stories over 50 years, and when you add in the halftime shows, the commercials, and everything thing else that makes this game an event, you'll understand why the Super Bowl is worthy of this epic book. No other game is like it, and I'm grateful that my stories live on as part of this larger Super Bowl tale.

Dwight Clark, two-time Super Bowl champion (XIV, XIX)

INTRODUCTION

When Green Bay fullback Jim Taylor rode Vince Lombardi's famed power sweep play to a 14-yard touchdown run that put his team up for good in Super Bowl I, he celebrated at the Los Angeles Coliseum in front of 61,946 fans—and 31,661 empty seats. Fans objected, it seemed, to the steep $12 ticket price.

The game was broadcast on two different networks, but neither NBC nor CBS thought twice about wiping the tapes and recording different footage over what would have become prized treasures for collectors. At the time, the network executives didn't see much point in saving copies of the first AFL-NFL Championship Game.

The game was big enough by football standards, certainly, but nothing that transpired on any gridiron threatened the supremacy of baseball, which truly was, in that era, America's game. In just a half century, football would stage a thorough coup and take over as the most dominant feature on the sports landscape, and nothing demonstrates that shift as vividly as the ascendancy of the game known first informally, and then officially, as the Super Bowl.

The Super Bowl is a spectacle, a behemoth, a cultural phenomenon so towering that tickets sell legally for close to $3,500 and fetch five or six figures through less conventional avenues. And since most fans will never get to breathe the rarified air of a live Super Bowl, the game has barreled into virtually every living room in America, thus sparking a trend of watch parties that has made the first Sunday in February the second-highest day for national food consumption, after Thanksgiving.

Then there are the commercials ($4.5 million and rising for a 30-second spot), the halftime shows (elaborate productions featuring the biggest names in pop music), and a full slate of festivities in the host city that gives everyone from players and coaches to media and sponsors a moment in the white-hot glow.

Of course, all this would eventually be exposed as mere window dressing without the football. The Super Bowl is flush with both flash and substance, thanks to trends such as the one that saw seven out of the past 11 games decided by less than a touchdown. Blowouts, such as the 43-8 drubbing the Seahawks gave the Broncos in 2014, do happen, but the hope of the next year—when the world's most talented football players will battle at the top of their game in front of 111 million TV viewers—is always there to build the anticipation to an ever-higher fever pitch.

Featured in a starring role are the players: legends such as Bart Starr, Joe Montana, and Tom Brady alongside more obscure names such as James Harrison and David Tyree, who made unforgettable cameos on the world's biggest sports stage. They join with a succession of legendary coaches, from Lombardi to Noll to Belicheck, whose leadership has given weight and legacy to the game that, over five decades, has become something that those fans in 1967 Los Angeles would find unrecognizabie.

Each winter, all things Super Bowl become bigger, grander, and more exorbitant, from media coverage, to security preparations, to the amount of guacamole consumed nationwide. The game itself, with its grand objective of crowning a world champion in a distinctly American sport, has embraced this happy excess and absorbed every new development, such as a record 24.9 million tweets sent via Twitter during the 2014 broadcast, into its powerful orbit.

Futurists will surely speculate about the new heights the Super Bowl will scale in the next 50 years, with the assurance that our country's growing obsession with technology will somehow manage to make the game even more ubiquitous than it is today. Amid the glitz and the dollars, though, the heart of this event is unchanged—two teams measuring their grit and skill against each other and millions of fans buoyed by the hope that this is the year their team will hold the Lombardi Trophy aloft.

PART 1

THE G

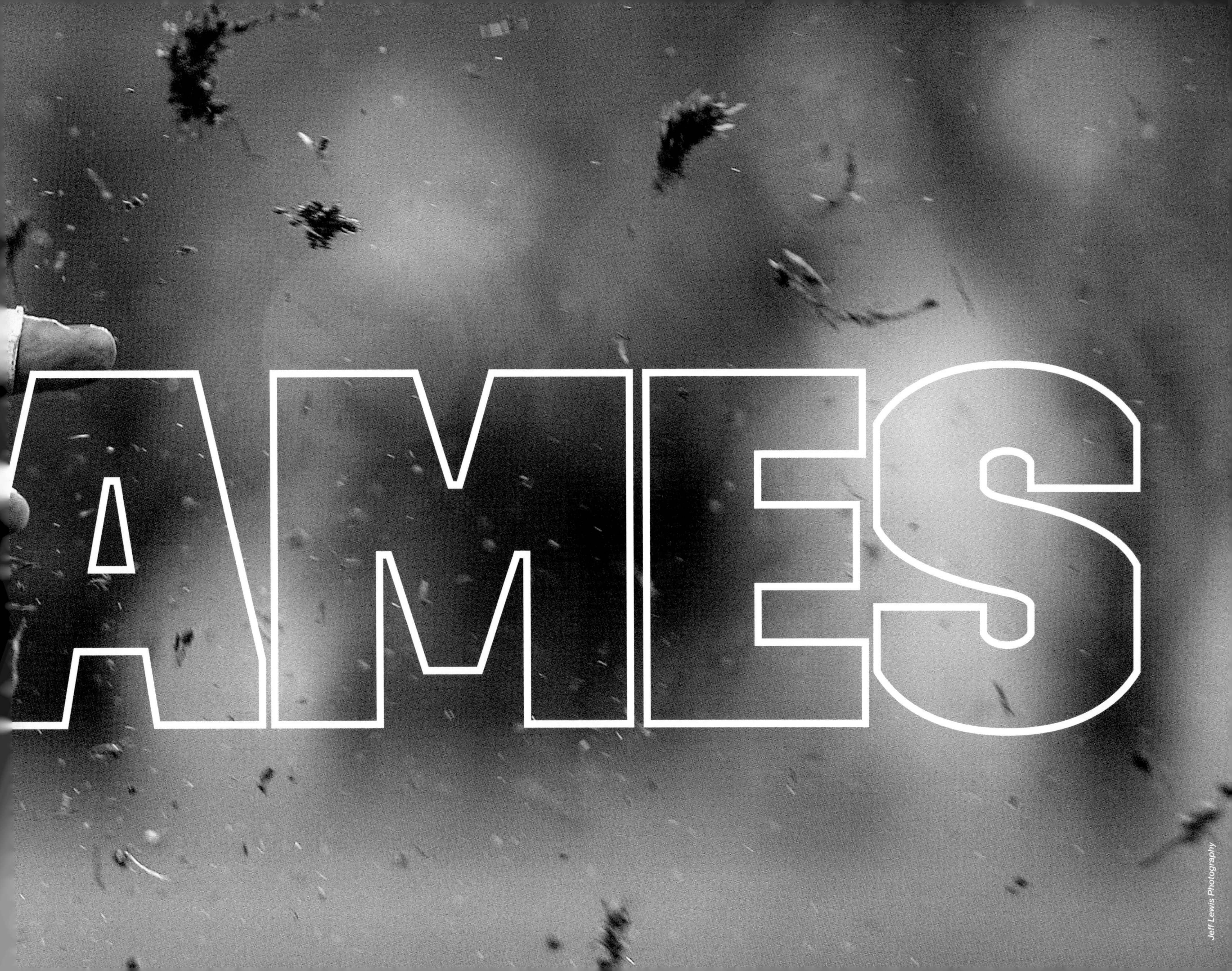

Jeff Lewis Photography

"WE'RE GOING TO WIN ON SUNDAY. I GUARANTEE IT."

Joe Namath

CHAPTER 1: THE 1960s

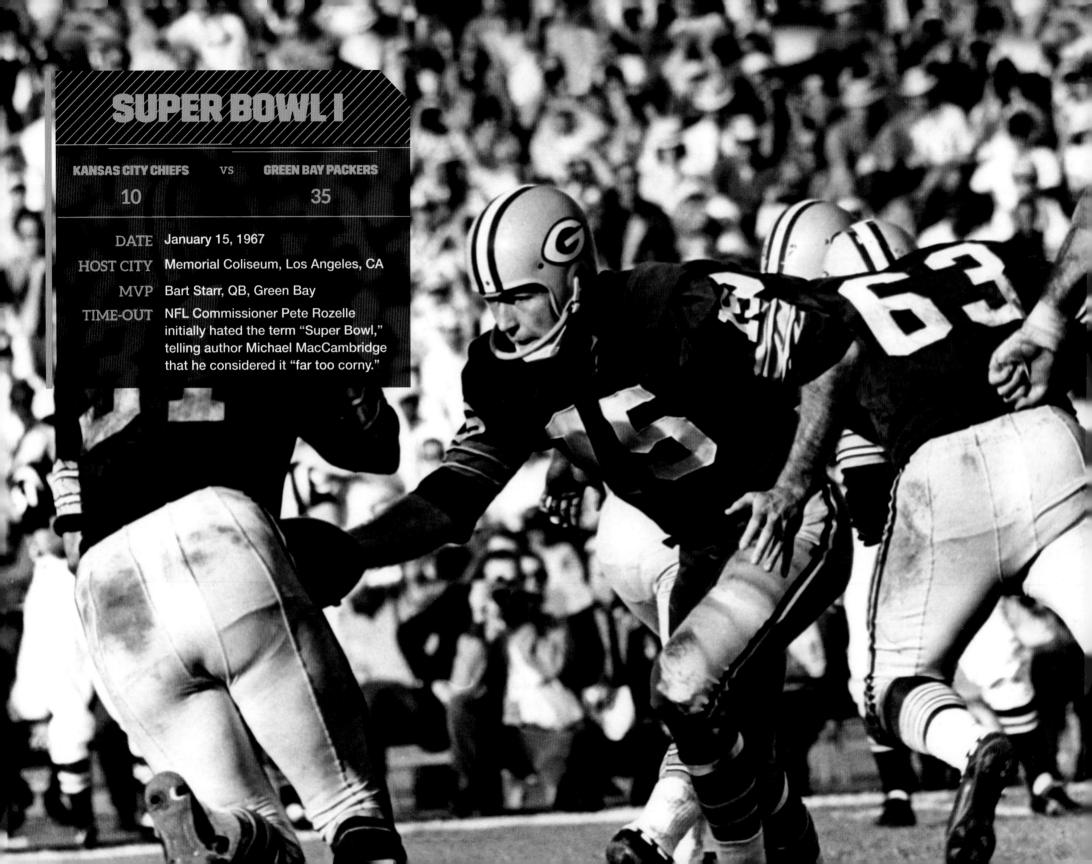

SUPER BOWL I

KANSAS CITY CHIEFS VS **GREEN BAY PACKERS**

10   **35**

DATE   January 15, 1967

HOST CITY Memorial Coliseum, Los Angeles, CA

MVP   Bart Starr, QB, Green Bay

TIME-OUT   NFL Commissioner Pete Rozelle
           initially hated the term "Super Bowl,"
           telling author Michael MacCambridge
           that he considered it "far too corny."

Green Bay Packers defensive end Lionel Aldridge (82) pressures Kansas City Chiefs Hall of Fame quarterback Len Dawson (16).
AP Photo/NFL Photos

The first Super Bowl was conceived because of intense competition—but not the kind that occurred between the end zones.

It was 1966, and the upstart American Football League (AFL) had been striving to reach equal footing with the established National Football League (NFL) for six years. With a lucrative TV contract with NBC, several top draft picks (notably Joe Namath and Gale Sayers) choosing AFL teams over NFL, and new commissioner Al Davis's poaching of established NFL players to the other side, executives in both leagues were starting to realize that something had to give.

Unbeknownst to Davis, owners in the AFL and NFL began to hold secret meetings in 1966 with the goal of reaching terms for a merger. On June 8, 1966, a merger deal became public, with the condition that the two leagues would not officially become one until the 1970 season. One outgrowth of the newfound warmth between the leagues was a proposed championship game between the top teams of each league, and the game that would soon be known as the Super Bowl was born.

Despite the fact that its official moniker did not become attached to the big game until 1970, media outlets were referring to the championship game as the Super Bowl as early as the fall of 1966. Common lore credits Chiefs owner Lamar Hunt with coming up with the name "Super Bowl," and an oft-repeated yarn supported by Hunt himself says that his inspiration was a "super ball" toy he had watched his daughter bounce around. In 2011, *The Atlantic* writer Henry Fetter questioned Hunt's role in the naming, primarily because he found numerous press references to the Super Bowl months before the meeting where Hunt's idea for the name was purportedly introduced.

The premier game, ambitiously titled the NFL-AFL World Championship in official communication, was scheduled for January 15, 1967, two weeks after the league title games that had established the Green Bay Packers and the Kansas City Chiefs as the competitors. Despite the increasingly bold landgrabs the AFL had been making in recent years, NFL owners and coaches had long considered their league superior, and the game at Memorial Coliseum in Los Angeles was the first concrete opportunity to give credence to their boasts.

The Packers, representing the NFL, came in as 13-point favorites, despite a near miss to the Dallas Cowboys in the NFL Championship Game. Coach Vince Lombardi had led his team to three NFL titles in his seven years, and his marching orders as he prepared his troops for the Chiefs were clear. "The Packers were expected to uphold the honor and prestige of the 47-year-old NFL against the 7-year-old AFL, not only by winning but by winning big," wrote Bob McGinn in *The Ultimate Super Bowl Book*. "Losing? Well, that was out of the question."

With four-time Pro Bowler Bart Starr running the offense, the Packers scored evenly in the first half, with one touchdown per quarter, but the Chiefs found their rhythm in the second quarter and went to the locker room trailing just 14-10, the first

world championship still in their grasp. At halftime, Lombardi instructed defensive coordinator Phil Bengtson to turn on the pressure, and Green Bay came out in the third quarter with the first blitz of the game.

The show of defensive force, unusual for a Lombardi-led team, had its intended effect, and the Chiefs didn't find the end zone again that afternoon. The final score, 35-10 in favor of Green Bay, satisfied the NFL loyalists and cemented Lombardi's legacy as one of the greatest ever to coach pro football.

The first-ever most valuable player award went to Starr, the unlikely superstar who came into the league in 1956 as a seventeenth-round draft pick with a reputation for subpar throwing mechanics. But even though Starr, who went 16 of 23 for 250 yards in the game, was a worthy recipient of the honor, the Packer who made the most unexpected impact on the game's outcome was wide receiver Max McGee.

McGee was 34 years old, a backup receiver to Boyd Dowler, and he showed up in L.A. expecting to get very little playing time. But he had made the trip from the frozen tundra of Wisconsin to sunny Southern California, and he was determined to have a good time while he was there. Lombardi enforced a strict curfew, but McGee lay still under his covers, fully clothed, during bed check and then slipped out of the hotel and had a rendezvous with some airline stewardesses in Beverly Hills. When Starr

headed to breakfast at about 7:30 a.m. on game day, he passed a bleary-eyed McGee on his way in from his big night. "He didn't worry about his late night out affecting his performance because, with his career winding down, he didn't expect to play at all," Starr told a reporter later.

On the Packers' second play, Dowler went down with an injury, and McGee heard Lombardi call his name. He jumped up, put on a helmet ("I'm pretty sure it was someone else's," he said), and proceeded to have one of the biggest games of his life. On the day, McGee had seven receptions for 138 yards and two

touchdowns—the first of which was an acrobatic grab of an overthrown Starr pass that McGee ran in for a 7-0 Packers lead. That catch, from a player who expected to camp out on the bench all afternoon, is considered one of the most legendary in Super Bowl history.

McGee's offensive theatrics were an unexpected spark for a Green Bay team that was loaded with talent and characterized by precise, mistake-free football. One fan in attendance at the L.A. Coliseum told a reporter that he was backing Kansas City because "rooting for Green Bay is like rooting for an IBM

machine," but the efficiency of the Lombardi system made his team difficult to beat.

Emotionally, it didn't hurt that the Packers players took the field with the expectations of proving NFL supremacy on their shoulders. Despite talented Chiefs such as precision-passing quarterback Len Dawson and the 6-foot-7, 287-pound defensive tackle Buck Buchanan, the Chiefs just didn't have enough ammunition to stop the Packer machine. For at least one more year, the NFL backers could rest secure in their league's legacy.

Opposite page, Green Bay Packers wide receiver Max McGee (85) makes a juggling touchdown catch. *AP Photo/NFL Photos*

Top, Green Bay Packers Hall of Fame quarterback Bart Starr (15) barks signals. *AP Photo/NFL Photos*

SUPER BOWL II

GREEN BAY PACKERS VS **OAKLAND RAIDERS**

33 **14**

DATE — January 14, 1968

HOST CITY — Orange Bowl, Miami, FL

MVP — Bart Starr, QB, Green Bay

TIME-OUT — Super Bowl II was Vince Lombardi's last game as the head coach of the Green Bay Packers.

The Super Bowl may have been in its infancy, but the Green Bay Packers were already a bona fide dynasty as 1968 dawned and the Super Bowl matchup between the Packers and the Oakland Raiders was revealed. Green Bay was a team that had become accustomed to winning flashy trophies, and the spark that set the team ablaze was the man who so defined Super Bowl excellence that the game's winning trophy eventually bore his name.

Vince Lombardi, who presided over his team's ascendancy with equal parts discipline and emotion, had led the Packers to five NFL Championships in the past seven seasons, and his team had dominated the Kansas City Chiefs in the first AFL-NFL World Championship Game in 1967. Green Bay had come to occupy the highest ground in professional football by adhering to Lombardi's allegiance to the fundamentals: strong, consistent blocking and tackling and an offense fueled by power, not gimmicks.

But despite the Packers' status as an NFL juggernaut, the team was slipping some during the 1967 season. Offensive stars such as Bart Starr, Max McGee, and Jim Grabowski had lost a step as they aged; Paul Hornung had retired; and Jim Taylor, who, with Hornung, had put the Green Bay "power sweep" on the football map, had left for New Orleans. And if these departures and depletions seemed to signal the end of an era, there was an even more ominous omen—rumors of Lombardi's imminent retirement.

Through an arduous road to the Super Bowl that included an epic NFL Championship showdown with Dallas

known as the Ice Bowl, Lombardi had been considering stepping down to reduce the stress of the head coaching role and focus on serving as the team's general manager. Just after the Ice Bowl, he decided that Super Bowl II would be his last coaching outing, and before the game against Oakland, he quietly told his players. They vowed to win for their coach, but this year, with a scrappy Raiders team before them, there were no illusions of an easy victory.

"It's inconceivable to think that anyone would know it was Coach Lombardi's last game and just let it go as another game," Packers offensive lineman Jerry Kramer said later. "I'm sure it was on everyone's mind, and they wanted to do the best they could and play the game as well as possible for him."

Seeking to be a spoiler on this quest for one more Lombardi tribute, armed with their own determination to prove AFL legitimacy, were the Oakland Raiders. The AFL champions were led by an up-and-coming young quarterback named Daryle Lamonica and head coach Johnny Rauch, who had taken over the top spot in 1966 when Al Davis became the AFL commissioner. When the Packers watched film of the 13-1 Raiders, they recognized a worthy opponent and knew that this Super Bowl was shaping up as a battle between talented youth and weathered experience.

Aware that a crucial chapter in his team's history was being penned that day, Jerry Kramer turned on a recording device as Lombardi addressed his team just before they took the field at the Orange Bowl. "All the glory, everything that you've had, everything that you've won is going to be

small in comparison to winning this one," the venerable coach said. "This is a great thing for you. You're the only team maybe in the history of the National Football League to ever have this opportunity to win the Super Bowl twice. Boys, I tell you, I'd be so proud of that I just fill up with myself."

Despite Lamonica's versatility and a well-crafted game plan, the Oakland offense was thwarted from the start by legendary Packer linebacker Ray Nitschke and his supporting cast. But even as the Raiders struggled to convert, the Packers had to settle for field goals on their first two drives. Finally, midway through the second quarter, Starr connected with Boyd Dowler on a touchdown, which the Raiders answered with a 23-yard touchdown pass from Lamonica to Bill Miller.

It looked like the defending champs were going to take a 13-7 lead into halftime, until Oakland's Rodger Bird fumbled a punt with 23 seconds left in the second quarter and the mistake led to another Green Bay field goal. Later, that fumbled punt stood out as the turning point for the Raiders, who were trailing only 16-7 but never truly posed a threat to the Packers as the second half unfolded. Green Bay, sparked by an athletic third-quarter completion to the aging Max McGee in his final game in the gold and green, outscored their opponent 17-7 in the third and fourth quarters for a 33-14 victory—and an appropriate tribute for Lombardi.

After the celebration had died down, Kramer assessed the day with this statement: "We made more mental mistakes than I can ever remember our

team making in any other game." But even with the missteps that seemed glaring to the Packers, the world champions finished the day with no fumbles or interceptions and only one penalty. It was, for a team accustomed to uncommon precision and power, more than enough.

Of course, Lombardi didn't actually stay away from the sideline. He returned to coaching in 1969 with the Washington Redskins, a team in need of a savior. Lombardi had not experienced a losing record once in his nine seasons in Green Bay, and he had no intention of going down that road in Washington—leading the Redskins to their first winning season in 14 years. But before the great coach could complete his new reclamation project, he was diagnosed with an aggressive form of colon cancer, and he lived only two more months. He died on September 3, 1970.

For Packers fans, the enduring image of the man is that January day in 1968: a jubilant coach with a wide grin who was leaving the field on the shoulders of his players, the owner of the only two Super Bowl titles yet to be awarded, his name forever linked with the sport's biggest game.

Top, Super Bowl II ticket artwork.
AP Photo/NFL Photos

None of them planned to be in this position 50 years later: subjects of television ads, honored guests with access to end-zone tickets, fielding requests for photo shoots and press conferences.

The timetable was different for all three men, but at some point decades ago Tom Henschel, Larry Jacobson, and Don Crisman each realized that they had no intention of missing a Super Bowl. Through the years when they arrived in the Super Bowl city without a ticket and had to pay scalpers, through the cold Super Bowls and the wet Super Bowls and an untold number of traffic jams, these three became the picture of perseverance—and gained a measure of fame in the process.

"We're kind of like those one-hit musical wonders," said Crisman, who makes the trip to the big game each year from Kennebunk, Maine. "We have one 10-day period a year when we're in demand, and then we fade away again."

All three men are in their 70s, and each has a different story of his journey into this exclusive, extraordinary club. Henschel was living in Chicago, working as a part-time bartender and befriending some of the Bears players when a friend gave him free tickets to Super Bowl I. Jacobson bought two tickets to that first game for himself and a date. ("She wasn't impressed with football, and she wasn't impressed with me.") Crisman was a businessman and a father of two living in Colorado when a new friend, Stanley Whitaker, got tickets through the bank where he worked and invited Crisman to join him.

Super Bowl I in Los Angeles featured only a fraction of the flash that characterizes the game today, but all three men enjoyed themselves enough to make the effort again the following year, when Super Bowl II was held in Miami. For that game, Jacobson remembers spending $300 for airfare from San Francisco, a four-night hotel stay, tickets, and food. Before long, Henschel was saving all year so that he would have the money to make his annual winter trip, and Crisman even approached the small newspaper in his Maine hometown and received a letter that he used to secure a media pass. Year after year, each found a way to get into the stadium.

"We thought it might turn into something big, and it turned out to be bigger than I ever imagined," Crisman said.

The Never Miss a Super Bowl Club (named after the stickers Crisman's friend Whitaker put on his car for his trip to the Super Bowl decades ago) has three members today, but as recently as 2008 there were five. Whitaker, who continued to plan Super Bowl trips with him even after Crisman moved to Maine in the late '60s, attended 42 Super Bowls before his death, and Bob Cook made it to 44 big games before passing away in February 2011—just weeks after being forced to cancel his trip to see his beloved Packers in Super Bowl XLV.

NEVER MISS A SUPER BOWL CLUB

In 2010, the four members of the club (including Cook) were spotlighted in a series of TV spots for Visa, and that exposure resulted in a flurry of media attention. In one of the more memorable lines from the ads, Jacobson said, "I've missed weddings, I've missed babies being born, but I have no intention of missing the Super Bowl, ever."

Crisman and Henschel have known each other for more than 30 years, when they met while waiting in line for a taping of *The Tonight Show* before Super Bowl XVII in Pasadena. They met Jacobson in 2000 at Super Bowl XXXIV in Atlanta, and since that year the three have incorporated an annual Saturday lunch together into their Super Bowl itinerary.

Jacobson will catch a break on his travel costs for Super Bowl 50, since his home city of San Francisco is hosting the game. He even sent a list of suggestions to the organizing committee, based on his decades of navigating the crowds and delays the Super Bowl brings. His observations included this quip about the full slate of Super Bowl parties that occupy the week before the game: "Who are those folks, and what do they have to do with the Super Bowl?"

Despite the headaches that Henschel, Jacobson, and Crisman have had to endure as they make travel plans, pull out their credit cards repeatedly, and wait in lines, they wouldn't take anything for their eyewitness access to some of the biggest moments in football history. In recent

years, the NFL has secured seats for the three together in one of the end zones, a vantage point that allowed them a perfect view of plays such as Joe Montana's pass to John Taylor to win Super Bowl XXIII, Mike Jones's stop of Kevin Dyson in Super Bowl XXXIV, and David Tyree's legendary helmet catch in Super Bowl XLII.

They were on the opposite end zone for a few astounding moments as well, including Malcolm Butler's interception of Russell Wilson's pass to win Super Bowl XLIX. All three cite Super Bowl III, when Joe Namath led the underdog Jets to an unexpected victory, as one of the best memories on this extraordinary journey, but beyond that game they each rate their favorites according to their team loyalties.

A die-hard Patriots fan, Crisman relished his team's first win in Super Bowl XXXVI. Jacobson loves the 49ers, so he has had plenty of chances to celebrate. Henschel cheers for the Steelers and the Bears primarily, but he also likes the Lions and the Browns and is determined to keep attending Super Bowls until one of those teams makes it. He calls himself a "health nut," and he sees no reason why he can't continue his Super Bowl streak for many years.

Crisman sees his Super Bowl future a little differently. He is the oldest of the three, and his wife, Beverly, accompanied him to 27 games but opted to stay home a few years ago when face-value ticket prices climbed past $200. He has loved every second of his membership in the Never

Miss a Super Bowl Club, but he believes that reaching the half-century mark might present an opportune time to suspend his membership.

"I keep saying that I'm going to quit at 50," he said, "and Larry and Tom say they're not quitting until they're six feet under."

Opposite page, Don Crisman, 74, of Kennebunk, Maine, poses in his study with some of the autographed footballs he has collected over 44 years of attending all the Super Bowl games. *AP Photo/Pat Wellenbach*

Right, Bob Cook displays some of his Super Bowl ticket stubs in Brown Deer, Wisconsin. Cook is one of the men featured in a Visa credit card television ad for having never missed a Super Bowl. He passed away in 2011. *AP Photo/Jeffrey Phelps*

"I'VE MISSED WEDDINGS, I'VE MISSED BABIES BEING BORN, BUT I HAVE NO INTENTION OF MISSING THE SUPER BOWL, EVER."

LARRY JACOBSON
NEVER MISS A SUPER
BOWL CLUB MEMBER

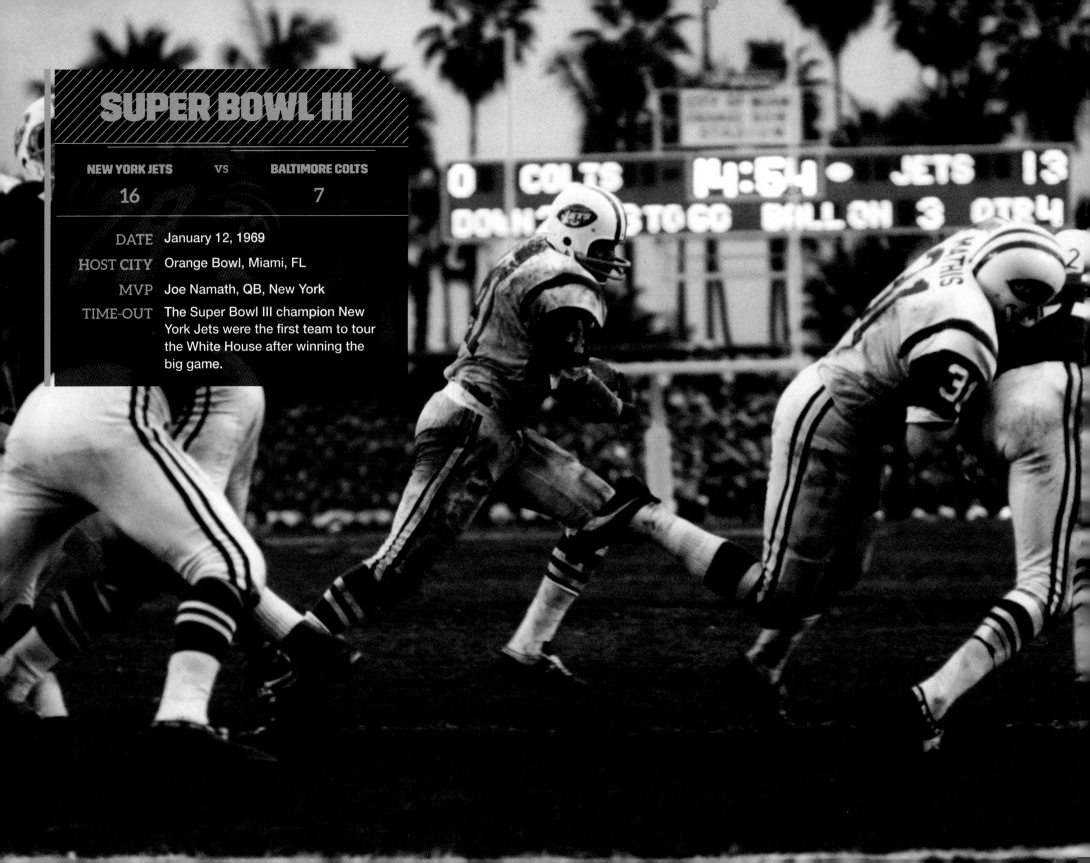

SUPER BOWL III

NEW YORK JETS   VS   **BALTIMORE COLTS**

16   **7**

DATE   January 12, 1969

HOST CITY   Orange Bowl, Miami, FL

MVP   Joe Namath, QB, New York

TIME-OUT   The Super Bowl III champion New York Jets were the first team to tour the White House after winning the big game.

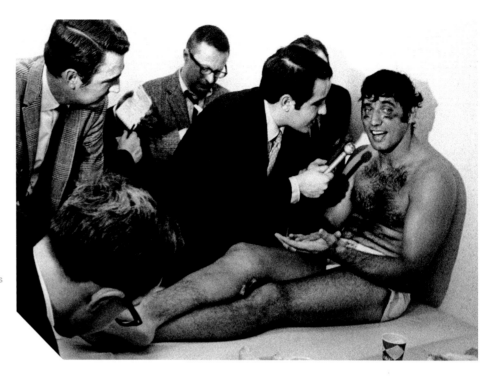

Joe Namath talks with reporters as he rests on a training table in the dressing room.
AP Photo

The only thing that moved faster than Joe Namath's arm in 1969 was his mouth. But in the end, he used one to back up the other, and the result was the first great upset in Super Bowl history.

AFL loyalists believed more than ever that the football in their league was underrated and one of their teams could soon topple an NFL squad. But not even the staunchest supporters of the lesser-known league thought that the team they would clear out of the path on their way to respect would be the Baltimore Colts.

The Colts featured not just one but two of the top veteran quarterbacks of the day in Johnny Unitas and Earl Morrall. They had rolled through their NFL season with a 13-1 record, defeating an intimidating Vikings team and the Cleveland Browns to punch their cards for their first Super Bowl. Vince Lombardi was gone, and most of his stars had moved on, so the Colts seemed poised to be Green Bay's heir apparent.

The media, the fans, and the members of the coaching community all seemed to know how the game was going to turn out. Atlanta Falcons head coach Norm Van Brocklin, chatting with a group of reporters at a Miami hotel a few days before the game, put it this way: "On Sunday, Joe Namath will be playing his first pro game." Two weeks earlier, the great Lombardi was asked to assess New York's chances of upsetting the Colts. His reply? "Infinitesimal."

Namath might have gotten that memo, but he made a steadfast decision not to read it. His Jets team might not have blazed a Colts-like trail through the AFL, finishing 11-3 with one of the losses coming at the hands of last-place Buffalo. But Namath's athleticism and field vision had gained him considerable attention in the football world, and his image—he showed up at the Fort Lauderdale airport sporting long hair, a Fu Manchu mustache, and a double-breasted suit—put him in a league of his own. At the airport that day, he told a friend, loud enough for everyone nearby to hear, "We should be favored by nine or 10 points."

But the airport pronouncement paled in comparison to the Miami Touchdown Club dinner three days before the big game. Namath was being feted as the club's pro football player of the year, the first AFL player to ever earn that distinction. During his acceptance speech, he said the words that made sports headlines the next morning: "Most people don't give us a chance. I think we have a chance. Matter of fact, I think we'll win it. I guarantee it."

The afternoon of the Super Bowl was cloudy with a threat of rain, but Namath and his teammates were too focused on finding the chinks in the Colts' armor to worry about the weather. As he watched film of the Baltimore defense, Namath had noticed their propensity to blitz, and he had detected some holes in the middle left by the blitzing defenders, holes he was confident he could hit with his quick-release passes.

Little by little, as the first half unfolded, Namath tested the opposing defense for weak spots that would accommodate the Jets' running game, and when the inevitable blitzes came, he completed one pass after another in the open lanes he had discovered. The Colts had seldom been handled this effectively, and it rattled them; at the end of the day, Baltimore had lost four interceptions and fumbled the ball once, and the turnovers spelled doom for any kind of offensive momentum. Their efforts to score failed repeatedly in the first half, and Namath drove his unit efficiently into the end zone, with a 4-yard touchdown run by Matt Snell signifying the first time an AFL team had led an NFL opponent in a Super Bowl.

Down 7-0 at halftime, the Colts entered the locker room completely stunned at the direction things had taken but with plenty of time and talent to hand fans the victory that had seemed assured. Head coach Don Shula looked for motivation by reminding his team that they still had superior talent. "We're making stupid mistakes; we're stopping ourselves," Shula said. "You've got them believing in themselves. You've got them believing that they're better than we are."

In the third quarter, after two Jets field goals and a 13-0 New York lead, Baltimore coach Don Shula benched Morrall and called in Unitas, an NFL legend who had been recovering from a torn tendon in his elbow. Though a shadow of the powerhouse he once was, Unitas moved the ball more effectively than Morrall, but the Colts either stopped his offense or stopped themselves, as in a fourth-quarter Randy Beverly interception in the end zone. On the next Baltimore possession, Unitas drove his team 80 yards, and they finally scored on a 1-yard run by Jerry Hill. The NFL champions would not score again, and the AFL had its triumph with a 16-7 victory.

The Jets had a victory party that night, and the guests included players from several other AFL teams who were stopping by to offer their thanks for the giant step the Jets had made for their league. Snell remembered Kansas City Chiefs defensive tackle Buck Buchanan walking around the room, shaking all of the Jets' hands, and saying, "Thank you for redeeming us."

It had all the elements of a Super Bowl for the ages: a telegenic, charismatic superstar who bragged about an impending victory and then made good; an aging quarterback with plenty of heart but not enough arm to pull his team through; bragging rights for an upstart league that had taken enough abuse. More than four decades later, Super Bowl III was still getting ink as one of the best in history, and it was certainly one of the types of upsets that make football fans grateful for the opportunity to be witnesses to the improbable.

Namath played eight more years of pro ball after that fateful game and went on to a different kind of fame with his appearances in movies, television shows, and advertising, but many believe Broadway Joe never shone as brightly as he did in the dress rehearsals and the unforgettable performance that was Super Bowl III.

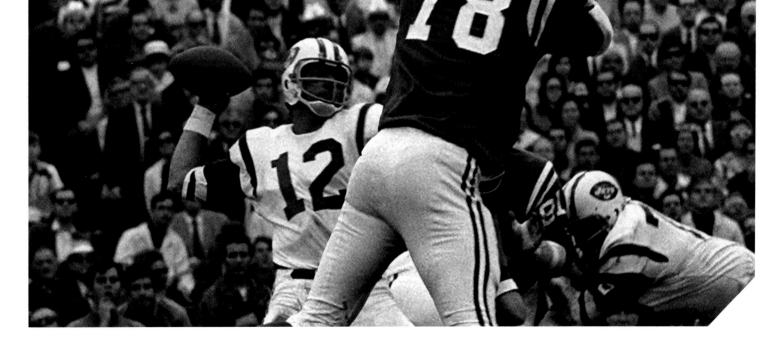

Opposite page, Bubba Smith (78) of the Baltimore Colts leaps in a vain attempt to block a pass from New York Jets quarterback Joe Namath. *AP Photo*

Top, Baltimore Colts fullback Tom Matte (41) shows some frustration. *AP Photo/NFL Photo*

Right, New York Jets Hall of Fame quarterback Joe Namath with his father and his coach Weeb Ewbank after a 16-7 win over the Baltimore Colts in Super Bowl III. Namath was named MVP. *AP Photo/NFL Photos*

"FOOTBALL IS AN INCREDIBLE GAME. SOMETIMES IT'S SO INCREDIBLE, IT'S UNBELIEVABLE."

Tom Landry

CHAPTER 2: THE 1970s

1970s

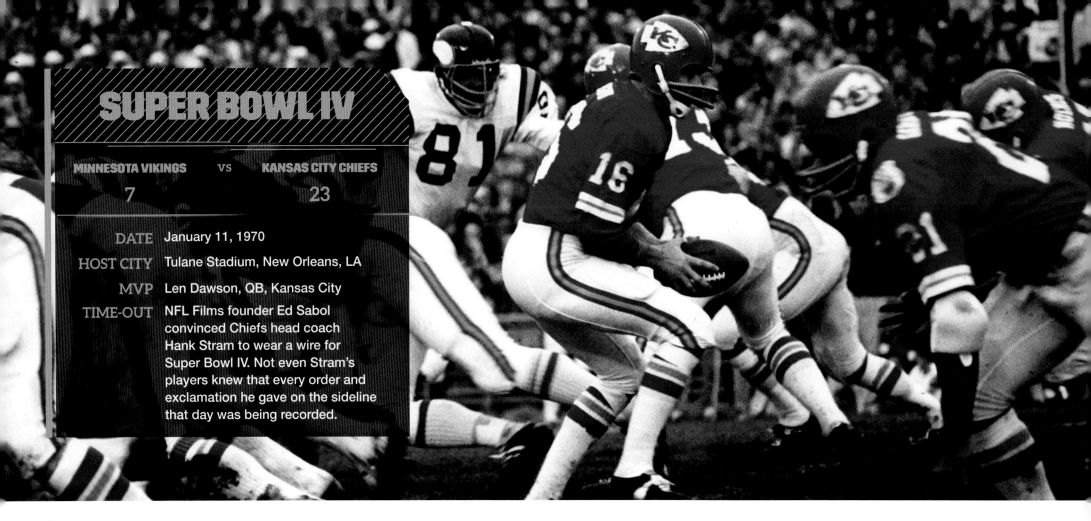

SUPER BOWL IV

MINNESOTA VIKINGS   VS   **KANSAS CITY CHIEFS**

7   **23**

DATE   January 11, 1970

HOST CITY   Tulane Stadium, New Orleans, LA

MVP   Len Dawson, QB, Kansas City

TIME-OUT   NFL Films founder Ed Sabol convinced Chiefs head coach Hank Stram to wear a wire for Super Bowl IV. Not even Stram's players knew that every order and exclamation he gave on the sideline that day was being recorded.

When Len Dawson and his Kansas City teammates entered the Tulane Stadium locker room to get dressed for Super Bowl IV, their bright red jerseys sported a new accessory: a patch reading "10 AFL" to commemorate a decade of competition in the American Football League.

If a week of media reports touting the Minnesota Vikings as the dominant talent and the Chiefs as posers who couldn't even win their own conference wasn't motivation enough, here was a reminder that Kansas City had been given the opportunity to make a bold final statement

for the league that had grown steadily in credibility through the decade.

Even among AFL loyalists, there were some who thought the Chiefs were the wrong team to defend the league's honor in the final Super Bowl before the NFL and AFL officially became one entity. The playoff structure in the AFL had recently been revised to allow the second-place teams in both divisions to battle the first-place teams in the other for a chance at the AFL title game. The Chiefs finished second to the Raiders in the Western Division, but they improbably defeated first

the defending Super Bowl champion Jets and then the Raiders to punch their ticket to New Orleans.

The typical two-week buildup to the Super Bowl was compressed into one week in 1970, and even then the Chiefs were plagued by distractions, most notably a story on NBC's *Huntley-Brinkley Report* alleging that their skilled field general, quarterback Dawson, was one of six professional players linked to a Justice Department investigation into an illegal sports gambling operation. Dawson quickly issued a statement that while he

was acquainted with one of the bookies implicated in the scheme, he had no involvement in the gambling web. He was never subpoenaed, and the charges were eventually dropped, but the accusations took their toll on Dawson as he tried to focus on the Vikings.

Kansas City head coach Hank Stram had a fondness for trick plays and multiple shifts and motions on offense (one media member called his outfit the "Kansas City Wild West Variety Show"), whereas the Vikings had steamrolled a 12-2 path through the NFL with an emphasis on size

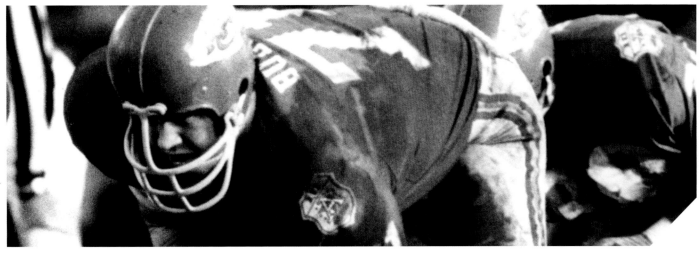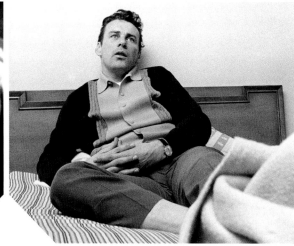

and brute strength personified by their vaunted "Purple People Eater" defensive line. Stram was one of the game's innovators, going toe to toe with Bud Grant's old-school, smashmouth model of football.

The Vikings' front defenders might have inspired fear in most opponents, but Dawson and his unit made it clear from the onset that afternoon that they intended to move the ball their way. They scored on four of their first five possessions by relying heavily on the soccer-style kicks of Norwegian placekicker Jan Stenerud, who connected on three consecutive tries from 48, 32, and 25 yards to give the Chiefs a 9-0 lead by the early minutes of the second quarter.

As sportswriter Ray Didinger assessed the unexpected shift of power in an NFL video ranking Super Bowl IV as the tenth-greatest upset in NFL history, "The Chiefs matched up the Vikings in almost lethal ways."

On the kickoff following Stenerud's third field goal, Vikings returner Charlie West fumbled the kick and lost it to Kansas City guard Remi Prudhomme. A quick drive, topped by a 5-yard touchdown run by the Chiefs' "mini-back," the 5-foot-9 Mike Garrett, gave the underdogs a 16-0 lead heading into halftime. Just as surprising as the Viking defense's newfound vulnerability was Minnesota's impotence on offense. Stram's strategy involved triple stacking linebackers and employing bump-and-run coverage against an offensive unit that relied on quarterback Joe Kapp staying planted in the pocket and running the old Green Bay sweep without any shifting or motion before the snap.

"The Chiefs did not make a serious mistake all afternoon," sportswriter Norm Miller wrote in the *New York Daily News* the next day.

"It was the Vikes who lost their cool in this game for the marbles with damaging giveaways, with frantic bombs by Joe Kapp that fizzled."

In the second half, the Vikings managed to cobble together just one scoring series, a 69-yard drive capped when Dave Osborn found the end zone from 4 yards out. With that triumph, the game was again in play at 16-7, but Dawson returned to his task of methodically picking apart the stalwart Viking defense on the next possession and fired a pass to Otis Taylor, who darted away from two Minnesota defenders who looked like they had him in their grasp for a 46-yard touchdown play and the 23-7 that would stay on the scoreboard through the fourth quarter and into history. Later in the locker room, Grant would pinpoint Taylor's evasive run after the catch as the death knell to his team's budding momentum.

For the second straight year, an underrespected AFL team had come to the Super Bowl and won convincingly, this time against a team with 12 straight wins and an intimidating physical presence. Football IQ and new offensive strategies had won the day over strength and power, and, suddenly, the league that had been the big, strong NFL's whipping boy through the mid-'60s and the advent of the Super Bowl had evened the score to 2-2. It would remain a tie game in perpetuity, since the two leagues would officially merge that fall and the next Super Bowl would be a battle between two members of a larger, more diverse National Football League.

"An insignia on your hat or jacket doesn't make any difference," Stram told reporters as he celebrated with his team. "Football is a game of people, not emblems."

Top left, Kansas City Chiefs guard Ed Budde (71) lines up. *AP Photo*

Top right, Kansas City Chiefs quarterback Len Dawson relaxes in his New Orleans hotel room. *AP Photo*

Bottom left, AFL's tenth anniversary patch specially made for the Super Bowl IV. *AP Photo/NFL Photos*

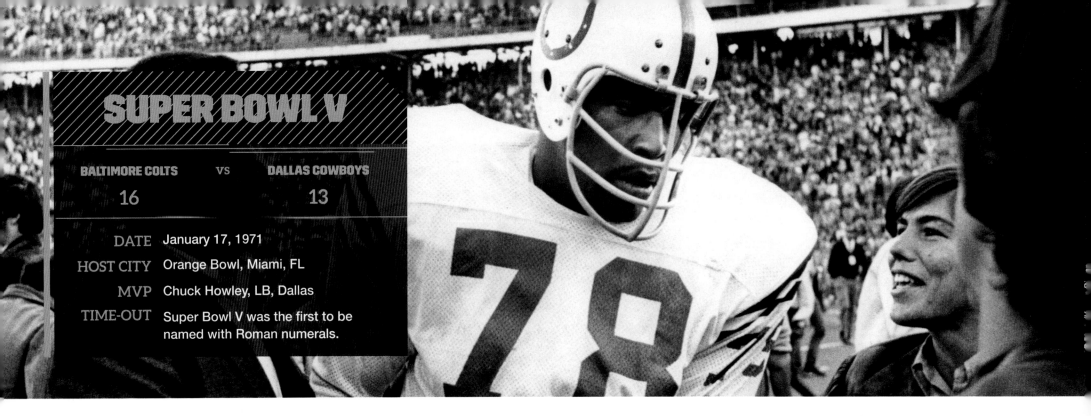

SUPER BOWL V

BALTIMORE COLTS VS **DALLAS COWBOYS**

16 **13**

DATE	January 17, 1971
HOST CITY	Orange Bowl, Miami, FL
MVP	Chuck Howley, LB, Dallas
TIME-OUT	Super Bowl V was the first to be named with Roman numerals.

If any NFL loyalists were still arguing their case for supremacy when the first Super Bowl in the new united league was played in 1971, they might have used for ammunition the fact that two of the original NFL teams lined up that year for Super Bowl V.

But physical domination and football skill were far from the order of the day when the Baltimore Colts eked out a 16-13 win over the Dallas Cowboys in the Orange Bowl. This championship would be decided in favor of the team that could get the most mileage out of their opponent's catastrophic mistakes.

The Packers of three years ago, they of the zero turnovers and one penalty, surely watched the game with a permanent cringe. When all was said and done and

the Colts had finally redeemed their embarrassing loss to the Jets in Super Bowl III, the two teams had combined for 12 turnovers, with six fumbles and six interceptions. And they were costly cough-ups, too—both teams fumbled within the 5-yard line in the second half on plays that could have locked up victories. The Colts finally tied the game, after the score had stayed 13-6 for what seemed like an eternity, when Dallas quarterback Craig Morton's pass was picked off by Baltimore's Rick Volk.

It might have been a slovenly game on the offensive side, but the two defenses battled heroically, and it provided the most exciting finish yet in the history of the Super Bowl: a winning field goal kicked with just nine seconds left on the clock. The Colts had their ring, and the Cowboys

had to wait one more year to disprove the whispers that they were the team that always made it near the promised land and were stopped just short of entering.

The MVP selection was Cowboys linebacker Chuck Howley, who had pulled in two interceptions and been the most effective member of a unit, called the Doomsday Defense, considered the best in the NFL. It was a surprise selection—the first defensive player and the first member of the losing squad to receive the award. But the player who will always be the most indelibly associated with that precarious Colts victory was charismatic placekicker Jim O'Brien.

Called "Lassie" by his teammates because of his long hair, O'Brien was more than just a strong leg; he was a starting wide

receiver at Cincinnati, where as a junior he set the NCAA record for yards per reception, with 25.2. He had just replaced veteran kicker Lou Michaels at the beginning of the season, and he had hit 55.9 percent of his field goal attempts while gaining a reputation as a carefree bachelor who was just a little bit cocky. Ever since Michaels had missed a crucial field goal the previous season because the opponents screamed at him before the kick, the Colts had incorporated a new practice responsibility for defensive tackle Billy Ray Smith—yelling disparaging things at O'Brien, loudly and obnoxiously.

After Baltimore finally tied the game with seven minutes remaining, Dallas quarterback Craig Morton assembled a drive into Colts territory that seemed destined to give the Cowboys the last

Left, Jim O'Brien (80) kicks the game-winning goal for the Baltimore Colts. *AP Photo*

Right, Pro Football Hall of Fame and Dallas Cowboys defensive back Mel Renfro (20) sitting on the bench contemplating the Cowboys' loss. *AP Photo/NFL Photos*

word. But this Super Bowl was a comedy of errors, and the Cowboys combined a sack and a holding penalty to put themselves at second down and 35 with just over two minutes to go. In an uncharacteristic gamble, Dallas coach Tom Landry called a pass play rather than burning the clock and sending the game into overtime.

Morton's pass was high, intended for receiver Dan Reeves. The ball glanced off of Reeves's fingertips and found the waiting arms of the Colts middle linebacker, who barreled to the Dallas 28-yard line. Teams had not yet introduced a sideline net for kickers to warm up in crucial moments such as this one, so O'Brien just started to stretch and get his mind off of the extra point he had missed

earlier in the game and on the task at hand. The Cowboys screamed lustily at him, but he tuned them out, conditioned by Smith's "scream drills." Lassie trotted out to the field, took the snap, and split the goalposts right in the center from 32 yards out, sealing Baltimore's triumph. "It would have been good from 52 yards out," he said afterward. "It was the best kick of my life."

It was a day of vindication for both of the seasoned Colts quarterbacks. Johnny Unitas, the backup to Earl Morrall in Super Bowl III, had earned the starting job, and after two early Cowboys field goals, he engineered the first touchdown of the game, a bizarre and controversial play that started with a 25-yard pass to receiver Ed Hinton. The ball bounced off of Hinton's

fingers, grazed the fingertips of Dallas cornerback Mel Renfro, and finally landed in the hands of Baltimore tight end John Mackey, who sprinted 50 yards to the end zone for a 75-yard touchdown play.

Cowboys coach Tom Landry argued that the pass was touched consecutively by two offensive players, thus making it illegal, but the officials watched the replays and confirmed that Renfro had touched the ball between Hinton and Mackey, so the six points went on the board. O'Brien stumbled on the subsequent extra point, which resulted in a 6-6 tie.

Dallas scored again, capitalizing on a Unitas fumble, and on the next Colts possession Unitas was drilled in the pocket by Cowboys defender George

Andrie. He rose from the field gingerly, holding his chest, and the medical team determined that he had sustained damage to his rib cartilage. Morrall, considered by many to be the goat of the Colts' Super Bowl loss two years earlier, had the opportunity to finish the game. His performance—7 for 15 for 147 yards and one interception—wasn't perfect, but it was the first and most coveted Lombardi Trophy for the 36-year-old veteran, who would actually win two more rings in the twilight of his long career after a trade to, of all teams, the Cowboys.

Basking in a long-awaited Colts celebration, he told the media after the game, "The good memories always blot out the bad."

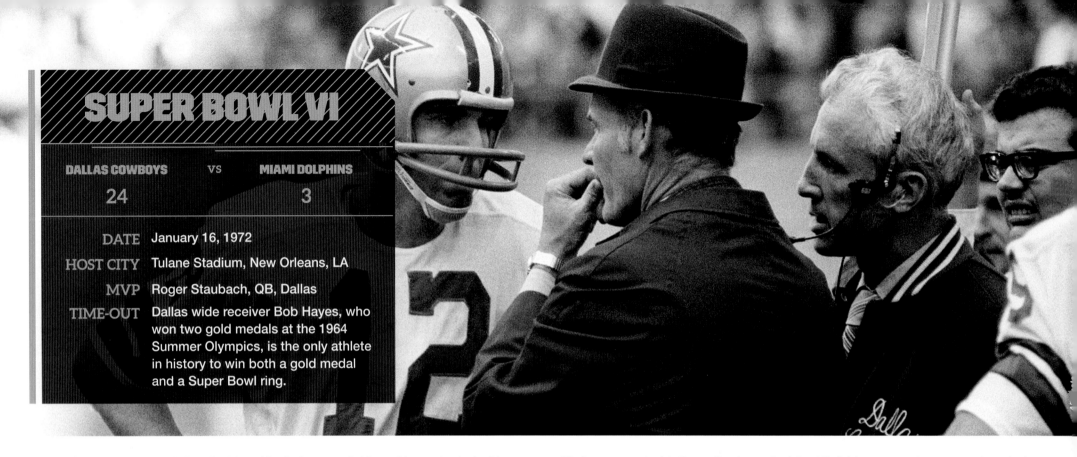

SUPER BOWL VI

DALLAS COWBOYS vs **MIAMI DOLPHINS**

24   **3**

DATE	January 16, 1972
HOST CITY	Tulane Stadium, New Orleans, LA
MVP	Roger Staubach, QB, Dallas
TIME-OUT	Dallas wide receiver Bob Hayes, who won two gold medals at the 1964 Summer Olympics, is the only athlete in history to win both a gold medal and a Super Bowl ring.

The Cowboys of the early '70s had heard it all: also-rans, bridesmaids, can't win the big one. Super Bowl VI was a far cry from the most exciting high-stakes football game ever played, but it was important because it finally got the monkey off the back of the team that turned into a bona fide Super Bowl legend.

In each of the past five seasons, the Cowboys had come tantalizingly close to national football glory. In 1966, in the NFL Championship Game to determine the competitor in Super Bowl I, an interception in the end zone halted a late-game comeback drive that would have given them, not the Packers, the spot in the first world championship. In 1967, it was the Packers with the improbable reversal of fortune in the Ice Bowl—giving the phrase "left out in the cold" a new meaning for Cowboys fans.

The next two forays into the postseason, in '68 and '69, both ended at the hands of the underdog Browns, and then there was Super Bowl V, where the Cowboys were incinerated in a bonfire of their own making, one painful turnover after another. The team's talent was well established: the much-vaunted Doomsday Defense, the coaching acumen of Tom Landry, the powerful arm of quarterback Roger Staubach. The media had plenty of positive story lines, but that negative theme, "the team that always finds a way to lose," kept bobbing to the surface.

Their opponent in this Super Bowl was the Miami Dolphins, a team long on youth and talent and short on experience in the trenches. Hapless in their early years—the team combined for just 15 wins in its first four seasons in the league—the decision to hire Don Shula away from the Colts in 1970 was the key to Miami's turnaround. Under Shula, the Dolphins won 10 games in both 1970 and 1971, and their path to Super Bowl VI included playoff wins over two former world champions, his former Colts team and the Kansas City Chiefs.

With the Cowboys projected as six-point favorites, the Dolphins approached the buildup to the game with the confidence of a team that had already defied expectations. But in the end, that six-point prediction didn't take into account the two-ton chip that America's Team had carried into Tulane Stadium on its shoulder pads. The Cowboys were a physical force with a clear mission, and in the end the Dolphins represented only a minor obstacle on their way to achieving it.

With the temperature at kickoff a frigid 39 degrees, Staubach and the Dallas offense advanced for 23 first downs and gained 252 rushing yards—both Super Bowl records. The vaunted Doomsday Defense thoroughly stifled every attempt the Dolphins made to put points on the board except a 31-yard Garo Yepremian field goal at the end of the second quarter, giving Miami fans a hopeful 10-3 halftime deficit.

But that glimmer of optimism was short-lived. Staubach, who had engineered a 76-yard drive in the second quarter for the Cowboys' first touchdown, made a dramatic return from the locker room by opening the second half with an eight-play, 71-yard drive accelerated by long runs from both Duane Thomas, who ended the game with 95 yards on the ground and 17 in the air, and Bob Hayes, a gold medalist in the 100 meters at the 1964 Summer Olympics.

With that drive, the score was 17-3, and even though Dallas scored only one more touchdown, the second half became their playground. If not for a fourth-quarter fumble by the Cowboys' Calvin Hill on the 1-yard line that seemed to be an inevitable touchdown, the game would have been the biggest upset in Super Bowl history to that point. That distinction still belonged to the Packers' 35-10 trouncing of the Chiefs in Super Bowl I, but the Cowboys, victors with a final score of 24-3, could be content in the fact that theirs was the first defense to keep a Super Bowl opponent from scoring a single touchdown.

The only uncertainty of the day was the question of which Cowboy would receive the MVP award. On paper, the award seemed to belong to Thomas, the mercurial, talented back who had dominated his team's championship offensive performance. No one knew how short-lived his time in Dallas was— two weeks after the Super Bowl, he would plead guilty to possession of marijuana, and Dallas would trade him to the

Chargers—but he had given what was perhaps the most philosophical sound bite in post–Super Bowl history the previous year after his team's disheartening loss to the Colts.

"I want to contemplate what has happened," Thomas said that day in 1971. "I hope that I have been enriched by the disappointment. There is something noble in defeat. You cannot find victory unless you first understand defeat."

The Cowboys had found victory—and in a big way—but in the end, *Sport* magazine, which was in charge of the honor during that era, selected the clean-cut, retired naval officer who was the quintessential face of "America's Team." It was by no means a superior Roger Staubach performance—he completed 12 of 19 for 119 yards and missed several open targets in the first half—but he was a known media commodity who would be gracious and camera friendly at the annual awards dinner *Sport* sponsored for the MVP. Thomas had been steamed at the media since the previous summer and had not said a word to a reporter since, and even Staubach conceded publically that his teammate's chilliness had probably won him his only MVP prize—which came with a new sports car.

"Probably Duane Thomas's attitude toward the media during Super Bowl week got me the MVP," Staubach said. "Duane was the guy Miami couldn't stop. He had a great game, but they probably said, 'Well, Roger did OK, so let's give it to him.'"

Dallas Cowboys defensive back Cornell Green (34) leaps to deflect a Bob Griese pass intended for Paul Warfield in the second quarter. *AP Photo*

SUPER BOWL VII

MIAMI DOLPHINS VS **WASHINGTON REDSKINS**

14 **7**

DATE: January 14, 1973

HOST CITY: Memorial Coliseum, Los Angeles, CA

MVP: Jake Scott, S, Miami

TIME-OUT: Washington quarterback Billy Kilmer, who always loved a good party, greeted writer Steve Perkins into his hotel room by saying, "The beer's in the bathtub."

In a locker room that felt more like a tomb, just after their humiliating Super Bowl VI loss to the Dallas Cowboys, the Miami Dolphins didn't utter a word. Some remembered the silence lasting as long as 15 minutes, with every shoe falling into a locker or strip of tape being ripped off an ankle echoing through the room.

Head coach Don Shula stepped up and gave a speech that his players have remembered in essence for decades, even if they have differed on the exact words. He told them to remember the pain of that moment, to carry it everywhere, as a safeguard against ever letting them feel that disappointment again. He told them that the pain of that day would make the triumph of next year's Super Bowl win even greater.

As Miami running back Larry Csonka recalls it, Shula went one step further than guaranteeing a Super Bowl conquest in 1973. He stood before them, according to Csonka, and said, "We're going to go one game at a time and win every damn game."

Armed with boatloads of frustration from that 24-3 shellacking and a coach with the audacity to guarantee an undefeated season, the Dolphins started to dispatch one opponent after another. They were talented but not dominant, and with their "No-Name Defense" that executed game plans nearly flawlessly and a running game powered by Csonka and Jim Kiick, Miami completed their 17-0 season in convincing, if unspectacular, fashion.

The legendary status of that undefeated season has been amplified over the years, in large part because the feat—at least until 2015—had never been replicated. Like any truth that gives way to folklore, the temptation is to view the Dolphins as world beaters, not as a team that lost its starting quarterback for most of the regular season and actually entered the Super Bowl as three-point underdogs.

The 14-7 victory over the Washington Redskins—the first Super Bowl played at Memorial Coliseum in Los Angeles since the inaugural game—was actually quarterback Bob Griese's first outing since his leg was shattered on a tackle during the Dolphins' fifth game of the season. Miami had made it through the rest of their schedule behind the strength of backup

quarterback Earl Morrall, now 38 years old, and the stifling defense, led by power players such as Nick Buoniconti and Manny Fernandez, which had allowed an average of just 12.2 points a game that year.

With only a seven-point margin, it appeared that the Redskins had ample opportunity to ruin Dolphins perfection, but in fact Miami had the upper hand far more convincingly than the scoreboard revealed. The defense didn't allow the Redskins to cross the 50-yard line until two minutes remained in the first half, and Washington's one touchdown came as a result of a spectacular gaffe by Miami kicker Garo Yepremian with just two minutes left in the game.

Miami Dolphin Jim Mandich makes a diving catch of a 19-yard Bob Griese pass near the goal line during the second quarter, setting up the Dolphins' second touchdown. *AP Photo*

In what was primarily a defensive battle, all of Miami's points came in the first half, with the first touchdown resulting from Griese's longest pass of the game, a 28-yarder to Howard Twilley late in the first quarter. Washington was driving late in the second quarter when Dolphins linebacker Doug Swift blitzed Redskins quarterback Billy Kilmer on a third and 3, disorienting him just as he passed the ball. Instead of hitting Kilmer's intended receiver, the ball landed in the hands of Buoniconti, who returned it 32 yards to set up his team's second touchdown drive.

Buoniconti's pick was one of three on the day for Kilmer, who collected more passing yards than Griese—104 to Griese's 88—but he gave up the ball at inopportune times. The other two interceptions were snatched by safety Jake Scott, whose performance made

him the second defensive player in Super Bowl history to earn MVP honors.

Most of the second half unfolded without a change to the scoreboard, with the Dolphins' 14-0 halftime lead seemingly suspended in perpetuity. With five minutes remaining, Kilmer fired a pass into the end zone and gave Scott his most damaging interception, complete with a 55-yard return that seemed to spell last rites for Washington. But then Yepremian committed a blunder so colossal that his teammate Buoniconti would later say, "If I had a rope, I would have hanged Garo right then and there."

The clock read 2:10, and Yepremian lined up for a 42-yard field goal that would have padded his team's inevitable victory and, as Shula later pointed out, resulted in a 17-0 win for a 17-0 team. But such

symmetry was not meant to be. The snap and Yepremian's kick were both low, allowing Washington's Bill Brundige to get in front of the ball for the block. The ball bounced into Yepremian's hands, and at this point all parties agreed he should have fallen on it and cut his losses.

But inexplicably, the bald Cypriot kicker attempted to pass the ball downfield and then reached up and batted it when his pass was woefully short. Yepremian's second touch drove the ball right to Washington's Mike Bass, who sprinted down the sideline 49 yards for a touchdown that suddenly gave a glimmer of hope to George Allen and his Redskins.

In the No-Name Defense's most critical test, an attempted Redskins drive with 1:14 remaining withered under Miami's full-force blitz attack, and the clock expired

to give Shula the trophy that had already eluded him twice. It was the second straight year in which the previous Super Bowl runner-up had prevailed, giving credence to Shula's "Let's never feel this way again" form of psychology. The game lived on as legendary for Dolphins fans as the perfect ending to a perfect season, but as a display of football, some deemed the game to be moderately boring.

"Miami would prove to be all too representative of its era—using a conservative offense that passed sparingly, and stifling opponents with a defense that choked the run and a zone that thwarted long passes," wrote Michael MacCambridge in *America's Game*.

The headline in *Pro Football Weekly* after the game told the story more succinctly: "Dolphins Were Super—Game A Drag."

HAIR OF FAME

It's a salute to the lovely locks of the Super Bowl. Do you know your manly manes?

(a)

(b)

(c)

(h)

(i)

(j)

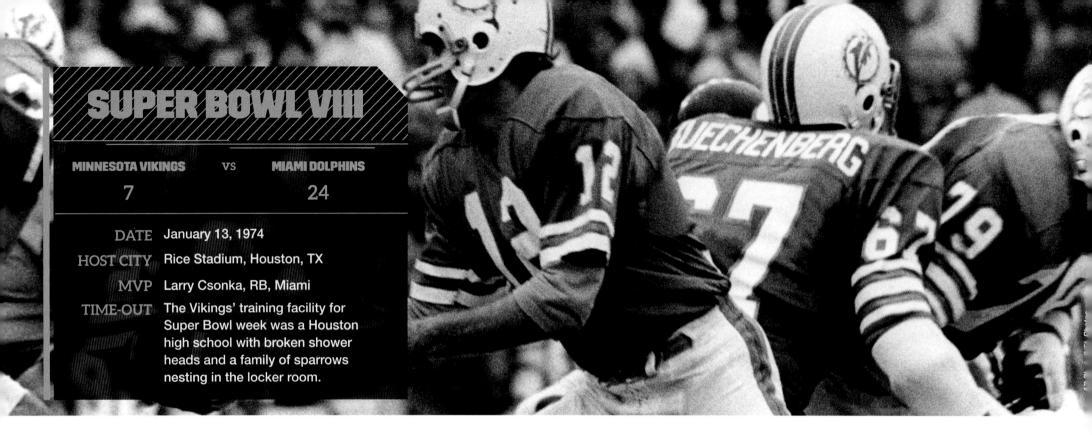

SUPER BOWL VIII

MINNESOTA VIKINGS VS **MIAMI DOLPHINS**

7 **24**

DATE January 13, 1974

HOST CITY Rice Stadium, Houston, TX

MVP Larry Csonka, RB, Miami

TIME-OUT The Vikings' training facility for Super Bowl week was a Houston high school with broken shower heads and a family of sparrows nesting in the locker room.

In the wake of their undefeated season, the Miami Dolphins approached their 1973 schedule with nearly identical personnel and a deadly mix of confidence and talent. Everyone associated with both teams agrees that the team that won the second consecutive Super Bowl was considerably more intimidating than the team of the previous year.

Defensive tackle Manny Fernandez, one of the Dolphins' most punishing defenders in those years, speculated later that his team, which defeated Minnesota 24-7 in Super Bowl VIII, could have actually won by 50 points. "It was total domination," Fernandez said in *But We Were 17 and 0*. "They had no luck. They had one drive against us that amounted to anything and that was it. … It was a fun game."

Miami head coach Don Shula was a firm believer in the power of a sound rushing game, and rushing was everything for his team that day in Houston's Rice Stadium. The Dolphins ran the ball 53 times for 196 yards, and Bob Griese attempted only seven passes and completed six—a record low for Miami.

After several Super Bowls in a row without a distinctive hero, this championship belonged to one man, Dolphin fullback Larry Csonka. He was a human steamroller, running for 145 yards and two touchdowns on his way to an undisputed MVP trophy. A *New York Daily News* reporter wrote that Csonka "pounded and pulverized the Vikings into Rice Stadium's Astro Turf" on his way to setting a new Super Bowl record for total rushing yards.

When Vikings defensive tackle Alan Page reflected on that afternoon's matchup, he said that the Vikings knew they were in trouble after just a few plays. The Dolphins' attack, honed through a playoff run in which they outscored three opponents by an 85-33 margin, was both powerful and efficient, with an offensive line that repeatedly rolled out the red carpet for Csonka. "Our line was probably the heart of our team," Griese said afterward. "Our whole attack was structured around it."

The Miami defense had gained so much respect that defensive coordinator Bill Arnsparger was coaching his last game with the Dolphins before taking over as the head coach of the New York Giants. The unit held the Vikings to just 72 rushing yards and forced two key turnovers: a fumble and an interception. Minnesota quarterback Fran Tarkenton finished the day with a respectable 18 of 28 for 82 yards, but the No-Name Defense kept him to short passes all day and repeatedly stifled Tarkenton's attempts to put together an effective drive. After three quarters, the Vikings' ineffectualness was spelled out on the scoreboard: 24-0, Miami.

Reminiscent of the 1967 Packers, the last team to win two consecutive Super Bowls, the Dolphins committed no turnovers and were assessed only one 4-yard penalty. As Minnesota general manager Jim Finks put it, "Nobody would have beat the Miami club the way it played in this game, whether it was the Packers or the '27 Duluth Eskimos."

Left, Miami Dolphin Larry Csonka races through the Minnesota Vikings. *AP Photo*

Right, Fran Tarkenton, Chuck Foreman (44), and Oscar Reed (32). *AP Photo/NFL Photos*

The Dolphins lined up for kickoff like a team that already knew they would be celebrating later, so they acted quickly to make the inevitability of the result known to everyone else in the stadium. They received the opening kickoff, and Griese and Csonka turned it into a 10-play, 62-yard touchdown drive culminating in a 5-yard Csonka burst into the end zone. Then Minnesota went 3 and out (the Vikings earned only one first down in their first three possessions), and Miami put together almost a mirror image of its first drive, this time traveling 56 yards in 10 plays with a 1-yard Jim Kiick run for the finale.

Only 13 minutes had ticked off the game clock; Miami was ahead 14-0, and Minnesota was trying to see what had hit them. "The first quarter wasn't over, but for all intents and purposes, the game was," wrote Bob McGinn in *The Ultimate Super Bowl Book*. The second quarter was quieter, with only a 28-yard Garo Yepremian field goal widening the Dolphins' advantage.

On Miami's second-half kickoff, Vikings returner John Gilliam stepped up to inject some life into his team's hopes with a 65-yard return. But just as quickly, the comeback flame went out when the big run was called back because of a clipping penalty, and the Dolphins' scorched earth attack resumed. The next time they got the ball, the Dolphins drove 43 yards to score on a 2-yard Csonka run on a drive

powered by the game's single showpiece pass play, 27 yards from Griese to Paul Warfield.

Minnesota avoided a shutout on a Tarkenton 4-yard keeper as the third quarter turned into the fourth. But the ball stayed firmly in the Dolphins' court, especially in the final 6:24 of the game when they burned the block by running 11 straight times to gain 41 useless yards and ensure that Csonka would break the Super Bowl rushing record. The record would last only a year—toppled in Super Bowl IX by the Steelers' workhorse Franco Harris.

Csonka's place in the record books wasn't the only thing that was fading into history, even as the Lombardi Trophy was presented to Shula and his Dolphins for the second time. The offensive heart of

the team would soon be gone as well. In March, the bottom fell out for Shula with a phone call informing him that Csonka, Kiick, and Warfield had signed futures contracts with the fledgling World Football League.

The three played out the final year of their contract with the Dolphins and then bolted for more money (Csonka's salary reportedly went from $55,000 to $500,000 with a $500,000 signing bonus), but the WFL experiment was a failure, and Csonka returned to the NFL in 1976 for three seasons with the Giants before ending his career in 1979 with the team that had afforded him his greatest glory, the Dolphins. Shula and his squad wouldn't win another playoff game until 1982, and he would never coach in another Super Bowl.

SUPER BOWL IX

PITTSBURGH STEELERS vs MINNESOTA VIKINGS

16   6

DATE	January 12, 1975
HOST CITY	Tulane Stadium, New Orleans, LA
MVP	Franco Harris, RB, Pittsburgh
TIME-OUT	Vikings defensive end Dwight White spent most of Super Bowl week in a New Orleans hospital, felled by a combination of pleurisy and an overabundance of oysters and gumbo.

The Super Bowl was not quite 10 years old, and even if teams such as the Packers and the Dolphins had made a bold imprint on the championship, a genuine Super Bowl dynasty had yet to emerge. The 1975 Super Bowl marked the inauguration for the peerless Pittsburgh Steelers squad that would win four Super Bowls in the next six years.

In the race toward football innovation, defensive minds were outpacing offensive strategists in the mid-'70s, and nowhere was the defensive revolution better epitomized than in Pittsburgh, the land of the Steel Curtain and coordinator Bud Carson's Cover-Two Defense. The score of Super Bowl IX—Pittsburgh 16, Minnesota 6—demonstrates clearly which side of the ball prevailed on that wet, cold day in New Orleans.

Perennial cellar dwellers in the '60s, the Steelers and their fortunes started to turn in 1970 when head coach Chuck Noll drafted Terry Bradshaw, followed by a string of picks in the next four drafts that yielded Hall of Fame talents such as Joe Greene, Franco Harris, Lynn Swann, Jack Lambert, and Mel Blount. After prevailing over the favored Raiders 24-13 in the AFC Championship Game, the Steelers would face the Vikings in their second consecutive Super Bowl appearance in what was originally planned to be the grand opening of the Superdome.

The NFL had awarded the game to New Orleans to christen the modern 73,000-seat domed stadium that was started in 1971. But burdened by construction delays and political squabbles, the construction took many months longer than planned, and the game had to be contested at Tulane Stadium, the site of the coldest Super Bowl on record in 1972. Players were certainly wishing for the dome when they stepped out on the soaked field for warm-up on a blustery 46-degree day that Carson considered one of the coldest football days he had ever experienced.

After being stifled by Miami's running game the previous year, the Vikings approached the game with hopes of establishing their own rushing attack, but the Steel Curtain held its opponent to only 21 yards on the ground, and versatile quarterback Fran Tarkenton was frustrated with only 11 pass completions out of 26 attempts, for 102 yards on the ground. Minnesota converted only nine first downs all afternoon, and it would be Tarkenton's second straight Super Bowl without a touchdown pass.

Pittsburgh's intense defensive pressure also forced five Minnesota turnovers—three interceptions and two fumbles—and the one fumble that they recovered was still costly, leading to a second-quarter safety when Tarkenton lost the snap and fell on the ball in his own end

Left, Fans of the Pittsburgh Steelers cheer on their team during a 16-6 win over the Minnesota Vikings in Super Bowl IX. *AP Photo/NFL Photos*

Right, "Mean" Joe Greene, Pittsburgh Steelers tackle, encourages his teammates. *AP Photo/Harry Cabluck*

zone. In case anyone had yet to label this a defensive scuffle, the halftime score of 2-0 was evidence enough of the game's central theme.

"In Super Bowl IX, the Steelers' front four painted a masterpiece of mayhem," wrote Gary Pomerantz in *Their Life's Work: The Brotherhood of the 1970s Pittsburgh Steelers, Then and Now*. "They beat the Vikings' offensive lineman off the snap, slipped their blocks, and physically handled them. As his pass protection disintegrated, Tarkenton scrambled wildly, as if escaping a burning building."

Even with a seemingly impenetrable defensive front, Pittsburgh needed more than a two-point edge if owner Art Rooney's dreams of a Super Bowl trophy were going to be fulfilled. Bradshaw was steady, and Harris was outstanding, breaking Csonka's Super Bowl VIII rushing record with 158 yards, but the game's first

touchdown was still enabled by the Steeler defense. On the kickoff to start the second half, the Steelers' Roy Gerela slipped on the wet surface for an unsteady kick, which then eluded Vikings fullback Bill Brown and finally found purchase in the arms of Pittsburgh linebacker Marv Kellum, thus setting up a short scoring drive that ended with Harris running 9 yards in for a 9-0 lead.

Despite the Steelers' confidence, their lack of offensive production and an error-prone special teams unit put them in a precarious 9-6 game with just 10 minutes left in the game. Minnesota linebacker Matt Blair got in front of Bobby Walden's punt for a clean block, which bounced four times downfield before Minnesota safety Terry Brown finally collected it for a touchdown. Kicker Fred Cox missed the point after, and the Steelers again looked to Bradshaw to fill their offensive vacuum.

The Blonde Bomber delivered, marshaling an 11-play, 66-yard drive that consumed seven minutes and gave Pittsburgh a 16-6 lead that made it the second-lowest-scoring Super Bowl of all time but was more than sufficient to earn the Steelers their first title. The final straw for Tarkenton and his Vikings came on the next play from scrimmage, when Pittsburgh's Mike Wagner picked off a pass intended for John Gilliam and sealed the triumph for his team. Color commentator Al Derogatis proclaimed, "If there's ever been a better defensive performance in the Super Bowl, I'd like you to name it."

After the victory, Pittsburgh linebacker and defensive captain Andy Russell had been tasked with choosing a defensive player as the recipient of the game ball. He was en route to defensive tackle Mean Joe Greene, who had dispatched every Viking with the misfortune to line up across from

him that day, but he glanced off to the corner of the locker room and saw 73-year-old owner Art Rooney, who had suffered through the team's dark years and overseen its rise to the top. "This one's for the Chief," Russell said as he handed the ball to Rooney. "It's a long time coming."

On the flight back to Pittsburgh, where some 120,000 fans would be waiting in subfreezing temperatures to hail their conquering heroes, Greene, Harris, and Swann pulled out souvenirs they had picked up in the stadium—plastic Viking helmets complete with horns. They wore them proudly, according to Pomerantz, calling them "spoils of war." The Steelers were just getting started. They would become fixtures on the front lines of NFL battle into the next decade.

SUPER BOWL X

DALLAS COWBOYS VS **PITTSBURGH STEELERS**

17   21

DATE   January 18, 1976

HOST CITY   Orange Bowl, Miami, FL

MVP   Lynn Swann, WR, Pittsburgh

TIME-OUT   Percy Howard caught just one pass in his entire NFL career: a 34-yard touchdown for the Cowboys in Super Bowl X.

Terry Bradshaw arriving in Miami, Florida.
AP Photo/Jim Kerlin

Up until the mid-'70s, the Super Bowl had become a major attraction with unparalleled media coverage because of the magnitude of the event itself. The world paid attention simply because it was the championship of a growing national sport, but, in reality, most of the games themselves left something to be desired.

The trend, through the first decade, was toward defensive scuffles in the trenches. With the exception of the scoring-heavy Packers in the first two bowls, the average combined scoring through the next seven games was only 26 points. And even though the 16-13 result in Super Bowl V was the outlier, most of the games were somewhere on the scale between definitive victory and blowout; every world champion except the Colts in 1971 won by at least a touchdown, with six out

of nine games ending with a double-digit margin.

Super Bowl X, besides marking a notable anniversary, represented a shift in offensive emphasis and a move toward more intense competition. The next decade of the Super Bowl wouldn't spell an end to routs, but the scoreboard operators would certainly be busier, and fans would be more engaged as explosion plays and frequent scoring became the norm. As Norm Miller recounted the contest for the New York Daily News, "All the big plays, the wacky mistakes and the suspense, right to the final play, today proved that a Super Bowl doesn't have to be dull."

The Pittsburgh Steelers of that era will forever be known as a defensive juggernaut, but with their 21-17 victory over the Dallas Cowboys that January in Miami, they would show their potency on

both sides of the ball. With an offensive connection—Bradshaw to Swann—providing the fireworks, the Steelers became the third team in NFL history to win two consecutive Super Bowls and further established themselves as one of the sport's true dynasties.

Racking up 161 yards on only four Terry Bradshaw passes, Lynn Swann was both MVP and human highlight reel that day in the Orange Bowl. Two of his earlier receptions, for 32 and 53 yards, included moves worthy of a circus acrobat, both pulled down miraculously in the midst of cornerback Mark Washington's aggressive coverage. But the reception with the most staying power, because it gave Pittsburgh the lead it would need for the win, was a 64-yard bomb with 3:02 left in the game. Afterward Swann called it "the best catch I've made in professional football."

Swann's performance was made even more sensational by his medical history in the two weeks leading up to the game. The AFC Championship Game between the Steelers and their archrival Raiders had looked more like a brawl, and even though Pittsburgh pulled out a 16-10 win, the greatest casualty of the day was the Steelers' leading receiver. Raiders defensive back George Atkinson leveled Swann with such force that Swann was knocked unconscious and spent two days in the hospital.

After he was discharged, he sat out of practice for a week, but even in workouts in Miami, just days before the game, Swann was showing the aftereffects of the concussion—dropping passes and appearing disoriented. But before game day was over, he had etched himself permanently into the collective memory

Left, Cowboys QB Roger Staubach (12) hands off to FB Robert Newhouse (44). *AP Photo/Vernon Biever*

Right, Actor Robert Shaw runs during a scene in the filming of the movie *Black Sunday*. Its theme of a terrorist plot at the Super Bowl was filmed during time-outs and halftime at the Super Bowl X game. *AP Photo/NFL Photos*

Opposite page, Dwight White (78), a member of Pittsburgh's acclaimed Steel Curtain Defense, chases down Dallas Cowboys quarterback Roger Staubach in the second quarter. *AP Photo*

of American football fans and became the first wide receiver ever to be named MVP.

Super Bowl X looked like a high-scoring affair compared to earlier results, but most of the points—21 in all—were accrued in the fourth quarter. The Cowboys, only the second Super Bowl competitor at that point to lose a game when they led at halftime, came into the locker room ahead 10-7, energized by a Roger Staubach–to–Drew Pearson touchdown pass set up by Steelers' punter Bobby Walden's lost fumble.

Pittsburgh answered with a touchdown of its own, accelerated by Swann's first miraculous grab, that culminated in a 7-yard pass from Bradshaw to Randy Grossman. Dallas kicker Toni Fritsch

converted on a 36-yard field goal in the second quarter, and neither team would score again until early in the fourth, when the Steelers special teams provided a breakthrough.

The key play was an unusual one—a blocked punt for a safety—and it gave the Steelers two points and excellent field position to strike again. When Pittsburgh's Reggie Harrison threw his body in front of Dallas punter Mitch Hoop's kick, the ball went straight through the end zone for an automatic safety, and the subsequent free punt led the Steelers to a quick Roy Gerela field goal. Suddenly, Pittsburgh owned a 12-10 lead and the momentum.

Just like that, Dallas was trailing, and their shaken confidence was evident when

Staubach threw an errant pass into the hands of Steelers safety Mike Wagner and the defending champions drove to another Gerela field goal. The next Pittsburgh blow was Swann's 64-yard deathblow, and the Cowboys found themselves with only three minutes to overcome a 21-10 deficit.

Tom Landry and his troops continued to battle by converting quickly on a 34-yard touchdown play from Staubach to Percy Howard and then getting the ball back, with no time-outs, at their own 39-yard line with 1:22 to put together another touchdown drive. Staubach was still confident, he said later, but in the end his team couldn't find the formula to collect the necessary yards when time was in such short

supply. At crunch time, there was no getting past the Steel Curtain.

When it was all over and Chuck Noll was collecting the Lombardi Trophy again, stat sheets revealed a total of 609 yards: 339 for Pittsburgh and 270 for Dallas. Only in Super Bowl III, when Joe Namath and his Jets upset the Colts, did the two teams collect more yards, and no one who had witnessed all 10 would dispute the status of this game—with Swann's displays of greatness, lead changes, and a trailing team with a last-minute comeback in its sights—as the most exciting Super Bowl yet.

GAME BREAK

Left, Actor Robert Shaw and director John Frankenheimer watch the Pittsburgh Steelers take on the Dallas Cowboys in Super Bowl X. Shaw was starring in Frankenheimer's film, *Black Sunday*, which was filmed during the game. *AP Photo/Tony Tomsic*

Below right, Actor Charlton Heston stars in *Two Minute Warning*. *AP Photo*

MOVIES AND BOOKS
USING THE SUPER BOWL
AS A SETTING

The measure of a truly pervasive cultural event is that event's presence in other aspects of American life, especially popular entertainment. When it comes to the Super Bowl, the game's artistic footprint is considerably larger than just the Chicago Bears' "Super Bowl Shuffle." Even if the NFL has placed more restrictions on the use of the game's name and setting in recent years, the Super Bowl's influence can still be found in these movies and books from earlier decades:

TWO-MINUTE WARNING, 1976

This low-budget film was panned, despite the presence of notable actors such as Charlton Heston and Jack Klugman. The plot, which features a sniper who sneaks into a game at the Los Angeles Coliseum called Championship X and decides to take out innocent people when the president of the United States fails to arrive as planned, has been largely forgotten by all but the most ardent sports-film buffs.

"How incompetent is it?" asks one reviewer on the film website imdb.com. "How about this for a setup: on Super Bowl Sunday (or Championship X, as it's referred to in the film), a sniper guns down a bicyclist from a nearby hotel, then escapes to the Coliseum, where he hides out in the bell tower waiting for the game to start, and evidently to start shooting. How does he get in? He simply breaks open a couple of locks, feeds the guard dogs some hamburger and climbs the ladder into the tower. There is no security, no police, no media, nobody around except one maintenance man the morning of the biggest football game of the year."

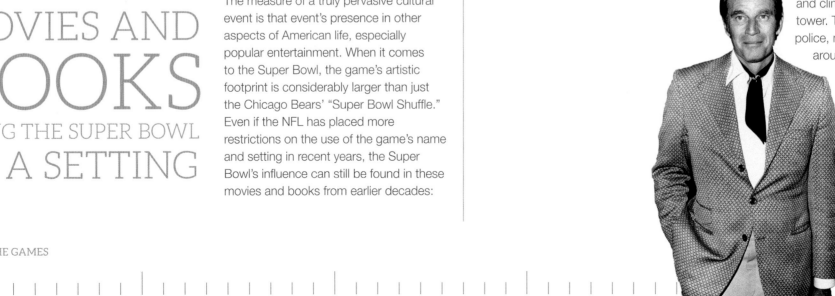

BLACK SUNDAY, 1977

Unlike *Two-Minute Warning*, this film was made with the approval of the NFL, and producer Robert Evans even managed to secure permission to shoot footage of the Cowboys playing the Steelers at Super Bowl X. The movie stars Bruce Dern as a Goodyear blimp pilot who is scarred from his prisoner-of-war experience in Vietnam and collaborates with a Palestinian terrorist group on a suicide plot involving his dirigible and a packed Orange Bowl on Super Bowl Sunday.

Billed as the second *Jaws*, the movie was popular with focus groups but a disappointment at the box office, and *Star Wars: Episode IV* usurped it as the big blockbuster of 1977.

MURDER AT THE SUPER BOWL, 1986

Fran Tarkenton can be forgiven if he has some dark feelings toward the Super Bowl, since he was the quarterback for the Minnesota Vikings during losing bids for rings at Super Bowls VIII, IX, and XI. In 1986, with coauthor Herbert Resnicow, Tarkenton penned a story about the drama that ensues when the head coach of the fictional Brooklyn Wizards is murdered a week before his team's Super Bowl matchup with the Oregon Orcas.
"*New York Daily Sentry* sports scribe Marc Burr discovers the body and tries to get a scoop for his paper," according to a write-up in *Publisher's Weekly*. "Soon he finds himself caught between a tough Brooklyn cop, who wants Marc's help in sleuthing, and the killer himself."

THE SUM OF ALL FEARS, 1991

Author Tom Clancy is renowned for his elaborate thrillers, and his favorite hero Jack Ryan finds himself in a treacherous situation in this novel when terrorists explode a small nuclear device at the Super Bowl in Denver. To illustrate the growingly cautious climate in the post-9/11 world and the NFL's vigilance against the use of the Super Bowl for entertainment purposes, the 2002 film of the same name starring Ben Affleck scripted the incident at a generic football game in Baltimore rather than at the Super Bowl.

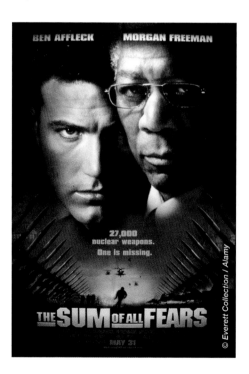

Above, This scene from the motion picture *Black Sunday* starring Robert Shaw, was filmed the day before a 21-17 Pittsburgh Steelers win over the Dallas Cowboys in Super Bowl X. *AP Photo/NFL Photos*

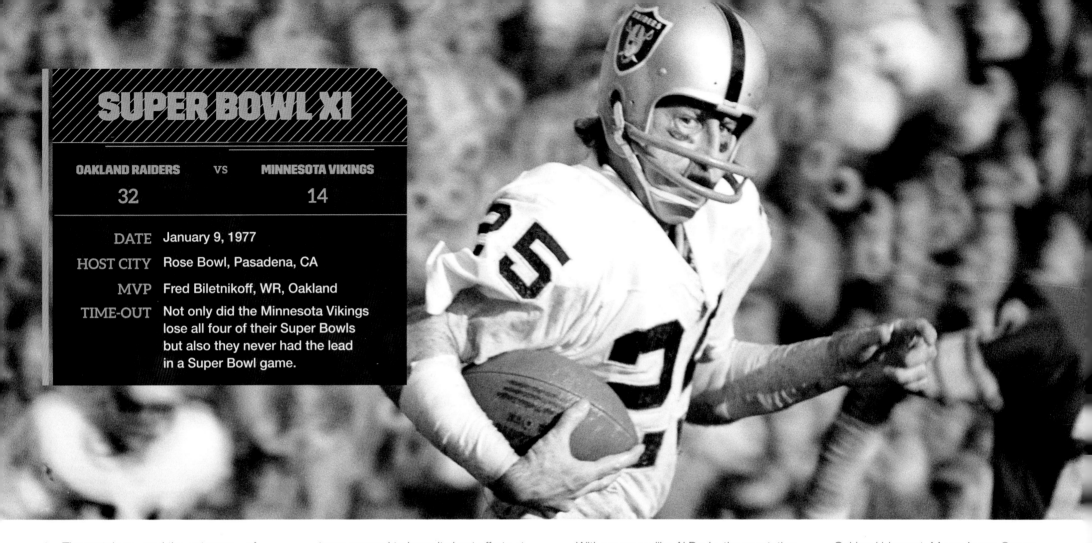

SUPER BOWL XI

OAKLAND RAIDERS VS **MINNESOTA VIKINGS**

32 **14**

DATE January 9, 1977

HOST CITY Rose Bowl, Pasadena, CA

MVP Fred Biletnikoff, WR, Oakland

TIME-OUT Not only did the Minnesota Vikings lose all four of their Super Bowls but also they never had the lead in a Super Bowl game.

The matchup—and the outcome—of Super Bowl XI begged the philosophical question: Is it better to barely miss the Super Bowl year after year or to make it four times and lose every one?

Ultimately, of course, it's best to win it all, and despite repeated frustrated attempts to get there, the Oakland Raiders finally prevailed in dramatic fashion when they punched their ticket in 1977. And when all was said and done in the Raiders' 32-14 victory in the Rose Bowl, Minnesota Vikings fans were left wondering why their

team seemed to leave its best efforts at home every time the Super Bowl came around.

Six times in the past eight years, Al Davis and his bad boy Oakland Raiders made it to the AFC Championship Game and lost. Despite their status as one of the toughest, most talented teams in the game, every one of those campaigns ended one step short of the Super Bowl, with Pittsburgh and its Steel Curtain standing in their way in both 1974 and 1975.

With an owner like Al Davis, the reputation of the 1970s Raiders teams was a foregone conclusion. They were characterized as wild, rebellious misfits, and when players with nicknames such as "the Assassin" (Jack Tatum) and "Dr. Death" (Skip Thomas) took the field for their first Super Bowl, no one expected a calm, civilized sporting event.

The Vikings weren't known as a particularly tough squad, and media members such as legendary *Los Angeles Times* columnist Jim Murray predicted an

Oakland blowout. Murray's pre–Super Bowl column proposed, among other modifications, making Raider touchdowns count for four points. Linebacker Phil Villapiano told the *New York Daily News* after the game, "We knew by Wednesday we were going to win," and years later Raiders head coach John Madden reflected, "It was the closest to being overconfident that I ever was in my life. I was like, 'We're going to kill these guys.'"

But when Minnesota's accomplished special teams unit came out and blocked a punt by the legendary Ray Guy 10 minutes into the game, the assumed Raider dominance seemed to be in question. It was the first one of Guy's punts ever to be blocked, and it seemed to portend trouble for the Raiders. But the Oakland defense fortified its front, dug in, and kept the Vikings from scoring on that possession when Brent McClanahan lost a fumble on first and goal from the 3-yard line and linebacker Willie Hall recovered it for Oakland.

That play, which put a sudden stop to the early momentum that was building for the Vikings, symbolized their Super Bowl troubles in a nutshell. In three of its four Super Bowl campaigns, Minnesota had lost a critical fumble within the 10-yard line, and the most telling stat of all, over the Vikings' four Super Bowl losses, was a total turnover differential of -12.

While the Raider defense was gunning for a shutout, the offensive line was putting together a masterful performance that would ultimately allow the backs to set a

Super Bowl record of 266 rushing yards and rack up 16 points in the second quarter alone. After the Vikings' fumble, Oakland's Clarence Davis broke out for a clutch 35-yard gain on third and 7 to spark Errol Mann's 24-yard field goal. On their next possession, Raiders quarterback Ken Stabler connected with Dave Casper on a 19-yard touchdown pass, thus building a 10-0 lead that would soon be insurmountable.

When the teams were stacked up against each other, Minnesota's age and inability to answer the Raiders' explosiveness truly sealed the victory for Oakland. As owner Al Davis said years later in a video celebrating his team's first Super Bowl win, they respected the Vikings' strengths but knew without a doubt that they could outlast them. "They weren't easy," he said. "It was just that what we could do, and what we did, I didn't see how they were going to stop us."

Returning to the field outpacing the Vikings 16-0 after halftime, Fran Tarkenton did manage to convert to score on passes in the third and fourth quarters, but the damage inflicted by the bruising Raiders —embodied by Tatum's kamikaze-style collision with Nate Wright that sent White's helmet flying across the field—was already done. For his team's dramatic finale, Hall picked off a Tarkenton pass in the fourth quarter and returned it 75 yards for a touchdown for the longest interception return in a Super Bowl to that point.

Receiver Fred Biletnikoff, who shone in a balanced Raiders offensive attack even

though he didn't score a touchdown, was the second consecutive wide receiver to win MVP honors. The future Hall of Famer caught four passes for 79 yards, and two of those receptions—including a 48-yarder in the fourth quarter—put his team just a hop from the goal line and in excellent position for Pete Banascak to barrel it in.

In the Vikings' locker room, the unique anguish that comes from getting four chances at the championship in 11 years and failing to come home with the trophy would have been compounded if they could have been allowed to glimpse the next four decades. Minnesota, which had been outscored 95-34 in its four Super Bowl appearances, would not play in the big game again in its first half century.

Even though it was the Raiders' first Super Bowl, they had something to prove that day, and the Vikings had made the trip so frequently that anything short of a victory would spell devastation. Ultimately, the day was a race to see which team could get the monkey off of its back first.

"You had that stigma—can't win the big one, always there, bridesmaid, all of those things, one shot and they're all gone now," Madden said. "And you can never say never anymore. The greatest thing about that win is that you have it for the rest of your life, and they can never say you can't do it."

Bottom left, Quarterback Ken Stabler of the Oakland Raiders celebrates completing a touchdown pass.
AP Photo

Bottom right, Coach John Madden of the Oakland Raiders is carried from the field by his players after his team defeated the Minnesota Vikings.
AP Photo/File

SUPER BOWL XII

DALLAS COWBOYS	VS	DENVER BRONCOS
27		10

DATE — January 15, 1978

HOST CITY — Superdome, New Orleans, LA

CO-MVPs — Randy White, DT, Dallas
Harvey Martin, DE, Dallas

TIME-OUT — The first Super Bowl to be played at the Superdome drew a sellout crowd of 75,583, and 102 million more Americans were watching on television. It was the largest audience ever to watch a sporting event and the first time the big game was ever played indoors.

The Denver Broncos had taken professional football by storm during the 1977 season, unexpectedly toppling higher-ranked opponents with their Orange Crush Defense and an aging quarterback who had already been discarded by two other teams.

So great was the mystique of this surging squad that the talented Dallas Cowboys, who were leading the NFL in both total offense and total defense, were only five-and-a-half-point favorites in the game that would be the first Super Bowl played

in the evening and the first one contested indoors (New Orleans was finally getting a chance to show off its Superdome, three years later than planned).

But despite some early sloppiness by Tom Landry and his Cowboys, in the end the enduring image of the Broncos in their first Super Bowl would be as the team hobbled by turnovers and stifled by a defense far more crushing than the one in orange. Denver's rise was abruptly halted by an all-around Cowboys team that took possession of its second Super Bowl title

with a 27-10 victory like it was a foregone conclusion.

The Orange Crush Defense, anchored by players such as Randy Gradishar, Tom Jackson, and Paul Smith, came into the game as the NFL's top unit against the run, but at the end of the day, Dallas prevailed with a balanced attack of 182 passing and 143 rushing yards in a national coming-out party for rookie running back Tony Dorsett.

Dorsett, the second overall pick in the draft, gave a crucial third dimension to a team that had long relied on its Roger

Staubach–powered air attack and the Doomsday Defense to stay competitive. Dorsett, who would be the Cowboys' leading rusher for the next 10 years, sustained a knee injury in the third quarter, so he gained only 66 yards on 15 carries that evening in New Orleans, but his early efficiency helped diversify Staubach's toolbox so that the Denver defense simply couldn't fill in all of the holes.

"I'd put that team against any team of any era," said Dallas safety Charlie Waters. "There was no weakness on that team."

Waters's assessment might have been questioned in the game's initial minutes, when the Cowboys fumbled the ball three times but managed to recover it each time. Staubach said later that the difference in decibel level between an outdoor stadium and the cavernous dome threw the Cowboys off on those early possessions, and he called the first quarter "pure chaos." Despite those missteps, Dallas managed to take a 10-0 lead into the second quarter with the assistance of Denver quarterback Craig Morton, who threw two consecutive interceptions that led first to a 3-yard Dorsett touchdown run and next a 35-yard Efren Herrera field goal.

Herrera hit a 43-yarder in the second quarter for a 13-0 Dallas lead, but he also missed three other field goals on Bronco turnovers during the game, so his impact on the final outcome could have been greater. Dallas had the momentum heading into halftime, but when Broncos kicker Jim Turner cleared a 47-yard field goal early in the third, the Cowboys' 10-point advantage was starting to look a bit slim.

Staubach and wide receiver Butch Johnson turned to theatrics to widen the gap on an unforgettable third-and-10 play, a 45-yard fingertip prayer that Johnson snatched from the air before falling into the end zone for a 20-3 Dallas lead. Denver answered with a touchdown of its own, sparked by Rick Upchurch's 67-yard kickoff return, but the stellar Cowboys defense would redouble its efforts and prevent its opponent from getting on the

scoreboard again. The Doomsday crew held the Broncos to just 38 yards on three possessions in the fourth period.

A key defensive tactic for Dallas was impeding quarterback Craig Morton, and the defensive players succeeded in aiding one of the most hapless quarterback performances in Super Bowl history. Morton had been a reliable passer for the Broncos throughout the season, but earlier in his career he spent nine seasons in Dallas (he was the Cowboys' starting quarterback in Super Bowl V), and the Doomsday Defenders were pretty confident that they had his number.

"We pressured him," said Dallas quarterback Mel Renfro. "Blitzed him. Went after him. Didn't give him time. He wasn't able to scramble because of his knees. We knew he wasn't mobile. … Our defense overwhelmed him."

Morton was so thoroughly rattled that Denver head coach Red Miller took him out of the game in the third quarter, just after he threw a screen pass that was nearly his fifth interception of the night. His passer rating for the game was 0.0. He was replaced by Norris Weese,

a virtual unknown who completed four passes for 22 yards and directed the Broncos' sole touchdown drive but also lost a crucial fumble in the fourth quarter.

The defense's role was so critical in the game's result that the *Sport* magazine writers who chose the most valuable player originally wanted to honor the entire defensive unit. In the end, they still broke precedent by selecting two players, defensive tackle Randy White and defensive end Harvey Martin, as co-MVPs. The two combined for three sacks and seven tackles in the victory.

The Cowboys would become one of the top three most successful teams in the first half century of the Super Bowl, and even if the team that triumphed in Super Bowl XII wasn't considered the most dominant of those championship teams,

it was certainly one of the most complete, and the victory in the game's first domed environment was the day they proved that they were a team that would be hanging around in the winner's column for a while.

In Denver, schoolchildren were required to wear orange to school, and teenagers had been trying to drink as much Orange Crush as they could hold, but the fan hysteria could go only so far. When the game was over, linebacker Thomas "Hollywood" Henderson picked up an orange cup from the turf, crumpled it in his hand, and said, "There's your Orange Crush." America's Team was back on top.

Top right, Dallas Cowboys wide receiver Butch Johnson (86) leaps out to make a catch. *AP Photo/NFL Photos*

Bottom center, Dallas Cowboys quarterback Roger Staubach smiles up at Tony Dorsett during a photo session for Super Bowl XII. *AP Photo*

SUPER BOWL XIII

PITTSBURGH STEELERS VS **DALLAS COWBOYS**

35 **31**

DATE January 21, 1979

HOST CITY Orange Bowl, Miami, FL

MVP Terry Bradshaw, QB, Pittsburgh

TIME-OUT The Cowboys' attempted comeback drive included two Roger Staubach touchdown passes in just two minutes late in the fourth quarter.

It's the scenario savvy sports observers hope for when the postseason rolls around, but often these games are too full of flukes, too open for underdog surges, for the two strongest teams to emerge and go toe to toe for the championship.

January 21, 1979, in the Miami stadium that had already hosted more Super Bowls than any other venue, was the day when the professional football planets aligned properly, when the two teams vying for the unofficial "team of the decade" designation met up with what seemed like more than a Lombardi Trophy on the line.

Neither the Pittsburgh Steelers nor the Dallas Cowboys had played perfect regular seasons, but as the fall advanced, the true strengths of both dynasties had emerged until their rematch in Super Bowl XIII became a foregone conclusion. It was the first time in the history of the big game that two teams met for the second time; in Super Bowl X, also in the Orange Bowl, Pittsburgh had prevailed 21-17.

That earlier game was stellar, but the two teams were still on the rise in 1976. When they met again three years later, they carried boatloads of expectations, and the football public anticipated the matchup with mouths watering, flush with the idea of powerhouses such as Staubach, Bradshaw, Dorsett, Swann, Harris, and Hill all taking the field together, with the ultimate bragging rights in the balance. When the dust had cleared, the Steelers had a 35-31 victory in the game that www.nfl.com would one day pronounce the best Super Bowl in the game's first half century.

The first half ran like a Hollywood script, with the game's two most accomplished quarterbacks engineering touchdown drives in turn. First Terry Bradshaw hit John Stallworth on a 28-yard pass for a Pittsburgh lead, and then Roger Staubach and Tony Hill responded when they combined for an explosive 39-yard scoring play.

The Cowboys, sniffing a possibility to build some momentum, took an early lead on a turnover forced by their tenacious defense. Thomas "Hollywood" Henderson, who made headlines before the game when he said that Bradshaw "couldn't spell 'cat' if you spotted him the *c* and the *t*," blitzed on a third and 10 and "shook him, trying to make something happen," he said later. Bradshaw lost control, and Dallas linebacker Mike Hegman came from behind him, grabbed the ball, and sprinted 37 yards home for a touchdown and a 14-7 Cowboys lead.

Dallas fans had mere minutes to enjoy their advantage. Three plays later, Bradshaw hit Stallworth again, this time on a short pass that turned into a 75-yard explosion play for a touchdown and one of the rare ties in Super Bowl history. Pittsburgh had the emotional edge after that big play, and Bradshaw capitalized on it late in the second quarter by turning a Mel Blount interception into a 56-yard drive capped with a 7-yard touchdown toss to Rocky Bleier. Halftime arrived just in time for fans, who needed to catch their breath as Pittsburgh entered the locker room with a 21-14 lead.

If the first half was a display of effective offense and explosion plays, the tale of the second half is constructed around a few crucial and historic mistakes, mostly by the Cowboys, that cracked the door open for Pittsburgh to gain control. In fact, the third quarter was an offensive misadventure for the Steelers; they converted only one first down in three possessions and failed to score. But one of the most famous fumbles in Super Bowl history, committed by the Cowboys, mitigated the effects of that lackluster effort for the eventual champions.

Staubach had marshaled his troops to the Pittsburgh 10-yard line, and as he checked off receivers on a third and 3, he spotted tight end Jackie Smith wide open, running a route to the back of the end zone. Smith was a 38-year-old bar owner and former St. Louis Cardinals player who had been called out of retirement late that season when the Cowboys lost their starter to an injury. He was known for his toughness and what Henderson described as "iron hands."

As Staubach fired the pass, as he later recalled, he took some power off of it because it appeared that Smith wasn't completely turned. But it came shorter and quicker than Smith expected, and as he scrambled for it, he slipped on the wet Orange Bowl turf. With no defender anywhere near him, the ball bounced away from him incomplete, and the Cowboys' hope for a second-half surge seemed to disappear with it.

With that fumble, Dallas settled for a field goal, and the game was still very much in play as Pittsburgh carried a scant 21-17 lead into the fourth quarter. But with three Dallas mishaps that would be replayed in the consciousness of America's Team for decades, the Cowboys' hopes of winning the nation's greatest rematch evaporated.

First, the field judge called a controversial and costly pass interference penalty on cornerback Benny Barnes that later prompted a letter of apology from NFL commissioner Pete Rozelle. Then Franco Harris barreled 22 yards for a touchdown, and seconds after that, Pittsburgh kicker Roy Gerela slipped on the kickoff, and the Cowboys' Randy White struggled to get control of the ball. Landry's decision to put White in that position was the subject of rampant second-guessing later; the Cowboys' Pro Bowl tackle had fractured his thumb two weeks earlier and was playing with a cast. He lost the ball, Steelers linebacker Dennis Winston recovered and ran it into the end zone, and in just 19 seconds Pittsburgh's lead had become 35-17.

Staubach and his troops kept fighting, converting twice more on pass plays for a final score of 35-31, but that short stretch of misadventure early in the period had sealed the Cowboys' fate. The hero of the day was the quarterback on the other sideline, Bradshaw, who completed 17 of 30 passes for 318 yards and his first MVP trophy. He also gave a definitive response to the much-publicized barb about his mental acuity when he told a group of reporters afterward, "Go and ask Henderson if I was dumb today."

"We tried hard, but we didn't take advantage of the opportunities we had," Landry told *The Sporting News*. "I said all along that turnovers and breaks would determine the winner. That's what happened today. On any given day the Steelers are no better than we are."

Pittsburgh Steelers wide receiver John Stallworth goes high to haul in a pass from Terry Bradshaw.
AP Photo

"AS A PLAYER, IT SAYS EVERYTHING ABOUT YOU IF YOU MADE THE HALL OF FAME. BUT, THEN AGAIN, BOY ... THERE'S SOMETHING ABOUT WINNING A SUPER BOWL."

CHAPTER 3: THE 1980s

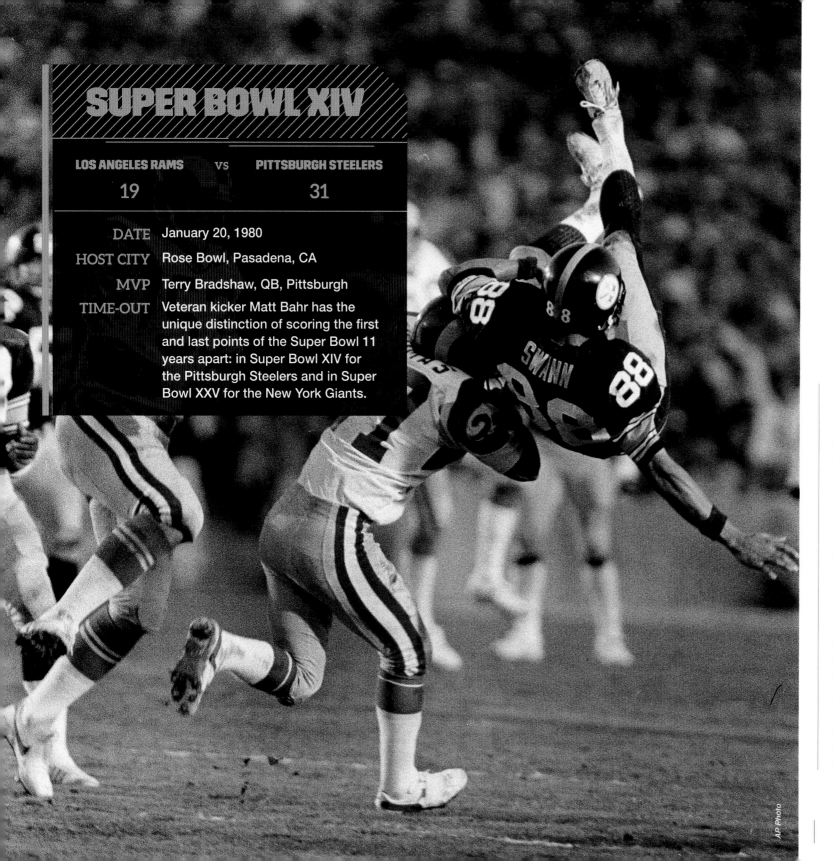

SUPER BOWL XIV

LOS ANGELES RAMS VS **PITTSBURGH STEELERS**

19 **31**

DATE	January 20, 1980
HOST CITY	Rose Bowl, Pasadena, CA
MVP	Terry Bradshaw, QB, Pittsburgh
TIME-OUT	Veteran kicker Matt Bahr has the unique distinction of scoring the first and last points of the Super Bowl 11 years apart: in Super Bowl XIV for the Pittsburgh Steelers and in Super Bowl XXV for the New York Giants.

AP Photo

After the slugfest between two powerhouses in Super Bowl XIII, it would seem that the Pittsburgh Steelers would put together a blowout when they punched their ticket to return to the game the following year. After all, their opponent was a 9-7 Los Angeles Rams team with the worst regular-season record of any Super Bowl team in history.

But projections don't always equal reality, and the truth was the Steelers juggernaut that had owned the '70s was showing signs of advancing age as the '80s dawned. In the early minutes of the fourth quarter, the brash Rams were disrespecting Chuck Noll's dynasty by holding onto a 19-17 lead. In the final period, Terry Bradshaw overcame uncharacteristic mistakes to pull his team through for Pittsburgh's fourth ring of the decade and his second consecutive MVP award.

The Steelers might have made it look easy at times, but that hard-fought fourth Super Bowl victory was emblematic of the magnitude of their accomplishment. The San Francisco 49ers would emerge as the 1980s' answer to Pittsburgh's dominance, but in the end the two teams would stand together unrivaled at the top of the pile of the greatest Super Bowl dynasties of the game's first half century. The Rams, with their scrappy veteran Jack Youngblood as the soul of the team, were the last squad with a shot at displacing them from the history books.

In many ways the Rams were the anti-Steelers: the glitz of Tinseltown versus blue-collar steel communities; a veteran Pro Bowl quarterback against a young upstart named Vince Ferragamo in only his eighth professional start; an established coaching giant matching wits with Ray Malavasi, the Rams' third coach in two years. But the two teams had more in common than met the eye. Three of Los Angeles' assistant coaches, Lionel Taylor, Dan Radakovich, and the legendary defensive mastermind Bud Carson, had coached under Noll in the '70s. Rams such as Youngblood, who played in Super Bowl XIV with a broken leg, typified the trademark Carson toughness that had forged the Steel Curtain a decade earlier.

The Rams, whose Hollywood image had been reinforced the year before by the release of the movie *Heaven Can Wait* (Warren Beatty's silver-screen L.A. Rams won the Super Bowl), took the field at the Rose Bowl without a hint of intimidation at the sports legends lining up across the line of scrimmage. Thanks to their Steeler-

savvy assistants, they had a good idea of the schemes they would face, and the Rams defenders showed their tenacity when they allowed Pittsburgh to gain only 23 yards on eight running plays on the first Steelers drive, which ended with a 41-yard Matt Bahr field goal.

Los Angeles struck with its own offensive fireworks just minutes later, when a 39-yard Wendell Tyler run sparked a touchdown drive that ended with a 1-yard Cullen Bryant run over the goal line. The lead seesaw continued in the second quarter, when Pittsburgh converted on a drive accelerated by Larry Anderson's 45-yard kickoff return (Anderson would set a Super Bowl record that day by collecting 162 yards on five returns). With the defending champs holding on 10-7, the Rams continued to pound away at a Steelers defense that was just a step or two past its prime. Two Frank Corral field goals, from 31 and 45 yards, gave Los Angeles a 13-10 halftime edge.

In the locker room at the game's midpoint, the Pittsburgh players certainly recalled the odds: the Steelers were favored by 10, the largest spread in a decade, as well as their status as Super Bowl regulars. The Rams would certainly slow their pursuit in the second half as the Steelers called on their considerable depth and experience. This optimism held up for a while, when Anderson gained 37 yards on the opening kickoff and Bradshaw found Swann for a highlight-worthy 47-yard touchdown pass. Steelers fans rejoiced as their MVP quarterback and their best receiver combined for a four-point lead.

But Ferragamo wasn't ready to concede. On a third down shortly after that Steelers drive, he connected with Billy Waddy on a 50-yard pass into Steeler territory and followed it with a 24-yard scoring pass to Ron Smith. As the third quarter expired, the Rams, who missed the extra point on the Smith touchdown, were ahead by two.

In the fourth quarter, the Steelers finally found a little bit of breathing room, thanks to more explosion plays from Bradshaw. He threw three interceptions in the game and called it "the toughest Super Bowl I've ever been in," but when he hit John Stallworth for a spectacular 73-yard catch for the go-ahead touchdown, the gods seemed to be smiling on the nation's Super Bowl team once again. Pittsburgh iced the win with one more touchdown drive for a 31-19 decision whose score belied the tension that had characterized most of the game.

Super Bowl XIV had seven lead changes, and while it wasn't Pittsburgh's final world championship, it marked the end of the Steeler stranglehold on the event. Bradshaw had appeared in four Super Bowls, led his team to victory in all of them, and taken home the MVP trophy twice. He would play for three more years, but this surprisingly tough battle with the Rams would be his last time to play in the game that had come to seem like his turf.

As the clock expired, Bradshaw told reporters later, he had a moment of clarity, a sense that he should soak up the atmosphere and the feeling of triumph. "There are few great moments in an athlete's life," he said. "Just this one time,

Super Bowl XIV, I decided that this was my moment and I wanted to take it all in. I wanted to pack it away in my mind forever. I felt that for this bunch of Steelers the run was over; we would never be in this situation again. So I did just that. I stood there and absorbed the stadium."

Pittsburgh Steelers quarterback Terry Bradshaw throws up both his arms and indicates his team is number one after the Steelers won their fourth Super Bowl over the Los Angeles Rams.
AP Photo/NFL Photos

SUPER BOWL XV

OAKLAND RAIDERS	VS	PHILADELPHIA EAGLES
27		10

DATE	January 25, 1981
HOST CITY	Superdome, New Orleans, LA
MVP	Jim Plunkett, QB, Oakland
TIME-OUT	MVP Jim Plunkett was cut from two other NFL teams and didn't become Oakland's starter until week 6, when Dan Pastorini went down with a broken leg.

The Philadelphia Eagles' defense was ranked second in the NFL, and in November of 1980 they had held the Oakland Raiders to one touchdown and prevailed in a 10-7 defensive scrap. But when veteran Eagles linebacker Bill Bergey gathered his fellow defenders in an effort to energize them after Oakland took a dizzying 14-3 lead in Super Bowl XV, he didn't like the look in their eyes.

"Everybody was like zombies," Bergey said. "I just said, 'This game is over. There is just no way we're going to win this game.'"

No one expected a trouncing that day in the Superdome, especially since the Eagles were favored and the Raiders were wild cards who had been overachieving all the way to the Super Bowl. But with

unlikely hero Jim Plunkett directing the Raiders offense, they acted nothing like underdogs and led wire to wire for their second Lombardi Trophy in five years.

The outcome was certainly not what Philadelphia fans, backing their team in its first Super Bowl appearance, were anticipating, especially with proven performers such as Herman Edwards and John Bunting providing strength in the trenches. Quarterback Ron Jaworski was professional football's golden child, the winner of three different player-of-the-year awards after throwing for a career-high 27 touchdowns that year. But from the early minutes of that game in New Orleans, Philadelphia's confidence seemed to be shaken.

When Philadelphia players reflect on that run to the championship, they concur that the team was drained by the effort of getting there. The Eagles had been hapless through the late '60s and most of the '70s, failing to make the postseason in the Super Bowl era and not recording a winning season at all between 1966 and 1978. Under Dick Vermeil, the Eagles finally figured out how to win, and 1980 had been a storybook 12-4 season, with the happy ending seeming to come with their 20-7 defeat of the Dallas Cowboys in the NFC Championship Game.

Vermeil and his troops poured maximum effort into the preparation and execution of that victory over Dallas, and their surprisingly resounding performance prompted the kind of celebration in

Philadelphia often reserved for the presentation of the Lombardi Trophy.

Of course, two weeks later they had to take the field again against the upstart Raiders, only the second wild card squad to make the Super Bowl since the playoff system was restructured 10 years earlier.

"The thing of it was we had put so much mentally and physically into that Dallas game, and guess what?" Bergey said. "We couldn't get back, not even close, to that level."

Rod Martin, the Oakland outside linebacker who had been a twelfth-round draft pick out of USC, became the thorn in Jaworski's side that evening when he intercepted three of his passes as Philly followed their game plan of keeping the

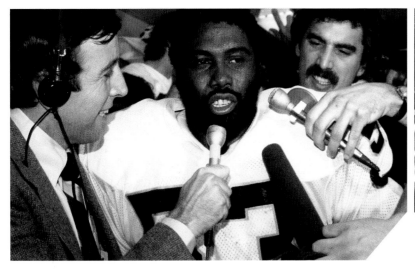

ball away from five-time Pro Bowler Ted Hendricks on the other side. The first of those picks happened on Jaworski's first pass of the day, intended for tight end Johnny Spagnola. Jaworski misread the coverage, an uncharacteristic mistake that represented his team's state of mind.

"I was trying too hard to make a big play," Jaworski told the *Philadelphia Daily News* 10 years later. "I think that happens to a lot of teams in their first Super Bowl. Instead of sticking with the things that got you there, you try to do more, and it backfires."

Martin's return brought the Raiders to the Philadelphia 30-yard line, and from there Plunkett had an easy touchdown drive that ended with a 2-yard Cliff Branch run. The game was just minutes old, and already Oakland had a 7-0 lead. It seemed like a battle was on when Jaworski found Rodney Parker on a 40-yard touchdown pass a few drives later, but the score was called back on an illegal motion penalty, and less than a minute later Oakland grabbed the reins.

The game's most pivotal moment came on a spectacular improvised pass play from Plunkett to Kenny King that resulted in an 80-yard touchdown conversion. The Eagles answered faintly in the second quarter with a 30-yard Tony Franklin field goal, but it wasn't enough to infuse momentum into the NFL champs as they headed into the locker room.

Harold Carmichael, the recipient of that crucial flag, said that the quick chain of events at the end of the first quarter was demoralizing for the Eagles. "I still have nightmares about that game," he told the *Philadelphia Daily News* in 1991. "We played mistake-free football all season, but that day we couldn't do anything right."

In the second half, Plunkett and Oakland continued to make plays while the Raider defense foiled Philadelphia's ground game, allowing their opponent only 69 yards on 26 carries all day. Martin also took further advantage of the Eagles' blunder of overlooking him by intercepting Jaworski two more times and derailing potential

comeback attempts. With his performance, Martin set a Super Bowl record for interceptions that stood for five decades and effectively deflated the Eagles for good.

"He was everywhere," Oakland linebacker Matt Millen, who like Jaworski went on to a career as a broadcast analyst, said on a film about the game. "He played as good a Super Bowl as any defender has ever played."

To this day, there are some NFL observers who believe the MVP award for Oakland's victory should go to Martin, but the story line of the actual winner, Plunkett, was every bit as compelling. As the 1970 Heisman Trophy winner out of Stanford and the 1971 AFC Rookie of the Year with the Patriots, Plunkett followed those accomplishments by stumbling for the rest of the decade but finally righted his career midway through the 1980 season when an injury to Dan Pastorini gave him the starting nod.

"I was ready, once I stepped out onto that field," said Plunkett, who finished the day with 13 of 21 for 261 yards and three interceptions of his own. "I still had something to prove to myself, and to whoever else." If the game itself provided scant drama, the trophy presentation had the potential for fireworks, since NFL commissioner Pete Rozelle was handing the hardware to the man who had become his nemesis, Raiders owner and lifelong maverick Al Davis. Davis had been lobbying for a year to move his team to Los Angeles, and Rozelle was blocking his attempts. The two didn't shake hands that day in New Orleans, but they were civil, and at that moment Davis didn't much care which West Coast city his team claimed.

"This was our finest hour," he said. "This was the finest hour in the history of the Oakland Raiders."

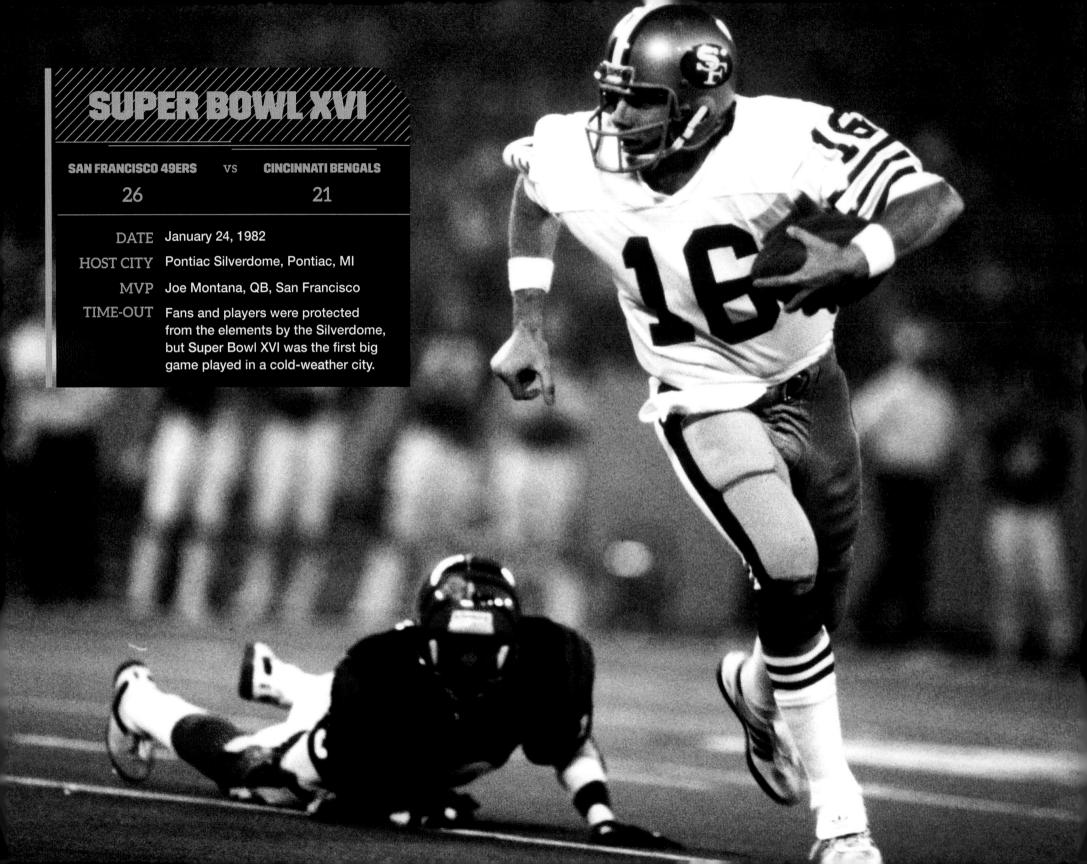

SUPER BOWL XVI

SAN FRANCISCO 49ERS   VS   **CINCINNATI BENGALS**

26   **21**

DATE   January 24, 1982

HOST CITY   Pontiac Silverdome, Pontiac, MI

MVP   Joe Montana, QB, San Francisco

TIME-OUT   Fans and players were protected from the elements by the Silverdome, but Super Bowl XVI was the first big game played in a cold-weather city.

Right, San Francisco 49ers' Dwight Clark leaps high in the end zone to catch a Joe Montana pass that tied the game late in the fourth quarter against the Dallas Cowboys in the NFC Championship football game at Candlestick Park. *AP Photo/ Dallas Morning News, Phil Huber*

Far right, Cincinnati Bengals quarterback Ken Anderson rolls out to pass. *AP Photo/Al Messerschmidt*

Still smarting from his team's improbable loss to the upstart San Francisco 49ers in the NFC Championship Game, Dallas Cowboys coach Tom Landry assessed Bill Walsh and his squad like this: "There is really nothing there but the quarterback."

The 49ers of the early '80s were certainly only a shadow of the force they would soon become, but the San Francisco team that felled the Cincinnati Bengals 26-21 in Super Bowl XVI was certainly no one-trick pony. Joe Montana did his thing, but an epic goal-line stand and astute play by the secondary were just as crucial for the 49ers in their first Super Bowl triumph.

Only three years earlier, San Francisco had limped through two straight seasons with records of 2-14. Walsh arrived in 1979, chomping at the bit to run his own team after years of serving as an offensive

assistant and two years at the helm at Stanford, but despite his revolutionary offensive practices, his first two 49ers squads went 2-14 and 6-10. It was a franchise whose history had been marked by haplessness, but Walsh slowly started to turn things around as he found personnel to match his philosophy, most notably when he drafted a quarterback named Joe Montana in the third round of the 1979 draft.

It was a Montana–to–Dwight Clark pass, forever immortalized in football lore as "The Catch," that vaulted San Francisco over Dallas in the NFC title game, and it was that third year of collaboration between Walsh and Montana that made the football world pay closer attention to the precision, pass-heavy approach that would soon change the game.

Neither the 49ers nor the Bengals had ever appeared in the Super Bowl before, and neither was expected to be there this year, but both climbed to the top with improbable postseason runs and composed play by quarterbacks Montana and Cincinnati's Ken Anderson. And Super Bowl XVI wasn't historic only for the inclusion of two first-time teams; it was also the first world championship to take place in the North.

The wind chill in Pontiac, Michigan, at kickoff was below zero, but it was a balmy 72 degrees inside the Silverdome, playing host to the Super Bowl for the only time. Nothing was quite as expected that day, and the oddsmakers—seemingly flummoxed by the convergence of two teams that had never been seen as powerhouses—favored Cincinnati by one.

The first half completely defied that prediction, ending with a 21-0 San Francisco lead enabled by the Bengals' inability to hold onto the ball at crucial moments. First Dwight Hicks intercepted an Anderson pass, and a touchdown drive resulted. Then San Francisco recovered Cris Collinsworth's fumble in the red zone and drove 92 yards the other way for a 14-0 lead. Finally, in just 13 seconds, Bengals kick returners fumbled two consecutive Ray Wersching squib kicks, and both resulted in Wersching field goals. Just like that, the 49ers found themselves with a comfortable lead and escalating confidence.

To Cincinnati's credit, they used that halftime break to find their inner drive. "In the locker room, we just talked about doing what we do well," head coach

Forrest Gregg said. "We were just getting ready to go back out on the field, and Reggie Williams jumped up and said, 'You just gotta believe that we can do this.' We came out and roared."

That burst of emotion helped fuel an 83-yard scoring drive at the beginning of the third quarter, putting the Bengals on the board on Anderson's 5-yard keeper on third down. Cincinnati did its part, too, tying up Montana's game plan with two consecutive three-and-out possessions. The scoreboard was still lopsided, but the Bengals owned the momentum as the fourth quarter opened. Anderson hit Collinsworth on an explosive 49-yard pass to put his team in the red zone, and the hunt seemed to be on.

It was at that moment that the San Francisco defense dug in its heels for what 49ers defensive line coach Bill McPherson called the best goal-line stand he had seen in 50 years. Cincinnati had five chances to find the end zone, starting at the 5-yard line, and at their last gasp it was fourth down and a foot. Running back Pete Johnson, who had been stuffed repeatedly in the last few plays, took the handoff and found a brick wall made of San Francisco jerseys.

The Bengals' comeback hopes were on shaky ground, but Anderson took charge again on their next possession and found a way to break through the defense, scoring on a 4-yard touchdown pass to tight end Dan Ross. The San Francisco

Joe Montana pauses for a refresher as he talks on the sidelines.
AP Images

lead was just 20-14, and there was plenty of time left on the clock. Montana, always cool under pressure, stepped up, threw a 22-yard pass to Mike Wilson, and helped direct a drive that ended in a 40-yard Wersching field goal. Both teams scored again, and the Bengals kept battling, but their last scoring drive consumed so much time that any further last-minute theatrics were impossible.

Gregg, a major contributor as a player in two Super Bowls with Green Bay and one with Dallas, was philosophical about the less-than-storybook ending to his team's unlikely ascent. "We weren't even picked for third in our division," he said. "We lost, but there is lots to be proud of. I think the players started thinking about what could have been instead of what was. After that

it looked as if they were trying not to make mistakes."

The 49ers earned their rings, but apart from Cincinnati's first-half turnovers, the two teams had similar stats and played each other closely. One of the two would become the dominant team of the decade, but even as a half million people feted the champs in a San Francisco victory parade, it would be difficult in 1982 to guess which team would emerge.

Bottom left, Cincinnati quarterback Ken Anderson fires a pass on a Bengals scoring drive.
AP Photo/Al Messerschmidt

Opposite page, Blair Bush (58) watches as the San Francisco 49ers react to their stopping a Bengals drive within the 1-yard line during the second half.
AP Photo

TOP SUPER BOWL UPSETS

Sports fans love watching the underdog rise up and conquer, but ranking the most decisive upsets is an inexact science. The betting line is one consideration, but Las Vegas is far from omniscient. Team records, momentum through the playoffs, public and media perception—all come into play when considering the most cataclysmic results in Super Bowl history. Here are five big games that unfolded in a truly unexpected fashion:

SUPER BOWL III

New York Jets 16
Baltimore Colts 7

This game gets top billing both for beating the betting line—the Colts were favored by 17 points—and for blindsiding American football fans who had been sold on the NFL's supremacy. But Jets quarterback Joe Namath had confidence to spare, and he guaranteed an upset and then backed it up with 206 yards and no interceptions while his defense forced five Colts turnovers.

SUPER BOWL IV

Kansas City Chiefs 23
Minnesota Vikings 7

Without a victory-guaranteeing quarterback in a fur coat, this Super Bowl is often overshadowed by the one that preceded it. But quarterback Len Dawson and the 12-point-underdog Chiefs rolled over a Vikings squad with 12 straight victories and a reputation for physical dominance. With the win, the AFL evened the score to 2-2 just before the merger of the two leagues.

Left, Kansas City running back Mike Garrett (*right*) is embraced by Otis Taylor after he scored a touchdown in the first half of Super Bowl IV. *AP Photo/JS*

Top right, Pro Football Hall of Fame and New York Jets quarterback Joe Namath (12) drops back for a pass. *AP Photo/Amy Sancetta*

Bottom right, Kansas City defensive back James Marsalis (40) gets his thumb on the ball as he deflects a pass intended for Minnesota receiver John Henderson. *AP Photo/stf*

SUPER BOWL XXXII

Denver Broncos 31
Green Bay Packers 24

Top left, Denver Broncos Hall of Fame quarterback John Elway holds up the Vince Lombardi Trophy after the Broncos defeated the Green Bay Packers in Super Bowl XXXII. *AP Photo/NFL Photos*

Top middle, New England Patriots kicker Adam Vinatieri (4) celebrates with teammate Ken Walter (back) after kicking a game-winning field goal to beat the St. Louis Rams 20-17 in Super Bowl XXXVI.
AP Photo/Amy Sancetta

Top right, New York Giants quarterback Eli Manning celebrates after his 13-yard touchdown pass to Plaxico Burress in the fourth quarter of Super Bowl XLII.
AP Photo/Julie Jacobson

The Broncos had lost four Super Bowls and the AFC had lost 13 straight when they took the field as 11-and-a-half-point underdogs to the favored Packers, but the day had finally come for John Elway to shine on sport's grandest stage. With the help of Terrell Davis (157 yards and three touchdowns), Elway directed his offense to an exhilarating victory that featured three ties and a game-winning drive with 1:45 remaining.

SUPER BOWL XXXVI

New England Patriots 20
St. Louis Rams 17

Patriots Super Bowl victories seemed like foregone conclusions in the decade following this game, but in this matchup the Rams were cast in the role of Goliath. As 14-point favorites, the dynamic offense featuring Kurt Warner and Marshall Faulk kept hitting the wall of the Patriots' well-crafted defensive plan, and in the end a 48-yard Adam Vinatieri field goal gave New England its first of three Super Bowl titles in four years.

SUPER BOWL XLII

New York Giants 17
New England Patriots 14

The Patriots were 18-0, looking for a storybook ending to an idyllic season, and Eli Manning and David Tyree stormed into the narrative with the "helmet catch" with an assist from New York's punishing defensive front. In the end, Tom Brady's legendary offense managed only two touchdowns, and the Giants became the ultimate Super Bowl spoilers in the most memorable fourth-quarter drive in the history of the big game.

SUPER BOWL XVII

MIAMI DOLPHINS	VS	WASHINGTON REDSKINS
17		27

DATE — January 30, 1983

HOST CITY — Rose Bowl, Pasadena, CA

MVP — John Riggins, RB, Washington

TIME-OUT — The Redskins' famed offensive line, "the Hogs," enabled running back John Riggins to set Super Bowl records for rushing yards and attempts. His record of 38 carries still stood more than 20 years later.

It had been 10 years since the Washington Redskins and the Miami Dolphins had last sparred at the Super Bowl. A few months after that 14-7 Dolphins victory in 1973, a third-year running back named John Riggins was mired in a contract holdout with the New York Jets.

When Riggins and the Jets finally agreed to terms, the brawny back went into coach Weeb Ewbank's office to sign the contract while wearing leather pants, no shirt, and a derby hat adorned with a big feather. Throughout his 14-year professional career, Riggins never missed the chance to make an impression.

By Super Bowl XVII, Riggins was a Washington Redskin, and second-year coach Joe Gibbs knew that he would need to rely heavily on the player who had already accumulated 610 yards through Washington's four playoff wins. In a season shortened by a 57-day player's strike, commissioner Pete Rozelle had improvised with a creation called the Super Bowl Tournament, and Redskins assistant head coach Dan Henning later speculated that if Riggins had carried that level of production over a full season, he would have gained 2,400 yards that year.

Even though the Redskins doubled the Dolphins' production in virtually every statistical category in their 27-17 victory and their defense was tenacious throughout the afternoon, Miami had the lead until early in the fourth quarter. The Dolphins did all of their scoring—a spectacular 76-yard touchdown pass from David Woodley to Jimmy Cefalo, a Mark Moseley field goal, and a 98-yard Fulton Walker kickoff return—in the first half, and the Redskins didn't have definitive answers for Miami's explosion plays.

The Dolphins were favored by three, but Gibbs and the Redskins had specialized in defying expectations throughout the truncated nine-game season. As they felled the Lions, Vikings, and Cowboys on the playoff march, Washington's average margin of victory was 19 points. What made their dominance surprising was the relative anonymity of most of the players on the roster; 26 came to the team as free agents, 14 had never been drafted, and three of the members of the vaunted "Hogs" offensive line had been released by other teams.

Behind the Hogs, Riggins gained 42 yards in the first quarter alone in the Super Bowl, but the Redskins didn't convert. Washington quarterback Joe Theismann did engineer two scoring drives in the

second for a manageable 17-10 halftime deficit. In the locker room, Gibbs evoked the underdog vibe. In a postgame interview, he said that he told his players that "this was the way it was supposed to be. If we were going to be world champions, we had to earn it by coming back."

The Redskins' freight train started rolling slowly in the third quarter, with one Moseley field goal comprising the scoring total. But with 10 minutes left on the clock, Riggins took charge by producing one of the most renowned running plays in Super Bowl history.

The Dolphins' "Killer B's Defense", led by dangerous linebacker A.J. Duhe, had held the Redskins to short gains, and the would-be drive seemed destined to end on the Miami 43-yard line with Washington halted at fourth and 1. The Miami coach was expecting a punt and called a time-out, but Gibbs used that time to review the play he had planned for this situation, the "70-Chip."

The Hogs blocked flawlessly on the play and set Riggins free around to the left with only cornerback Don McNeal, who was at least 50 pounds lighter than Riggins, standing in his way. McNeal took a swipe at Riggins, but Riggins shed him like he was taking off a jacket and in doing so proved why he was the Kansas state champion in the 100-yard dash in high school. All 250 pounds of Riggins sprinted 43 yards for the touchdown, the Washington lead, and the Lombardi Trophy.

The scoreboard read only 20-17 at that point, but the Redskin defense rendered Woodley and his unit totally ineffective through the entire second half. The Dolphins gained only 34 yards in the half, and their quarterbacks—Shula benched Woodley in the final minutes and replaced him with Don Strock—did not complete a single pass. Miami had the league's highest-rated defense coming into the game, but it was Washington that demonstrated how a defense can definitively turn the tide and aid their team in putting together a 14-0 run in 10 minutes.

"To be able to play the way we wanted to play, with John, that was allowed by the fact that our defense was so stout in the second half," Henning said. "Our defense dominated—I mean dominated."

Gibbs was still virtually unknown, but he would go on to lead the Skins to three Super Bowls with three different quarterbacks. With a heroic effort that paid homage to tough, smashmouth, old-fashioned football, Washington established itself as a force whose formerly unknown players would become targets on every opponent's film study in the 1983 season.

The MVP trophy went to Riggins, the first running back to win the award since Franco Harris eight years earlier. After the game, the

writers on press row tried to process the number of ways he had made Super Bowl history. His 166 yards and his 38 carries were the most ever by a running back to date. His 43-yard touchdown play was the longest scoring play on the ground.

Thirty years later, the record for number of carries in a Super Bowl would still be standing, even if future stars toppled the others. Riggins exalted in his MVP trophy, especially because he had a public rivalry with teammate Joe Theismann, and the quarterback traditionally got the nod from the MVP committee. In his characteristically colorful way, he absorbed the events of the day with a nod to current President Ronald Reagan.

"I'm very happy," Riggins said. "At least for tonight, Ron's the president, but I'm the king."

Washington Redskins running back John Riggins (44) drags Miami Dolphins Don McNeal (28) as he fights for yards. *AP Photo/Al Messerschmidt*

SUPER BOWL XVIII

WASHINGTON REDSKINS VS **LOS ANGELES RAIDERS**

9   **38**

DATE	January 22, 1984
HOST CITY	Tampa Stadium, Tampa, FL
MVP	Marcus Allen, RB, Los Angeles
TIME-OUT	Seven players on the bad-boy Raiders were fined $1,000 for being late to a meeting during Super Bowl week.

If the Washington Redskins found themselves playing the unexpected role of the swatter in Super Bowl XVII, one year later in Tampa, they became the fly.

For the second straight year, the three-point underdog took command of the game and pulled out a decisive win, but in Super Bowl XVIII, the Oakland Raiders followed that script to an extreme. And their victims certainly weren't a wild card Johnny-come-lately; the Redskins took the field at Tampa Stadium after having recently broken the NFL record for points scored in a season.

Riding the energy of their world championship, Joe Gibbs and his confident team barreled through the season 14-2, scoring a record 541 points (a mark that stood for 15 years), and set another league record with a turnover margin of +43. In contrast, the Raiders had continued in their tough, wild, undisciplined fashion that reflected owner Al Davis's status as the NFL bad boy. They lost an epic battle to Washington early in the season 37-35 and had an abysmal turnover margin of -12, but by the playoffs, Tom Flores and his team were operating at a different level.

A Redskins offense guided with efficiency and power by Joe Theismann and John Riggins against Miami sputtered and died against Oakland. The Raiders defense, led by a line that featured hard-charging players such as Reggie Kinlaw and Howie Long, sacked Theismann six times and held the Redskins to just six points. Even if Washington had come up with an answer up front, the backfield duo of Lester Hayes and Mike Haynes became the gold standard for shutting down a passing game with aggressive, smothering cover corners.

"We had our rear ends handed to us on a platter," Theismann said. "We embarrassed ourselves."

Many who admired the Raiders' dominance that day thought that a game-changer like Kinlaw deserved the MVP award, but the committee—typically biased toward offensive production—had a worthy candidate on the other side of the ball as well. Running back Marcus Allen finished the day with 20 rushes for 191 yards and two touchdowns, and his total yardage for the game set a Super Bowl record at the time.

Allen almost didn't make it to the game in time to become its most valuable player. Instead of taking official team transportation, he and safety Odis McKinney rented a car to take them from the hotel to the stadium, but when they encountered a parking attendant, she insisted they couldn't get by without a parking pass. "I said, 'Lady, we're playing in the game. We don't need a parking pass. You've got to let us in.' And she said, 'I'm sorry; you've got to have a parking pass to get in.'"

When it became clear that the attendant wasn't going to budge, Allen and McKinney grabbed their bags, jumped out of the car, and left the rental car running at the gate. Decades later, he said he never knew what happened to the car, but he did see some symbolism in the holdup. "It was just proof that nothing was going to stop us," he said.

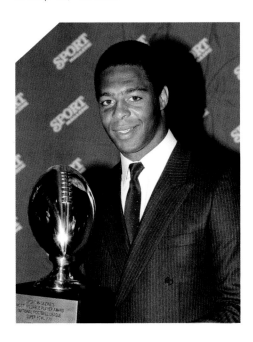

Starting with an anomaly—a blocked punt recovered by Derrick Jensen for the game's opening touchdown—the Raiders seemed to score at will while stifling the Redskins' efforts to keep up. The previous Super Bowl MVP, running back John Riggins, gained only 64 yards that afternoon, and the Redskins backs gained fewer than 3 yards per attempt. "That was as much physical domination as I had seen defensively," said Raiders tight end Todd Christensen.

After a third-quarter drive that resulted in Washington's only touchdown of the game, the Oakland lead was 21-9, and Redskins optimists still had reason to hope for a turnaround. But then the game pivoted on the legs of Allen, first on a touchdown drive boosted by a Redskins pass interference call and then on a remarkable play that has come to symbolize the transcendence of that day for the Raiders community.

It was the final play of the third quarter, and Allen took the handoff from quarterback Jim Plunkett and cut right in the backfield. Seeing opposition, he reversed course and cut left, barely eluding the grasp of Ken Coffey far behind the line of scrimmage. Allen, whose running ability had been the target of critics, took charge, ran through a traffic jam, and broke free, escaping at least a dozen Redskins en route to a 74-yard touchdown run. "For Marcus, it was a confirmation of his greatness," Long remembered.

The Raiders certainly exulted in their third Super Bowl title when the clock expired after the fourth quarter, but Christensen

remembers the celebration following Allen's epic run more vividly, because it was then that the game was effectively over. "It was at that point in time that I think everybody realized we were going to be world champions," he said. "The sheer delight, almost to the point of frivolity, that's a picture that I think will linger for quite a while."

When the Redskins were finally permitted to escape the field for the locker room, they were the victims of what was, to date, the biggest blowout in Super Bowl history. (In a decade characterized by drubbings, that record would be topped three times in the next six years.) On the victors' side, NFL commissioner Pete Rozelle was ready to award another trophy to Raiders owner Al Davis, who had succeeded in moving the team to Los Angeles since his team's last Super Bowl title. Davis, never one to shy away from hyperbole, gave props to

the team that seemed to thrive against the odds.

"This is the greatest team we ever had, one of the greatest in history—hell, one of the greatest in all time in any professional sport," he pronounced. "There is nothing it lacks."

Amid the celebration, Flores took a phone call from President Ronald Reagan, who evoked that day's political tension with the Soviet Union in offering his congratulations. "Coach? I have already had a call from Moscow," Reagan said. "They think that Marcus Allen is a secret weapon, and they insist that we dismantle it."

Bottom left, Raiders running back Marcus Allen holds the Vince Lombardi Trophy. *AP Photo*

Top right, Howie Long (75) of the Raiders battles George Starke (74) of the Redskins on the line during the first half. *AP Photo/Mario Suriani*

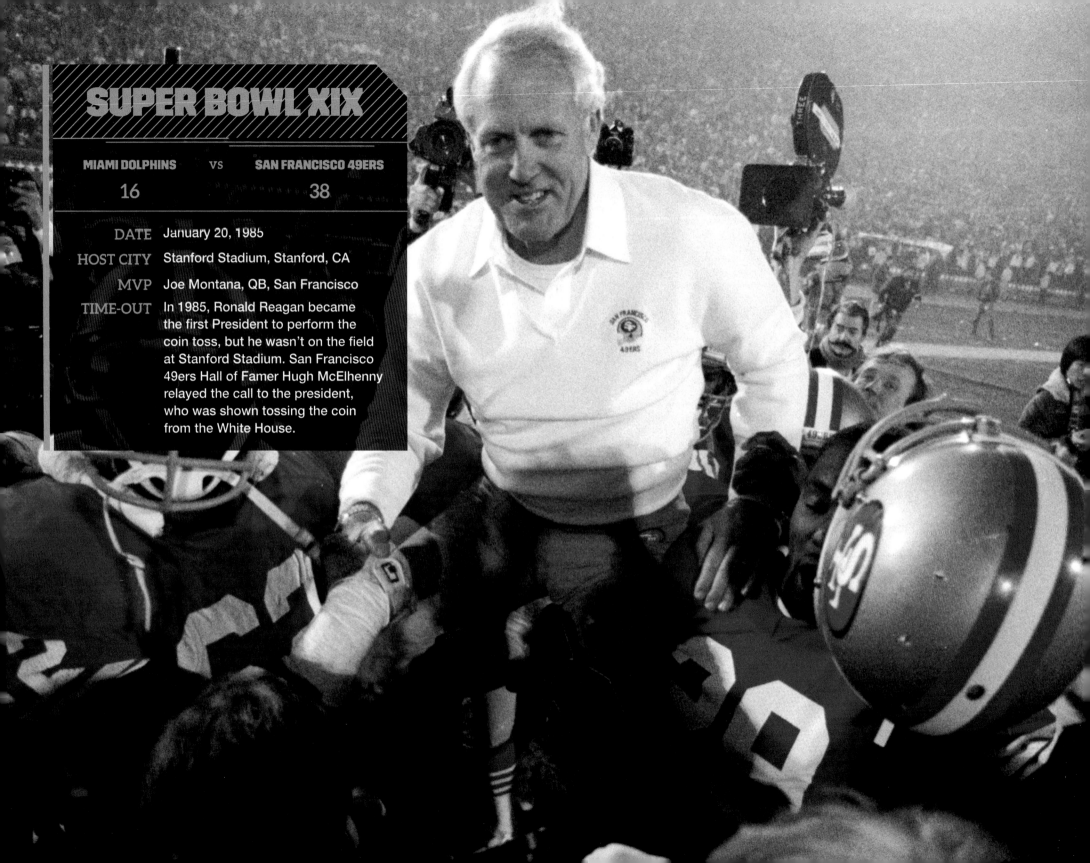

SUPER BOWL XIX

MIAMI DOLPHINS	VS	SAN FRANCISCO 49ERS
16		38

DATE January 20, 1985

HOST CITY Stanford Stadium, Stanford, CA

MVP Joe Montana, QB, San Francisco

TIME-OUT In 1985, Ronald Reagan became the first President to perform the coin toss, but he wasn't on the field at Stanford Stadium. San Francisco 49ers Hall of Famer Hugh McElhenny relayed the call to the president, who was shown tossing the coin from the White House.

History would cast Super Bowl XIX as a showdown between Dan Marino and Joe Montana, but in the weeks preceding the game, the media seemed to have already declared a victor.

In the days leading up to the matchup between the San Francisco 49ers and the Miami Dolphins, the full spotlight was on Marino, the 23-year-old golden child of the game who had won the NFL Most Valuable Player award in just his second season, with 48 touchdown passes and 5,084 total passing yards. San Francisco head coach Bill Walsh heard the question over and over: "How are you going to stop Marino and the Miami offense?"

"When you heard all week 'Miami, Miami, Miami,' you had to think, 'Hey, what about us?'" 49ers quarterback Montana said later.

On a cool day in Stanford Stadium, Walsh strolled down the field during warm-ups and took stock of his opponent. "I could see a distinct difference between the two squads," he said. "We were a much more physical, more athletic football team than Miami. At that moment my confidence soared. We truly feared Dan Marino and his battery of receivers, but they were a one-dimensional team with no running attack to worry us, and I thought we could attack their defense effectively."

Some years would pass before Walsh would wear the mantle of one of the generation's greatest football minds, but his powers of gridiron analysis were on full display with that pregame assessment. Not only did the

49ers capably handle Miami's defense and pave the way for Montana's record-breaking day but also the San Francisco defense unleashed a savvy game plan that effectively deflated the Dolphin offense that everyone had deemed unstoppable.

Montana had already won one MVP trophy three years earlier, but in leading his team to a 38-16 defeat of the Dolphins, he guaranteed that the 49ers' Super Bowl XVI performance looked like a mere warm-up. He was the quarterback who could do no wrong that afternoon; he completed 24 of 35 passes for 331 yards, three touchdowns, and no interceptions. He also rushed for 59 yards, and both his passing and rushing yardage totals broke Super Bowl records.

The Dolphins enjoyed only two leads— both in the first 15 minutes of play. As *New York Daily News* sportswriter Joe Belock quipped in his story the day after the game, "The quarterback battle of the century lived up to the hype. For one quarter." After Marino led his team far enough downfield on the game's opening possession to set up a 37-yard Uwe von Schamann field goal, San Francisco scored on a 33-yard pass from Montana to Carl Monroe, and then Marino—running the first no-huddle offense most players and coaches remember seeing completed a series of short passes that culminated in a 2-yard Dan Johnson touchdown reception.

The scoreboard read 10-7 in the favor of Marino and Miami, but then San Francisco defensive coordinator George Seifert made an astute

adjustment that put a vise grip on the Dolphins' offensive production. He benched all of his linebackers but Keena Turner and Jeff Fuller, added Tom Holmoe as an extra defensive back, and trusted his speedy backfield to match up with Miami's receivers in the nickel defense for the rest of the game.

The adaptation worked to perfection, preventing Marino from scoring any more touchdowns and also extinguishing a Dolphins ground game that had averaged 138.5 rushing yards in their first two playoff games. In Super Bowl XIX, Miami's offense rushed only nine times and gained a total of 25 yards—less than half the number of rushing yards collected by Joe Montana.

"Dan Marino had some problems," Dolphins head coach Don Shula told the media after the game. "He didn't play the way he did during the regular season. We would have liked to go to our running game, but the runs we tried didn't work and we got behind. Their defensive backs were playing so far off, it was tough to think about going deep."

From the opening drive of the second quarter through the end, it was the Montana and Roger Craig show on one side of the ball and the conquest of the nickel defense on the other. At halftime San Francisco had both a 28-16 lead and the momentum, and in the third quarter they outscored Miami 10-0. The fourth quarter was an exercise in futility for a frustrated Dolphins team and a prelude to the victory party for San Francisco.

Craig, who was selected 22 picks after Marino in the 1983 draft, had the game of

a lifetime and would have certainly had a claim to the MVP trophy if Montana had been less commanding. He scored three touchdowns—two in the air and one on the ground—and gained a total of 135 yards. His record of three touchdowns in a game has been equaled by three players, Jerry Rice, Ricky Watters, and Terrell Davis, but it has never been surpassed.

The victory was such a poetic display of what made Walsh and the 49ers of that era special that the San Francisco coach later fretted over a fumble on the recovery of an onside kick at the end of the second quarter. When Jim Jensen gained possession of Guy McIntyre's fumble, and the Dolphins subsequently converted on a von Schamann field goal "that ruined a perfect game," Walsh said, "That troubled me."

No defeat could erase what Marino had accomplished in the regular season, and his supporters could take solace in their certainty that he would be back to the Super Bowl for another opportunity to take his talent to the pinnacle of the game. Marino went on to a stellar 16-year career in Miami, with nine Pro Bowl appearances and induction into the Pro Football Hall of Fame in 2005, but that second chance never came.

Walsh took great pleasure, after the game, in transferring the hyperbole he had been hearing about Marino for two weeks onto his own quarterback with this pronouncement: "Montana is the greatest quarterback in this league, maybe of all time."

San Francisco 49ers running back Roger Craig.
AP Photo/Al Messerschmidt

SUPER BOWL SOUVENIRS

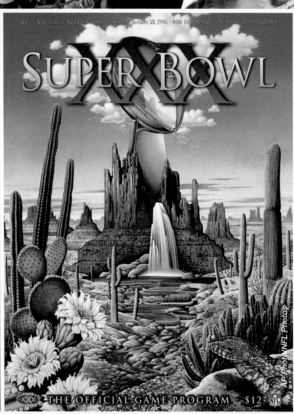

THE OFFICIAL GAME PROGRAM · $12

SUPER BOWL

SUPER BOWL XXI

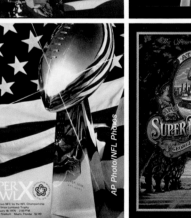

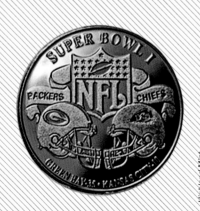

AP Photo/David Longstreath

AP Photo/Michael Conroy, File

Highland Mint

AP Photo/Paul Spinelli

AP Photo/Julie Jacobson

MANNING

AP Photo/Amy Sancetta

AP Photo/Al Golub

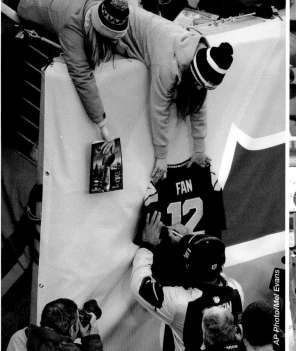

FAN
12

AP Photo/Mel Evans

AP Photo/Matt York

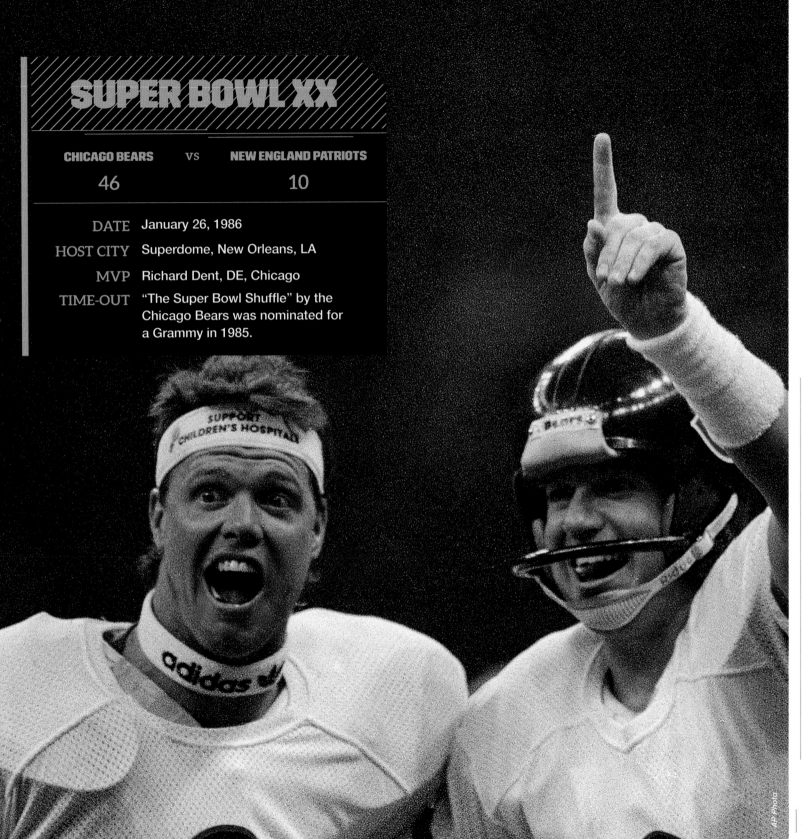

SUPER BOWL XX

CHICAGO BEARS VS **NEW ENGLAND PATRIOTS**

46 **10**

DATE | January 26, 1986
HOST CITY | Superdome, New Orleans, LA
MVP | Richard Dent, DE, Chicago
TIME-OUT | "The Super Bowl Shuffle" by the Chicago Bears was nominated for a Grammy in 1985.

For evidence that the 1985 Chicago Bears carried themselves with confidence bordering on cockiness, consider this: the day after their first loss of the season, they went into a recording studio to film a rap called "The Super Bowl Shuffle."

The first player to approach the mike for his solo rap, legendary Bears running back Walter Payton, embodied the team's attitude with a month left in the regular season. Payton's lines included, "Well, they call me Sweetness, and I like to dance. Runnin' the ball is like makin' romance. We've had the goal since training camp to give Chicago a Super Bowl Champ."

That 38-24 defeat by Miami turned out to be the only one of the year for Mike Ditka and his team, who embodied "swagger" before it was en vogue. And that rap, with its accompanying video, was a self-fulfilling prophecy for the players who knew two things with certainty: they would make it to Super Bowl XX in New Orleans and, once they took the field, they would make a Super Bowl–sized statement.

Even though Payton and bad boy quarterback Jim McMahon received much of the focus in the pregame media press, the Bears' 46-10 trouncing of the New England Patriots was actually a monument to Buddy Ryan and his defense. After dispatching the New York Giants 21-0 and the Los Angeles Rams 24-0 in the playoffs, the only low point of the day for the Bears' defensive unit was allowing a first-quarter Patriots field goal that erased the chance for another shutout.

When the assault on New England was finally over, the Bears had allowed only 7 rushing yards and 116 yards in the air, and they had permitted New England to convert only one third down on 10 attempts. They had also set new Super Bowl records for sacks, with seven; fewest rushing yards allowed; and largest margin of victory. New England right guard Ron Wooten said his team's struggle for yardage was like "trying to beat back the tide with a broom."

Offensive coaches had struggled to find an answer for Ryan's "46" defense all season, but in the end the combination of his innovative schemes and savvy, tough players such as Richard Dent, Mike Singletary, and Dan Hampton presented one of the most daunting fronts in the history of the game. "Whenever anybody asks me what the finest defense in NFL

history was, I always answer with the '85 Bears," former Philadelphia Eagles quarterback and sports broadcast analyst Ron Jaworski wrote. "It was the single most talented defensive unit I've ever seen. But what also made them great was the system in which they played."

The legend of Ryan and his world-beating defense at Super Bowl XX was amplified by his imminent departure. Ryan's name had been frequently linked to the head coaching vacancy in Philadelphia, and at a defensive film session the day before the Super Bowl, he told the players with a catch in his voice, "No matter what happens tomorrow, you'll always be my heroes." With that, the Bears defenders knew they were looking at their last chance to prove their coordinator's genius in Chicago, and they ran at that challenge full bore.

New England's inability to get anything started on offense was a surprise, particularly because their running game, powered by Craig James and Tony Collins, had accounted for 510 yards in the wild card Patriots' three playoff victories. But head Coach Raymond Berry was aware of the defensive complexity he was about to face, so he decided to misdirect the Bears by focusing on quarterback Tony Eason and the passing game.

Before he was replaced by Steve Grogan in the third quarter, Eason proved the futility of that approach by becoming the only quarterback in Super Bowl history to fail to complete a pass.

"They called the right defenses at the right time," Berry said. "The fumbles I saw, they knocked the tar out of us. I just don't think there is one more darn thing we could have done today."

Woven through the Chicago defense's repeated denials of the Patriots' scoring overtures were a series of explosive plays by McMahon and his offense, including three Kevin Butler field goals, two rushing touchdowns by McMahon himself, and an improbable 1-yard run to cap an offensive series by defensive tackle William "The Refrigerator" Perry. Nine of the Chicago points came on defensive possessions: a 28-yard Reggie Phillips interception return and, in the game's final points, a safety when Henry Waechter tackled Grogan in the end zone.

The only controversy in a game whose result was never in question was the lack of scoring by Payton, who gained 186 yards that day and whose productivity had sparked the Bears all season; he somehow never found the end zone through that entire postseason run. When the game was over, Payton reportedly locked himself in a storage closet of the Superdome rather than join in the celebration. More than one Patriot would have happily joined him rather than sit through the final minutes of the game.

"I blacked that second half out," New England cornerback Raymond Clayborn said. "I was on the sideline waiting for the clock to run out when it got up to 37-3. I said, 'Let this end mercifully. Please.'"

When the clock finally read 0:00, the leaders on the Chicago defensive unit did something unprecedented. They hoisted Ryan up on their shoulders and carried him off the field in triumph while their teammates carried off Ditka, the head coach with whom Ryan had a reportedly frosty relationship. That edition of the Bears had an abundance of egos and more than a little drama, but that day in New Orleans they seemed to have done enough to be pronounced a Super Bowl legacy after only one win.

"Despite the conflicts," Singletary said, "there was nothing that the 1985 Bears couldn't accomplish."

Bottom center, Chicago Bears' William "The Refrigerator" Perry spikes the ball after scoring a touchdown. *AP Photo/Al Messerschmidt*

Top right, Chicago Bears coach Mike Ditka reaches to shake hands with New England Patriots Coach Raymond Berry. *AP Photo/Amy Sancetta, File*

SUPER BOWL XXI

DENVER BRONCOS vs **NEW YORK GIANTS**

20 **39**

DATE	January 25, 1987
HOST CITY	Rose Bowl, Pasadena, CA
MVP	Phil Simms, QB, New York
TIME-OUT	This Super Bowl was the first to feature players giving the winning head coach a postgame Gatorade shower.

When the New York Giants started playing professional football in 1925, flappers were dancing their way through the prosperous decade and the Great Depression was still years away. Only the Green Bay Packers have a longer history of playing in the same city with the same name.

But through the first two-plus decades of the Super Bowl and even years before that, the Giants' quest for postseason glory resulted in repeated frustration. Their last appearance in the NFL Championship, a defeat, was four years before the first Super Bowl was played. In the two decades of the Super Bowl era, the Giants had put together only six winning seasons. Year after year, one of football's most venerable franchises watched while relative upstarts such as the Cowboys and the Dolphins hoisted the game's most coveted prize.

The tide finally started to turn for the Giants in the mid-'80s under the leadership of Bill Parcells in his first NFL head job. Parcells's first season was more of the same, ending 3-12-1, but then the franchise got in the habit of winning, and in 1984 and 1985 they made it to the postseason but lost in the divisional championship. Through the slow climb Parcells stuck with his game plan of high-pressure defense and intentional player motivation, and he stood by the quarterback who became the key to his franchise's long-awaited Super Bowl victory—a 39-20 win over the Denver Broncos in Super Bowl XXI.

Phil Simms's rocky path closely resembled the one traveled by his team. Drafted by the Giants in 1979 out of the little-known Morehead State, his early years were so tumultuous that he started to wonder whether he wanted his wife, Diana, to even attend the games. "My wife had to sit up in the stands and listen to them cuss me," he told *New York* magazine in 1987. But Simms was known as tough and cocky, so when he entered the Rose Bowl for Super Bowl XXI in the shadow of Broncos starter John Elway, he knew he and his teammates had what they needed to take control of the matchup. By game's end Simms had done more than engineer a victory; he had put together one of the most dominant quarterback performances in NFL history.

After it was over, Simms could talk in specifics about each of his incomplete passes that day, since there were only three. It was the completions that tended to run together, since he made a connection 22 times on 25 attempts for 268 yards in the air. He also threw for three touchdowns and no interceptions, and his passer rating of 150.9 made him the most accurate passer in the history of the NFL playoffs. Parcells said afterward, with no hyperbole, "This may be the best game a quarterback has ever played."

"I was like a fastball pitcher," Simms said of his performance. "I had great location all day. Almost every pass landed exactly where I wanted it to. I've never played better."

Defensive end George Martin said years later that none of the Giants had any question about whether they would emerge victorious that day, but the Broncos actually brought a 10-9 lead into halftime, and Elway showed why he was considered one of the league's hot young quarterbacks, with 187 passing yards in the first half alone. But even with an edge, the Broncos were plagued by missed opportunities that would have given them a more commanding lead: two missed field goals and a stifling goal-line defensive series by New York that started with Denver at first and goal from the 1-yard line and ended with nothing.

It was the closest halftime margin in Super Bowl history, but the Giants wasted no time after intermission in erasing the perception that they were competing in a close game. On a play that came to represent the pivot point of the afternoon, Parcells sent out a punt team on a fourth and 1—a unit that included backup quarterback Jeff Rutledge. After a long snap, Parcells gave Rutledge a nod, and the quarterback tucked the ball in and ran for the first down on a sneak. From that point on, Simms and the Giants took turns leading short clinics for the crowd of 101,000 and the national TV audience. "We really had Elway on the run," said Giants director of pro personnel Tim Rooney. "One of the quarterbacks played as if he was in a practice, and the other played as if he was in a panic."

New York outscored Denver 17-0 in the third quarter, with both touchdowns coming on passing plays from Simms.

He completed every pass he threw in the second half. On the other side, the Giants defense ruined Elway's Super Bowl coming-out party with star power of its own—NFL MVP linebacker Lawrence Taylor and powerhouses such as Harry Carson and Carl Banks. "We were just a hard hat group of guys who just wanted to go out and smack people around," Carson remembered.

Giants owner Wellington Mara, a man so inextricably linked with his team and his league that the inscription "The Duke" on every Wilson NFL football pays him honor, finally had a Super Bowl ring. Parcells, Taylor, Simms, and defensive coordinator Bill Belichick had proved that sometimes the latecomer to the party makes the most memorable impression.

It would be 15 years before Belichick would carve out his own domain in Super Bowl lore by leading the New England Patriots to three world titles in four years. At Super Bowl XXI he was a 34-year-old unknown, a fact reinforced by the reaction of Rose Bowl security guards when he slipped back out on the field to soak up the moment after the locker room celebration and was initially refused reentry. He returned to the field because he thought he might never experience a moment like that one again. In fact, both Belichick and the Giants would be back multiple times, but this first triumph— achieved with a combination of true toughness and savvy football skill—would always be remembered as exceptional.

New York Giants defensemen Erik Howard (74) and Lawrence Taylor (56) stand over Denver Broncos quarterback John Elway after he was sacked in the end zone for a safety in the second quarter.
AP Photo/Amy Sancetta

SUPER BOWL XXII

WASHINGTON REDSKINS VS **DENVER BRONCOS**

42   10

DATE	January 31, 1988
HOST CITY	Jack Murphy Stadium, San Diego, CA
MVP	Doug Williams, QB, Washington
TIME-OUT	MVP Doug Williams was the first black quarterback ever to start in the Super Bowl.

1988 WORLD CHAMPIONS

John Elway was the NFL MVP in 1987, the field general for a Denver Broncos team that had suffered an embarrassing setback to the Giants in Super Bowl XXI but had marched effectively through the postseason en route to a chance for redemption. And in the first quarter of Super Bowl XXII against the Washington Redskins in San Diego, it looked like their day had arrived.

Before fans had even settled into their seats, Elway had launched a 56-yard touchdown pass to Ricky Nattiel, and a few minutes later he caught a 23-yard pass from running back Steve Sewell on one of the trick plays that had come to characterize head coach Dan Reeves's squads. That drive ended in a field goal after the Washington defense created a tenacious red-zone barrier, but a 10-0

lead, compounded by a series of sloppy offensive mistakes by the Redskins, seemed to put Denver in the driver's seat. After all, no team in the 21-year history of the Super Bowl had come back to win from a deficit of more than seven points.

But this championship was a tale of two quarters, and the second period brought one of the most stunning reversals of fortune—and the single most overpowering quarter—that had ever been seen in the Super Bowl. Doug Williams, the man with access to a raft of legitimate excuses for underachievement, stepped up and delivered such a definitive deathblow to the Broncos that the second half seemed irrelevant.

"The second quarter was something dreams are made of," a Redskins fan named Frank Hastings wrote decades

later on a Washington fan website called www.thehogs.net. "I've never seen anything like it in any game, let alone the Super Bowl."

Williams took the second-quarter stage hobbled by a knee injury he had sustained near the end of the first quarter; a trainer put a brace on the leg, but he was still limping noticeably. He was also feeling the effects of a three-hour root canal he had undergone to treat an abscessed molar the day before. Add the constant media questions casting him as a pioneer because he was the first black quarterback to start in the Super Bowl and you have the perfect formula for grace under pressure.

"A little more than an hour before game time came the curious announcement that Doug Williams underwent emergency root

canal treatment for an abscessed lower right molar Saturday night," wrote Paul Needell the next day in the *New York Daily News*. "Team dentist Barry Rudolph said there were no complications, however, and Williams was pronounced fit to start. Fit to start? Maybe John Elway should have given [a root canal] a whirl, too."

Before the teams retired to their locker rooms for halftime, Williams led his team to five touchdowns on five straight possessions. The Redskins had the ball for fewer than six minutes, but in that short span Williams managed to complete nine of 11 passes for 228 yards. Combined with an explosive ground game from little-known back Timmy Smith, the Redskins amassed 356 yards in just the second quarter, or an astounding 18.7 yards per snap.

"In all the time I've ever been around football, I've never seen a more perfect quarter," said Washington assistant coach Dan Henning. "It was staggering."

As if the Redskins' 15-minute zeitgeist wasn't unique enough in Super Bowl annals, consider the path taken to that field by its two top offensive playmakers. Williams had spent five seasons in Tampa Bay (with Joe Gibbs as his offensive coordinator) and guided the Buccaneers to the playoffs three times. But a dispute over his contract—and his wife's sudden death from the complications of a brain tumor—led him to take a year off in 1983, and when he returned to football, it was with the Oklahoma Outlaws of the upstart USFL. When the new league folded in 1986, his old coach Gibbs signed him as the backup quarterback in Washington.

He requested a trade early in 1987 in hopes of finding a team that would give him more playing time, and Gibbs was close to working out a deal to send him to the Raiders when he reconsidered. A few weeks later Williams surpassed Jay Schroeder as the starter.

The spark behind the running game that day, Timmy Smith, was an even more unlikely savior for Redskins fans. Smith ran for 204 yards (still a Super Bowl record nearly 30 years later) and two touchdowns that day, with 122 of those yards coming in that electric second quarter.

George Rogers had been the starting running back throughout the season, but right before the team left for the Super Bowl, Gibbs quietly decided to give the starting job to Smith, a rookie out of Texas

Tech who had come to the Redskins in the fifth round of the 1987 draft. Hobbled by injuries for much of his collegiate career, Smith was known to be fast and strong, but the Redskins coaches considered him unproven and difficult to coach until they gave him a shot on the biggest proving ground of them all.

The Broncos' confidence was decimated by the speed with which their 10-0 lead became a 35-10 deficit, and the second half was a study in the debilitating power of a psychological edge. The Washington defense did its part, holding Denver scoreless for the rest of the game, and Smith even capped off his dream game with a 4-yard touchdown run near the end of the fourth quarter for a 42-10 result. No one present expected the favored Broncos to plummet so dramatically, but in the end

Reeves looked back at the unstoppable force that had upended their game plan philosophically.

"They're definitely the world champions," Reeves said. "We couldn't stop them. They had five straight drives to score. You just can't win championships playing that way. It would have been difficult for anyone to beat Washington today."

Top left, Washington Redskins quarterback Doug Williams looks downfield for a receiver. *AP Photo/Paul Spinelli*

Top right, Quarterback John Elway (7) stands dejected on the sidelines during the final two minutes of of the Super Bowl against the Washington Redskins. *AP Photo/Ed Andrieski*

SUPER BOWL XXIII

CINCINNATI BENGALS VS **SAN FRANCISCO 49ERS**

16 **20**

DATE January 22, 1989

HOST CITY Joe Robbie Stadium, Miami, FL

MVP Jerry Rice, WR, San Francisco

TIME-OUT The San Francisco 49ers are the only team to win back-to-back Super Bowls under different head coaches. They won Super Bowl XXIII under legendary coach Bill Walsh and returned to victory the next year under George Seifert.

Twenty-two Super Bowls were in the books, and each included its share of big plays, larger-than-life coaches, and over-the-top atmospheres. But until 1989, not one Super Bowl had been decided in the final minutes by a comeback drive. After five straight blowouts, all of America —except Cincinnati fans—was grateful for the chance to stay on the edge of their seats through the game's waning seconds.

Throughout a season that presented the most daunting challenge to their eventual "Team of the Decade" designation, the 49ers toppled expectations en route to the Super Bowl and then claimed their third Lombardi Trophy by beating the Cincinnati

Bengals in the most dramatic way possible: a 92-yard drive in under three minutes orchestrated by a quarterback who was traditionally invigorated by pressure.

"What makes this the sweetest is everything we went through to get this far," San Francisco safety Ronnie Lott told *Sporting News*. "The first two, we breezed through the season and expected to win. This one, we had to struggle. It makes it better."

The lowlights of the 49ers' regular season included four losses in six games in October and November and a 10-9

Monday Night Football defeat at the hands of the Bears in which 49ers quarterback Joe Montana was sacked four times and a controversy ignited when head coach Bill Walsh started Steve Young instead of Montana after the Bears loss. They regained their footing in the playoffs and outscored Minnesota and Chicago 62-12, but when they earned their rings in January, the 49ers still held the distinction of becoming the world champions with the worst regular-season record in history (10-6).

Walsh was the architect of an offense that was already revolutionizing the league, but for more than a year after Super Bowl

XXIII, he wouldn't watch the film of the game because his team executed the scheme so poorly. But if the value of a story is embodied in its ending, Walsh and Montana were scriptwriters of the highest order that day and the ones who made the football universe forget that the action leading up to "the Drive" had not been particularly compelling.

The first half of the game had been, quite unexpectedly, a defensive battle between the NFL's top two offenses. The halftime score, more suited to baseball or soccer, was 3-3, with Walsh and Cincinnati head coach Sam Wyche puzzling about how to string together enough effective plays to get on the board. Despite Montana's reputation for transcendence and Bengals quarterback and NFL MVP Boomer Esaison's accomplishments that season, neither team actually scored an offensive touchdown until early in the fourth quarter.

With the score tied to open the second half, the Bengals inched out ahead first, determined to improve on a first half in which they gained only 93 yards. They got close enough for a 43-yard Jim Breech field goal that felt like a defeat after driving for 9:21 and continually facing frustration from the 49er defense. Later in the third quarter, San Francisco linebacker Bill Romanowski intercepted Esiason's pass, and the resulting drive ended in a Mike Cofer field goal and another tie.

The last thing that happened in that period was the first touchdown of the day and a cause for renewed Bengal optimism. Stanford Jennings ran the 49ers' kickoff back 93 yards to give his team a 13-6 lead that, in this game, looked nearly insurmountable.

It was, in fact, a short-lived advantage, because in the fourth quarter Jerry Rice finally found the end zone. He was far from silent throughout the game, catching 11

passes for 215 yards and ultimately winning the MVP award. But he scored only one touchdown—a 14-yard conclusion to a drive sparked by a 31-yard Montana-to-Rice connection. The game was tied for the third time when the Bengals marched down the field on a subsequent drive and pulled ahead again with a 40-yard Breech field goal. Just when it seemed that the lead changes and ties could continue indefinitely, time became the most pressing issue. San Francisco was down 16-13 and starting a drive from its own 8-yard line, with 3:10 left on the clock.

On the Cincinnati sideline, a teammate leaned over to wide receiver Cris Collinsworth and attempted to be encouraging, saying, "We've got 'em now." Collinsworth fired back, "Have you taken a look at who's quarterbacking the 49ers?"

Montana commenced with a West Coast offense tutorial—passes up the middle to Roger Craig and John Frank, a 7-yarder to Rice, a short pass to Craig to convert a third down—and on he went, mixing up the plays, converting with efficiency, and making it clear that he was in command

of the situation. "We were functioning like a machine by then," said offensive tackle Bubba Paris. "You could feel the intensity in the huddle."

With his adrenaline at full tilt (Walsh called a time-out just after the two-minute warning because he thought his quarterback might pass out), Montana continued the onward assault by hitting Rice and Craig on passes of 17 and 13 yards and then throwing his only incompletion of the drive. The 49ers kept racking up yards and first downs, even overcoming a 10-yard penalty, until they sat at the Bengals' 10-yard line with 39 seconds remaining.

Montana had already resolved that his offense was going to get the go-ahead touchdown rather than a tying field goal to prompt overtime, and in the time-out before that play he told his teammates they were running a play called 20 Halfback Curl X-Up. Craig was the primary target; Rice was a decoy; and John Taylor, who hadn't caught a single pass yet that day, was the secondary receiver. Montana checked off Craig, noticed that Rice was double covered, and spotted Taylor in the back of the end zone.

He fired the ball into Taylor's hands, just inches from the outstretched arms of Bengals cornerback Ray Horton, and San Francisco had its hardest-fought Super Bowl title. The Bengals, meanwhile, had to replay Montana's precision march all the way downfield and agonize over what they could have done to stop it.

"We're kind of feeling sorry for ourselves," Cincinnati's rookie running back Elbert "Ickey" Woods said afterward. "To lose the game like that is devastating. We played a whale of a game and we should have won, but we didn't."

Bottom left, Cincinnati Bengals quarterback Boomer Esiason (7). *AP Photo/Al Messerschmidt*

Top left, Quarterback Joe Montana. *AP Photo/Al Messerschmidt*

Top right, Running back Roger Craig of the San Francisco 49ers. *AP Photo/NFL Photos*

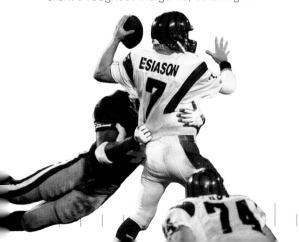

"TODAY I WILL DO WHAT OTHER'S WON'T, SO TOMORROW I CAN ACCOMPLISH WHAT OTHERS CAN'T."

Jerry Rice

CHAPTER 4: THE 1990s

SUPER BOWL XXIV

SAN FRANCISCO 49ERS   VS   **DENVER BRONCOS**

55   **10**

DATE   January 28, 1990

HOST CITY   Superdome, New Orleans, LA

MVP   Joe Montana, QB, San Francisco

TIME-OUT   Hall of Famer Jerry Rice is the only player to score three receiving touchdowns in a single Super Bowl game, in both Super Bowls XXIV and XXIX.

Even without Super Bowl XXIV, the '80s would have been the domain of the San Francisco 49ers. They had already played in three Super Bowls in the decade—and won them all. Joe Montana had become known as the quarterback who played nearly flawlessly when everything was on the line, and Jerry Rice had claimed a Super Bowl MVP award in only his third season in the league.

Chalk it up to the spirit of California excess, or the West Coast's love of a dramatic Hollywood ending, but the 49ers saved their most incredible feat of the '80s for last. They became only the second team to win back-to-back Super Bowls, but that was just one in a flurry of achievements that make that particular title team stand out among all of the others in 50 years. The records that were upended that day in New Orleans and still stood a quarter of a century later include:

- Most points in the Super Bowl, with 55

- Largest margin of victory in the Super Bowl, with 45

- Most touchdowns in a Super Bowl, with eight

- Most Super Bowl MVP awards, with three. Montana shares this distinction with the Patriots' Tom Brady

- Starting quarterback with most Super Bowl titles. Montana shares the record of four titles with both Terry Bradshaw and Brady

- Most points and most touchdowns scored by a player in a Super Bowl. Jerry Rice scored three touchdowns against Denver, and he tied that mark five years later in Super Bowl XXIX

- Most career touchdown passes in Super Bowls. Montana tops all other quarterbacks, with 11 passes into the end zone in four Super Bowls

- Lowest interception percentage for a quarterback. Montana never threw an interception in four Super Bowls, with 122 attempts

In an event where shellackings had become expected fare, San Francisco's 55-10 thrashing of the Denver Broncos was a blowout on a different level. Everyone involved—coaches, players, and observers—concurred that the 1989 edition of the 49ers was a team that played outstanding football on every side of the ball and that their performance that day made the Broncos look hapless and frustrated.

It was Montana's fourth Super Bowl and also his last, although if you had told anyone who watched Super Bowl XXIV that he would not have another chance to play for a title, he or she would have been skeptical. His performance was close to flawless: 22 of 29 for 297 yards, five passing touchdowns, and no interceptions, for a passer rating of 147.6. And he came out of the game for backup Steve Young with more than 10 minutes remaining, leaving some to wonder how close to 100 points this team could have come if they had kept up the Montana-fueled momentum.

The team's personnel was nearly identical to the roster of the Super Bowl XXIII champions who had relied on a last-minute comeback drive to squeak out a win, but former head coach Bill Walsh said that the 49ers who steamrolled through the matchup with the Broncos were loaded with intangibles that optimized their talent. "That Super Bowl was just an incredible demonstration of football in every facet of the game," said Walsh, who had retired after the previous championship and turned over the reins to George Seifert. "No one could have even come close."

Unfortunately for head coach Dan Reeves, his Broncos broke some records that evening too. They tied the Minnesota Vikings as the team with the most Super Bowl losses, with four each. And by the time 50 Super Bowls had been played, Denver would have the distinction of being on the losing end of three of the five biggest blowouts in the history of the game.

In the weeks leading up to the game, with the Broncos sitting as 11-and-a-half-point underdogs and the media salivating over a prospective back-to-back champion, Reeves strived to keep his players on the right track mentally, asserting, "We could do what the American hockey team did against the Russians." But by game's end, with only 12 first downs, 167 total offensive yards, and five turnovers, even Reeves had to pay homage to the greatness of this San Francisco squad. "They're playing at a level that's incredible," he said after the rout.

San Francisco jumped out to a lead almost immediately on a 20-yard Montana-to-Rice touchdown pass, and a series of similar displays resulted in a 27-3 halftime lead and a hunch that the 49ers had already done what they came to New Orleans to do. Just for emphasis, Montana threw two more touchdown passes in the early minutes of the third quarter, one to Rice and one to Taylor, and then jogged to the sideline and took off his helmet to watch Young play out the remaining minutes.

Denver quarterback John Elway's legacy as one of the top quarterbacks in league history is secure, but in those years he was developing a reputation as a signal caller who could perform at his best during the regular season and even in the playoffs but not in the Super Bowl. He was reportedly sick during Super Bowl XXIV, and his attempts to get anything past the 49ers defense—he completed just 10 passes and threw two interceptions—were anemic at best. Montana was the clear winner in this quarterback duel, but Elway would get another shot at the top, and in the next decade he would help dilute his team's reputation as perennial Super Bowl losers.

That landmark day in the Superdome, of course, belonged to Montana. He was a crystal-clear choice for MVP, and his single-game numbers from that victory and the career Super Bowl numbers bolstered by that performance would survive for decades. And even though it was not to be, there was nothing in the 49ers locker room to keep the players from planning for something that had never been done—three straight Super Bowl titles. Said safety Ronnie Lott: "I don't know if it's a tri-peat or a three-peat, but we want to do it again."

"Each victory is sweeter," Montana said. "This is just sweet. Let's go get another."

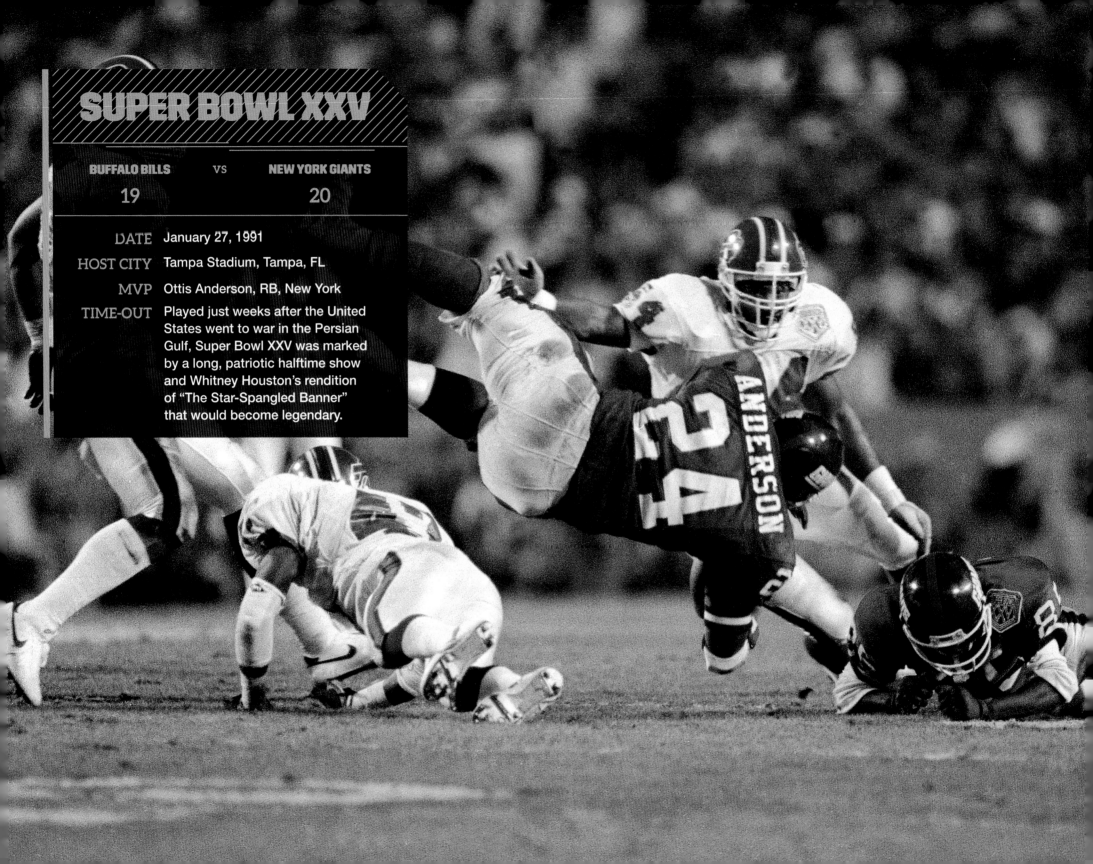

SUPER BOWL XXV

BUFFALO BILLS	VS	NEW YORK GIANTS
19		20

DATE January 27, 1991

HOST CITY Tampa Stadium, Tampa, FL

MVP Ottis Anderson, RB, New York

TIME-OUT Played just weeks after the United States went to war in the Persian Gulf, Super Bowl XXV was marked by a long, patriotic halftime show and Whitney Houston's rendition of "The Star-Spangled Banner" that would become legendary.

Every kicker has visualized the scenario: the waning seconds of the Super Bowl, the game on the line, one kick the difference between going home with your head down or celebrating as a triumphant world champion. But reality, at odds with kickers' imaginations, didn't allow for that setup to occur for a quarter century, until Scott Norwood trotted out on the field with eight seconds remaining in Super Bowl XXV.

Norwood's Bills, a team packed with talent and confidence that had manhandled the Raiders 51-3 in the AFC Championship, came to Tampa as the favorites, but the Giants had kept possession of the ball for twice as long as their opponents and seen surprising performances from backup quarterback Jeff Hostetler and aging running back Ottis Anderson. New York had a miniscule 20-19 lead, and Buffalo quarterback Jim Kelly had managed to move the ball close enough for a 47-yard field goal attempt.

Bills players and fans would relive every millisecond of the kick for years: the snap; the hold; Norwood's powerful kick that had plenty of distance but a little too much torque to the right; and, ultimately, the pit in their stomachs when the ball flew outside the uprights and handed the Giants their second Lombardi Trophy in four years.

"I wanted to hit the ball solid, and I did," Norwood said after the game while patiently answering every reporter's question for more than an hour. "I wanted to get the kick off fast, and I wanted to get it high so it wouldn't be blocked. And I did. I just didn't get my hips into it enough."

It was certainly a kicker's worst nightmare, even though the Buffalo fans embraced Norwood upon the Bills' return to New York and chanted his name at a rally until he approached the microphone. But Norwood can't accurately be cast as a goat, especially considering the fact that he had never made a kick that long on natural grass (the Bills' home stadium had artificial turf). "We asked him to do something in the Super Bowl that he had never done before," said Buffalo special teams coach Bruce DeHaven.

Of course, any time a game comes down to a single kick, the tapestry of the entire game must be taken into consideration, and for Buffalo, Super Bowl XXV presented a surprising challenge from a New York team proficient in ball control and coached in fundamentals and power by Bill Parcells. The Giants had the ball for 40:33 compared to the Bills' 19:27, setting a Super Bowl record for time of possession.

Marv Levy's No-Huddle Offense had been prolific through most of the season, but

New York's toughness forced six Bills punts and contained the efforts of quarterback Jim Kelly, receiver Andre Reed, and running back Thurman Thomas. As one Bills assistant coach said later, "There is no question we got outcoached in that game." The Giants' defenders had an answer for anything that might have ignited the Bills' momentum until Thomas broke free in the fourth quarter for a touchdown that cut his team's lead to a paltry one point.

Fans who had grown weary of thrashings in the '80s were certainly heartened in the first half, as the two teams proved to be well matched and ready for a true battle. First the Giants and then the Bills drove far enough in the first quarter for field goals, thus bringing a 3-3 tie into the second

quarter. Buffalo then showed a flash of the offensive brilliance that had characterized the team through the regular season, by scoring nine quick points on a 1-yard Don Smith run and a safety from Bruce Smith's end-zone tackle of Hostetler. Halfway through the second, the Bills had a 12-3 lead.

Then Hostetler, the quarterback who finally got the starting nod after six years as a backup when Phil Simms went down with a foot injury in mid-December, made the most of the final minutes of the half by directing a 10-play, 87-yard drive topped with a 14-yard touchdown pass to Stephen Baker with just 25 seconds until halftime. With the scoreboard reading a satisfying 12-10 in the Bills' favor at the half, it was still anybody's game.

The third quarter was integral to the Giants' success that day, and it put their ball-control skills on display with an opening drive that consumed 9:29 of the clock and featured key plays from receivers Mark Ingram and Dave Meggett. With a 17-12 lead, New York handed the reins to a defensive unit that made up for the small amount of time it spent on the field with a careful Bill Belichick–crafted game plan that is now displayed in the Pro Football Hall of Fame.

"Kelly was the best quarterback in the league during the 1990 season, piloting a high-powered no-huddle attack that led the league in scoring and hung 51 points on the Raiders in the AFC Championship Game," Peter King wrote in 2014 on www.mmqb.com. "Belichick had different

plans for the Super Bowl: He deployed extra defensive backs to take away Kelly's deep options, and instructed his defenders to hit hard to limit the short passing game."

The Bills offense had one last spark—a fourth-quarter drive powered by Thomas's explosive 31-yard touchdown run. The Giants, still patiently executing their plan, answered with another long drive that added only three points on a Matt Bahr field goal but consumed 7:32.

With the score at 20-19, the Giants continued to manage the clock until Kelly and his troops got the ball back with 2:16 remaining and executed a two-minute drill sparked by a 22-yard Thomas run. But Kelly, who spiked the ball to set up Norwood's kick before the Giants iced the kicker with their final time-out, couldn't get his team quite close enough to make it a comfortable situation for Norwood. This is the Super Bowl that will be forever known by two words—"wide right"—but insiders know that there was much more to the story.

"They call us predictable and conservative, but I know one thing," Parcells said. "I've coached this game a long time. Power wins football games. Power wins football games."

Opposite page, Buffalo Bills running back Thurman Thomas carries the football and heads for the end zone on a 31-yard touchdown run on the first play of the fourth quarter. *AP Photo/NFL Photos*

Top, Jeff Hostetler (15) runs from the field carrying the game-winning ball. *AP Photo/Ron Heflin*

Right, New York Giants coach Bill Parcells is carried on the shoulders of Lawrence Taylor (56) and Carl Banks (58). *AP Photo/EdReinke, File*

SUPER BOWL XXVI

WASHINGTON REDSKINS VS **BUFFALO BILLS**

37 **24**

DATE	January 26, 1992
HOST CITY	Hubert H. Humphrey Metrodome, Minneapolis, MN
MVP	Mark Rypien, QB, Washington
TIME-OUT	This Super Bowl included the only touchdown called back by officials in the big game.

As Washington kicked off at the Metrodome in Minneapolis, Buffalo Bills running back Thurman Thomas, the NFL's Most Valuable Player that year, couldn't locate his helmet. The game started anyway, with Kenneth Davis getting the first two carries on the Bills' initial possession.

The helmet incident didn't have a measurable effect on the game's outcome, but it was emblematic of the Bills team that faced the Washington Redskins that day. Despite a 13-3 regular season record and considerable depth on both sides of the ball, the Bills' 37-24 defeat was characterized by turnovers, sloppiness, and frustration.

Listen to the assessment of two Buffalo coaches, reflecting on the game years later: "We were dominated," said head coach Marv Levy. "It was a catastrophe," said offensive line coach Tom Bresnahan.

Of course, the other side of the equation was a surprisingly commanding, tight performance by a Redskins squad that was not populated by big names. Quarterback Mark Rypien, a former sixth-round draft pick who spent his first two years with the Redskins on injured reserve, had been disparaged by Bills defenders who told the media they would blitz him and render him ineffective. Ricky Ervins and Earnest Byner shared the rushing duties with little fanfare, and Art Monk was a three-time Pro Bowler who was considered past his prime.

The part of the Redskin offense with the most notoriety was the current version of "the Hogs," the offensive line that once again proved—along with a defensive line running a scheme masterminded by coordinator Richie Petitbon—that championships are won in the trenches. So aggressively did the Redskins shut down the vaunted Bills offense that after a scoreless first quarter, Washington had outgained Buffalo 168 yards to 34.

Despite considerable toughness on both sides of the line, Washington made enough mistakes during the first quarter to keep the door wide open for Buffalo, if the Bills had only found an effective way to move the ball. In the first quarter, a touchdown pass from Rypien to Monk was overturned, a 21-yard field goal

attempt failed on a dropped snap, and a Rypien pass was intercepted by Kirby Jackson. The Bills were even more hapless, as Washington set the tone to smother Buffalo quarterback Jim Kelly all day (he would be sacked five times and knocked down 11 more before the day was over).

In the second quarter, the Redskins found a rhythm and started to pull away, scoring one field goal and two touchdowns for a 17-0 halftime lead. Thomas might have been the most prolific back in the NFL during the season, but after two quarters his team had only 8 rushing yards and no first downs on the ground. Despite a Kelly interception and other mistakes, the Bills were in field goal range near the end of the second quarter when Andre Reed threw

Left, Quarterback Mark Rypien (11) throws a pass during the Redskins' 37-24 victory over the Buffalo Bills. *AP Photo/NFL Photos*

Right, Hall of Fame quarterback Jim Kelly (12) of the Buffalo Bills sets up to throw a pass as Redskins linebacker Wilbur Marshall (58) applies pressure. *AP Photo/NFL Photos*

his helmet down in frustration at a pass interference call and drew an unsportsmanlike conduct penalty that backed his team out of scoring contention. All in all, it was an inauspicious day for the Bills and their headgear.

Things became even more lopsided when Kurt Gouveia intercepted Kelly on the Bills' first play from scrimmage, returned the pick 21 yards, and set up a Gerald Riggs touchdown run for a 24-0 lead only 16 seconds into the half. Then the Bills finally got on the board with a 21-yard Scott Norwood field goal, and Thomas found the end zone at the end of a 56-yard scoring drive. Bills fans identified a glimmer of hope that a comeback could erase the prospect of two consecutive Super Bowl defeats, but a Redskins drive capped by a

30-yard touchdown pass to Gary Clark and a Kelly fumble that led to a Chip Lohmiller field goal created a 31-10 chasm that meant the curtains were closing on the Bills again.

The fourth quarter included more Bills turnovers (they finished the day with four interceptions and one lost fumble), two more Redskin field goals, and two late-game passing touchdowns from Kelly that served only to make the losing score more respectable. When the clock expired, the world would learn the names of several Redskins players who had never been household names before—especially MVP Mark Rypien, who suffered a knee injury two years later and then began a circuitous seven-team tour through the

NFL in search of the greatness that had characterized him that day in the Metrodome.

"No matter what happens, I'll always have this moment," he said afterward. "They can never say I can't win the big one, because they don't come any bigger than this." With the triumph, Rypien's coach, Joe Gibbs, entered the rarified air of becoming one of only three coaches to win three Super Bowls. Unlike Chuck Noll and Bill Walsh, though, he spread his victories out over 10 years and won the trophies with three different quarterbacks. This one, for Gibbs, was the hardest fought and the most cherished.

"We knew we weren't a great team and that we'd have to play hard and together

to win, and that's what we did," he said. "I never enjoyed coaching a team more. I really believe it was a well-balanced team with great team chemistry and great team leadership. I was along for the ride."

From the losing side, the Buffalo players could never have imagined that they would fall in the next two Super Bowls as well, but even at the halfway point of that stressful odyssey, Thomas was comparing the Bills to other teams that became notorious for getting to Super Sunday and stumbling just one step short of the trophy. "We're falling into the category of the Minnesota Vikings and Denver Broncos," he said. "Once we get to the big games, we don't play as well."

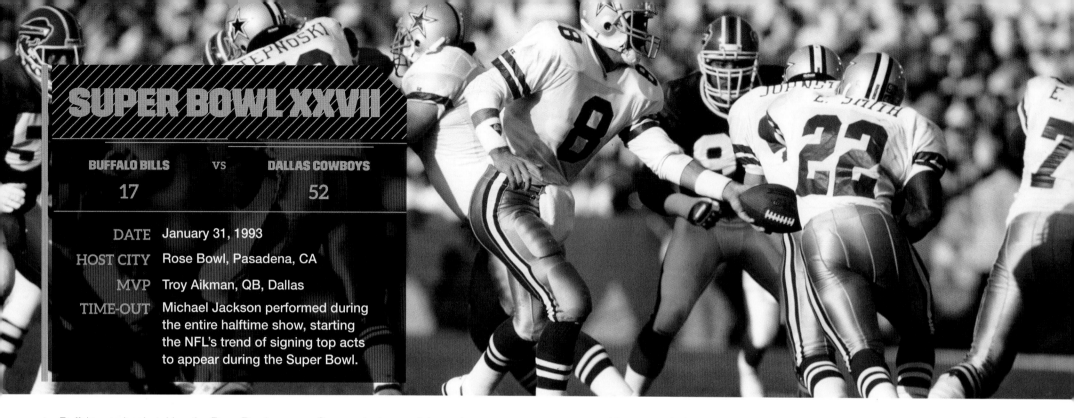

SUPER BOWL XXVII

BUFFALO BILLS VS **DALLAS COWBOYS**

17 **52**

DATE	January 31, 1993
HOST CITY	Rose Bowl, Pasadena, CA
MVP	Troy Aikman, QB, Dallas
TIME-OUT	Michael Jackson performed during the entire halftime show, starting the NFL's trend of signing top acts to appear during the Super Bowl.

Buffalo was back, taking the Rose Bowl field for its third straight Super Bowl with 11 Pro Bowl players and a blocked punt that led to an early touchdown on the game's first possession. But Dallas Cowboys head coach Jimmy Johnson, who had been persona non grata just four years earlier when his first team went 1-15, never entertained a doubt about the outcome of Super Bowl XXVII.

"I truthfully can say that I don't know that I've ever been as confident in a big game as I was in that one," he said years later. "I just thought we were far and away the better team. The night before the game I said, 'We've got this game won. All we have to do is play it a little bit close to the vest and protect the football early and eventually Buffalo will turn it over.'"

So prescient were Johnson's pregame words that the Bills set a Super Bowl record for turnovers that day—four interceptions and five lost fumbles—that still stood more than 20 years later. With a cast of characters whose average age was just 26, the confident young Cowboys team steamrolled over the Bills 52-17 in what was, far and away, the most demoralizing of Buffalo's three Super Bowl defeats.

The game featured some unforgettable football moments, but a controversy over its setting turned out to be historic as well. Arizona was selected as the original host of Super Bowl XXVII, but after the announcement that voters in the state rejected an initiative to observe Martin Luther King Jr. Day as an official holiday, NFL owners swiftly changed course and

named the second-place host city, Pasadena, California, as the site of the game. Later that year, Arizona voters reversed their earlier decision and recognized the holiday but not before their state lost hundreds of millions of dollars of revenue the nation's largest sporting event would have brought in.

Dallas, featuring a No-Name Defense with no Pro Bowl selections, was nonetheless exceptionally fast and well versed on the Bills' legendary No-Huddle Offense. Add to that the limited mobility of Buffalo quarterback Jim Kelly, who was back after missing most of the playoffs with strained knee ligaments, and the stage was set for Buffalo's exercise in futility. "You can't beat a college team with that many turnovers," said Kelly, who was sacked twice and completed only four passes before he

was replaced by Frank Reich after re-injuring his knee in the second quarter.

When the No-Name Defenders were taking a breather on the sidelines, Cowboys offensive players such as Emmitt Smith, Troy Aikman, and Michael Irvin were becoming instant superstars. Under the tutelage of offensive coordinator Norv Turner, the Cowboys turned into a model of play-action passing effectiveness and power rushing, relying on fundamentals over gimmicks. Their 52 points were just three shy of breaking the Super Bowl scoring record, set by San Francisco three years earlier.

The magic of Aikman-to-Irvin was on brilliant display just after Kelly's injury in the second quarter, when a 38-yard Smith run led to a 19-yard touchdown pass to

Right, Wide receiver Michael Irvin holds the Lombardi trophy. *AP Photo/Al Messerschmidt*

Far right, Bills receiver Don Beebe (82) stripped the ball from Leon Lett (78) just before Lett crossed the line in a meaningless but memorable play. *AP Photo/Paul Spinelli*

Irvin with 1:54 left in the half and then Jimmie Jones's recovery of a Thurman Thomas fumble on the next play led to a nearly identical play—an 18-yard touchdown pass. The two scores in the air happened in just 18 seconds, and they catapulted the result from an unintimidating 14-10 to a discouraging 28-10.

"Those two plays back-to-back were probably our bread-and-butter run and our bread-and-butter pass," Johnson said of the first of the two scoring drives. "We didn't do a lot of things to trick people. We did a lot of things that we believe in and that challenged people to stop us."

Just as Joe Montana used the Super Bowl stage to establish himself as the undeniable quarterback of the '80s, that

game at the Rose Bowl would be the backdrop for Aikman's coming-out party. He completed 22 of 30 passes for 273 yards, four touchdowns, and no interceptions and earned the MVP award running away in the first of his three Super Bowl victories in the '90s. "This team has meant everything to me," Aikman said. "It's a tremendous weight off my shoulders."

If the first half featured glimmers of Cowboy greatness, the second half was saturated with it, and the Bills were helpless to reverse the course. "An earthquake over in Santa Monica tonight —that's the only thing that will stop the Dallas Cowboys," said Buffalo wide receiver James Lofton. Even if the third was the only period in which the Bills outscored them (Dallas had a field goal,

and Frank Reich hit Bills receiver Don Beebe on a 40-yard touchdown pass), the fourth quarter was all Cowboys—three touchdowns in 2:33 to put the matchup into the blowout category.

The fourth quarter should have been even more catastrophic for Buffalo, and the play that kept the score from breaking the records for most points scored was inconsequential but still legendary as one of the Super Bowl's most memorable moments. With five minutes left in the game, Dallas defensive tackle Leon Lett recovered a Reich fumble and took off for the end zone. No one seemed to be in pursuit of Lett, so at the 10-yard line he extended his right arm out, with his right hand gripping the ball, in a premature show of celebration. That flourish almost worked, but at the 1-yard line Beebe

caught up with Lett and stripped him of the ball.

Although Bills coach Marv Levy used Beebe's perseverance as inspirational fodder for overcoming a third loss, it was an all-around tough day for the team that had become the first team in history to lose three consecutive Super Bowls. "It's not how many times you lose; it's how many times you get back up," Buffalo nose tackle Jeff Wright said. "And we're going to get back up."

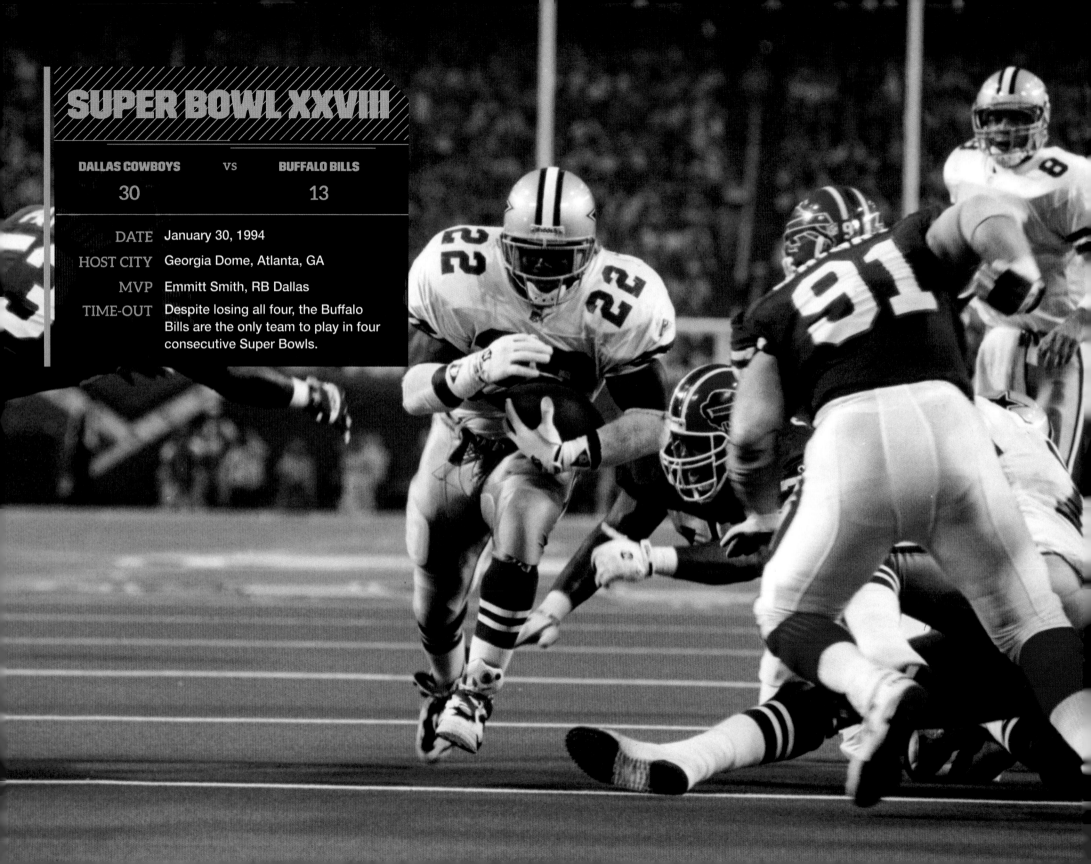

SUPER BOWL XXVIII

DALLAS COWBOYS	VS	BUFFALO BILLS
30		13

DATE — January 30, 1994

HOST CITY — Georgia Dome, Atlanta, GA

MVP — Emmitt Smith, RB Dallas

TIME-OUT — Despite losing all four, the Buffalo Bills are the only team to play in four consecutive Super Bowls.

The Super Bowl had been the chief pursuit in professional football for nearly three decades, and in that time only one team had made it to the big game for more than two consecutive years. And in the playoffs leading up to Super Bowl XXVIII in Atlanta, the Buffalo Bills were blazing a trail toward an unprecedented fourth appearance.

Four straight Super Bowls. It is a stellar achievement, a testament to stamina, skill, toughness, and the wise, steadfast leadership of Marv Levy. But of course, the extraordinary nature of that streak is tempered by its accompanying truth, the unpleasant reality one headline writer called "Woe for four."

To keep prevailing through the regular season and the playoffs and then to stumble every time with everything on the line, what does it say about a team? The Bills players from that era have said that they would have rather been a part of those Super Bowl losses than to have never made it at all, but quarterback Jim Kelly said something else, when the run finally ended at the hands of the Dallas Cowboys in early 1994. "Had we won just one of those games," he said, "they'd be talking about us as one of the greatest teams of all time."

A rematch with Dallas appeared as either divine providence or abject cruelty after the 52-17 shellacking of the year before. But even if the actors were the same, this Super Bowl featured a different script with more drama and a much scrappier underdog. In the end it was still loss number four, but a considerable measure of the potency that had given Buffalo

four straight opportunities was on display that evening in the Georgia Dome.

The Bills entered the locker room at halftime with a 13-6 lead and the momentum, buoyed by a Super Bowl–record 54-yard kick from Steve Christie in the first quarter and an 80-yard touchdown drive capped by a 4-yard Thurman Thomas run. At halftime, Kelly was 12 for 12 on passes under 10 yards, and the Bills led the Cowboys in total yardage 216-170 and also had an edge in both total snaps and time of possession. Buffalo's famous No-Huddle Offense was operating efficiently, and the Cowboys weren't showing the brilliance that had characterized them the previous year.

Dallas quarterback Troy Aikman, still feeling the effects of a concussion he suffered in the NFC Championship Game against San Francisco, remembers feeling dissatisfied with the way his team had played in the first half. But even as he entertained a concern that this could finally be Buffalo's year, he caught a glimpse of the Bills players filing into the locker room. "I looked over and saw their players go in, and you would have thought they were the team who was behind," he said. "At that moment, I kind of thought they were a team that just felt something bad was going to happen, that they were snakebit in Super Bowls."

The snake would show itself soon enough, and its venom was familiar to the Bills. In a stroke of karmic justice for a team that had made "turnovers" synonymous with "January," the tide turned on a Thomas fumble less than a minute into the third quarter. Thomas took the handoff on the first down, but he was stripped by

Leon Lett, who famously experienced the sensation of having the ball taken from him at the end of Super Bowl XXVII, and free safety James Washington scooped up the ball and dashed 46 yards for a Dallas touchdown. Just 55 seconds had ticked off of the clock, and the game was tied at 13.

"The key was the fumble," Cowboys defensive end Charles Haley told *The Buffalo News*. "After that, it seemed like they panicked a little bit, went off their game plan, and tried to go downfield."

The Bills wouldn't see the end zone again, but Dallas was just getting started. Less than six minutes after Washington's game changer, Emmitt Smith scored on a 15-yard run, serving as the apt finale in a drive that featured him carrying the ball on seven out of eight plays. The powerful back rushed for only 41 yards in the first half, but he and his team both came to life after halftime, and Smith's 132 yards on the ground were enough to earn him his first MVP award.

In the fourth quarter, Washington, who many believed should have garnered co-MVP honors for his tenacious defensive performance, intercepted a third-and-6 Kelly pass intended for Don Beebe and returned the ball 12 yards to the Buffalo 34. Smith jumped a short yard in for another touchdown eight plays later, and Dallas iced its second consecutive world title with a 20-yard Eddie Murray field goal with less than three minutes left in the game.

In the end, the Bills were downed by their old archenemy, turnovers—Dallas scored 17 points on three takeaways—and by an offensive scheme that set the pace early but sputtered and never recovered after the lead was lost. Thomas will always be remembered as one of the best backs in Buffalo's history, but he gained only 37 yards that evening, and his total yardage in Super Bowls XXVI, XXVII, and XXVIII was fewer than 70 yards.

Buffalo's trouble in igniting its ground game was just one of the symptoms of its Super Bowl paralysis. Despite plenty of talent and innovative coaches, none of the four Bills teams that vied for a Super Bowl ring played like the team that had propelled them there. In those four defeats, they had an abysmal -13 turnover differential, 18 fumbles, and no touchdowns from leading receiver Andre Reed.

Afterward the Bills players, ruminating on the futility of it all, considered what their legacy would look like decades later, and receiver Steve Tasker issued an accurate prediction. "That's probably going to be part of our identity for years and years to come," he said, "that we lost four Super Bowls in a row."

Jim Kelly leaves the field after his team lost.
AP Photo/Amy Sancetta

Left, Tennessee Titans running back Eddie George sits dejectedly on the bench after the Titans' loss in Super Bowl XXXIV. *AP Photo/Mark Humphrey*

LOSING
A SUPER BOWL

It's a question that is mere speculative entertainment for fans who will never come close to actually experiencing it: Would you rather make it to a Super Bowl and lose or never make it at all?

At the heart of the debate is America's obsession with winning the big one, the unique nature of professional football, and the difference between people who want a win to brag to their coworkers the next day and those who need a win to keep their job.

Ernie Accorsi, AP Photo/Mike Derer

Ernie Accorsi spent close to four decades as an executive in the NFL, first as the public relations director with the Baltimore Colts and then as the general manager of the Colts, the Cleveland Browns, and the New York Giants. When he arrived in Baltimore in 1970, more than a year had passed since the team was thunderstruck by the New York Jets in Super Bowl III, and it still felt to him like the aftermath of a funeral.

"They had not gotten out of a state of shock," Accorsi said. "Then when we won Super Bowl V against the Cowboys, the feeling in the organization was not joy; it was relief."

Through close associations with hundreds of executives, coaches, and players since the NFL was founded, Accorsi has reached the conclusion that no loss in sports is as singularly distressing as losing on Super Bowl Sunday. In the NBA and Major League Baseball, teams have seven chances to play their best for a championship trophy, so the spotlight is not nearly as searing as it is in the winner-takes-all atmosphere of the Super Bowl.

"We have created a mentality that if you lose the Super Bowl, you're a loser," he said. "Baseball celebrates winning a pennant, they raise a flag. We never do that."

It's a little-known fact that in professional football the AFC and NFC champions are given rings to celebrate their accomplishments. Accorsi has an NFC championship ring from the year his Giants made it to Super Bowl XXXV and lost to the Baltimore Ravens. It's a nicer and more comfortable ring than his Super Bowl XLII ring, he said, but he refuses to wear it.

As for that philosophical question, Accorsi knows where he stands. He has experienced the pinnacle of the mountain, when the New York Giants team he helped assemble won Super Bowl XLII shortly after his retirement, and he sees only one way to feel satisfied in making it to Super Sunday: leaving with a Lombardi Trophy. "I'd rather not make it if I was going to lose," he said.

Accorsi remembers a conversation with former Green Bay Packers general manager Ron Wolf, whose team first won Super Bowl XXXI and then lost Super Bowl XXXII the following year. The win was nice, he told Accorsi, but the good feelings from that triumph would never be enough to make up for the pain of the loss.

Of the 49 teams that have been on the somber side of that trophy ceremony, only nine have never redeemed that loss with a Super Bowl title. And of those nine unfortunate franchises, only two, the Minnesota Vikings and the Buffalo Bills, have compiled a worse all-time record than 0-2. So when it comes to the emotions of losing the Super Bowl, the coaches who compiled four losses each offer valuable perspective.

Bud Grant actually won four national football championships in his career—the four Grey Cups he captured while coaching in the CFL. When he took the head job with the Minnesota Vikings in 1967, he turned around a struggling team and made it to the Super Bowl four times in seven years, but each time they were defeated. In interviews decades later, Grant was philosophical and upbeat about having the trophy within his grasp so many times. He told Loran Smith of the *Athens Banner-Herald* that it took him "about a day" to get over the losses.

"Football is entertainment, and you can't let your defeats defeat you," he told the *Banner-Herald* in 2013. "That is what has made this country great—competition to

Minnesota Vikings quarterback Fran Tarkenton (10), finishing his third Super Bowl without a win, sits on his helmet during the final minutes as his team falls to the Oakland Raiders. *AP Photo*

"IT JUST SO HAPPENED IT WASN'T OUR TIME TO WIN A SUPER BOWL. THAT'S PAST HISTORY, AND THE SUN WILL COME UP TOMORROW. AT LEAST WE WERE THERE, DOGGONE IT."

PAUL KRAUSE
Minnesota Vikings safety

Left, Minnesota Vikings Hall of Fame safety Paul Krause. *AP Photo/NFL Photos*

see who is the best. In sports, we want to see who is No. 1, but those who lose the big game are winners by being able to play in the championship game. You play your best and move on."

The only man in the world who can understand Grant's perspective is Marv Levy, a scholar and a poet who was admitted to Harvard Law School but was unable to deny the lure of coaching football. As the man in charge through four consecutive Buffalo Bills losses between 1991 and 1994, Levy was nonetheless selected for the Pro Football Hall of Fame in 2001, and he gained respect throughout the league for the way he built one winning team after another despite the burden of losing on America's biggest stage.

But that doesn't mean the losses didn't sting. In his biography, *Where Else Would You Rather Be?*, Levy described a loss in the NFL as "a despair so gripping that you can feel it physically," and he says that when the loss happens in the Super Bowl, those emotions are "multiplied by infinity."

In vivid detail, Levy described the effects a momentous defeat had on his joints, his muscles, and his breathing, and he remembered specifically when that sensation hit him after Buffalo's first Super Bowl loss, a 20-19 loss to the Giants when kicker Scott Norwood missed a field goal attempt in the final minutes. After that game, the full weight of the defeat hit him after he had addressed his team, answered questions from the media,

headed back to his hotel room, and tried to sleep.

"I spent most of that tormented night trying to refrain, sometimes unsuccessfully, from kicking away my blankets and from pummeling my mattress," Levy wrote. "In the darkness I winced as I listened to an occasional sob from my dear wife, Frannie."

No one denies that to make it to the Super Bowl is both an honor and a testament to the fortitude a team must show to persevere through the brutality that professional football offers up week after week. Some, like Accorsi, are honest about the fact that making it is simply not enough. Other executives, players, and coaches hold onto the pride of being there, even if the ending turns out to be tragedy rather than fairy tale.

"We had good football teams," said former Minnesota safety Paul Krause, a Hall of Famer who set an NFL record with 81 career interceptions. "It just so happened it wasn't our time to win a Super Bowl. That's past history, and the sun will come up tomorrow. At least we were there, doggone it."

Right, Buffalo Bills coach Marv Levy reacts during the fourth quarter of Super Bowl XXV. *AP Photo/Mark Duncan*

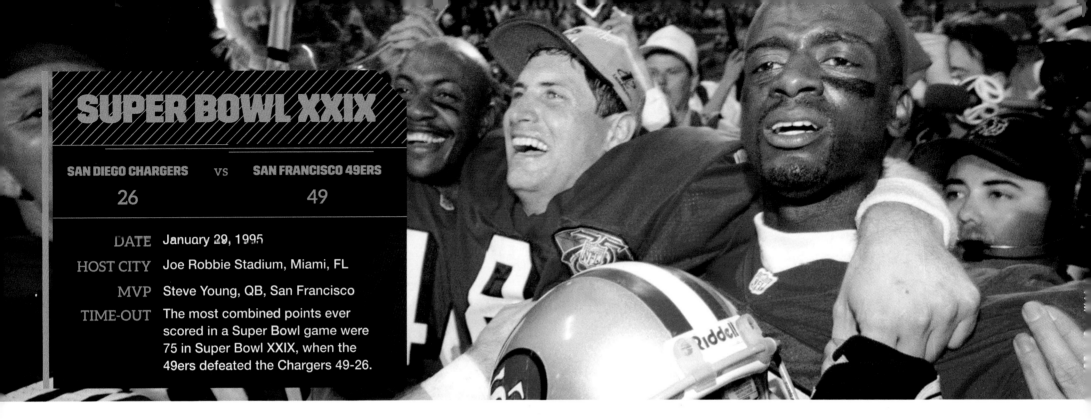

SUPER BOWL XXIX

SAN DIEGO CHARGERS VS **SAN FRANCISCO 49ERS**

26 **49**

DATE	January 29, 1995
HOST CITY	Joe Robbie Stadium, Miami, FL
MVP	Steve Young, QB, San Francisco
TIME-OUT	The most combined points ever scored in a Super Bowl game were 75 in Super Bowl XXIX, when the 49ers defeated the Chargers 49-26.

The days of two pro football leagues and the NFL shouting its supremacy over the AFL were decades in the past, but the modern-day NFC had picked up the mantle in the mid-'80s, winning 10 straight Super Bowls over AFC opponents. The dominance had become so total that the NFC Championship Game was threatening to displace the Super Bowl as the game that really mattered, and the two teams that had come to define that conference rivalry were Dallas and San Francisco.

The 49ers hadn't made a Super Bowl in five years, but for the past two winters they had advanced as far as the NFC title game and collided with Emmitt Smith and his Cowboys. Looking to recapture the magic that had made San Francisco the team of the '80s, in the offseason before Super Bowl XXIX owner Eddie DeBartolo

and president Carmen Policy went on a shopping spree and inked eight new players for $12 million just months before the NFL enacted the salary cap.

With new acquisitions such as Ken Norton Jr., Gary Plummer, and Deion Sanders fortifying the troops, the 49ers finally toppled the Cowboys 38-28 to punch their ticket to Miami, and the San Francisco players were justified in their feeling that the main event was already behind them. "I feel, honestly, that this was the Super Bowl," Sanders said after the Dallas victory.

But over in the AFC, a young San Diego Chargers team had blazed a surprising path to become the next AFC offering at the Super Bowl altar. The Chargers brought talented players such as Natrone

Means and Junior Seau, but this was a one-sided matchup from the start, and it seemed that nearly everyone on both sides knew it. San Diego was a 19-and-a-half-point underdog, and the final score of 49-26 just exceeded that projection.

Steve Young, who had earned the 49ers starting job in 1991, was leading the offense in his first Super Bowl, and he was feeling nervous just before the game started until offensive coordinator Mike Shanahan approached him. "Steve, don't worry," Shanahan said calmly. "We're going to crush these guys."

One Chargers assistant, director of player personnel Billy Devaney, said after the game, "To be honest, we knew we were in trouble when we lost the coin toss."

It was a game that was never truly in question. Young came out like a bolt out of the blue in the first quarter, hitting Jerry Rice on a 44-yard touchdown bomb on the third play of the game, and then gave Ricky Watters a turn to play when the two connected on a 51-yard touchdown pass the next time San Francisco took the field. San Diego did score in the first quarter on a 1-yard Natrone Means run that made the score 14-7, but the underdogs would never come that close again.

In each of the first three quarters, the 49ers scored two consecutive touchdowns. San Diego scored once each quarter, but even with flashes of inspiration such as Andre Coleman's 98-yard kickoff return in the third quarter, the 49ers' sizable lead was never in any jeopardy. Even the Chargers seemed to have flipped the

Left, Steve Young (8) runs over San Diego's Darrien Gordon (21) for a first down. *AP Photo/Andrew Innerarity, File*

Right, San Diego Francisco running back Natrone Means celebrates after scoring a touchdown. *AP Photo/Andrew Innerarity*

pages and read the ending before they were done with the book, playing flat against a team with a huge arsenal of weapons.

San Francisco's revamped defense shut down Means and the Chargers' ground attack, allowing them only 67 rushing yards, and Sanders and the backfield combined for three interceptions as San Diego's Stan Humphries struggled to find the rhythm that had characterized his team's stunning 17-13 AFC Championship win over the Pittsburgh Steelers.

"We lost that game because we were an immature football team," San Diego special teams coach Chuck Priefer said of the Super Bowl. "We had some super leaders and players in Humphries and Seau, but my belief is San Francisco would have beat the hell out of anybody that day."

When it was over, Young celebrated wholeheartedly, his exultation a direct result of the obstacles he had faced on the road to the top. He was hot and cold in the early '90s at the starting position, even losing the spot briefly to Steve Bono in 1991, and despite being the NFL MVP in 1992, DeBartolo announced the next year that Montana would again be the starter, thus causing a divide in the 49ers locker room. Montana himself helped resolve the conflict by requesting and receiving a trade to Kansas City, but Young was haunted nonetheless by the presence of the greatest Super Bowl quarterback in league history.

In Super Bowl XXIX Young had a golden opportunity for redemption, and he seized it. Not only did he complete 24 of 36 passes for 325 yards, six touchdowns, and no interceptions but also he was the

49ers' leading rusher with 49 yards on the ground. As the game winded down, he turned to teammates on the sideline and shouted, "Somebody take the monkey off my back, please!" Plummer obliged, ripping the imaginary monkey off of Young's jersey before the quarterback threw his arms up in joy.

"I really wish that anyone who has ever played football could feel like this," said Young, a runaway choice for Super Bowl MVP. "I wish this on everybody. To throw six touchdowns and when you get to the big game and play your best game ever, you couldn't ask for more. I'll always remember this as probably my best ever. I hope there's more to come."

In fact, Young would not mirror his rival's accomplishments. He wouldn't return to the Super Bowl, but San Francisco fans had a dramatic assurance that their good

fortunes weren't a thing of the past. The 49ers leadership had proven that they would go to great lengths to build a winner—and the team that was on display that day was a showpiece of what great football looked like in the age between unrestricted free agency and the salary cap.

"That team was put together specifically to win a Super Bowl," head coach George Seifert said. "We hadn't won the Super Bowl since my first year. It was mandated that we were to win the Super Bowl. It was an all-out vendetta to put that team together."

SUPER BOWL XXX

DALLAS COWBOYS vs **PITTSBURGH STEELERS**

27 **17**

DATE January 28, 1996

HOST CITY Sun Devil Stadium, Tempe, AZ

MVP Larry Brown, CB, Dallas

TIME-OUT When Dallas cornerback Larry Brown received the MVP award for his two key interceptions, he became the first defensive player to be chosen for the honor in 22 years, since Dolphins safety Jake Scott in Super Bowl VII.

An unknown MVP on a team of superstars. A much-maligned coach with an enormous chip on his shoulder. They might have collected four rings already, but the Dallas Cowboys had never won a Super Bowl like this one.

Troy Aikman, Emmitt Smith, and company were 13-and-a-half-point favorites against the Pittsburgh Steelers, but this was the tightest world championship in four years. Dallas had only a three-point lead with 6:36 to play, and the Steelers defense held the powerful Smith to just 49 rushing yards.

The X factor in Tempe that day was a cornerback named Larry Brown, a twelfth-round draft pick in 1991 who had just earned his first starting job that fall but left with the MVP trophy thanks to two vital interceptions in the second half. Both of Brown's picks from Pittsburgh quarterback Neil O'Donnell led to Cowboys touchdowns, and without his theatrics Dallas and head coach Barry Switzer would have gone home defeated.

The game was within two errant passes of becoming the greatest Super Bowl upset since Joe Namath made good on his pronouncement in Super Bowl III. The Cowboys, the team of the '90s, had been to three Super Bowls in four years, and Switzer ran a famously loose ship in the week leading up to the big game. Players stayed out having a good time, practicing haphazardly, while the Cowboys cheerleaders prepared a video featuring their version of "The Super Bowl Shuffle" —before the game was even played.

"Most thought this Super Bowl would be rated XXX, figured what the Cowboys would do to the Steelers would be obscene, that Troy and Michael and Emmitt and Deion were going to run roughshod over the AFC again," wrote Paul Needell in the *New York Daily News*. "Few expected Dallas to be holding on in the fourth quarter, only to be rescued by a courageous cornerback named Larry Brown."

A young Bill Cowher, who would win his only Lombardi Trophy a decade later, brought a scrappy team that had rallied back from a 3-4 early-season start and spent his Super Bowl preparation week preaching discipline and highlighting their role as underdogs who didn't stand a chance. When his team trailed just 13-7 at halftime, he called on his best motivational skills in a fiery pep talk that sent his players tearing out of the locker room.

"They thought they were going to run all over you!" he said, according to Jeff Pearlman's book *Boys Will Be Boys*. "They thought you were a joke. Well, they're not laughing anymore! We took their best shots! Now it's our turn! Let's go take what's ours."

If the Steelers had prevailed, MVP voters would have been inclined to honor the entire defense for their almost-complete stifling of Aikman, Smith, and the rest in the second half. In six possessions, Dallas ran just 19 plays and gained only 61 yards after halftime. Talented linebackers such as Greg Lloyd and Kevin Greene teamed with backfield standouts Carnell Lake and Rod Woodson—back from reconstructive knee surgery after an early-season injury—to make sure Dallas didn't rally. Unfortunately, the defensive unit couldn't control their own passing game or the quick hands of Brown.

"They had a field full of guys that probably will be in the Hall of Fame," defensive coordinator Dick LeBeau said in *The Ultimate Super Bowl Book*. "But after the second drive we completely contained them. We didn't have a weakness on that defense. We won everything but the score."

O'Donnell's first miscue came halfway through the third quarter when he threw a sloppy pass under pressure from the Dallas defensive line, which was borrowing generously from its opponent's trademark zone blitz package in the game. As tackle Chad Hennings plowed into him, O'Donnell released the ball in desperation—and it went straight to Brown. "Neil made a bad, bad read," said Pittsburgh wide receiver Ernie Mills. Brown ran the ball back to the Pittsburgh 18, Aikman completed a 17-yard pass to Michael Irvin, and on the next play Smith barreled in for a touchdown and a 20-6 Dallas lead.

As the fourth quarter commenced, the Steelers had a burst of offensive production, and football fans who had endured four straight blowouts sat up a little straighter in their seats. Cowher got his team within three points with some unconventional coaching decisions, including the nod for an onside kick that was the earliest ever attempted in a Super Bowl at that point.

First, O'Donnell engineered a 10-play, 52-yard drive that threatened to expire when Tony Tolbert drilled him on a third-down sack but resulted in a 46-yard Norm Johnson field goal. On the ensuing kickoff, Cowher approved the idea of the onside kick and told special teams coach Bobby April, "I'm not leaving anything in the bag." Cornerback Deon Figures recovered the ball, Pittsburgh drove again, and Bam Morris scored on third and goal to make the score 20-17, Dallas, with 6:36 on the clock.

The updated version of the Steel Curtain stopped another attempted Dallas drive and handed its offense a golden opportunity with 4:15 remaining. But on second and 10, O'Donnell was again rattled by the zone blitz, wide receiver Andre Hastings misread the coverage, and Larry Brown had one of the most crucial interceptions in Super Bowl history. He ran it back 33 yards, and the Cowboys had to cover only 6 yards to pad their lead at 27-17 and claim their fifth ring.

The victory spelled sweet vindication for Switzer, who had been the target of relentless criticism when team owner Jerry Jones hired him to replace Jimmy Johnson in the preseason. Switzer was portrayed as a buffoon who lacked the experience and the knowledge to build a champion, but in the end the famously garrulous good ol' boy relished the chance to have the last word.

As the celebration began, he turned to Jones and famously screamed out, "We did it our way, baby! We did it! We did it! We did it!"

Top right, Dallas Cowboys quarterback Troy Aikman, (*right*), and wide receiver Michael Irvin celebrate their 21-17 win. *AP Photo/Elaine Thompson*

Bottom left, Neil O'Donnell (14) leads a Pittsburgh scoring drive. *AP Photo/Doug Mills*

SUPER BOWL XXXI

NEW ENGLAND PATRIOTS VS **GREEN BAY PACKERS**

21 **35**

DATE — January 26, 1997

HOST CITY — Lousiana Superdome, New Orleans, LA

MVP — Desmond Howard, KR-PR, Green Bay

TIME-OUT — Despite three NFL MVP awards and 11 Pro Bowl selections, quarterback Brett Favre's only title was for Super Bowl XXXI

The Green Bay Packers' place in Super Bowl history was undisputed, but through the '80s and '90s there were plenty who wondered about their prospects for a Super Bowl future. After winning the first two championships, the team from Titletown had not returned to fight for a title in 29 years.

The Packers squad that took the field at the Superdome against the New England Patriots was loaded with both talent and confidence that this could be the year the past met the present. And with a solid performance from Brett Favre and a spectacular special teams play by MVP Desmond Howard, a 35-21 triumph ensured that the Lombardi Trophy would return to the squad of its namesake.

"We were on such a roll," Packers tight end Mark Chmura said. "That team seemed to have so much destiny to it, and we had so much depth."

The Patriots, in the news in the week before the game because of strain between team owner Robert Kraft and head coach Bill Parcells that was reportedly reaching a breaking point, nonetheless made it interesting when they trimmed the lead to six points in the third quarter. But just when the door was opening for the Pats, Howard traveled 99 yards on a kickoff return to slam it shut.

Howard's heavy lifting—he gained 90 yards on punt returns and 154 on kickoffs—was complemented by the poise and accuracy of Green Bay's 27-year-old quarterback. Favre could not have known that Super Bowl XXXI was the only one he would ever win, but starting with a clutch audible that resulted in a 54-yard Andre Rison touchdown catch on the Packers' first possession, he kept his cool and finished with 246 yards and no interceptions.

"We paid so much attention to the strength of Brett Favre that we didn't pay enough attention to the strength of their return game," New England director of college scouting Charley Armey told Bob McGinn in *The Ultimate Super Bowl Book*.

On the other sideline, the Patriots passing game engineered by Drew Bledsoe betrayed some of the unraveling that seemed to characterize the team that day. Bledsoe and his unit carried a lopsided measure of pressure due to the ineffectiveness of New England's running game at that point, and Bledsoe jumped into the void by completing 25 of a dizzying 48 pass attempts. Unfortunately,

four of those incompletions landed in the hands of Packers defenders.

Even though Bledsoe's first giveaway came on the Patriots' first touch of the game, the first period ended as the highest-scoring first quarter in Super Bowl history and smacked of promise for an exciting evening. After Green Bay jumped out to a 10-0 lead on the Rison long bomb and a 37-yard Chris Jacke field goal, Bledsoe put together two consecutive scoring drives of his own, ending in go-ahead passes to Keith Byars and Ben Coates, who was New England's leading receiver that day.

The Packers, the first team since the undefeated 1972 Miami Dolphins to lead the NFL in both points scored (456) and fewest points allowed (210), entered the game as two-touchdown favorites, and players remember being fairly unfazed by the 14-10 Patriots lead heading into the second quarter.

"When I watch the game now, I can't believe we were behind," Chmura said. "There was just absolutely no panic whatsoever. Deep down, we knew before the game that we were going to win."

It wasn't until the third drive of the second quarter that Favre delivered a definitive answer to that lead, an 81-yard touchdown pass to the speedy Antonio Freeman that made mincemeat of New England's man-to-man coverage plan, and then scored 10 more uncontested points to build a 27-14 halftime lead. "At halftime we said, 'We're not doing that anymore,'"

Patriots assistant head coach and secondary coach Bill Belichick said. "We're just going to play zone and make them earn it."

New England's defensive adjustment was enough to slow Favre and company down in the second half, stopping the Packers on fourth and 1 on an early third-quarter drive and then turning the tables to score on a 28-yard Curtis Martin run that represented the majority of his team's 43 total rushing yards for the game. The scoreboard read 27-21 and the Patriots were collecting momentum when Howard stepped in as the game's uncontested spoiler.

Howard's was the ultimate redemption plotline in a script loaded with them. Favre put together an impeccable quarterback performance after spending six weeks in a rehabilitation center in the offseason for a prescription painkiller addiction. Reggie White was a force of nature in New Orleans with three sacks, including two consecutive takedowns of Bledsoe in that crucial third quarter, and his Super Bowl ring represented 14 years of trying to carry the Packers to the mountaintop on his back.

The only special teams player in the first half century of the Super Bowl to be named MVP, Howard was cut by both the Redskins and the Jaguars before landing with the Packers in July on

a one-year $300,000 contract. "He was as good at what he did as anyone I have ever seen win my life," Packers general manager Ron Wolf said. "That's what happens sometimes when you get a guy off the scrap heap that has to prove to everybody that he can still play."

Since the Packers made their return to Titletown look easy, the most physically grueling part of the whole experience might have been their victory parade back in Wisconsin. Schools closed early in Green Bay, and more than 100,000 people (roughly the population of Green Bay) lined up along the road while the buses inched toward the 60,000 who had packed Lambeau Field to welcome the team. The motorcade crept along for nearly three hours as players leaned out the bus windows to give high fives on a 20-degree day.

"This is a new era," Green Bay native Brian Hamilton told at the parade. "We've been celebrating since last night. I don't know when we'll stop."

Top right, A Packers fan holds up a Vince Lombardi trophy poster. *AP Photo/Mark Humphrey*

Left, Desmond Howard returns a kick. *AP Photo/NFL Photos*

THE GREAT DIP
DEBATE

When Jolie Kerr of *Deadspin* developed a March Madness-style dip bracket for Super Bowl 2014 and asked her readers to vote, she could hardly have anticipated the passion with which football fans embrace their dips of choice. With comments full of vitriol for anyone who would choose seven-layer dip over crab dip and insights like, "Spinach and artichoke dip in a bread bowl is the first warning sign that you may be accidentally attending a book club rather than a Super Bowl party," more than 12,000 *Deadspin* visitors weighed in on each round. When the Final Four was unveiled, it contained a few surprises. The four dips that survived to the final rounds were guacamole, salsa, buffalo chicken dip, and queso. The big winner? Guacamole, which beat out salsa 62 to 38 percent in the finals.

GUACAMOLE
CHAMPION

SALSA
RUNNER-UP

QUESO
SEMIFINALIST

BUFFALO CHICKEN DIP
SEMIFINALIST

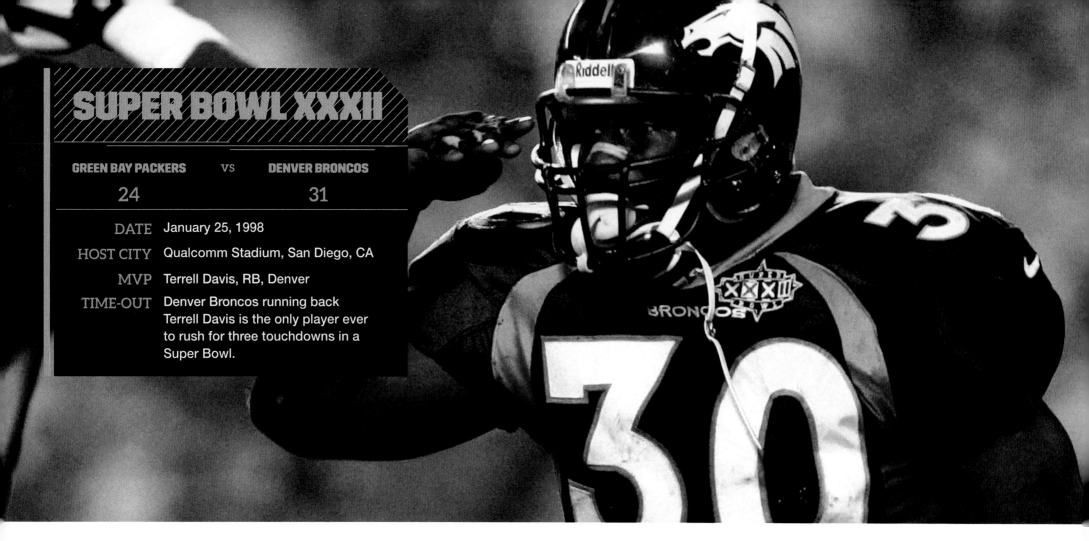

SUPER BOWL XXXII

GREEN BAY PACKERS	VS	DENVER BRONCOS
24		31

DATE — January 25, 1998

HOST CITY — Qualcomm Stadium, San Diego, CA

MVP — Terrell Davis, RB, Denver

TIME-OUT — Denver Broncos running back Terrell Davis is the only player ever to rush for three touchdowns in a Super Bowl.

When the Super Bowl was in its infancy, talk centered on the supremacy of the NFL over the AFL. When the two leagues merged in 1970, all but three of the original NFL teams formed the NFC, and two decades later NFC fans were still making a case for dominance.

After all, by the time the defending champion Green Bay Packers met the Denver Broncos in San Diego for Super Bowl XXXII, NFC squads had won a stunning 13 straight Super Bowls, with 11 of those victories decided by 10 points or more. It was no wonder that the Packers were favored by 11 and a half points.

But oddsmakers and NFC apologists didn't account for a Broncos game plan that smothered the Packers with the blitz and capitalized on the power and speed of running back Terrell Davis on the way to a 31-24 victory. For Green Bay, it would always be the one that got away. For Denver, it was the one that erased the shame of four Super Bowl losses and gave veteran quarterback John Elway the trophy that made his career complete.

"Other than my wife and four children, there's nothing better than this," Elway told the New York Daily News afterward. "That was the ultimate win, no question. It's three times better than anything I could've imagined."

The game, widely considered one of the top five Super Bowl upsets in the game's first 50 years, certainly shocked the Packers, but everything that day went according to Mike Shanahan's well-scripted plan. The Denver head coach even played media and popular opinion in the weeks leading up to the game, giving quiet credence to the idea that the Packers were world beaters on their way to a second ring.

"Mike Shanahan was perfect in his mental approach to that game," linebacker Bill Romanowski reflected years later. "It was all about building the Packers up. They were feeling real good about themselves, and we were telling them how great they were. Really, we felt we had them right where we wanted them."

That Super Sunday will always be associated with Elway because of the valleys he endured to reach the mountaintop: three lopsided Super Bowl defeats, murmurs that despite the accomplishments of an 18-year career he couldn't guide his team to the ultimate championship. But the MVP of Super Bowl XXXII, and the offensive player most responsible for stymying the vaunted Green Bay defense, was a 25-year-old who had entered training camp a year earlier as the sixth-string tailback.

Since that time, Davis had become the linchpin of the Broncos' ground attack, and his power was on full display on Super Sunday at Qualcomm Stadium, where he covered 157 yards on 30 attempts and scored three of his team's four touchdowns. Ultimately, the Green Bay defense couldn't contain Davis, and some feel that head coach Mike Holmgren failed to make adjustments that would have used All-Pro players such as LeRoy Butler and Reggie White effectively. Packers general manager Ron Wolf called the loss "the day our defensive line went away."

The hundreds of thousands of Cheeseheads who had lined the streets of chilly Wisconsin to welcome their conquering heroes a year earlier might have been poised for a blowout, but instead they got a thriller with three ties—the last with just 1:45 left in the game. The Packers struck first on a 22-yard pass from Brett Favre to Antonio Freeman, but the Broncos soon answered with Davis's first touchdown run and then posted 10 more points in the second

quarter for a 17-7 edge that was the largest lead of the day. Green Bay tight end Mark Chmura caught a 6-yard pass from Favre to make it 17-14 heading into the locker room—with the feeling that it was still anybody's game.

Davis missed part of the second quarter with a severe migraine headache that blurred his vision. He took some medication, rested through halftime, and sprinted back out on the field with his team in a moment that Broncos owner Pat Bowlen called one of the greatest feelings of relief he had ever experienced.

The teams exchanged touchdowns again in the third quarter, thus setting up a blockbuster fourth quarter. The period was barely two minutes old when Elway—trying to hit Rod Smith in the end zone for a score that would have given the Broncos a comfortable lead—instead threw into the grip of Green Bay safety Eugene Robinson, setting up a 13-yard Favre-to-Freeman pass that tied the game at 24. For the next 10 minutes, Favre tried three times to put together another successful drive, but the Denver defense smothered him with its particular model of blitzkrieg. During the game, the Broncos rushed five or more defenders on nearly 50 percent of Favre's dropback passes.

The Broncos' go-ahead touchdown in the game's waning minutes resulted from one of the more controversial coaching decisions in Super Bowl history. After starting the drive in optimal position at the Packer 49, Elway's 23-yard pass to Howard Griffith and a 17-yard Davis run brought Denver to the 1-yard line. During

the ensuing time-out, Holmgren reasoned that since they had been unable to stop Davis all day, they should let him score uncontested to allow more time for their own offense to assemble a touchdown drive.

Holmgren revealed later that he thought it was first down, but it was actually second, a misstep that could have altered Green Bay's defense significantly. Davis waltzed in for the touchdown, and then the Packers recovered and advanced to the Broncos 35; however, Favre and his unit were unable to gain any more ground, and their hopes of bringing consecutive celebrations to Titletown were dashed.

It's a defeat that still haunts the players and executives of that Packers squad. A decade after the game and seven years after his retirement, Wolf told the *Milwaukee Journal Sentinel* that he believes the Packers were outcoached and Holmgren could have made adjustments that would have changed the outcome.

"Certain calls were to be made that weren't made," said Wolf, who told reporter Bob McGinn that other NFL coaches had talked to him about the mistakes made in the game in the years since. "Mike Holmgren refused those calls. There would have been an adjustment on the blocking scheme and it would have been over.

"I'm probably still not over it."

Green Bay Packers QB Brett Favre (4) during Super Bowl XXXII. *AP Photo/Tom DiPace*

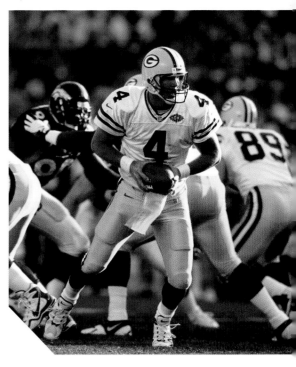

SUPER BOWL XXXIII

DENVER BRONCOS	VS	ATLANTA FALCONS
34		19

DATE · January 31, 1999

HOST CITY · Pro Player Stadium, Miami, FL

MVP · John Elway, QB, Denver

TIME-OUT · John Elway didn't announce his retirement for three months, but Super Bowl XXXIII was his last professional football game.

It's too bad the sun had already disappeared behind the Miami horizon by the end of Super Bowl XXXIII. If any player in history deserved a ride off into a brilliant orange sunset, it was Denver Broncos quarterback John Elway.

Official word of Elway's retirement wouldn't come for three more months—he didn't want to divert attention from his teammates' celebration—but those close to him knew he was done. And rarely does a top athlete get to leave under such storybook circumstances.

The MVP of his team's second straight Super Bowl title, Elway completed 18 of 29 passes for 336 yards and one interception in the Broncos' 34-19 toppling

of the Atlanta Falcons. Aware that the Falcons would key on star running back Terrell Davis after his performance in Super Bowl XXXII, the 38-year-old Elway knew he would have to come through in a big way, and he embraced the pressure.

"I know they were saying, 'Make Elway beat us,'" he said. "My thought was, 'Good, let's go.' I was so motivated it wasn't even funny."

The unlikely challenger, in its only Super Bowl appearance, was a Falcons club that surprised prognosticators first by assembling a 14-2 season and then by persevering against the Minnesota Vikings—a 10-point favorite—in overtime in the NFL Championship Game. Head

coach Dan Reeves, who had fired Broncos head coach Mike Shanahan when Reeves was the head coach and Shanahan the offensive coordinator in Denver in 1991, had stirred the pot by airing some of that dirty laundry in a pregame press conference, giving Shanahan and his team even more to prove.

But the coach drama ignited by Reeves was a mere spark compared to the inferno caused by Atlanta safety Eugene Robinson's colossal misstep on the eve of the game. Well before the team curfew of midnight, Reeves received word that Robinson, a seasoned veteran who had played for the Packers in the previous Super Bowl and was considered the leader of the defense, had been arrested

for soliciting a prostitute who was actually an undercover police officer.

The incident kept players and coaches up half the night and constituted the biggest public relations nightmare in the history of the big game, especially because Robinson had received an award for "high moral character" from the Christian group Athletes in Action earlier that day. Robinson's teammates, some of whom told *The New York Times* that at least five of the Falcons had paid for sex in that same area during the week, sought to keep their focus on the upcoming game as Reeves made the surprising announcement that Robinson would be in the starting lineup against Denver.

"Instead of getting mentally ready for the Broncos," a Falcon player who spoke under the condition of anonymity told Mike Freeman in the *Times* article, "we were talking about Eugene. The Broncos beat us, but anyone who says what happened to Eugene was not a factor is lying."

When football finally returned to the forefront, Atlanta jumped out with a scoring drive sparked by five Jamal Anderson carries. But in a trend that would dog the Falcons all day, the offense failed to get into the end zone and had to settle for a Morten Andersen field goal for an early but tenuous lead. The Falcons' only offensive touchdown of the day, a 3-yard pass from Chris Chandler to Terance Mathis, was an inconsequential score late in the fourth quarter.

As it turned out, Robinson was the defender left behind on the Broncos' pivotal touchdown, an 80-yard pass from Elway to Rod Smith on which Smith misdirected his opponent and exploited the loss of speed that had been one of the main reasons for his release from Green Bay. It was a crucial play because it vaulted the Broncos to a 17-3 lead that would only grow after halftime.

The third quarter was scoreless, a slight reprieve for the Falcons even though the Broncos had the ball for most of the period. When Denver kicker Jason Elam missed two field goals from 38 and 48 yards, a small dose of hope was still alive for Atlanta fans. In the fourth quarter, the door slammed shut on that glimmer of light when Darrien Gordon intercepted a Chandler pass and returned it 58 yards to set the table for a 1-yard touchdown run.

Atlanta got the ball back, and in a nightmare of déjà vu for Falcons fans, Chandler again misfired and saw the ball land in Gordon's hands, this time for a 50-yard return and an eventual 3-yard rush over the goal line from Elway. In four dynamic minutes, Gordon had set a Super Bowl record for interception return yards and put his team ahead 31-6 with 11:20 remaining.

"Today our defense played like an offense," Denver defensive coordinator Greg Robinson told *The New York Times*. "When we got the interceptions, those were athletes making those plays and those were athletes who took the ball and became offensive."

By spring, Elway would officially be an ex–football player, and by the end of the year, the Broncos would be on the other side of a 6-10 free fall aided by Davis's catastrophic knee injury in week 4. This Broncos team—from double-digit underdogs to seven-point favorites—wasn't a Super Bowl dynasty in the mold of the '70s Steelers or the '80s 49ers, but it was a team that held sway with the football public for a sliver of the '90s, making the trip to the top of the world twice with a quarterback who knew how to make a memorable exit.

"We didn't have that many big-time, well-known guys," said Denver linebacker Bill Romanowski. "There was John Elway, and then a group of guys that kicked ass for one another. That's what comes to mind when I think of those two years."

Denver Broncos defensive end Trevor Pryce (93) gives defensive tackle Maa Tanuvasa (98) a high five. Falcons quarterback Chris Chandler (12) is at bottom right. *AP Photo/Dave Martin*

"THE TRUE COMPETITORS, THOUGH, ARE THE ONES WHO ALWAYS PLAY TO WIN."

Tom Brady

CHAPTER 5: THE 2000s

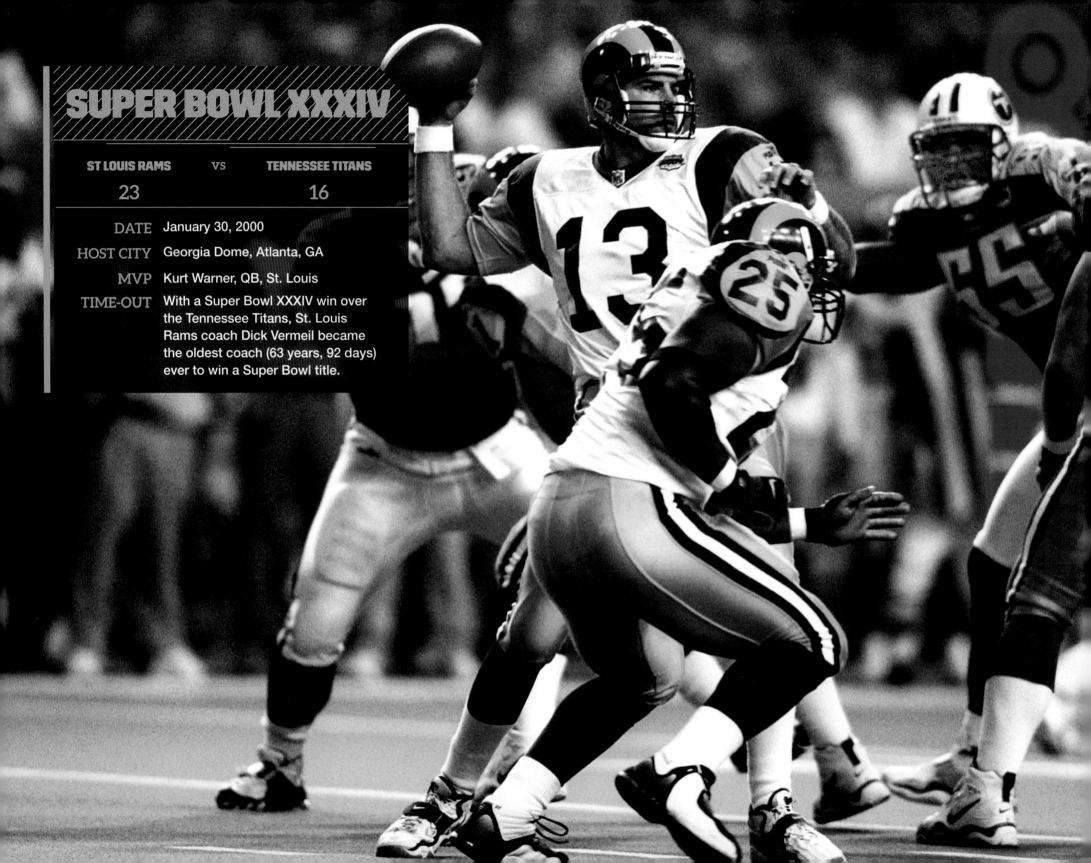

SUPER BOWL XXXIV

ST LOUIS RAMS	VS	TENNESSEE TITANS
23		16

DATE | January 30, 2000

HOST CITY | Georgia Dome, Atlanta, GA

MVP | Kurt Warner, QB, St. Louis

TIME-OUT | With a Super Bowl XXXIV win over the Tennessee Titans, St. Louis Rams coach Dick Vermeil became the oldest coach (63 years, 92 days) ever to win a Super Bowl title.

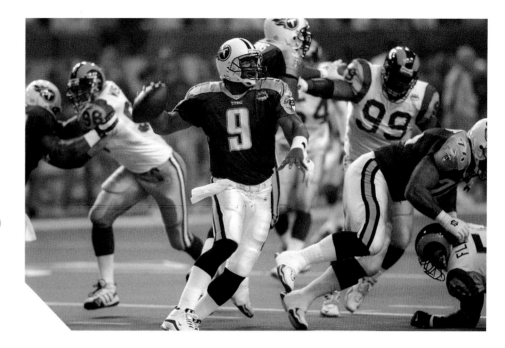

Tennessee Titans quarterback Steve McNair (9) throws a pass against the St. Louis Rams.
AP Photo/Paul Spinelli

An MVP who had completed only four NFL passes before being named his team's starter by default in the preseason. A challenger on the final stop of an improbable playoff run, coming within a half yard of making Super Bowl history in several different ways. If purists were sickened by the elevation of glitz over true gridiron drama in the modern Super Bowl era, this championship was the perfect prescription.

If Tennessee Titans wide receiver Kevin Dyson had run a route that was just 1 yard longer, or broken Mike Jones's tackle as he hurled himself at the end zone as the clock expired, this would have likely been the only Super Bowl in history to be decided in overtime. Instead, Kurt Warner and the Rams celebrated their 23-16 victory with the zeal of a squadron that had just dodged a barrage of bullets.

It was truly a game for the ages, a parry between two teams vying for their first Super Bowl wins, both with exceptionally courageous quarterbacks, stellar running games, and astute defensive coordinators bent on shutting the other squad down.

So plentiful were the rich story lines in this Super Bowl that Kurt Warner, one of the most compelling rags-to-riches narratives ever in professional sports, was merely one of the highlights. Five years before receiving his ring and his MVP trophy, Warner had been stocking groceries for $5.50 an hour. Four years earlier, he had been fighting for respect in the Arena Football League, and two years earlier, he was leaving a stint in Amsterdam with NFL Europe to enter the Rams camp—as the third-string quarterback.

Warner held the clipboard plenty in 1998, but he saw little action on the field as the third quarterback behind Tony Banks and Steve Bono, completing four of 11 passes all season for a total of 39 yards. He entered the 1999 campaign as the backup to Trent Green, but when Green tore his ACL in the preseason, he was reluctantly promoted to the number one spot, prompting a press conference in which head coach Dick Vermeil said haltingly, "We will rally around Kurt Warner, and we'll play good football."

From that colossal understatement, Warner started to piece together an astonishing season: three touchdowns in each of his first three NFL starts and a total of 4,830 passing yards for a completion percentage of 65.1. His Rams, who had been in the cellar with a 4-12 record the previous year, finished the season 16-3 and punched their ticket to the Super Bowl in what seemed like an inevitable date with destiny.

In Atlanta on Super Sunday, Warner continued to amaze, throwing for 414 yards to set a new Super Bowl record and firing off an electric 73-yard touchdown pass to Isaac Bruce that ultimately gave his team the Lombardi Trophy. And he did it all with two cracked ribs he sustained from a bruising hit in the second quarter. St. Louis offensive coordinator Mike Martz was so convinced that his starter was finished at halftime that he told backup quarterback Paul Justin to warm up because Warner wouldn't last a series. "He could hardly breathe," Martz said.

"It is sort of a storybook ending," he said afterward. "When you think about where I was and where I am now, it seems pretty incredible."

In the first half, it looked like the game would be another display case for Martz's offensive masterwork. The Rams gained

294 yards and 18 first downs in the first two periods, but the Titan defenders, ranked first in the NFL and reinforced by punishing ends Jevon Kearse and Kenny Holmes, stifled their red-zone attack and kept them to three field goals for a surmountable 9-0 lead heading into the locker room.

The tables turned after halftime, with Steve McNair and the Titans finding their stride on offense and outpacing the Rams 16-7 in the first 28 minutes of the half. Then came the final 1:54 and two electrifying plays that would move this Super Bowl from interesting to extraordinary.

With the score knotted at 16, observers expected Martz to order a slow march into Titans territory culminating in a well-timed field goal for the win. But on the first play of the drive inside the two-minute drill,

Warner managed to set sail an improbable pass just before he got bulldozed in his cracked ribs by Kearse. Bruce, who finished the game with 162 receiving yards, outfoxed his defenders, made the catch, and eluded two would-be Titans tacklers on his 73-yard victory sprint.

"I saw the safety overrun me, and I ducked under him, and after that it was a race to the end zone," Bruce said. "I wasn't going to lose that race."

Unfortunately for the Rams, no celebration was in order because McNair and the Titans had been claiming ground with little resistance since halftime. A Tennessee penalty forced the dogged McNair to start the drive on his own 12-yard line with just 1:48 remaining, but even then the first Super Bowl overtime seemed imminent. "The only thing I remembered thinking was

that I wouldn't put anything past this guy, even if he has to run it down there himself," Titans wide receiver coach Steve Walters said.

A series of short completions and Rams penalties allowed the Titans to progress to the St. Louis 31, after which McNair fought through a stifling blitz to complete a pass to Dyson, who was brought down at the 10. The Titans called their final time-out with six seconds left and called their last play—another McNair-to-Dyson connection that ended when Jones brought him down just inches from the goal line. Despite the longest reach Dyson could muster, when the clock read 0:00, the Rams were world champions.

"I look back at the field, and there was confetti everywhere," Titans running back Eddie George said of those final seconds.

"At that moment, you just don't believe that you went through a game like that. The more I think about it, it almost hurts. We were so close."

Left, St. Louis Rams wide receiver Isaac Bruce (80) celebrates as receiver Torry Holt (88) scores on a 9-yard touchdown pass. *AP Photo/NFL Photos*

Right and opposite page, Tennessee Titans wide receiver Kevin Dyson (87) reaches for the goal line in the final play of the fourth quarter while wrapped up by St. Louis Rams linebacker Mike Jones (52). *AP Photo/Paul Spinelli/Kevin Terrell*

SUPER BOWL XXXV

BALTIMORE RAVENS   VS   **NEW YORK GIANTS**

34   **7**

DATE   January 28, 2001

HOST CITY   Raymond James Stadium, Tampa, FL

MVP   Ray Lewis, LB, Baltimore

TIME-OUT   Baltimore is the only American city to have two different franchises win the Super Bowl (the Colts in Super Bowl V and the Ravens in Super Bowls XXXV and XLVII).

The Steel Curtain in the '70s and the Chicago Bears in the '80s had showed what it looks like when a defense dominates a Super Bowl, but it had been more than a decade since an NFL season had ended with a nationwide tribute to a unit of stoppers. At Super Bowl XXXV, the Baltimore Ravens stepped in and filled that void in a big way with a 34-7 rout of the New York Giants.

So bruising and confident was the Ravens defense that after Baltimore quarterback Trent Dilfer hit Brandon Stokley for the game's first touchdown and a seven-point Ravens lead, defensive leaders such as Rod Woodson were sure that the game was theirs, because they had no intention of letting the Giants score. At that point, only eight minutes had ticked off of the clock.

"Once we scored, we honestly looked at each other and said, 'This game's over. They're not going to score on us,'" Woodson said afterward. "Our main goal was to have the first shutout in Super Bowl history."

Baltimore's defensive unit had steamrolled its way to the Super Bowl in Tampa with a heroic regular season in which they allowed only 165 points, setting a new NFL record for fewest points allowed. At Super Bowl XXXV, the Ravens intercepted four Kerry Collins passes and sacked him four times and allowed the Giants backfield only 66 rushing yards. New York had the ball 16 times and crossed midfield only twice, and their only points came off of a third-quarter kickoff return.

This suffocating environment was made possible by coordinator Marvin Lewis and a unit packed with speed and power, led by Tony Siragusa and Sam Adams on the line, Ray Lewis and Peter Boulware in the linebacking corps, and Woodson and Duane Starks in the backfield. Giants head coach Jim Tressel and a number of his players said the same thing after the game: until you lined up across from the Ravens, it was impossible to understand their speed off of the line or the frustration of trying to make effective plays against them.

The heart and soul of the group was Lewis, who became the seventh defensive player and only the second linebacker to win the MVP award. His numbers weren't spectacular—he logged three tackles, two assists, and four passes defensed—but the players who shared the field with him that day said that the statistics did little to quantify the impact of Lewis's presence.

"It seemed like there were nine Ray Lewises out there," Giants defensive end Michael Strahan said. "Ray Lewis, at that point, was absolutely the best defensive player in the game."

The Giants' ineptitude in the contest was unexpected, especially since they had trounced the Minnesota Vikings 41-0 in the NFC Championship Game on a day when Collins threw for 381 yards and five touchdowns. Two weeks later on the game's biggest stage, he completed 15 passes for 112 yards and finished with a quarterback rating of 7.1, the second lowest in Super Bowl history.

The Ravens defense made sure that the only real suspense was whether they would achieve the Super Bowl's first shutout, but there were nonetheless a few moments worthy of a highlight reel that evening. The real story might have been in players such as Siragusa and Lewis thwarting Collins repeatedly, but those looking beyond the trenches could find something to celebrate in the players such as Trent Dilfer and Jamal Lewis, offensive contributors who gave their defense a larger cushion than they really thought they needed.

Dilfer, who became the starter at midseason just months after Tampa Bay released him and Baltimore picked him up, was viewed through the lens of low expectations at Super Bowl XXXV. He wasn't spectacular, but he did everything the Ravens needed him to do, completing 12 of 25 passes for one touchdown. Most importantly, he held onto the ball, refusing to give the Giants' defense a chance to make up the ground its offense kept losing.

Tony Banks, the quarterback Dilfer had replaced, had to fill in late in the third quarter when Dilfer broke his finger, and two months later, Baltimore released Dilfer as an unrestricted free agent, making him the only NFL quarterback in history who didn't re-sign with the team he helped lead to a Super Bowl championship. Despite giving the defense its due for the win in a 2010 interview with *The Baltimore Sun*, Dilfer said that he always questioned their decision to bring in Elvis Grbac for the 2001 season.

"To not re-sign there, I was so flabbergasted by the situation," Dilfer said. "To this day, I can't wrap my brain around how that decision was made."

Jamal Lewis was another pleasant surprise, barreling through the Giants' front for 102 rushing yards and a touchdown while playing smashmouth football at its finest. The intensity of Lewis's repeated collisions with Giants linebacker Michael Barrow made it a showdown for the ages.

"We knew he wasn't bringing any paper plates to the party," Barrow said. "It was a rumble in the jungle, choking him in the bottom of the pile … and he just took it and wanted more. Boy, he took it personal. He earned a lot of respect that day."

Just five years earlier, Art Modell had ferreted his Cleveland Browns out of town—despite a promise never to move the team—for greener pastures in Baltimore, breaking the hearts of one of the most venerable football cities never to have won a Super Bowl title. The Ravens faltered in the first few years after the relocation, but in 1999 Brian Billick took the head job with an eye toward shoring up the offense and bringing a winner to Baltimore for the first time since Johnny Unitas and the Colts took Super Bowl V.

The former Browns had their title, with only new fans to join the celebration, but they earned it in the most old-school football way possible—by showing how game changing a display of absolute defensive power could be.

"Their aptitude for the opponent made them special," Marvin Lewis told Sports on Earth in 2014. "Obviously, they were great, great players. But they were so in tune to what the opponent did tendency wise, personnel wise and formation wise."

Jermaine Lewis reacting after returning a kickoff 84 yards for a touchdown.
AP Photo/Roberto Borea, File

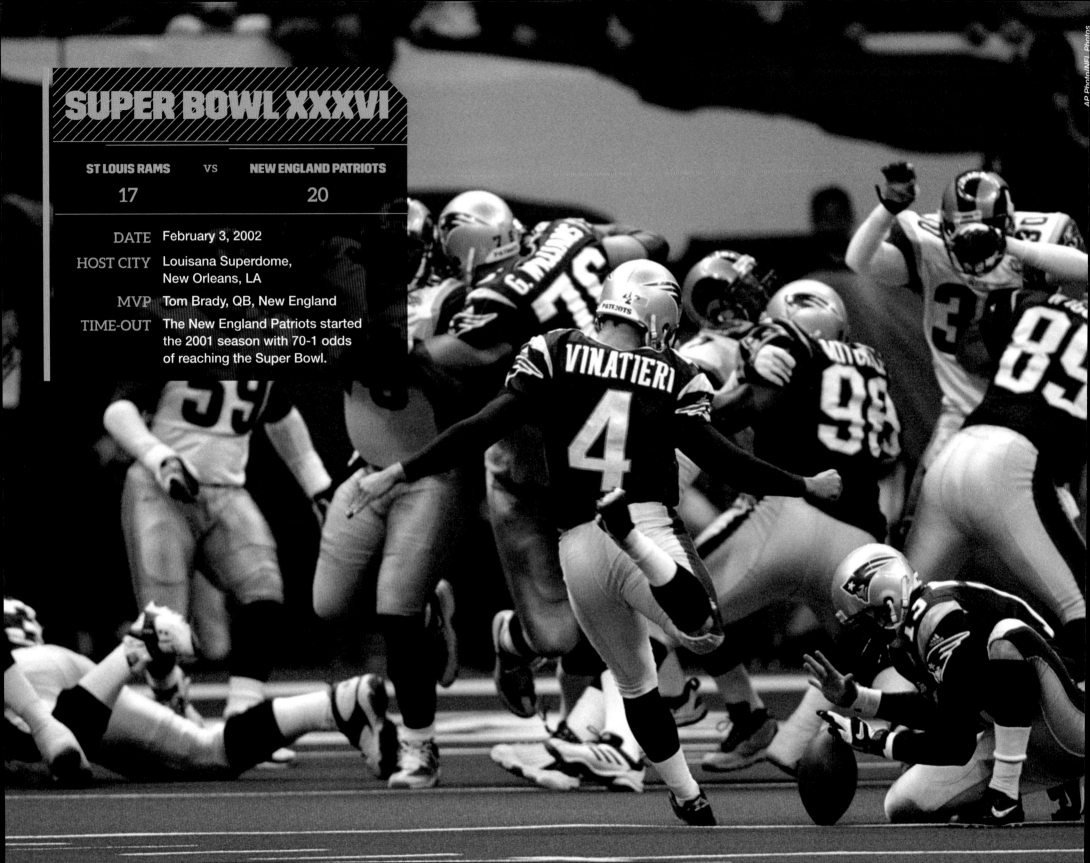

SUPER BOWL XXXVI

ST LOUIS RAMS	VS	NEW ENGLAND PATRIOTS
17		20

DATE   February 3, 2002

HOST CITY   Louisana Superdome, New Orleans, LA

MVP   Tom Brady, QB, New England

TIME-OUT   The New England Patriots started the 2001 season with 70-1 odds of reaching the Super Bowl.

For those with a short Super Bowl memory, it might be surprising to consider that a new century had to dawn before the New England Patriots won a Lombardi Trophy and that, as late as 2002, most of America didn't realize that Tom Brady epitomized coolness under pressure.

Most startling of all to those who have come to make "Patriots" synonymous with "Super Bowl," almost no one gave them a chance of winning that first ring in Super Bowl XXXVI. As 14-point underdogs to the powerhouse St. Louis Rams, Bill Belichick and his Pats outplayed and outcoached the team across the line—and then kept right on doing it through the decade.

After Adam Vinatieri hit a clutch 48-yard field goal as time expired to seal the upset over the Rams team known as "The

Greatest Show on Turf," safety Lawyer Milloy screamed out, "We shocked the world!" Before the season started, oddsmakers had given New England a 70-1 shot of winning the Super Bowl, and they had finished 5-11 the previous year in Belichick's first head-coaching campaign.

With a defensive game plan that put prolific running back Marshall Faulk squarely in their crosshairs, the Patriots scored their first 17 points off of St. Louis turnovers and quickly put the Rams in the unfamiliar position of trying to scramble out of a hole. Kurt Warner and his offense battled with a fourth-quarter surge that tied the game inside of two minutes, setting up one of the most spectacular moments for a kicker in the history of football.

"He was our best player," Belichick said of Vinatieri after the game-winning boot. "There's no other player that we would say was better at what they did than Adam was at what he did."

Holding the MVP trophy that night in the Superdome, though, was the 24-year-old Brady, a still-unproven young man who had come to New England in the sixth round in 2000 and was reportedly so unperturbed by his first Super Bowl appearance that he took a nap in the locker room before kickoff. He amassed 145 yards on 16 completions but forged his legacy with his leadership over the last 1:21 of the game, when he calmly pushed his team into Vinatieri's range to set up the victory with no time-outs.

New England Patriots kicker Adam Vinatieri (4) celebrates his 48-yard game-winning field goal in the final seconds of Super Bowl XXXVI.
AP Photo/Amy Sancetta, File

Ernie Conwell sits dejectedly in the confetti shower after the Rams lost.
AP Photo/David J. Phillip

The *Boston Herald* apologized to the New England Patriots on the front page of their Wednesday, May 14, 2008, newspaper for falsely reporting that the Patriots videotaped a St. Louis Rams walk-through the day before their 2002 Super Bowl XXXVI.
AP Photo/Stephan Savoia

The Rams got on the board first with a 50-yard Jeff Wilkins field goal in the first quarter, but then the New England defense began its shock-and-awe campaign, forged over just a week of preparation because the NFL schedule had been altered in the fall after the 9/11 attacks. When Patriots cornerback Ty Law stole a Warner pass and carried the ball home 47 yards for a 7-3 lead, the scales began to tip away from the St. Louis team that had gained 2,027 rushing yards and finished the regular season as the NFL's top-ranked offense.

When another second-quarter turnover—Terrell Buckley's recovery of a Ricky Proehl fumble—led to Brady's 8-yard pass to David Patten, New England had a 14-3 lead headed into halftime, a margin the Patriots padded early in the third quarter when Warner threw his third interception and Vinatieri kicked a field goal to cap his team's possession. While Rams fans sat stunned at the misfortune that had befallen

their formerly dominant team, Martz and his staff believed that their dynamic offense still had a rally in them.

They were right, but the fireworks didn't start until the fourth quarter, when Warner led his team in two touchdown drives in eight minutes to tie the game 17-17. But when Warner hit Proehl for the second touchdown with 1:30 remaining, St. Louis left the door open for the persistent Patriots to win in regulation. It was an unlikely scenario because of a decision Belichick had made three minutes earlier, when he realized his defensive players were dragging the ground and desperately needed a rest. He used his final time-out to provide that respite and set the stage for extra drama in the final seconds.

A series of short precision passes to receivers who got out of bounds just in the nick of time gave Brady the yardage he needed to leave the game on Vinatieri's tee. The sixth-year kicker, who had hit a

59-yarder in pregame warm-ups, knew the minute his foot made contact that he was on the fast track to a celebration.

"It was so true, there was never a doubt about it," Belichick said of the kick.

As far as some of the Rams from that era are concerned, that painful loss will always be covered with a cloud of suspicion because of the accusation that was levied against the Patriots brass six years after the game. New England video assistant Matt Walsh had been at the stadium setting up equipment while St. Louis was doing a walk-through, and it was believed that he had videotaped the Rams' plays and shared the recording with the Patriots coaches. The charges were never substantiated, even if Belichick did plead guilty to similar behavior in the "Spygate" scandal in 2007.

Faulk, who had been the Associated Press Offensive Player of the Year for the past

three seasons but was held to only 76 yards that day in New Orleans, told Comcast SportsNet's Tom Curran in 2013 that he has remained convinced that the Rams would have won their first title if the New England staff had not had access to certain key Rams plays before the game.

"I'll never be over being cheated out of the Super Bowl," Faulk said.

Belichick has consistently denied having any kind of edge except the painstaking preparation his team put into the game. Long known as a capable coordinator for Bill Parcells, he made a solid debut that night as a strategist who loves the challenge of rendering an outstanding team ineffectual on the sport's biggest stage.

"If we played next week," Belichick said, "we'd probably be the underdog."

SUPER BOWL XXXVII

OAKLAND RAIDERS	VS	TAMPA BAY BUCCANEERS
21		48

DATE January 26, 2003

HOST CITY Qualcomm Stadium, San Diego, CA

MVP Dexter Jackson, FS, Tampa Bay

TIME-OUT The Tampa Bay defense set Super Bowl records for interceptions, with five, and defensive touchdowns, with three.

Less than a year before Super Bowl XXXVII, the Oakland Raiders' leadership was in a shambles, as owner Al Davis axed head coach Jon Gruden—despite Gruden's success—reportedly as a response to Gruden's magnetic popularity in Oakland. Things weren't much better at the top in Tampa Bay; owner Malcolm Glazer had released Tony Dungy, a quintessential player's coach, because he had failed to bring the Buccaneers into the postseason four out of the past five years.

In a confluence with Shakespearian undertones, Gruden became Tampa Bay's head coach and sparked his new team to a 12-4 record and a trip to the Super Bowl in San Diego—against none other than the Raiders.

It was more tragedy than comedy for the Raiders and new head coach Bill Callahan, with pregame events such as Pro Bowl center Barret Robbins's ill-fated night of partying that landed him in a treatment center on Super Bowl Sunday rather than lining up in Qualcomm Stadium. Without Robbins, the leader of the defense, and with a tepid performance by NFL MVP quarterback Rich Gannon, the Raiders stumbled through the day and helped Tampa Bay to a 48-21 victory that was pure vindication for Gruden, the youngest coach, at that time, ever to win a Super Bowl.

"Our guys just made play after play after play," said Gruden, whose team entered the matchup as three-and-a-half-point underdogs.

The key dynamic in this, the first trip to the Super Bowl for the historically hapless Buccaneers, was the strength of the Tampa Bay defense against the travails of Gannon and the Oakland offense. Despite a stellar regular season—4,689 passing yards and a 67.6 percent completion rating—Gannon threw five interceptions in the Super Bowl and finished with a quarterback rating of 48.9.

The Raiders' rushing game was even more ineffective. Oakland's backfield gained only 19 yards on 11 attempts, and in the end Tampa Bay's top-ranked defense outscored the Raiders' offense 21-15. "We were just absolutely terrible," Gannon told the *New York Daily News*. "It was a nightmarish performance."

Oakland struck first with a 40-yard Sebastian Janikowski field goal, but the upper hand for the favorite ended there. After driving for a field goal of their own by Martin Gramatica, the Buccaneers put on a second-quarter clinic, outscoring the Raiders 17-0 with the help of Tampa Bay safety Dexter Jackson's two straight interceptions that resulted in a field goal and a touchdown. To ice the first half, Buccaneers quarterback Brad Johnson engineered a 10-play, 77-yard drive capped by a 5-yard pass to Keenan McCardell. At halftime, it was 20-3, and the stunned Raiders were searching for a way to right the ship as Tampa Bay tried to hold on to their momentum.

"I wanted to go back out there and finish it, and so did the players," Gruden told

ESPN in a film reflecting on the win a decade later. "But that halftime lasted for three days. It was a long break."

Johnson, who came to Florida State on a basketball scholarship before switching to football as a junior, had languished in his early NFL seasons and spent a year with the London Monarchs in the World League before finally getting his chance as a starter with the Vikings in 1996. He became the first Buccaneers quarterback to lead the NFL in passer rating that season, with 92.9, but the spotlight was on Gannon heading into the contest.

The lack of hype allowed Johnson to put his head down and turn in a solid performance, completing 18 passes for 215 yards and one interception with possessions like halftime bookends—the 77-yard drive at the end of the second quarter and the 14-play, 89-yard drive padded with a 33-yard completion from Johnson to Joe Jurevicius. On the next play, Tampa Bay cornerback Dwight Smith snagged a Gannon pass intended for Jerry Rice and returned it 44 yards for a 34-3 lead.

Oakland made one last-ditch comeback attempt early in the fourth quarter, made possible by a Tampa Bay special teams blunder. Linebacker Tim Johnson and cornerback Eric Johnson teamed up to block and recover Tom Tupa's punt, and after Eric Johnson's 13-yard return touchdown, the Raiders struck again on their next possession when Gannon found Rice for a 48-yard touchdown pass. Rice's career was nearing its twilight, but he had one more Super Bowl explosion play in his arsenal.

With just over six minutes remaining, the Raiders were trailing 34-21 and suddenly seemed capable of doing something miraculous. Oakland, after all, had a potent offense that had put up 41 points against the Titans in the AFC Championship Game. Gruden told his players, "We got to get something done," and the Buccaneers top-notch defense did exactly that, scoring twice on successive interception returns from Derrick Brooks and Smith.

When Smith crossed the goal line after his 50-yard sprint, the clock showed two seconds, and Gruden celebrated with the satisfaction of one who has been given the emphatic last word against an adversary. Later, as he reflected on the Raiders' dramatic slide after that season—a 4-12 campaign as star players aged and burned out—he told writer Bob McGinn in a biting tone, "That's the way it goes. My heart goes out to them."

It was a brief and brilliant moment in the spotlight for a program that had seen precious few. As the team flew into Tampa Bay, they circled near Raymond James Stadium, and players and coaches noticed the stadium lights on and the seats full of fans ready to fete their returning heroes and the first true triumph the city of Tampa Bay had ever experienced.

"We showed what you can do as a team if you have mental toughness and the right group of guys," Gruden told The *Tampa Tribune*. "That's become a trademark day in the history of Tampa Bay. To get off the plane in Tampa and see that type of enthusiasm makes you feel you were part of something that will never be forgotten."

Tampa Bay Buccaneers wide receiver Keenan McCardell celebrates a touchdown. *AP Photo/Kevin Reece*

THE INTERNATIONAL
APPEAL
OF THE SUPER BOWL

Nothing is as uniquely American as the Super Bowl. The excess, the glitz, the pop stars, the parties, and even the sport itself—it is like a portrait of everything that makes America stand out from the rest of the world.

But that doesn't mean that the network executives, the advertisers, and the NFL don't want the game to catch on beyond the borders of the United States. Super Sunday might never become anything approaching a worldwide phenomenon, but viewership numbers indicate slow but steady progress in that direction.

Some 160 million people watched the Super Bowl XLVIII telecast—more than 111 million of them Americans. In contrast, five months later 1 billion viewers worldwide tuned in for the 2014 World Cup final between Germany and Argentina.

Between efforts such as the now-defunct NFL Europe league and a series of annual regular-season games in London, the NFL has been intentional through the past two decades about building an international fan base. And even though the European league struggled to make a profit and disbanded in 2007, there is room for optimism, according to Mark Waller, the executive vice president of the NFL's international division.

"We're encouraged by the work we've done in London, the belief we can build long term fandom for the game way beyond a one-off experience," Waller told the Reuters news service.

When it comes to the Super Bowl, one major obstacle is the time difference that has the live telecast starting near midnight in Europe and early the next morning in countries such as China and Australia. Despite the fact that Aussie viewers have to enjoy their Super Bowl with their Monday morning breakfast, 210,000 people there tuned in for Super Bowl XLVIII.

Even if some international markets are tough for the NFL to crack—one Chinese college student told Reuters, "Most Chinese people don't have the foggiest idea of American football"—there is one place where Super Bowl viewing audiences are guaranteed: on U.S. military bases.

Some of the largest and most raucous Super Bowl parties every year are held in remote outposts in places such as Iraq, Afghanistan, and Germany, where the game is broadcast through the Armed Services Network and American troops enjoy snacks, beer, and that most American of escapes from the stress of defending their nation.

Former Detroit Lions offensive lineman Scott Conover was invited to an American base in Bosnia in 2000 as part of the USO's Super Bowl tour, and in his account of the experience on his wife, Courtney's, blog he recalled meeting die-hard fans who backed every one of the NFL's 32 teams. It was evident to Conover that the Super Bowl gathering, with former NFL players as guests, was meaningful to the soldiers.

"I felt proud to be there with them because our presence kind of gave them a piece of home—even though they were so far away," he wrote. "And some of them even articulated this to me, that watching our games was such a comfort for them."

At Bagram Air Field in Afghanistan, base personnel spent two months preparing for a mammoth Super Bowl XLIX party that included football-themed decorations, live entertainment, and a spread featuring pizza, burgers, and chicken wings. At least some of that pizza came from the United States, from a Buffalo, New York–based food company called Rich Products that shipped 5,000 pizzas to Afghanistan in early 2015 to make sure that every

American soldier had plenty of pizza for the big game. In the Pizzas 4 Patriots campaign, the pies were delivered to the door of the bases by DHL Express to ensure that they were fresh and ready to eat at kickoff.

"Having served overseas, I personally know that having a taste of home on Super Bowl Sunday is a powerful experience for troops stationed abroad," retired Master Sergeant Mark Evans, the founder of Pizzas 4 Patriots, said in a release heralding the giant pizza delivery.

Top left, Japanese patrons watch the replay of Super Bowl XLIX played earlier in the day shown on a large screen at Hooters sports bar in Tokyo's Ginza district. *AP Photo/Shizuo Kambayashi*

Bottom left, U.S. Army Lt. Julie Glaubach, 30 (*center*) Staff Sgt. Michael Sauret, 23 (*left*) both from Pittsburgh, Pennsylvania, cheer for the Steelers as they watch the Super Bowl XLII on television at Camp Victory in Baghdad, Iraq. *AP Photo/Maya Alleruzzo*

Top right, Ian Clough, (*left*) CEO of DHL Express, Mark Evans, (*center*) of Pizza 4 Patriots, and Illinois Governor Pat Quinn, help load boxes that will hold thousands of Chicago-style pizzas headed overseas to members of the military in time for Super Bowl Sunday. *AP Photo/M. Spencer Green*

Bottom right, U.S soldiers react as they watch Super Bowl XLII on television at a U.S military base in Bagram, north of Kabul, Afghanistan. *AP Photo/Rafiq Maqbool*

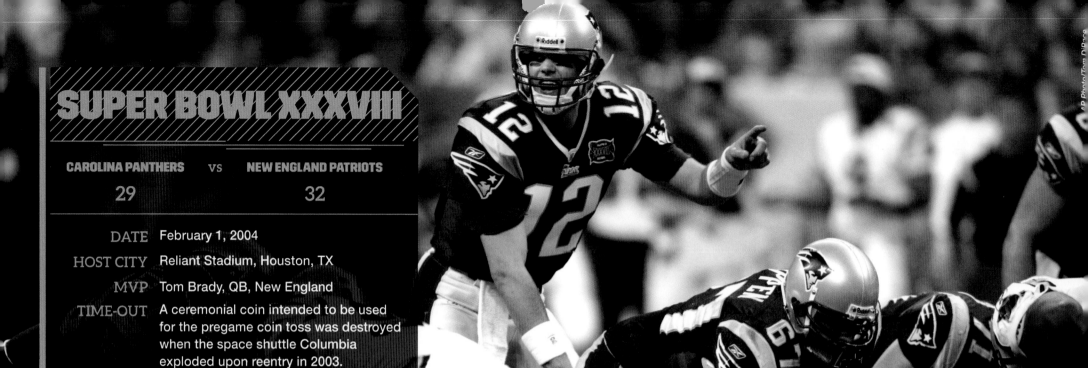

SUPER BOWL XXXVIII

CAROLINA PANTHERS vs **NEW ENGLAND PATRIOTS**

29   **32**

DATE   February 1, 2004

HOST CITY   Reliant Stadium, Houston, TX

MVP   Tom Brady, QB, New England

TIME-OUT   A ceremonial coin intended to be used for the pregame coin toss was destroyed when the space shuttle Columbia exploded upon reentry in 2003.

It was a skirmish for the ages, between two teams with head coaches who specialized in defensive fortitude and offenses with very few standouts. A final score with single digits on both sides wouldn't have been too surprising.

So why was the fourth quarter a manic shoot-out with 37 total points and the feeling that either team could score without resistance? As the New England Patriots pulled a second Super Bowl victory from Adam Vinatieri's magic leg, this was a contest that started out slow but accelerated to a speed as blazing as the air inside Houston's Reliant Stadium. Neither team scored in the first or third quarters, and the 14-10 halftime score signaled how closely matched the two squads actually were. But this game will be remembered for the fifteen minutes of

madness that came within an errant kickoff and a clutch field goal of turning the underdog Panthers–in their first Super Bowl–into spoilers for a New England team carrying a 14-game winning streak.

Other than quarterback Tom Brady, the Patriots' roster wasn't distinguished by offensive stars or special teams efficiency, but they had put together enough scoring over the course of the season to set the table for an outstanding defense engineered by Bill Belichick and Romeo Crennel. Before the game, Belichick reportedly said to longtime friend and advisor Ernie Adams, "Can you believe we're here? We can't run the ball, we can't punt the ball, and we can't snap for field goals."

Throughout the first half, any Patriot deficiencies were overshadowed by the

ineffectual play of Carolina quarterback Jake Delhomme, who completed one pass for 1 yard on nine attempts and sustained three sacks in the first 27 minutes of play. The scoreboard still read 0-0 until New England linebacker Mike Vrabel mugged Delhomme and defensive end Richard Seymour recovered the ball at the Carolina 20. Two plays later, Brady found Deion Branch on a 5-yard touchdown pass.

On the Panthers' next possession, Delhomme finally proved why the New England coaches considered him dangerous despite his lackluster start. He completed passes of 13, 23, and 39 yards to Ricky Proehl, Muhsin Muhammad, and Steve Smith for an efficient seven points and a tie game. There was only a minute left before halftime, but the teams made up for the early drought by scoring 10 more points in that time—New England on

a 52-yard touchdown from Brady to Branch and Carolina on a 50-yard John Kasay field goal as time expired.

At halftime, fans in the seats at Reliant Stadium and millions at home on their couches were seeing more of Janet Jackson's physique than they ever imagined in the world's most famous wardrobe malfunction, but the players were missing the opportunity for either entertainment or strategic fine-tuning. Instead, many of them were hooked up to IV bags, precipitously dehydrated from the excessive heat inside the stadium. Reliant officials had opted to close the roof of the building before the game, reportedly because one of the pregame musical acts wouldn't play unless it was closed.

It was cold for Houston—59 degrees—but it was certainly acceptable football

weather. Conversely, when the retractable roof closed, the air-conditioning was insufficient to cool the huge structure, and players suffered in hot, humid conditions similar to those of summer training camp. Later, after Houston poured on a barrage of fourth-quarter explosion plays, observers would wonder whether New England, the oldest team in the league, was too depleted by the heat to apply its typical defensive pressure.

The defenders took their assumed starring roles through the third quarter, but the "score-at-will" show began 11 seconds into the fourth with a 2-yard Antowain Smith touchdown push that put the Panthers down 21-10. But Delhomme's confidence was growing at the eleventh hour, and on the next drive he moved the ball to the New England 33 on the air

attack and then handed off to DeShaun Foster in the shotgun to cut Foster loose to the end zone. In a decision that would come back to haunt him, Panthers head coach John Fox went for a two-point conversion, which failed, and his team trailed 21-16.

The theatrics continued when the Patriots reclaimed the ball and Brady's drive was ruined by a Reggie Howard interception. With seven minutes remaining, Delhomme and Muhammad teamed up for the most explosive play of the night—an 85-yard touchdown play that gave their team a 22-21 lead after a second two-point conversion was ineffective.

On it went at a dizzying pace, with Brady finding Vrabel on a short pass and the Patriots making the two-point conversion

to pull ahead 29-22 with 2:55 left in the game. It was the Panthers' turn, so Delhomme responded by plowing 80 yards in just over two minutes and scoring on a 31-yard touchdown pass to Proehl. It was 29-29 when Carolina kicker John Kasay lined up to kick off and he uncharacteristically kicked it out of bounds, giving the Patriots the ball at their own 40 and the knowledge that they had, in Vinatieri, a kicker with a penchant for thriving under pressure.

Brady went to work, completing three passes to Troy Brown, one to Daniel Graham, and a clutch 17-yarder to Branch to bring the ball to the Panthers 23, where Vinatieri lined up for a 41-yard kick that sailed cleanly through the uprights with nine seconds remaining.

Just as they had done in Super Bowl XXXVI, Brady and Vinatieri combined to prove that even in a steamy stadium, ice water still ran through their veins. And the Panthers, their Cinderella campaign thwarted, exceeded expectations by holding their own through one of the most thrilling quarters in Super Bowl history.

"I didn't think the game would be that close," New England linebacker Tedy Bruschi said a few years later. "Looking back, I see how good of a football team they were. If we were the best team in the NFL, there was no doubt that the next best team was them."

SUPER BOWL XXXIX

NEW ENGLAND PATRIOTS	VS	PHILIDELPHIA EAGLES
24		21

DATE February 6, 2005

HOST CITY Alltel Stadium, Jacksonville, FL

MVP Dion Branch, WR, New England

TIME-OUT The city of Jacksonville was overwhelmed by the Super Bowl XXIX crowds and had to bring in cruise ships to make up for a shortage of hotel rooms.

AP Photo/Julie Jacobson

The Philadelphia Eagles had all of the hallmarks of a team on fire as Super Bowl XXXIX approached: a prolific quarterback with 3,875 passing yards, three straight trips to the NFC Championship Game, a confirmed playoff berth just 11 games into the 2004 season.

Even the zero-hour decision to play wide receiver Terrell Owens just six weeks after ankle surgery seemed to portend the coronation of the Eagles as first-time Super Bowl champs, but the fire was extinguished by turnovers and other careless mistakes. The New England Patriots didn't put up stellar numbers that evening in Jacksonville, but the surging Eagles stumbled too often to become the spoilers for an opponent that was nearing dynasty status.

The Patriots' 24-21 victory made them only the second team in the Super Bowl era to win three Lombardi Trophies in four years, joining the Dallas Cowboys of 1992, 1993, and 1995 in that exclusive club. And as if to prove that the days of regular Super Bowl drubbings were in the past, New England won each of its titles by only three points.

With extraordinary teamwork from a roster lacking marquee players, the Patriots pulled out definitive wins over Indianapolis and Pittsburgh on their path to Alltel Stadium. By meeting every challenge and winning their ninth straight playoff game (a mark that tied an NFL record), they merited serious consideration as the Super Bowl team of the 2000s.

"We took on all comers," head coach Bill Belichick said. "I'll leave the historical comparisons to everyone else."

Hope never dimmed from Philadelphia fans in a game that saw two ties, including a 7-7 mark at halftime, and an Eagles team that outgained the Patriots on offense 369 yards to 331 and collected 24 first downs to New England's 21. An air attack team, Philadelphia showed weakness in only two crucial areas: their running game and the turnover battle.

For most of the contest, Eagles head coach Andy Reid called for passes on nearly every down, and when time had expired, his squad had gained only 45 yards on the ground and scored no rushing touchdowns. More detrimental were the three interceptions and one lost fumble taken from quarterback Donovan

McNabb, who was reportedly struggling with sickness or fatigue in the fourth quarter as his team attempted a comeback drive.

Both McNabb and New England quarterback Tom Brady completed touchdown passes in the second quarter, and the Eagles' confidence was high. But during the long break, Patriots offensive coordinator Charlie Weis scripted out the first 10 snaps of the third quarter, and what resulted was a 69-yard touchdown drive capped by a 2-yard touchdown to Mike Vrabel, a linebacker who occasionally came in at tight end.

McNabb evened things up again a few minutes later on a 10-yard pass to Michael Westbrook, but from there the Patriots built the largest lead of the game with 10 straight points—a 2-yard Corey Dillon touchdown run and a 22-yard Adam Vinatieri field goal fueled by a 19-yard reception by Deion Branch, who had a stellar day with 11 catches for 133 yards and went home with the MVP trophy.

When Vinatieri's kick gave New England a 24-14 advantage, the Eagles tried to recapture lost ground on the legs of Owens, who had emerged as an exceptional rookie talent through his first 14 games before a fractured fibula and torn ankle ligament ended his regular season. The Eagles medical staff gave Owens the green light to play in the Super Bowl only by the morning of the game, and he responded to the vote of confidence by grabbing nine passes for 122 yards. But on some plays, such as a 36-yard pass play just after the New

England field goal that ended when Dexter Reid pushed him out of bounds, Owens was thwarted in situations that would have likely led to touchdowns before his injury.

"Had we got some more opportunities we could have won that game," Owens told *USA Today* in 2013. "We lost by three points. I wasn't sure if they were confident in my ankle to be as healthy as it was. Had I been healthy, I'm pretty sure I would've been more involved in the game plan, but I just tried to make the best of my opportunities."

When the drive including Owens's run was foiled by a Tedy Bruschi interception, the Eagles didn't get another chance to battle back until only 5:40 remained on the clock, and then they proceeded on offense with a relaxed pace that many later used to vilify Andy Reid for poor clock management. When McNabb finally hit Greg Lewis on a 30-yard touchdown pass, only three points separated the teams, but a failed Eagles onside kick gave the Patriots the ball with just 1:47 left on the clock.

It wasn't enough. The Patriots ran the ball three times and punted, but when the punt rolled dead to the Philadelphia 4-yard line, the underdog Eagles were tasked with traveling 96 yards in 46 seconds. "To me, that was the play of the Super Bowl," Bruschi said of the downed punt. "Our punt coverage was throwing a party around the ball. Now they had to go 60, 70 yards for a field goal, and it wasn't going to happen with that time. They put the nail in the coffin."

To assure that his team would put its name in the postseason history books, Patriots safety Rodney Harrison grabbed the third McNabb interception of the game, and New England had another giant three-point victory. They didn't need Vinatieri to make this one a reality, just steady offensive production and an opponent that was just a few steps behind.

"What it really came down to is when we got to the big games in the playoffs, we didn't play well," said Philadelphia tackle Jon Runyan. "It was the same way in the Super Bowl. … It was turnovers in the first half that killed us. We should have blown them out of the water."

Philadelphia Eagles quarterback Donovan McNabb (5) is chased by New England Patriots linebacker Roosevelt Colvin (59). *AP Photo/Gene J. Puskar*

SUPER BOWL XL

SEATTLE SEAHAWKS	vs	PITTSBURGH STEELERS
10		21

DATE: February 5, 2006

HOST CITY: Ford Field, Detroit, MI

MVP: Hines Ward, WR, Pittsburgh

TIME-OUT: Before the game, a moment of silence was observed in the memory of civil rights pioneers Rosa Parks and Coretta Scott King.

It's the most scrutinized game in America's most popular sport, and every few plays a crucial decision is made by a third party with human subjectivity. So it's not a surprise that Super Bowl XL produced lingering anger over the officiating; it's only surprising that it was the first Super Bowl to be mired in such a controversy.

Four years after a series of hotly disputed calls paved the way to a 21-10 Pittsburgh Steelers win over the Seattle Seahawks, the head referee from the game visited Seattle's training camp and apologized for flubbing two fourth-quarter penalties. "It left me with a lot of sleepless nights, and I think about it constantly," Bill Leavy said. "I'll go to my grave wishing that I'd been better."

The dark cloud of those officiating missteps—real and perceived, confessed and concealed—will always hang over the narrative of this Super Bowl. But for the Steelers, plenty of the most inspirational story lines survive as well: the final bus ride for the legendary Jerome Bettis, the unlikely ascent of a team that entered the playoffs as a sixth seed, the long-awaited "one for the thumb"—Pittsburgh's fifth ring after a 26-year drought.

With the victory, the Steelers became the highest-seeded team ever to win a Super Bowl, which was certainly not a result anyone would have predicted when they were sitting on a 7-5 record with just four games left in the regular season. But then Bill Cowher set on a new motivational theme—play for the moment—and some key Pittsburgh players came back from

injuries. With transcendent play from quarterback Ben Roethlisberger, the Steelers knocked off Cincinnati, Indianapolis, and Denver—all on the road—to earn an invite to the first Super Bowl ever played at Ford Field in Detroit.

"We just got some guys back at the right time, and our team played its best at the critical time," Pittsburgh defensive coordinator Dick LeBeau said. "We weren't dead in the water, but we were certainly looking at a very daunting task. Our guys just kind of thought at the end that nobody was going to beat them. And that's the way it turned out."

In a growing Super Bowl trend, scoring was sparse in the first half, and Seattle's 3-0 edge after the first quarter made it the fifth straight Super Bowl in which neither

team scored a touchdown in the first 15 minutes. The Seahawks, in the first of many frustrations for the day, believed the field goal should have been a touchdown. Head coach Mike Holmgren and others on his sideline were incensed by an offensive pass interference call against Darrell Jackson that negated Jackson's apparent 16-yard touchdown pass.

A touchdown did finally make the scoreboard in the first half, but it was on another contested call that went Pittsburgh's way. Roethlisberger executed a 1-yard dive for the goal line in the second quarter—only to hit two obstacles in Seattle linebackers Leroy Hill and D.D. Lewis. As the linesmen ran toward him, Roethlisberger pushed the ball over the goal line, and it was ruled a touchdown,

but Seattle coach Mike Holmgren was one of many who believed the ball never crossed the plane.

Willie Parker had taken a rocky road to his spot as the Steelers' starting running back; he was an undrafted free agent who played as the backup during most of his collegiate career at North Carolina, but injuries to both Bettis and Duce Staley had landed him the starting job early in the 2005 season. The pinnacle of that climb for the speedy Parker was a flashy 75-yard touchdown run in the third quarter that gave his team a 14-3 lead. Seattle answered in similarly dramatic fashion when Kelly Herndon intercepted a Roethlisberger pass and returned it 76 yards to the Steelers' 20-yard line, after which a 16-yard pass from Matt Hasselbeck to Jerramy Stevens trimmed

Pittsburgh's advantage to 14-10 and gave the momentum to the favored Seahawks.

Looking to capitalize their team's late-game surge, the Seattle offense assembled an efficient drive 97 yards downfield, bringing them inches from the leading touchdown with an 18-yard pass from Hasselbeck to Stevens. But the catch was canceled when right tackle Sean Locklear was called for holding—a penalty Holmgren passionately called the worst call of the night.

"The other holds, you could kind of probably say, 'OK, maybe this, maybe that,' although I don't think they should call them in a game like this. This one, there was no penalty. Absolutely no penalty. Behind closed doors that's been agreed on."

Of course, Leavy opened those doors with his mea culpa in 2010, admitting error in both the holding call and an ensuing illegal block call on Hasselbeck that turned a 24-yard Ike Taylor interception return into a 39-yard gain. The end result of that turnover—a 43-yard gadget play touchdown pass from wide receiver Antwan Randle El to Hines Ward—sealed a storybook 21-10 victory for the Steelers.

Pittsburgh won it all despite a lackluster performance from Roethlisberger, who compiled a quarterback rating of 124.8 through the first three games of the playoffs and only 22.6, with just nine completions and two interceptions, in the Super Bowl. The MVP award went to Ward, who caught five passes for 123 yards but also dropped two crucial passes.

After the game, Holmgren highlighted the statistical disparity between the two teams, saying, "You look at the numbers, and you'd swear we won the game, by normal standards," but he stopped short of overtly calling out the officials. When the team returned to Seattle to a gathering of 15,000 fans at their home stadium, he went a step further.

"We knew it was going to be tough going against the Pittsburgh Steelers," he said. "I didn't know we were going to have to play the guys in the striped shirts as well."

Despite the bad taste the game left in the mouths of the Seahawks Nation, it was a fitting finale for Bettis, who spent nearly a decade of his stellar 13-year NFL career with the Steelers. "It's truly an amazing

feeling," said Bettis, a Detroit native who got to win his only Super Bowl in his hometown. "I'm the happiest person on the field. I'm the happiest person in the world. We're the champions of the world. It's an unbelievable moment."

Top left, Pittsburgh Steelers quarterback Ben Roethlisberger (7) dives in for a 1-yard touchdown. AP Photo/Mark J. Terrill

Top right, Pittsburgh Steelers' Jerome Bettis rushes against the Seattle Seahawks. AP Photo/Gene J. Puskar

Bottom right, The Renaissance Center with a Super Bowl XL wrap is shown in Detroit. AP Photo/Carlos Osorio

MAKE SOME NOISE!

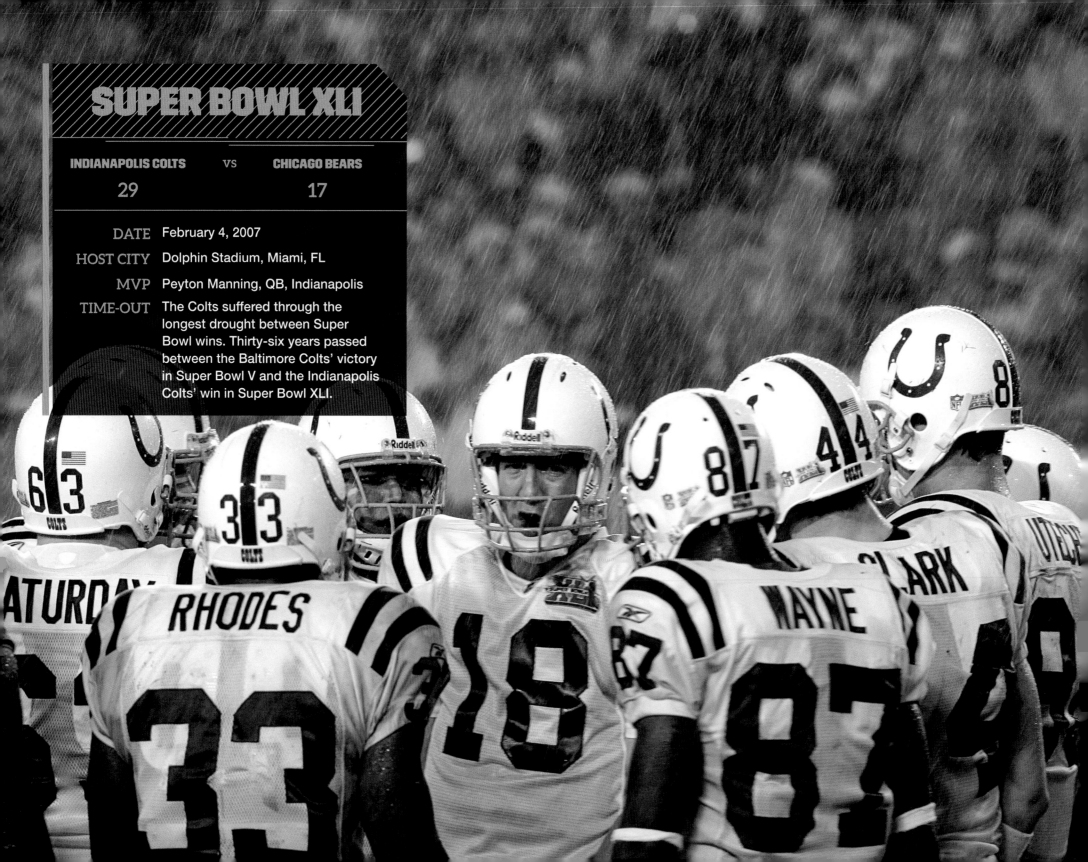

SUPER BOWL XLI

INDIANAPOLIS COLTS VS **CHICAGO BEARS**
29 17

DATE February 4, 2007
HOST CITY Dolphin Stadium, Miami, FL
MVP Peyton Manning, QB, Indianapolis
TIME-OUT The Colts suffered through the longest drought between Super Bowl wins. Thirty-six years passed between the Baltimore Colts' victory in Super Bowl V and the Indianapolis Colts' win in Super Bowl XLI.

This was a Super Bowl that was literally awash in milestones. First Super Bowl played in unremitting rain. First Lombardi Trophy won by an African American head coach. First touchdown scored less than 15 seconds into the game. And the first Super Bowl win for the quarterback who, despite being one of the best ever, had suffered through eight years of postseason futility.

It was Peyton's day—a long-awaited ring for the Indianapolis Colts quarterback who had passed for more than 4,000 yards in seven of his past eight seasons and had earned NFL MVP honors twice but had never made it to the big game. And even though most everyone in the football world believed Manning should have a title, through the regular season there were plenty of reasons to believe that this wasn't the Colts team that could get him to the top.

The Indianapolis defense ranked last in rushing yards allowed through the season, and the roster as a whole was known for featuring underweight, undersized players. Add to that the fact that the Colts fell in their last four road games and another juggernaut New England Patriots squad would await them if they made it to the AFC Championship Game and it would seem that Manning would have to wait at least another year.

But with some key personnel and scheme changes and savvy leadership from head coach Tony Dungy, general manger Bill Polian, and Manning, the Colts pooled their strengths and emerged as 29-17 victors over the more imposing Chicago Bears on a soggy evening in Miami's

Dolphin Stadium. "Last year's team was healthier and had more talent on it," Polian said afterward, "but this team was more resilient and tough-minded."

Both teams struggled with their passing games in the wettest Super Bowl in history, and the Colts were knocked back on their heels immediately thanks to Chicago's rookie return superstar Devin Hester, but in the second half an intersection of Indianapolis's solid rushing attack and Chicago's uncharacteristic defensive missteps locked the game away for the Colts and assured Indianapolis its first professional sports title since the Pacers won the NBA Finals 34 years earlier.

"It was nice to be able to hoist that trophy," said Manning, whose Colts teams had previously gone 3-6 in playoff appearances.

As the hazardous weather seemed to lock in over the stadium during the pregame, the Colts lost the coin toss and then opened the game by wagering with a man-made hazard—a kick into the hands of Hester. Only 14 seconds had ticked off the clock when the Bears' prolific return specialist cleared the initial traffic and then broke out for a memorable 92-yard touchdown run that became the earliest Super Bowl touchdown ever.

The Colts answered with their own explosion play—a 53-yard scoring pass from Manning to Reggie Wayne—but a bungled snap put the score at 7-6 until Chicago made another statement on its next possession with a 52-yard Thomas Jones run followed by a 4-yard touchdown

pass from Rex Grossman to Muhsin Muhammad. As the second quarter commenced, the Bears held a 14-6 lead.

The spark that had carried the Colts to come from behind in a dramatic 38-34 AFC Championship win over the Patriots finally started to show up in the second quarter, as Indianapolis outscored Chicago 10-0 to enter the locker room with a slim 16-14 halftime lead. The Colts' dramatic highlight reels were absent from the third quarter, with both of their scoring drives resulting in Adam Vinatieri field goals, but in a game where the Colts dominated the time of possession by nearly 17 minutes, it was telling that they had the ball for 11 of the 15 minutes. But when the Bears put together another field goal drive of their own late in the third quarter, Indianapolis held a 22-17 lead that sustained hope for Bears fans.

The fourth quarter was less than four minutes old when Grossman made the blunder that spelled his team's downfall, misfiring a pass into the hands of Colts cornerback Kelvin Hayden. Hayden ran the ball 56 yards into the end zone and a 29-17 Indianapolis lead that would survive and spark a wave of celebration in Indianapolis.

"We were dictating early in the game," Chicago director of pro personnel Bobby DePaul reflected. "We had all the confidence and the mojo. Peyton wasn't off to a good start. Then we had that mistake. You can't give a guy like Peyton Manning his confidence back."

Manning walked away with the MVP award, but offensive accolades in equal

measure were due to the Colts' running back tandem of Joseph Addai and Dominic Rhodes. A Bears defense known for stuffing the run couldn't find a sustained solution for Addai and Rhodes, whose combined 190 rushing yards were the most gained against Chicago all season. Addai, the rookie who had exceeded 1,000 yards through the regular season as a backup, was also his team's leading receiver, with 10 receptions for 66 yards.

As the rain made the requisite Gatorade shower redundant for Dungy, he exulted quietly in the victory that had eluded him through a decade as a head coach, first in Tampa Bay and then in Indianapolis. The historic weight of the moment wasn't lost on Dungy, either, especially because across the field on the opposite sideline stood Lovie Smith. As the first two African American head coaches to lead their teams to the Super Bowl, Dungy and Smith guaranteed a milestone even as they hoped that diversity in the coaching ranks would become so commonplace that it would no longer merit a mention in the media.

"I feel good I was the first one to do it," Dungy told ESPN after the game. "This may not have been our best team in five years, but it was the closest and the most connected—and it showed in the way we played. The disappointment you have along the way, it helps you appreciate it more after you finally do achieve it."

SUPER BOWL XLII

NEW YORK GIANTS	VS	NEW ENGLAND PATRIOTS
17		14

DATE February 3, 2008

HOST CITY University of Phoenix Stadium, Glendale, AZ

MVP Eli Manning, QB, New York

TIME-OUT Steve Tisch, a film producer and co-owner of the New York Giants, is the only person to have ever won both an Oscar and a Super Bowl ring—the rings in Super Bowls XLII and XLVI and the Oscar for *Forrest Gump* in 1995.

New York Giants receiver David Tyree (85) catching a 32-yard pass in the clutches of New England Patriots safety Rodney Harrison (37) during the fourth quarter of Super Bowl XLII.
AP Photo/Gene Puskar, File

Throughout the history of the Super Bowl, games have stood out because of stellar performances from players or defensive units, an extraordinary drive, the weather conditions, or even an electrifying moment from a halftime show. But until Super Bowl XLII, no Super Bowl was singularly associated with one remarkable play.

Just say the name David Tyree, or even the Helmet Catch, and America's collective sports memory will turn to the New York Giants' 17-14 underdog victory over the New England Patriots at the University of Phoenix Stadium. Like the Catch and the Immaculate Reception, both of which occurred during divisional playoff games, Tyree's acrobatic grab was both visually arresting and historically significant.

Certainly, other factors were at play as quarterback Eli Manning and the Giants played spoilers to the Patriots' campaign to be the only team in NFL history to finish 19-0. New York's defensive line, powered by forces such as Michael Strahan, Justin Tuck, and Osi Umenyiora, kept Brady out of his rhythm all night and limited the most prolific offense in NFL history to just 14 points. But the highlight reel? For most fans, it would start and end with one late-fourth-quarter moment, a third and 5 play that Tyree himself described as "supernatural."

New England was leading 14-10 when the Giants got the ball back at their own 17-yard line with 2:42 left in the game. As the drive unfolded, Strahan told the *New York Daily News* that he walked up and down the Giants' sideline telling his teammates that the final score would be 17-14. "I kept telling them, 'Repeat it,'" Strahan said. "I was walking up the sidelines saying, 'You say it. Repeat it. You have to believe it.'"

Manning moved the ball efficiently out of the shotgun until the comeback dream was nearly shelved by a fourth-and-1 situation in which Brandon Jacobs converted by near inches. After a deep right pass to Tyree that fell incomplete, the stage was set for the day's high drama.

The heroics started in the pocket, as a New England blitz subjected Manning to an onslaught that included Adalius Thomas, Richard Seymour, and Jarvis Green. While Green grabbed Manning around the waist and Seymour yanked at his jersey, he seemed to teleport himself out into the flat, where he suddenly had the time and space to find a receiver. "It was like a scene out of *Planet Earth* or *National Geographic*, where it's a lion jumping on the back of a wild horse," said referee Mike Carey, who had a front-row seat to Manning's liberation. "You could see him desperately trying to pull out, and somehow he did."

Manning hurled up a high prayer, 32 yards deep center to Tyree, a sixth-round draft pick who had caught a total of four passes throughout the regular season. As Tyree jumped straight up and snatched the ball over his head, he was already in a wrestling match with New England safety Rodney Harrison, who got a hand on it, too. In an effort to get control, Tyree pressed the ball against his helmet, got both hands firmly around it, and against all odds kept it from hitting the ground as he and Harrison crashed to earth.

Harrison refused to concede, trying to wrest the ball away from Tyree, but the

New York Giants receiver Plaxico Burress (17) fails to catch a pass in the end zone while under pressure from New England Patriots defenders Ellis Hobbs III (*right*), Brandon Meriweather (31), and Asante Samuel in the third quarter. *AP Photo/David Duprey/FILE*

catch was ruled a completion and suddenly the Giants looked a lot like a team of destiny. "The velocity of the throw, the defender draped all over me, the curved surface of the ball against a round helmet, the way we came down to the ground, it just doesn't make sense," Tyree said later.

Four plays later, with 39 seconds left on the clock, Manning found Plaxico Burress on a 13-yard pass for a touchdown and the Giants' third Super Bowl championship. Amid the celebration, Giants' co-owner John Mara pronounced it "the greatest victory in the history of this franchise, without question."

The Patriots, who had fueled an eleventh-hour drive of their own that consumed five minutes and ended with a 6-yard Brady–to–Randy Moss touchdown pass just before the Giants took over, were stunned at the unexpected way in which their 19-0 dream had been dismantled. New England had been the favorite in every game they had played that season, but New York had come to Phoenix from the other direction, toppling Tampa Bay, Dallas, and Green Bay from the underdog position through the playoffs and winning 11 straight games on the road to become world champs.

Manning was crowned the MVP for a solid performance that included 19 passes for 255 yards and that gutsy third-down escape act that would live in infamy, but the real heroes on the New York squad played on the defensive side. The Patriots had averaged 36.8 points and averaged 295 passing yards a game through the 2007 season. At the Super Bowl, they scored 14 points and compiled 229 yards in the air, and the Giants held them scoreless in both the first and third quarters.

"We knew that if we played our best, we'd have a chance to beat them," Manning added. "We believed the whole time."

As the 1972 Miami Dolphins toasted their sustained standing as the only NFL team ever to run the table, pundits tried to put New York's spectacular win into perspective. NFL media analyst Elliott Harrison deemed it the second-best Super Bowl of all time, after Super Bowl XIII. A Bleacher Report piece ranked it number three, and *FOX Sports* and *Sports Illustrated* agreed in their assessments of the Giants' victory as the best Super Bowl of all time.

"When arguably the greatest play in Super Bowl history is crucial to the winning drive against an undefeated, seemingly invincible team, you've got a valid case for this one being the best ever," read the story on www.si.com that ranked the top 10 games.

Left, New York Giants defensive end Michael Strahan (92) reacts during the Giants 17-14 win over the New England Patriots. *AP Photo/Stephan Savoia*

Bottom right, New England Patriots quarterback Tom Brady watches the final seconds of the Patriots' loss to the New York Giants. *AP Photo/Paul Sancya*

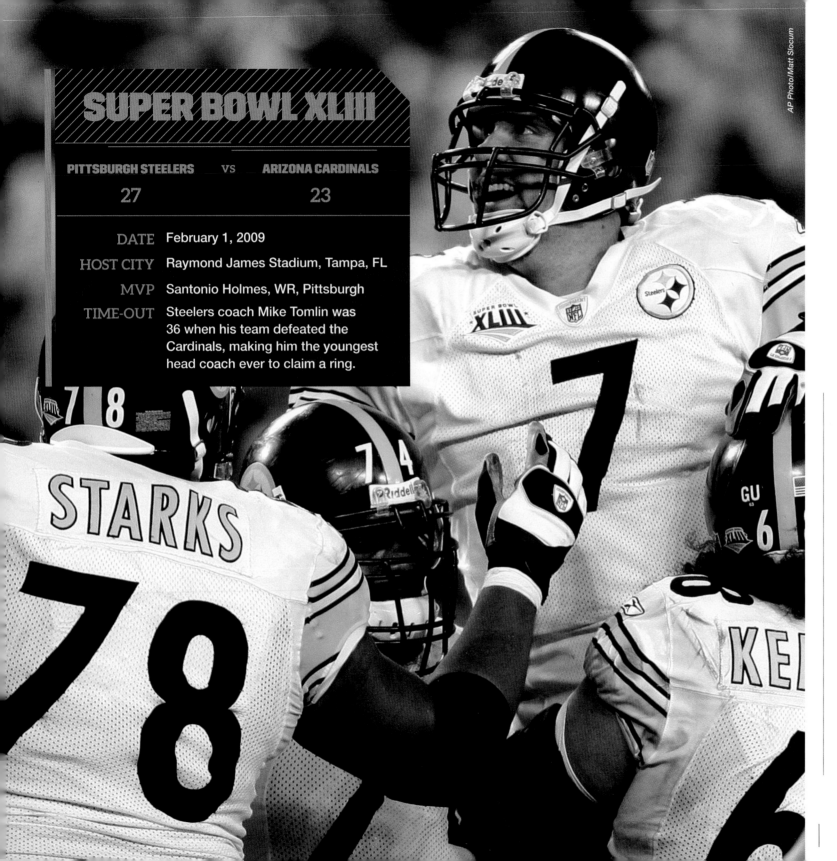

SUPER BOWL XLIII

PITTSBURGH STEELERS	VS	ARIZONA CARDINALS
27		23

DATE — February 1, 2009

HOST CITY — Raymond James Stadium, Tampa, FL

MVP — Santonio Holmes, WR, Pittsburgh

TIME-OUT — Steelers coach Mike Tomlin was 36 when his team defeated the Cardinals, making him the youngest head coach ever to claim a ring.

There was a time, through much of the '90s, when a Super Bowl was likely to be a blowout. But after fans wore out the edge of their seats through two of the most spectacular last-second, game-winning plays ever witnessed in professional football, those blowout years seemed like a distant memory. The Pittsburgh Steelers' theatrics in Super Bowl XLIII might not have topped the Giants' miracle of the year before, but they certainly kept the fans from entertaining any regrets.

"We're going down in history with one of the greatest games ever played in the Super Bowl," said wide receiver Santonio Holmes, the MVP and the player on the receiving end of the deciding touchdown pass.

If the ending was worthy of a fairy tale as the Steelers defeated the Arizona

Cardinals 27-23 for their sixth Lombardi Trophy, the action through much of the second half seemed more fitting for a horror story. Quarterback Ben Roethlisberger and his team saw a 20-7 lead evaporate and become a 23-16 deficit in the fourth quarter, as the Steelers fell victim to a suddenly anemic offensive plan and the volatile combination of Cardinals quarterback Kurt Warner and wide receiver Larry Fitzgerald.

As seven-point favorites, the Steelers were in concert with expectations early, scoring the first 10 points of the game on an 18-yard Jeff Reed field goal and a seven-minute drive, launched by a 25-yard pass from Roethlisberger to Holmes, that was resolved by a 1-yard touchdown run by fullback Gary Russell. When Arizona regained possession, Warner, who had already won a ring in Super Bowl XXXIV, found a way to move the ball despite nearly constant pressure from the Steeler defense, and the score was 10-7 with eight minutes left in the half.

The play that ultimately carried the most weight for the Steelers might have been the final touchdown pass, but the pick six executed by linebacker James Harrison with 18 seconds left in the second quarter was historic in its own right. It was the longest interception returned for a touchdown in Super Bowl history, it stopped the Cardinals on a first-and-goal situation that would have given them the lead, and Pittsburgh defensive coordinator Dick LeBeau later called it the best defensive play he had ever witnessed in the big game.

Harrison became a human highlight reel, in essence, because he was in the wrong place at the wrong time. He was instructed to blitz Warner on the play, but he dropped into coverage instead and found himself in the neighborhood of Warner's pass to Anquan Boldin, who had lined up several yards too far inside for the play. As Harrison snatched the ball away with his feet on the goal line and lumbered through traffic 100 yards to the promised land, he embodied every defensive player's dream on the world's biggest stage.

"He did something that, as a linebacker, he's not trained to do," Arizona offensive coordinator Todd Haley said. "He made a fantastic play, probably one of the greatest plays of all time, in the Super Bowl."

Neither team accomplished much in the third quarter, although Pittsburgh consumed more than eight minutes off of the clock on a scoring drive that culminated in a 21-yard Reed field goal. Things intensified with 11:30 left in the game after the Steelers were forced to punt and the Cardinals took eight plays— including three passes from Warner to Fitzgerald for a total of 30 yards—to score a touchdown that put them only six points behind. Thanks to a punishing sack by Darnell Dockett for a 10-yard loss, Roethlisberger went three and out on the next possession and gave the Cardinals a chance to continue assembling their comeback.

Arizona failed to convert on its next possession, but an unnecessary roughness penalty on Harrison on the punt return helped drive Pittsburgh all the way

back to the 1-yard line, where a Pittsburgh holding penalty resulted in a safety and a shrinking 20-16 Steelers lead.

With 2:47 remaining, Warner and Fitzgerald struck again rapidly, but as it turned out, they should have taken their time. On second down, a short pass down the middle from Warner allowed Fitzgerald to pull off a spectacular 64-yard touchdown run that left the NFL's top-rated defense in the dust. Quietly, with a 23-20 lead and 2:37 left on the clock, the Cardinals started to celebrate the prospect of their first-ever Super Bowl title. The worst-case scenario at that point, Haley said, seemed like a drive for another Pittsburgh field goal, which would create the first overtime game in the history of the Super Bowl.

"I was scared to death," Haley said. "Everybody was celebrating. I took Larry on the side and tried to temper everybody. I said, 'Hey, start prayin' right now.'"

Roethlisberger, who had become the Steelers' first $100-million player when he signed a contract extension earlier that season, calmly executed a two-minute drill, going 6 for 8 for 83 yards with the most dramatic of those completions hitting Holmes for 40 yards. Pittsburgh was first and goal from the 6-yard line with 48 seconds left when Roethlisberger threw a perfect pass to Holmes but it went through the receiver's hands. When that play failed, many fans at Raymond James Stadium thought they were headed for that historic overtime.

But on second down, with 42 seconds remaining, Roethlisberger gave Holmes another chance to deliver, and he came through in a big way, stretching up impossibly high to snag the ball in the back corner of the end zone while still somehow managing to keep his feet on the ground. After the official confirmed the touchdown, Holmes cradled the ball like a baby and kneeled on the ground.

"I dared the team," said Holmes, who was 9 for 131 on the day. "I came up and told Ben I want to be the guy: 'I want to win this game for you guys, man. Just give me the ball.'"

The Steelers had one for their other thumb, their head coach Mike Tomlin was the youngest head coach in history to win a Super Bowl, and Roethlisberger had earned his keep. The Super Bowl team of the '70s had served notice that they were effective in other decades as well.

Arizona Cardinals wide receiver Larry Fitzgerald runs past the Pittsburgh secondary. *AP Photo/Mark Humphrey*

"IN NEW YORK, THEY LIKE WINNERS. THEY DON'T LIKE SECOND PLACE."

Eli Manning

CHAPTER 6: THE 2010s

SUPER BOWL XLIV

NEW ORLEANS SAINTS	VS	INDIANAPOLIS COLTS
31		17

DATE February 7, 2010

HOST CITY Sun Life Stadium, Miami, FL

MVP Drew Brees, QB, New Orleans

TIME-OUT The victory over the Colts was the first Super Bowl appearance for the Saints and the first championship ever for a team from New Orleans.

By 2010, only a handful of NFL cities had never seen their team compete in a Super Bowl. But it's a certainty that none of those five fan bases needed a taste of world championship glory as badly as hurricane-ravaged New Orleans.

The Saints' opponent, the Indianapolis Colts, had more experience and more playoff credibility going into the matchup in Sun Life Stadium, but Sean Payton and Drew Brees prevailed with an abundance of grit, innovation in play calling, and a fourth-quarter interception that was both the only turnover of the game and a terminally costly mistake for the Colts.

In the end, the scoreboard read 31-17, and the 'Aints had found a way.

It had been five years since Hurricane Katrina devastated the Big Easy, and alongside the city's slow rebuilding efforts, Payton had been constructing a team on the principles of offensive efficiency, bold leadership, and a progressive defensive strategy behind coordinator Gregg Williams. The franchise had made the playoffs only once in the eight seasons before 2009, when the Saints ignited and started 13-0.

To demonstrate his willingness to swim against the current, Payton called for an onside kick to open the second half—the first onside kick to occur before the final minutes of the fourth quarter in Super Bowl history. The gamble succeeded in putting the Colts back on their heels and setting the table for the Saints' go-ahead touchdown. Facing a team with NFL MVP Peyton Manning calling the signals and seven 12-win seasons in a row, the Saints took control with that startling call, and the Colts couldn't get them to relinquish it.

As confetti showered down and Brees held his baby son, Baylen, in one of the defining images of the modern Super Bowl era, he gave up trying to fight back his tears as he considered the redemption that he had witnessed and helped orchestrate.

"Four years ago, who ever thought this would happen?" he said. "Eighty-five percent of the city was underwater, all the residents evacuated all over the country, people never knowing if they were coming back or if New Orleans would come back," he said. "But not only the city came back, the team came back.

"We leaned on each other. This is the culmination of that."

Brees, who came to New Orleans from San Diego the year after Katrina plowed through and quickly became a symbol of the city's fragile hope, set a Super Bowl record for completions, with 32, and amassed 288 passing yards, two touchdowns, and no interceptions. He also became one of only four 6-foot quarterbacks—along with Len Dawson, Joe Theismann, and Steve Young—to win a Super Bowl ring.

The Colts struck first with a 10-0 first quarter, but that early dominance ended quickly off the foot of Garrett Hartley, a 23-year-old free agent kicker who was one of the other heroes of the New Orleans victory. By clearing the uprights from 46 and 44 yards in the second quarter and 47 yards in the third, Hartley became the first kicker in Super Bowl history to make three field goals from 40 yards or farther.

The Saints had been working on an onside kick with punter Thomas Morstead in practice, and the play succeeded nearly every time. Emboldened by what he had seen from those trial runs and by his groundbreaking style of coaching, Payton told the team during the extended halftime that the opening play of the second half would be an onside kick.

The kick certainly disarmed the Colts' return unit, but Indianapolis nonetheless waged a valiant fight for possession of the ball. At least a dozen players ended up tangled in a pile, and at the bottom lay New Orleans' Chris Reis with the ball in his clutches. Reis, according to Williams, "looked like he had been in a fistfight gangster brawl. Scratches and cuts all over him."

With victory in that battle assured, the Saints set out to win the war, taking a 13-10 lead on a six-play drive that ended with a 16-yard screen pass from Brees to Pierre Thomas. But Manning and his teammates hadn't become one of the most legendary offenses of the decade for nothing, and they answered with a 76-yard drive and reclaimed the lead on Joseph Addai's 4-yard touchdown run. Then Hartley hit his third long field goal to end a wild quarter, and the Colts were grasping a 17-16 advantage.

After linebacker Jonathan Vilma stuffed Austin Collie on third down to thwart another Colts scoring march, Brees took command, hitting seven different receivers in nine plays and ultimately hitting tight end Jeremy Shockey on a 2-yard touchdown toss. The score was 24-17 Saints, but with 3:24 left on the clock, the people of New Orleans knew better than to exhale.

Indianapolis was just getting the drive under way when Williams called a six-man blitz on third down when Manning fired a pass to Reggie Wayne on an inside route. But Wayne wasn't in position, and cornerback Tracy Porter cut across for a textbook interception and 74-yard return down the middle for a touchdown and the 31-17 lead that endured.

The game featured the kind of error-free football that had characterized the early Super Bowls with Vince Lombardi's Packers. The shortest Super Bowl in history, in 3:14 the two teams combined for only one turnover and just eight penalties. The Colts gained 100 more yards than the Saints, but a sublime performance from Brees paired with the

type of swagger than can be found only in a team that has been to the depths equaled an unforgettable celebration.

"Forty-something years, being called the 'Aints, everyone coming to games with brown paper bags on," said veteran safety Darren Sharper. "They can come to games smiling now, because everyone's going to have a ring that's shining."

When the team returned to New Orleans, the fans came out, indeed, minus the paper bags, as a crowd of 800,000 welcomed their conquering heroes and reached a conclusion that they didn't need a FEMA pronouncement or a government grant to understand. New Orleans was back.

Top right, New Orleans Saints fans celebrate during Super Bowl XLIV.
AP Photos/Ben Liebenberg

Bottom right, Indianapolis Colts quarterback Peyton Manning releases a pass.
AP Photos/Ben Liebenberg

SUPER BOWL XLV

GREEN BAY PACKERS   VS   **PITTSBURGH STEELERS**

31   **25**

DATE	February 6, 2011
HOST CITY	Cowboys Stadium, Arlington, TX
MVP	Aaron Rodgers, QB, Green Bay
TIME-OUT	More than 200 fans sued the NFL for the seating fiasco that led many to be displaced at Super Bowl XLV, with the first lawsuit hitting the court in 2015.

AP Photo/Matt Slocum

It was bad enough that hundreds of fans were left without a seat and hundreds more had less than stellar views of the action of Super Bowl XLV. The snafu was made even worse by the fact that those luckless fans missed an exhilarating game combining two of football's storied giants with an ageless performance by an ascending quarterback and a tenacious comeback attempt by the team with more rings than any other.

The Green Bay Packers emerged with a 31-25 victory over the Pittsburgh Steelers in a game that saw an 18-point Packers lead evaporate to three points midway through the fourth quarter. It was a day on which winning the turnover battle—Green Bay didn't lose the ball once but managed three Pittsburgh takeaways—and the poised performance of Packers quarterback Aaron Rodgers made all the difference.

When the confetti had settled and MVP Rodgers was exulting in his first Super Bowl victory, his coach was rating it as the greatest performance ever by a quarterback in the big game. With 24 of

39 completions for 304 yards, three touchdowns, and no interceptions, Rodgers's long wait for the starting nod in Green Bay suddenly seemed insignificant.

"It's a dream come true," said Rodgers, a California native who grew up as a 49ers fan. "It's what I dreamt about as a little kid watching Joe Montana and Steve Young."

Host cities never want the location to be the villain in a Super Bowl tale, but between the 400 fans left without a seat when planned temporary seats were left unfinished, the ice storm that paralyzed the city of Dallas in the week preceding the game, and the unyielding playing surface that made the sidelines look like a triage center, the event was less than triumphant for the North Texas organizers.

The Packers had been plagued by injuries throughout the season, placing 16 players on injured reserve, but the loss of two starters during the Super Bowl itself was ultimately more motivational than costly as the battered team pushed through to victory. In the second quarter, wide receiver Donald Driver went down with an ankle injury, and then All-Pro cornerback Charles Woodson broke his collarbone while defending a play.

At halftime, less than an hour after his injury, Woodson gathered his teammates and tried to tell them how he felt about the team and how badly he wanted the prize that had eluded him through 12 seasons and seven Pro Bowl appearances. He was too choked up to speak, but his teammates got the message as they stormed out to try to protect their 21-10 lead.

Later, Packers coach Mike McCarthy said that wide receiver Jordy Nelson had injured his knee in the same part of the field where Woodson went down, and although Nelson kept playing, he dropped several key passes after the injury and ultimately had to come off the plane in a wheelchair when the team returned to Green Bay. It was undeniably a talented group, but as the second half unfolded, their troop strength was perilously low.

The Steelers seemed to sense a subtle momentum shift, and after James Jones dropped a pass, Pittsburgh relied on its running game to assemble a five-play, 50-yard scoring drive that culminated in an 8-yard Rashard Mendenhall run. Mendenhall claimed the only points of the third quarter, and at the start of a tense fourth period, the score was Packers 21, Steelers 17. Enter Green Bay receiver Greg Jennings, who had already snagged a 21-yard pass for a first-half touchdown and then played a featured role in the Packers' next scoring drive. Rodgers led his team 55 yards in under three minutes, hitting Jennings on an 8-yard touchdown pass one play after he was sacked for a loss of 6 by LaMarr Woodley.

Green Bay's more comfortable 28-17 advantage didn't last long. First Pittsburgh quarterback Ben Roethlisberger completed eight passes in nine attempts and found the end zone on the longest—a 25-yarder directed deep left to Wallace for the touchdown. A successful two-point conversion by Antwan Randle El brought the Steelers within a field goal with 7:34 left on the clock.

But Rodgers kept plugging away, driving his team into field goal range on the next possession and eating 5:27 off the clock in the process. The most explosive—and important—play of the drive was a quick 33-yard pass that found Jennings and sparked the drive. After a drop from Nelson on a play that could have easily resulted in a touchdown, the Packers went for three points that turned out to be enough when they held the Steelers until the final whistle sounded. Rodgers leapt in the air as his team claimed a 31-25 win that established Green Bay as a modern-day and historic Super Bowl team.

With that, Rodgers had earned the same number of Super Bowl rings as his predecessor Brett Favre and had reinforced the argument that he was edging into elite quarterback territory. Steelers fans would always wonder what might have been if not for one disastrous play, such as Nick Collins's 36-yard pick six in the first quarter. But the Packers had overcome adversity of every stripe, and the reward was the Lombardi Trophy's first trip to Titletown in 14 years.

Driver and Woodson forgot about ankle pain and fractured collarbones. The rings, which would be ordered without delay because head coach Mike McCarthy actually gathered the players' ring sizes the night before the Super Bowl, would be coming their way, and that was a salve that could ease any ailment.

"Just like all season, somebody stepped in and they stepped up," said Woodson. "It's an unbelievable feeling."

"It was the great resolve of this football team," coach Mike McCarthy said. "We had some practice of guys going down with other guys stepping up. Just a tremendous effort."

Top right, Pittsburgh Steelers' Rashard Mendenhall (34) runs away from Green Bay Packers' Clay Matthews (52) during the second half.
AP Photo/Charlie Krupa

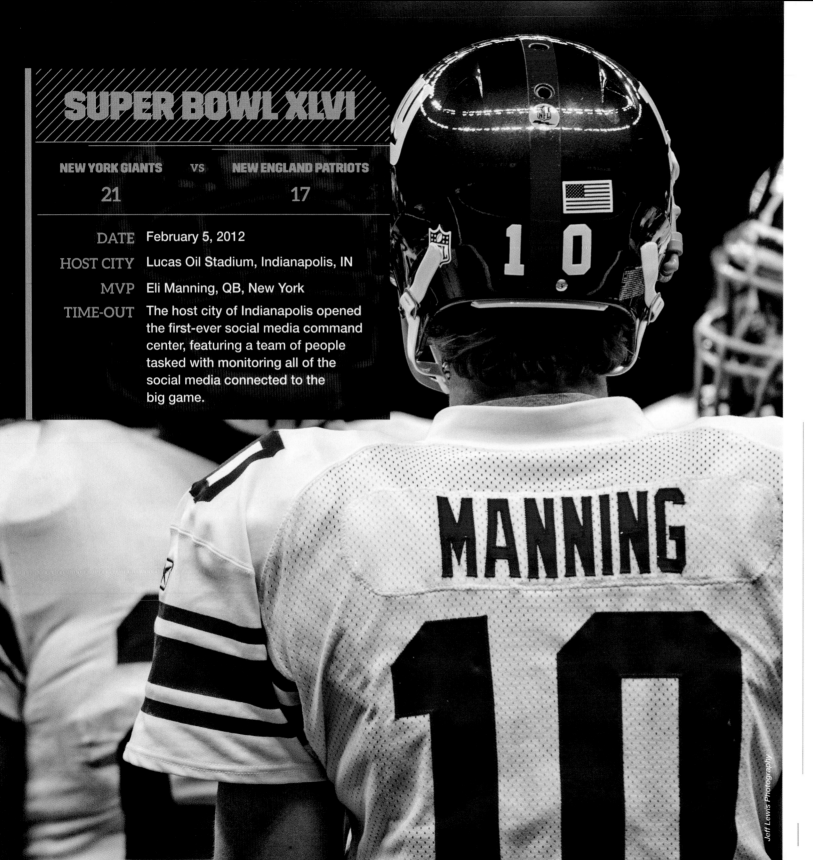

SUPER BOWL XLVI

NEW YORK GIANTS vs **NEW ENGLAND PATRIOTS**

21   **17**

DATE   February 5, 2012

HOST CITY   Lucas Oil Stadium, Indianapolis, IN

MVP   Eli Manning, QB, New York

TIME-OUT   The host city of Indianapolis opened the first-ever social media command center, featuring a team of people tasked with monitoring all of the social media connected to the big game.

Jeff Lewis Photography

In 2004, as Eli Manning was entering the NFL in the sizable shadow of his older brother, the notion that he would be responsible for Super Bowl–winning drives against the best team of the modern era—not once but twice—would have seemed widely improbable.

But with a second extraordinary fourth-quarter performance in Super Bowl XLVI to topple the New England Patriots 21-17, Manning and his New York Giants proved that there was nothing flukey about Super Bowl XLII and David Tyree's helmet catch. The victory was considered a significant upset, but once again Manning and his team came in acting like they belonged there and then went out and proved it.

"To get one Super Bowl win in the manner that we got it four years ago usually lasts a whole career," Giants owner John Mara said afterward. "But to get two of these? It is beyond description. It really is."

The Giants took more than half the season to gather momentum, standing at 7-7 before finally going on a six-game winning streak to finish the regular slate and carry them through the postseason. With the victory, they became the first 9-7 team ever to win the Super Bowl and the first Super Bowl champion that was outscored throughout the regular season by its opponents.

A disproportionate number of those victories—six, in fact—came through fourth-quarter theatrics on the part of Manning, who had engineered eleventh-hour drives to seal the win so many times that it was nearly a guarantee he would face the same situation on Super Sunday. Besides the spectacular 38-yard pass to Mario Manningham that fueled the drive, it was made even more unforgettable by the bizarre environment in which Ahmad Bradshaw crossed the goal line—tentatively afraid to score, with no resistance from a defense that had been told to let him go.

"It was definitely weird," running back Brandon Jacobs said.

In a game in which the total offensive yards were within 50 yards of each other and the two teams combined to score an even 19 points in each of the two halves, any prevailing wisdom about Patriot dominance was quickly debunked. Despite the Giants' average season, they were a talented team on a mission, and

the Patriots were an offensive juggernaut with a defense populated with players who had been cut from teams all over the NFL.

After a start that ignited the Las Vegas gambling community—Brady was penalized into the end zone for intentional grounding to make the first time a safety ever opened the scoring in the Super Bowl—New York put together a five-minute drive to pad a surprising early lead. The Giants jumped out to 9-0 on a tapestry of short Manning passes to five different receivers that culminated with a 2-yard toss to Victor Cruz for the score. The Patriots pass defense was successful in keeping Manning in the short field through the first 56 minutes of play, with no completion for more than 19 yards.

The second quarter was the dominion of the favorites, as New England advanced for a 29-yard Stephen Gostkowski field goal early in the quarter, put on the defensive pressure to stop Manning and his unit twice, and then chewed up the final four minutes of the half on a 96-yard drive that featured 5-foot-7 running back Danny Woodhead on three passing and four running plays. The halftime score was Patriots 10, Giants 9.

The extended break did little to cool the Patriots as they chased a fourth Lombardi Trophy. Fewer than four minutes into the half, they had scored another touchdown on a 12-yard pass from Brady to tight end Aaron Hernandez, giving them their biggest lead of the game at 17-9. But the advantage diminished some when the Giants put together two consecutive field goal drives and Lawrence Tynes's

accuracy from 38 and 33 yards made it only a 17-15 edge.

Thus was the stage set for Eli's Miracle 2.0. The fourth quarter started badly for New England when Chase Blackburn intercepted a Brady pass, but then both teams put together five-minute drives that ended in punts. With 3:46 left, the Giants assembled at the 12-yard line to embark on their quest for the lead, and with the first play from scrimmage, the world received notice that Manning had slipped into his fourth-quarter superhero costume.

He dropped back and launched the ball deep left to Manningham, who was a half step ahead of a gaining Sterling Moore and squarely in the sights of safety Patrick Chung barreling in from the side. With his feet perched just in bounds, Manningham made the catch over his shoulder as Chung made contact. Patriots coach Bill Belichick asked for a review, but the play was upheld, and the Giants suddenly had something spectacular on which to build.

"What makes you think you can get the ball in there?" New York guard Kevin Boothe said about Manning's no-room-for-error placement of the pass. "I've seen Eli make so many plays you just grow to expect it. But I still can't believe the pass and the catch."

As the drive unfolded, Manning found both Manningham and Nicks twice to advance into Patriots territory before putting the ball into the hands of Bradshaw on second and goal from the sixth. Before the play, Belichick had

told his team to let the Giants score a touchdown, reasoning that they were guaranteed to make the field goal to take the lead even if the Patriots stopped them, and in that scenario there wouldn't be any time for a last-gasp effort to reclaim the lead.

"It was like opposite day," wrote Sam Borden of The New York Times. "The Patriots defenders, trained their whole lives to try to push and claw and fight to bring down the ball carrier, stood up and opened a double-wide hole for Bradshaw to reach the end zone. Bradshaw, trained his whole life to sprint into the end zone whenever he could, pulled up just short of the goal line and tried to fall down."

It might have been unconventional, but Brady's attempt at igniting something with 0:57 remaining failed, and Bradshaw's touchdown had made Manning an MVP for the second time and given his team an ironclad identity as a team with a talent for stealing Super Bowls.

New York Giants wide receiver Hakeem Nicks (88) catches a pass against New England Patriots defensive back Antwaun Molden (27). *AP Photo/Greg Trott*

GLUG GLUG

1,240,800,000

1,240,800,000 bottles of beer are consumed each year on Super Bowl Sunday.

BOTTLES OF BEER ON THE WALL

SUPER BOWL XLVII

BALTIMORE RAVENS VS **SAN FRANCISCO 49ERS**

34 **31**

DATE February 3, 2013

HOST CITY Mercedes-Benz Superdome, New Orleans, LA

MVP Joe Flacco, QB, Baltimore

TIME-OUT It was the first time ever that two brothers—Jim Harbaugh of the 49ers and John Harbaugh of the Ravens—have coached against each other in the Super Bowl.

It was known alternately as the Harbowl and the Blackout Bowl, but Super Bowl XLVII could just as aptly be remembered as Ray's Last Stand. The most dominant defensive player in the modern era willed his teammates to withstand a furious San Francisco 49ers comeback attempt to hold onto a 34-31 lead for a Baltimore Ravens triumph.

The wild and the unlikely dominated this Super Bowl, from the first incidence of brothers coaching across the field from each other to a blackout that took 34 minutes to resolve. But when the game was on the line in the fourth quarter, a

good old-fashioned defensive stop in the red zone became the ultimate highlight for Ray Lewis, the linebacker who had become the epitome of a defensive superstar and walked into retirement holding his second Lombardi Trophy.

"How else can you finish that off but with a goal-line stand?" Lewis said. "How else can you finish a Super Bowl off when your coordinator trusts the way he trusts, and we finished it off? We kept them out of the end zone. That is championship football."

The event in the New Orleans Superdome was divided through the pregame buildup

between two brothers, Baltimore head coach John Harbaugh and his brother, San Francisco head coach Jim Harbaugh. But once the ball was kicked off, the game was divided in a different way: before the lights went out and after they came back on.

Through the first half and the early seconds of the third quarter, before the dome was plunged into darkness, the Ravens were virtually unstoppable, building a 28-6 lead early in the second half when Jacoby Jones ran the opening kickoff back 108 yards for a touchdown and a Super Bowl record. Down 22 points,

the 49ers had managed nothing more potent than a 36-yard David Akers field goal. When the stadium went dark at the 13:28 mark, it could have been a metaphor for San Francisco's shot at winning a sixth ring.

But after 34 minutes of inactivity—broadcasters speculating endlessly on the cause of the outage, players trying to stay focused—the game resumed, and a new 49ers team took the field. Starting with a 31-yard touchdown pass from Colin Kaepernick to Michael Crabtree, San Francisco outscored Baltimore 23-3 in the 12:23 after the blackout. Suddenly the game stood at 28-23 at the end of the third quarter, and the chance for an easy Baltimore victory had been lost in the dark.

As the third quarter became the fourth, quarterback Joe Flacco and the Ravens were driving in hopes of reconstructing their lead, but despite two chances to get into the end zone from the 1-yard line, Baltimore was unable to break the plane, falling victim to a Justin Smith tackle and an Isaac Sopoaga pass breakup. A 19-yard Justin Tucker field goal made it 31-23, but San Francisco still had ample time to keep things interesting.

It only took 2:50 for Kaepernick to direct his unit 76 yards for a touchdown, and his 15-yard keeper was the longest quarterback touchdown run in Super Bowl history. When the 49ers' two-point conversion attempt failed, the Ravens clung to a 31-29 lead with 9:51 remaining in the game. The next Baltimore drive resulted in Tucker's second field goal in fewer than eight minutes, giving San Francisco the ball with a five-point deficit and 4:19 on the clock. It took the 49ers only five plays to travel 73 yards, sparked by a 33-yard Frank Gore run and a 24-yard pass from Kaepernick to Crabtree. Thus the stage was set for the clash in the trenches.

Running back LaMichael James gained 2 yards on a first down from the 7-yard line, but the 49ers wouldn't gain another yard that evening. On second down, Ravens cornerback Corey Graham got in the way of a Kaepernick-to-Crabtree attempt on a play that had Crabtree looking fruitlessly for a pass interference call. The third-down play, after a San Francisco time-out, was

also a pass to Crabtree, this one thwarted by Jimmy Smith.

Finally, on fourth down, Kaepernick tried to hit his favorite receiver one more time for the win, but Lewis came blazing up the middle on the blitz as Kaepernick passed. In the backfield, Smith wrapped Crabtree up and the pass fell incomplete. All that was left was a Baltimore possession designed to consume seconds and secure the victory, although it was interrupted by a Super Bowl unicorn—a safety to end the game and make the final score 34-31 when punter Sam Koch was tackled in the end zone with four seconds remaining.

Lewis had his dramatic curtain call, but his team's quarterback also earned his share of the spotlight in the victory. Joe Flacco had long been considered second tier in discussions of the NFL's elite quarterbacks, but after completing 22 of 33 passes for 287 yards, three touchdowns, and no interceptions for a passer rating of 124.2, Flacco emerged from the shadows for good.

"He fears nothing," Ravens offensive coordinator Jim Caldwell said afterward. "That's the thing about him. He really has no fear of anything. He's as tough as he can be. He's fearless in terms of taking chances. And he's going to squeeze that ball, but yet he's very, very smart."

In the postgame scrutiny of the stadium blackout, Superdome officials would only say it was caused by an "abnormality." But in the months after the game, both Lewis and Ravens linebacker Terrell Suggs theorized that the blackout was more than a random electrical malfunction, with

Suggs even mentioning NFL commissioner Roger Goodell specifically as a culprit. "Roger Goodell, he never stops, he always has something up his sleeve," Suggs told ESPN. "He just couldn't let us have this one in a landslide, huh?"

"You cannot tell me somebody wasn't sitting there and when they say, 'The Ravens [are] about to blow them out. Man, we better do something,'" Lewis said in an NFL documentary about the game. "That's a huge shift in any game, in all seriousness. And as you see how huge it was because it let them right back in the game."

Top right, Baltimore Ravens linebacker Ray Lewis (52) talks to safety Bernard Pollard (31) during the blackout in the third quarter of Super Bowl XLVII. *AP Photo/Kevin Terrell*

Bottom right, Ravens quarterback Joe Flacco holds up the Lombardi Trophy. *Jeff Lewis Photography*

SUPER BOWL XLVIII

SEATTLE SEAHAWKS	VS	DENVER BRONCOS
43		8

DATE	February 2, 2014
HOST CITY	Metlife Stadium, East Rutherford, NJ
MVP	Malcolm Smith, LB, Seattle
TIME-OUT	Despite the Broncos' loss, wide receiver Demaryius Thomas set a Super Bowl record with 13 receptions.

There was a time when Super Sunday was synonymous with blowouts, but by the early 2000s the days when the commercials sparked more excitement than the game itself seemed to be over. After all, the average margin of victory in the 10 Super Bowls between 2004 and 2013 was only 6.3 points.

Then the Seattle Seahawks and the Denver Broncos arrived at MetLife Stadium for Super Bowl XLVIII, and a lopsided scoreboard was suddenly back in vogue. Driven by a stifling defense, the Seahawks trounced the Broncos 43-8 to ruin Denver quarterback Peyton Manning's legacy-building project and claim the first-ever Super Bowl title for the Pacific Northwest.

"We are the best defense ever," defensive end Michael Bennett told ESPN after he and his teammates forced four Bronco turnovers and held Denver to only 306 total yards. "We could have played anybody today and done the same thing. We were mad at the eight points we gave up, but that's what makes us so great."

From the bad snap from Manny Ramirez to Manning that led to a safety on the first play of the game, the Broncos kept digging themselves a larger and larger hole as Seattle piled on points in every possible way. In addition to the more traditional field goals (two), passing touchdowns (two), and running touchdowns (one), the Seahawks added points with a Malcolm Smith interception return and a Percy Harvin kickoff return.

The scoreboard read 22-0 at halftime, padded with 3:21 left in the second quarter, when Smith, who ultimately became the third linebacker in history to receive the Super Bowl MVP award, grabbed a Manning pass dislodged by his teammate Cliff Avril and ran it back 69 yards for the touchdown.

Manning, who had won the regular season MVP award for the fifth time with his second team, was so flummoxed by Seattle's defensive tactics early in the game that the Broncos didn't even gain a first down until five minutes into the second quarter. Denver finally moved the ball inside the red zone on the final drive of the half but made the trip for nothing, and the Seahawks had constructed the first first-half Super Bowl shutout in 13 years.

"It's all about making history," Seattle safety Earl Thomas said. "This was a dominant performance from top to bottom."

Denver had an extended halftime to consider the futility of the previous 30 minutes, but the Broncos offense had set the league ablaze through the regular season, posting NFL records in passing touchdowns, passing yards, touchdowns, and points scored in a single season. They had proven repeatedly that they could score at will, so they strategized and motivated at halftime, intent on a comeback.

The third quarter was only seconds old when Seattle's Percy Harvin delivered a critical blow to those hopes with an 87-yard return for a touchdown on the opening kickoff. Seattle was ahead 29-0, and before the quarter was over, they would score again, on a 23-yard pass from quarterback Russell Wilson to Jermaine Kearse. With three seconds remaining in the third, Denver finally got on the board with a 14-yard pass from Manning to Demaryius Thomas and a Wes Welker two-point conversion, but the Broncos never scored again.

"It was embarrassing," said Thomas, who set a Super Bowl record with 13 receptions but found little satisfaction in the milestone. "It was the Super Bowl, and we didn't show up."

By the time Seattle iced the cake with a 10-yard pass from Wilson to Doug Baldwin four minutes into the fourth quarter, the celebration was well under way. Manning, who had made a stirring comeback from a neck injury that forced him to miss the 2011 season, was left with just one ring (from Super Bowl XLI with the Colts) and an unsatisfactory ending to the game that was supposed to cap his triumphant rebirth as a Bronco.

"I'm disappointed for our entire team," said Manning, who finished the game with respectable numbers—34 of 49 for 280 yards in the air—but two costly interceptions. "We worked hard to get to this point. Overcame a lot of obstacles. Put in a lot of hard work just to have this opportunity. But to finish this way, it certainly is disappointing. It's a bitter pill to swallow."

Calling signals across the field was the quarterback who, while outshined by his team's fierce defense, nonetheless did exactly what he had to do to claim his first Super Bowl ring at the age of 25. Russell Wilson passed for only 206 yards, but he never threw the ball away while standing as a steady presence in the pocket. He became the first quarterback who threw for more than 200 yards and two touchdowns and completed more than 70 percent of his passes in the Super Bowl yet was bypassed for the MVP award.

For the Seahawks, winning the turnover battle 4-0 was equivalent to winning the game, especially when they capitalized on first-half interceptions for 21 of their 43 points. More than any other Super Bowl in recent memory, this game spelled domination of an opponent through excellence in offense, defense, and special teams. It was also sweet

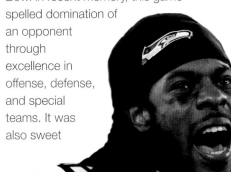

vindication for head coach Pete Carroll, a journeyman coach who had made 12 different stops through his college and professional career and was fired as head coach from both the Jets and the Patriots before rekindling his reputation with USC from 2001 to 2009.

"This is an amazing team," he said. "Took us four years to get to this point, but they never have taken a step sideways. These guys would not take anything but winning this ball game."

Among other dubious distinctions attached to the Broncos' calamity at the hands of the Seahawks, the result was tied for the third-worst blowout in Super Bowl history. Unfortunately for Denver fans with good memories, the widest margin of victory in the big game also came at the Broncos' expense—a 55-10 loss to Joe Montana and his San Francisco 49ers in Super Bowl XXIV.

Top right, Denver Broncos' Peyton Manning looks at the scoreboard during the second half of Super Bowl XLVIII. *AP Photo/Paul Sancya, File*

Bottom right, Seattle Seahawks' Richard Sherman during Super Bowl XLVIII. *AP Photo By Tom DiPace*

THE GAMES

GAME BREAK

Left, ABC Sports play-by-play announcer Al Michaels and sideline reporter Leslie Visser on the field just before the St. Louis Rams 23-16 victory over the Tennessee Titans in Super Bowl XXXIV. In this game, Michaels spoke the term that came to define that Buffalo Bills defeat: "wide right."
AP Photo/NFL Photos

SUPER BOWL LEXICON

Every transformative event or development in American history has an effect on our vocabulary, and the Super Bowl is no exception. When something particularly memorable occurs—either on the field or off—at the big game, the result is often a word or phrase that lives long after the details of the contest have been forgotten.

"THE SUPER BOWL OF _____"

As the big game has become all consuming on the cultural landscape, the term "Super Bowl" has come to denote the supremacy of any concept, competition, meeting, or phenomenon. In 2015 alone, media reports revealed happenings such as the "The Super Bowl of Hunting Sweepstakes," "The Super Bowl of Linguistics," "The Super Bowl of Surfing," and "The Super Bowl of Preaching." The last one could be the most unique—an event held annually at Crossroads Community Church in Cincinnati in which two preachers are each given two nine-minute "quarters" to preach. Each message must include a reference from the Bible and a random phrase that each competitor must work into his sermon.

"A referee then decides whether the criteria of the quarters has been met and awards points accordingly. The service includes pregame interviews with the competitors, live commentary during and in between the quarters, humorous and professional-quality 'commercials' and even a musical halftime show complete with lights, dancers and a live band," explained an article about the event in the *Xavier Newswire*.

"WIDE RIGHT"

For true fans of the game, these two words are all it takes to describe Super Bowl XXV, when Buffalo Bills kicker Scott Norwood missed a 47-yard field goal attempt that would have given his team the victory over the New York Giants. When commentator Al Michaels announced, "No good … wide right," he coined a phrase that later symbolized the first misstep on the Bills' long road of Super Bowl misfortune: four losses in four years.

Below, Buffalo Bills kicker Scott Norwood watches off line kick sail wide during Super Bowl XXV. *AP Photo/Paul Spinelli*

"HELMET CATCH"

This term joined "The Immaculate Reception" and "The Catch" for phrases that defined a matchless reception, and it was coined when little-known New York Giants receiver David Tyree used his helmet to help him hold onto the ball in a circus catch in Super Bowl XLII. The reception sparked the underdog Giant's comeback drive over the New England Patriots in one of the most dramatic endings in Super Bowl history.

Below, New York receiver David Tyree (85) catches a key third down pass on his helmet at the Patriots 24-yard line, setting up the go-ahead touchdown for the underdog Giants. *AP Photo/Paul Spinelli*

"WARDROBE MALFUNCTION"

When Justin Timberlake exposed far too much of Janet Jackson during the Super Bowl XXXVIII halftime show, Jackson's spokesman Stephen Huvane categorized the calamity as "a malfunction of the wardrobe." That explanation birthed a phrase so ubiquitous that it was acknowledged by *The Chambers Dictionary* in 2008.

"The incongruity of the phrase has proven just too delicious for us to let it go," wrote Andrea Denhoed in a 2014 *New Yorker* article. "Ten years later, 'wardrobe malfunction' still hasn't slunk out of usage. It appears in many a baiting headline, and it does so independently, with no explanation needed. It's self-supporting."

Below, Singer Janet Jackson, (*left*) covers her breast after her outfit came undone during a number with Justin Timberlake at the halftime show of Super Bowl XXXVIII. *AP Photo/Elise Amendola, File*

"DEFLATEGATE"

Deflategate. How would we identify our scandals in this country without President Nixon and his infamous break-in? The most famous "-gate" to befall professional football didn't actually occur at the Super Bowl, but its aftermath dominated the two weeks before Super Bowl XLIX between the Patriots and the Seahawks. Patriots head coach Bill Belichick and his quarterback Tom Brady were put in the awkward position of explaining the discovery that 11 of their team's 12 footballs were deflated prior to the AFC Championship Game against the Colts. An independent investigation, the Wells Report, concluded in May with the finding that it was "more probable than not" that Brady was aware of the football tampering.

Below, A Seattle Seahawks fan holds up a deflated football before the Super Bowl XLIX. *AP Photo/Brynn Anderson*

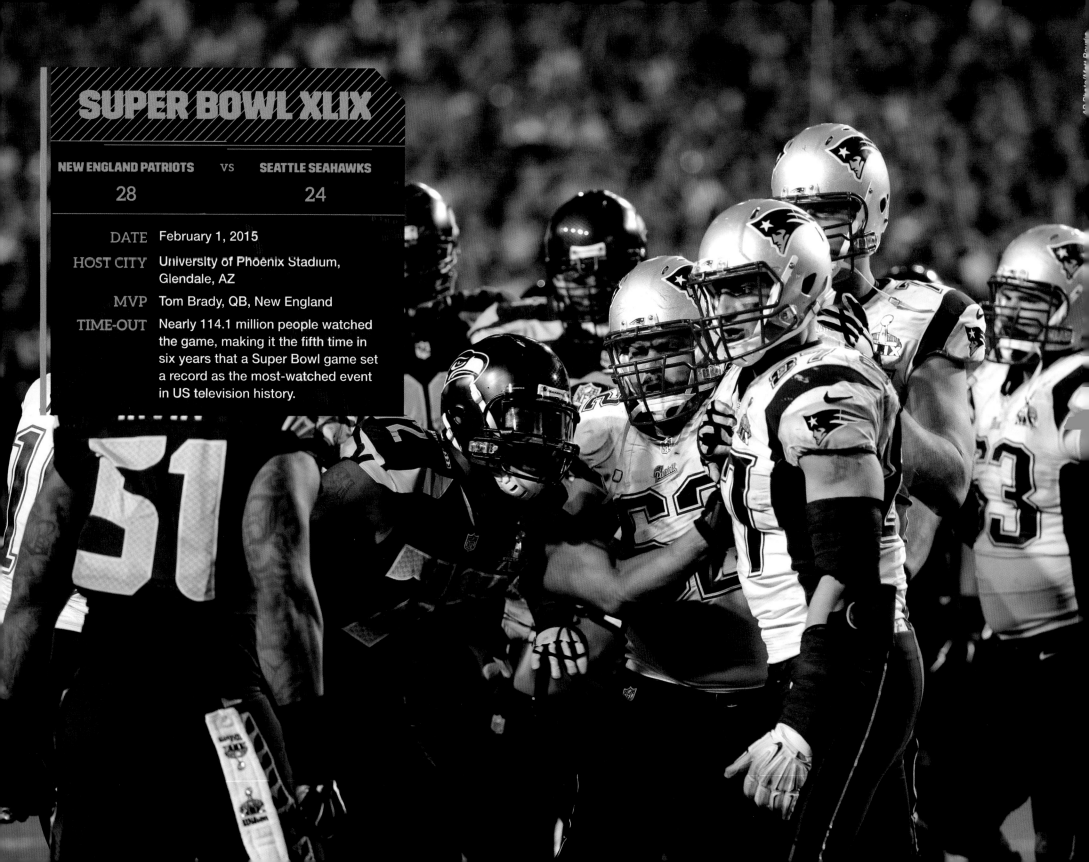

SUPER BOWL XLIX

NEW ENGLAND PATRIOTS   VS   **SEATTLE SEAHAWKS**

28   24

DATE   February 1, 2015

HOST CITY   University of Phoenix Stadium, Glendale, AZ

MVP   Tom Brady, QB, New England

TIME-OUT   Nearly 114.1 million people watched the game, making it the fifth time in six years that a Super Bowl game set a record as the most-watched event in US television history.

Seattle Seahawks wide receiver Chris Matthews (13) celebrates his touchdown catch.
AP Photo/Matt York

With a prelude colored by controversy and a finale polarized by a heated play-calling debate, Super Bowl XLIX cemented the legacies of Tom Brady and the New England Patriots and electrified fans with one of the most remarkable ending sequences in the history of the game to seal a 28-24 Patriots victory over the Seattle Seahawks.

The buildup to the event in Glendale, Arizona, was monopolized by two story lines: questions over the apparently intentional deflation of 11 Patriots footballs in the AFC Championship victory over Indianapolis (known forevermore as "Deflategate") and the extreme reticence of star Seattle running back Marshawn Lynch, who spent one press conference repeating the phrase "I'm just here so I don't get fined" 29 times.

But when an unknown defensive back named Malcolm Butler robbed the Seahawks of their hopes for a second consecutive title with a remarkable interception at the goal line, the nation's attention turned from the sideshows back to football—back to surprising stars, unexpected plays, and the resurgence of the modern era's greatest team.

"The Super Bowl That Took Our Breath Away has a good ring to it," wrote Peter King on *Sports Illustrated's* MMQB website.

Speaking of Monday morning quarterbacks, the second-guessing of Seattle's decision to throw a pass from the 1-yard line instead of sending Lynch barreling into the end zone for a near-certain victory was deafening from armchair critics and professional analysts

alike. Many, including King, called it the worst play call in Super Bowl history. That ill-fated call, and the pitched battle that followed it, created a gridiron spectacle worthy of the pregame hullabaloo.

It was a battle between past greatness and up-and-coming talent, as the defending champion Seahawks, with their bruising Legion of Boom defense, went toe to toe with a Patriots team with three Super Bowl titles since 2002 but none in the past decade. So evenly matched were the two teams that the betting line flip-flopped throughout the week before the game, eventually moving from a one-point New England favorite to a pick 'em 24 hours before kickoff.

After a scoreless first quarter in which Seattle quarterback Russell Wilson was

unable to complete a pass and Brady's goal-line throw was intercepted by Seahawks cornerback Jeremy Lane, both teams found a scoring rhythm and put up a combined 28 points in fewer than 10 minutes.

First Wilson hit Brandon LaFell on an 11-yard pass for a 7-0 New England lead with 9:47 remaining in the half, and then Lynch answered seven minutes later when he capped a 70-yard Seattle drive with a 3-yard scoring run. With just 31 seconds left, the dynamic combination of Brady to Rob Gronkowski grabbed a 14-7 lead on a 22-yard touchdown pass, and it looked like New England would enter the locker room with the advantage. But no one was accounting for Chris Matthews, an undrafted wide receiver who caught his second-ever NFL pass for a touchdown

on a quick-fire Wilson drive that covered 80 yards in a mere 29 seconds. With a 14-14 tie at halftime, the contest was making geniuses out of the Vegas prognosticators.

Seattle had finished the half with the momentum, and Wilson flew out of the blocks after halftime, his slow start ancient history. On the opening drive, he directed a 72-yard drive to its culmination with a 27-yard Steven Hauschka field goal, and his defense handed him the ball back three minutes later when linebacker Bobby Wagner intercepted a pass intended for Gronkowski. It was the first time Brady had thrown more than one interception in a Super Bowl.

Starting his next drive at midfield, Wilson completed three passes, and then Lynch ran twice for 15 yards to get the Seahawks within striking distance. With a 3-yard touchdown pass to Baldwin, Wilson and his team had a 10-point lead and a clear vision of their second straight trophy.

But Brady had been in this position before, and even if his past two Super Bowl appearances had ended in defeat to New York Giants teams making improbable plays, he knew how to stay cool when the pressure was the most intense and move the chains in the fourth quarter. He led two touchdown drives in fewer than six minutes, sparked by the Patriots' trademark short-passing game and connections

with receiver Julian Edelman. With 2:02 remaining, the Patriots had a 28-24 lead.

Then Wilson and his offense stepped up and traveled 75 yards in less than a minute, due largely to a circus catch by Jermaine Kearse that must have given Brady and Belichick uneasy flashbacks of David Tyree's helmet catch in Super Bowl XLII. Marshawn Lynch barreled 4 yards, and the Seahawks were poised at second and goal from the 1-yard line with 26 seconds left and the most physical back in football at their disposal.

Then came the play that might have caused more Americans to shout at their televisions than any in the history of the game. Rather than send Lynch into the fray, offensive coordinator Darrell Bevell called for a slant route up the middle to Ricardo Lockette in the end zone. Enter Butler, the first player from Division II West Alabama ever to play in the Super Bowl, making a perfect read for his first-ever interception on the world's most immense stage.

"I just had a vision that I was going to make a big play, and it came true," Butler said. "It's like a dream come true. It's like I was playing Madden in the eighth grade, winning the Super Bowl. It's unreal."

Ironically, it was a player no one had ever heard of who guaranteed history's treatment of the quarterback who had

long been a household name. With the victory, Tom Brady joined Joe Montana as the only three-time MVPs in Super Bowl history, set a Super Bowl record of pass completions with 37, and became one of only three quarterbacks (along with Montana and Terry Bradshaw) to capture four Super Bowl titles.

"I never put myself in those discussions," Brady said of the inevitable legacy debates. "That's not how I think. There are so many great players that have been on so many great teams. I think you've just got to enjoy the moment."

Opposite page, Seattle Seahawks wide receiver Jermaine Kearse (15) makes a 33-yard catch during the second half. *AP Photo/David J. Phillip*

Bottom left, New England Patriots quarterback Tom Brady holds up the Vince Lombardi Trophy. *AP Photo/Michael Conroy*

Left, New England Patriots strong safety Malcolm Butler (21) intercepts a pass that seals the Patriots' victory over the Seahawks. *AP Photo/David J. Phillip*

SAN FRANCISCO:
PLANNING FOR SUPER BOWL 50

In the mid-1850s, the San Francisco Bay Area was known for the Gold Rush. On February 7, 2016, the NFL will bring in a gold rush of its own when the Super Bowl's golden anniversary comes to town.

Only the second Super Bowl to be contested in the Bay Area (the first, Super Bowl XIX, was played at Stanford Stadium), the big game will unfold in Levi's Stadium, the state-of-the-art stadium that opened in Santa Clara in 2014 as the new home of the 49ers. As part of Super Bowl 50's goal to be the most technologically advanced championship in its history, the stadium will be ticketless and cashless and capable of providing Wi-Fi for the 75,000 people in attendance.

"We look forward to NFL fans from around the globe enjoying our region and our stadium, the likes of which cannot be found anywhere else in the world," 49ers

GUEST SERVICES HOTLINE (408) 579-4600

president Jed York told the media in 2013 when the Bay Area was selected over South Florida as the host.

In concert with the grandness of the golden anniversary, the Super Bowl 50 organizing committee is planning a full slate of pre–Super Bowl activities as well as fund-raising and marketing events throughout the year leading up to the game. As they set a new standard for technology and digital reach, the organizers also hope to make Super Bowl 50 the most generous big game in history.

Early in the planning, the committee announced its intentions to raise $40 million to offset the costs of hosting the Super Bowl and to give 25 percent of that amount to charitable causes. To kick off its philanthropic aim, in February 2015 the Super Bowl 50 group gave $2.5 million to five different organizations dedicated to helping underprivileged youth.

"To be distributing $2.5 million straight back into the community at such an early date is unheard of in the history of Super Bowls," committee spokesperson Nathan Ballard told the *San Francisco Chronicle*.

In addition to fund-raising, event planning, and the intricate web of logistics that accompanies an event of that magnitude, the Super Bowl 50 host committee is recruiting up to 10,000 volunteers to help with every aspect of the operation. Every Super Bowl is a production, but the expectations for the golden anniversary—that it be the splashiest and most sprawling one yet—equal the need for more money, more facilities, and more hands on deck.

Typically, the host city–based organizing committee is responsible for events leading up to the big game, and the NFL takes charge of every aspect of Super

Sunday itself. But the NFL won't limit its golden anniversary revelry to February 7. At the league's annual meeting in March, NFL officials announced a season-long plan to commemorate the fiftieth Super Bowl.

For starters, the NFL commissioned Tiffany and Co. (which crafts the Lombardi Trophy each year for the winning team) to create a giant 5 and a giant 0—each digit weighs nearly 33 pounds and is cast in bronze and coated in 18-carat gold. The golden "50" will go wherever the Lombardi Trophy goes throughout the season, and, ultimately, it will be awarded to the Super Bowl 50 champions.

Other aspects of the NFL's six-month-long golden anniversary fete include special 50-yard-line numerals and golden logos emblazoned on every field; gold accents

on sideline apparel; recognition of former Super Bowl MVPs through the year, culminating with a special halftime ceremony in San Francisco; and 19 Super Bowl rematches on the schedule in the regular season.

"There's going to be gold that's infused into everything this year, from jerseys, to memorabilia that you can buy, to logos, to the big 50," said Super Bowl XXXIV MVP Kurt Warner, who was tapped to help unveil the league's "On the Fifty" campaign at the league meetings. "So we're just really excited about this year. Nothing says 'NFL' like the Super Bowl."

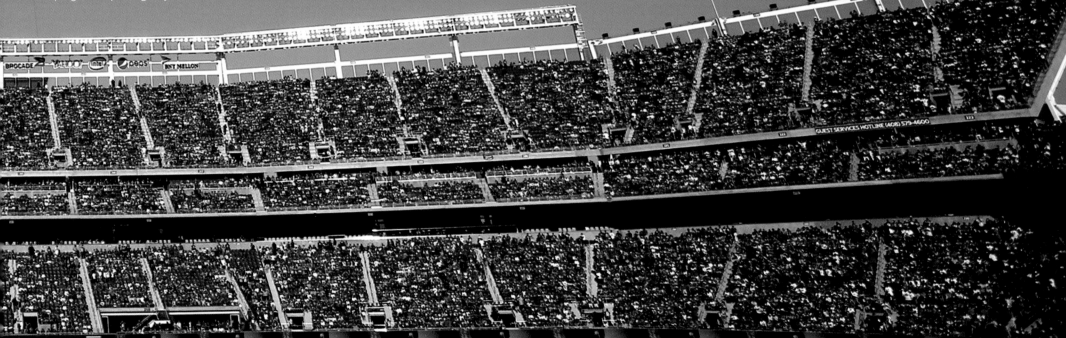

PART 2
PLAYERS 8

COACHES

"EVEN WHEN I WAS PLAYING, I NEVER THOUGHT MUCH ABOUT THE INDIVIDUAL HONORS. I WANTED TO GO TO THE SUPER BOWL."

Joe Greene

CHAPTER 7: STAR PLAYERS

ATT: Attempts // AVG: Average // AST: Assists // COMP: Completions // FF: Forced Fumbles // FG: Field Goals // FG%: Field Goal Percentages // FUM: Fumbles // FR: Fumbles Recovered
G: Games // INT: Interceptions // LNG: Longest // PCT: Percentages // REC: Receptions // RTG: Ratings // SFTY: Safeties // SCK: Sacks // TDS: Touchdowns // TCKL: Tackles // XP: Extra Points
YDS: Yards // YDS/A: Yards per Attempt // YDS/G: Yards per Game

15

HEIGHT	6'1"
WEIGHT	193
BORN	January 9, 1934
COLLEGE	University of Alabama
TEAM	Green Bay Packers, 1956–1971
POSITION	Quarterback

When the pressure was the most intense, Starr was at his best. Through all of his playoff appearances, he compiled a passer rating of 104.80—the highest of any quarterback in history. He was named the NFL MVP in 1966, the year before the Super Bowl premiered. But the accomplishment that brought him the most pride? Quarterbacking three straight national championship teams: when the Packers won the NFL Championship in 1965 and Super Bowls I and II. It's a feat that has never been replicated.

BART STARR

TDS
152

	G	COMP	ATT	PCT	YDS
	196	1,808	3,149	57.4	24,718
	INT	SCK	RTG	YDS/G	
	138	59	80.5	126.1	

NICKNAME

BART THE COOL

STARR WAS THE WINNING QUARTERBACK FOR THE ORIGINAL "ICE BOWL." THE FIELD WAS A SHEET OF ICE, AND THE AIR TEMPERATURE AT GAME TIME WAS -13°F.

SUPER BOWL APPEARANCES

I, II

4-time Pro Bowl selection (1960, 1961, 1962, 1966) | AP First-Team All-Pro (1966) | 2-time AP Second-Team All-Pro (1962, 1964) | 1966 NFL MVP
"Whizzer" White NFL Man of the Year (1966) | 5-time NFL champion (1961, 1962, 1965, 1966, 1967) | 2-time Super Bowl champion (I, II)
2-time Super Bowl MVP (I, II) | NFL 1960s All-Decade Team | Packers Hall of Fame inductee | Pro Football Hall of Fame inductee (1977)
Green Bay Packers #15 retired | Rated #51 NFL Player of All Time by NFL.com

AP Photo

HEIGHT	6'3"
WEIGHT	228
BORN	June 28, 1936
COLLEGE	West Virginia University
TEAMS	Chicago Bears, 1958–1959 Dallas Cowboys, 1961–1973
POSITION	Linebacker

54

54

Howley was inducted into the Texas Sports Hall of Fame in 2009, but his exclusion from the Pro Football Hall of Fame has prompted heated debate among Cowboys fans and students of the great defensive units of the '60s and '70s. It was such a golden age for linebackers that Howley wasn't even included on the All-Decade Team for the 1960s, even though Tom Landry once called him the greatest linebacker he ever coached.

In a 2014 fan poll conducted by the Talk of Fame Network, 70 percent of respondents said that Howley should be the next ex-Cowboy to make it to Canton—resoundingly defeating wide receiver Drew Pearson, defensive end Harvey Martin, and safety Cliff Harris.

CHUCK HOWLEY

DEFENSIVE TEAM NICKNAME

	SCK	TCKL	INT
G	N/A*	N/A	25
180			

DOOMSDAY DEFENSE

*SACKS AND FORCE FUMBLES WERE NOT KEPT AS OFFICIAL STATISTICS UNTIL 1982. THE NFL DID NOT RECORD TACKLES UNTIL 2001, ALTHOUGH SOME TEAMS KEPT THEIR OWN TALLIES BEFORE THAT YEAR.

LANDRY ONCE SAID THAT HOWLEY MIGHT HAVE MADE IT IN THE NFL AS A RUNNING BACK IF HE HADN'T BEEN TOO VALUABLE TO MOVE FROM LINEBACKER.

SUPER BOWL APPEARANCES

V, VI

6-time Pro Bowl selection (1965, 1966, 1967, 1968, 1969, 1971) | 5-time Associated Press First-Team All-Pro selection (1966, 1967, 1968, 1969, 1970) | Super Bowl V MVP | Super Bowl champion (VI) | Dallas Cowboys Ring of Honor | 20/20 Club

AP Photo

HEIGHT	6'3"
WEIGHT	218
BORN	September 2, 1948
COLLEGE	Louisiana Tech University
TEAM	Pittsburgh Steelers, 1970–1983
POSITION	Quarterback

12

Terry Bradshaw had been a Steeler for close to a decade and earned two Super Bowl rings before he finally earned the world's respect at the big game.

He was the obvious choice for MVP in Super Bowl XIII. "I don't think any other quarterback could have done what Bradshaw did to us," Dallas defensive end Harvey Martin reflected later. "We knocked him down, almost had him out at one point, but he came back. He deserved the MVP and everything he got after that game."

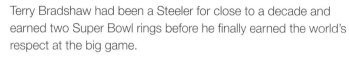

TERRY BRADSHAW

TDS 212

G	COMP	ATT	PCT	YDS
168	2,025	3,901	51.9	27,989

INT	SCK	RTG	YDS/G	
210	307	70.9	166.6	

NICKNAME

THE BLONDE BOMBER

BRADSHAW HAS APPEARED IN FOUR MOVIES AND 10 TELEVISION SERIES.

SUPER BOWL APPEARANCES

IX, X, XIII, XIV

AP Photo

4-time Super Bowl champion (IX, X, XIII, XIV) | 2-time Super Bowl MVP (XIII, XIV) | 3-time Pro Bowl (1975, 1978, 1979) | AP First-Team All-Pro (1978) | 4-time AFC champion (1974, 1975, 1978, 1979) | NFL MVP (1978) | NFL Quarterback of the Year (1978) | 2-time Pittsburgh Steelers Team MVP (1977, 1978) | 2-time NFL Passing Touchdown Leader (1978, 1982) | *Sports Illustrated* Sportsman of the Year (1979) | NFL 1970s All-Decade Team | Pittsburgh Steelers All-Time Team (50th Season) | Pittsburgh Steelers #12 retired | Louisiana Tech Athletic Hall of Fame (1984) | Senior Bowl MVP (1970) | Pro Football Hall of Fame inductee (1989) | College Football Hall of Fame inductee (1996) | Pittsburgh Steelers All-Time Team (2007) | Pittsburgh Pro Football Hall of Fame (2011) | Tied with Joe Montana as quarterback with four Super Bowl titles | One of only two quarterbacks to win back-to-back Super Bowls

FRANCO **HARRIS**

G	ATT	TDS	YDS/A	LNG	YDS/G	FUM
173	2,949	91	4.1	75	70.1	90

32

34

HEIGHT 6'2"
WEIGHT 230
BORN March 7, 1950
COLLEGE Penn State
TEAMS Pittsburgh Steelers, 1972–1983
Seattle Seahawks, 1984
POSITION Running Back

AP Photo/Harry Cabluck

YDS
12,120

SUPER BOWL APPEARANCES

IX, X, XIII, XIV

BEST PLAY

THE IMMACULATE
RECEPTION

HARRIS IS THE CO-OWNER OF A WOMAN'S FOOTBALL TEAM CALLED THE PITTSBURGH PASSION.

9-time Pro Bowl selection (1972, 1973, 1974, 1975, 1976, 1977, 1978, 1979, 1980) | AP First-Team All-Pro (1977) | AP Second-Team All-Pro (1972, 1975) | 4-time Super Bowl champion (IX, X, XIII, XIV) | Super Bowl IX MVP
2011 Pittsburgh Pro Football Hall of Fame | NFL Offensive Rookie of the Year (1972) | 1972 AFC Rookie of the Year | Walter Payton Man of the Year (1976) | NFL 1970s All-Decade Team | Pittsburgh Steelers
All-Time Team (50th Season) | Pittsburgh Steelers #32 retired | Pro Football Hall of Fame inductee (1990) | 10,000 Rushing Yards Club

LYNN **SWANN**

G	REC	YDS	AVG	LNG	YDS/G	FUM
116	336	5,462	16.3	68	47.1	11

88

HEIGHT 5'11"
WEIGHT 180
BORN March 7, 1952
COLLEGE University of Southern California
TEAM Pittsburgh Steelers / 1974–1982
POSITION Wide Receiver

AP Photo

TDS
51

SUPER BOWL APPEARANCES

IX, X, XIII, XIV

NICKNAME

SWANNY

RAN FOR GOVERNOR OF PENNSYLVANIA IN 2006 AND WAS DEFEATED BY INCUMBENT ED RENDELL.

Pop Warner Trophy (1973) | Consensus All-American (1973) | 3-time Pro Bowl selection (1975, 1977, 1978) | AP First-Team All-Pro selection (1978) | 2-time AP Second-Team All-Pro selection (1975, 1977) | 4-time Super Bowl
champion (IX, X, XIII, XIV) | Super Bowl X MVP | Walter Payton Man of the Year Award (1981) | Walter Camp Man of the Year (1996) | Pittsburgh Steelers All-Time Team (50th season) | 2014 Pittsburgh Pro Football Hall of Fame
NFL 1970s All-Decade Team | College Football Hall of Fame inductee (1993) | Pro Football Hall of Fame inductee (2001)

HEIGHT 6'3"

WEIGHT 237

BORN December 25, 1946

COLLEGE Syracuse University

TEAMS Miami Dolphins, 1968–1974, 1979
New York Giants, 1976–1978

POSITION Fullback

39

39

No Miami Dolphins team has ever reached the heights of those in the early '70s, and the backbone of those Fins offenses was Csonka, a bruising fullback known for bulldozing opposing defenses. He ran for 64 touchdowns and averaged fewer than two fumbles a season over 11 years in the NFL—and at Super Bowl VIII he became the first running back to win the MVP award.

"If Merriam or Webster had to select one all-time NFL player to be listed next to the definition of the word 'toughness' in the dictionary, former Miami Dolphins star Larry Csonka would easily get the nod," Football.com writer Corbin Smith wrote in a tribute to Csonka in 2014.

LARRY CSONKA

TDS	G	ATT	YDS	AVG
64	146	1,891	8,081	4.3
	LNG	YDS/G	FUM	
	54	55.3	21	

NICKNAME

THE LAWNMOWER

ZONK

CSONKA HAS BECOME A MOTIVATIONAL SPEAKER AND HAS HOSTED SEVERAL HUNTING AND FISHING SHOWS FOR THE NBC SPORTS NETWORK.

SUPER BOWL APPEARANCES

VII, VIII

5-time Pro Bowl (1970, 1971, 1972, 1973, 1974) | 2-time AP First-Team All-Pro (1971, 1973) | AP Second-Team All-Pro (1972) | 2-time Super Bowl champion (VII, VIII) | 3-time AFC champion (1971, 1972, 1973) | Super Bowl MVP (VIII) | PFW NFL Comeback Player of the Year (1979) | Miami Dolphins #39 retired | Pro Football Hall of Fame inductee (1987) | College Football Hall of Fame inductee (1989)

AP Photo

HEIGHT	6'3"
WEIGHT	197
BORN	February 5, 1942
COLLEGE	United States Naval Academy
TEAM	Dallas Cowboys, 1969–1979
POSITION	Quarterback

12

"Staubach was a fighter pilot who was often at his best when everything broke down around him," wrote Tim MacMahon of ESPN.com in a column comparing Staubach to Troy Aikman. "They didn't call him Roger the Dodger just because it was a catchy rhyme. He was a pure passer who also excelled at improvising, rushing for more than twice as many yards and touchdowns as Aikman over the course of his career and completing countless passes after scrambling out of trouble."

ROGER STAUBACH

TDS
153

G	COMP	ATT	PCT	YDS
131	1,685	2,958	57	22,700

INT	SCK	RTG	YDS/G	
109	313	83.5	173.3	

NICKNAMES

CAPTAIN COMEBACK

ROGER THE DODGER

A U.S. NAVAL OFFICER, STAUBACH SERVED A ONE-YEAR TOUR OF DUTY IN VIETNAM.

SUPER BOWL APPEARANCES

V, VI, X, XII, XIII

6-time Pro Bowl selection (1971, 1975, 1976, 1977, 1978, 1979) | 2-time AP All-NFC (1971, 1976) | 2-time Super Bowl champion (VI, XII) | 5-time NFC champion (1970, 1971, 1975, 1977, 1978) | NFL MVP (1971) | 1971 NFC Player of the Year | Super Bowl MVP (VI) | NFL 1970s All-Decade Team | Dallas Cowboys Ring of Honor | Pro Football Hall of Fame inductee (1985) | Rated #46 NFL Player of All Time by NFL.com

AP Photo

HEIGHT 6'4"
WEIGHT 275
BORN September 24, 1946
COLLEGE University of North Texas
TEAM Pittsburgh Steelers, 1969–1981
POSITION Defensive Tackle

75

If anyone wants to make a case for offensive bias in Super Bowl MVP selections, Joe Greene would make an excellent piece of evidence. Greene played a major role in the Pittsburgh Steelers' four titles, but he left the league after 12 games and 10 Pro Bowl selections without a single MVP trophy.

Under the guidance of defensive coordinator Bud Carson, in 1974 he started lining up at a sharp angle between guard and center, and it was an adjustment that helped spark Pittsburgh's first AFC Championship and first Super Bowl ring.

JOE GREENE

G 181	SCK N/A*	TCKL N/A	INT 1

NICKNAME

MEAN JOE GREENE

*SACKS AND FORCE FUMBLES WERE NOT KEPT AS OFFICIAL STATISTICS UNTIL 1982. THE NFL DID NOT RECORD TACKLES UNTIL 2001, ALTHOUGH SOME TEAMS KEPT THEIR OWN TALLIES BEFORE THAT YEAR.

GREENE WAS THE LEADER AND THE ANCHOR OF THE "STEEL CURTAIN" DEFENSE THAT WON FOUR SUPER BOWLS.

SUPER BOWL APPEARANCES

IX, X, XIII, XIV

Pro Football Hall of Fame (1987) | 10-time Pro Bowl (1969, 1970, 1971, 1972, 1973, 1974, 1975, 1976, 1978, 1979) | 5-time First-Team All-Pro (1972, 1973, 1974, 1977, 1979) | 3-time Second-Team All-Pro (1969, 1971, 1975) | 11-time First-Team All-AFC (1969, 1970, 1971, 1972, 1973, 1974, 1975, 1976, 1977, 1978, 1979) | 4-time Super Bowl champion (IX, X, XIII, XIV) | NFL 75th Anniversary All-Time Team | NFL 1970s All-Decade Team | Pittsburgh Steelers All-Time Team (50th Season) | Pittsburgh Steelers All-Time Team | 1969 NFL Defensive Rookie of the Year | 2-time AP NFL Defensive Player of the Year (1972, 1974) | 2-time KCC 101 AFC Defensive Player of the Year (1972, 1974) | 2-time NEA NFL Defensive MVP winner (1972, 1974) | Pittsburgh Steelers #75 retired | 2011 Pittsburgh Pro Football Hall of Fame | Ranked #13 NFL Player of All-Time by NFL.com

AP Photo

HEIGHT	6'4"
WEIGHT	220
BORN	July 8, 1952
COLLEGE	Kent State University
TEAM	Pittsburgh Steelers, 1974–1984
POSITION	Linebacker

58

He was a tenacious tackler, an Iron Man in a Steel Curtain and the physical and emotional center of the Pittsburgh Steelers' defense that claimed four Super Bowl titles. His numerous accolades and his single-mindedness on the field have led many to name Jack Lambert as the best middle linebacker of his era.

"When you start talking about attitude and focus, Jack is the epitome," Lambert's legendary coach Chuck Noll once said about him. "He was the most focused individual I've ever had."

JACK **LAMBERT**

G 146	SCK 8*	TCKL N/A	INT 28

NICKNAMES

JACK SPLAT
COUNT DRACULA

*SACKS AND FORCE FUMBLES WERE NOT KEPT AS OFFICIAL STATISTICS UNTIL 1982. THE NFL DID NOT RECORD TACKLES UNTIL 2001, ALTHOUGH SOME TEAMS KEPT THEIR OWN TALLIES BEFORE THAT YEAR.

MANY PRO FOOTBALL COACHES AND SCOUTS THOUGHT LAMBERT WAS TOO SMALL TO PLAY LINEBACKER IN THE NFL.

SUPER BOWL APPEARANCES

IX, X, XIII, XIV

9-time Pro Bowl (1975, 1976, 1977, 1978, 1979, 1980, 1981, 1982, 1983) | 7-time First-Team All-Pro (1975, 1976, 1979, 1980, 1981, 1982, 1983) | 1-time Second-Team All-Pro (1978) | 4-time Super Bowl champion (IX, X, XIII, XIV) | 2-time Pittsburgh Steelers Team MVP (1976, 1981) | Pittsburgh Steelers All-Time Team | Pittsburgh Steelers All-Time Team (50th Season) | 2011 Pittsburgh Pro Football Hall of Fame | NFL 75th Anniversary All-Time Team | NFL 1980s All-Decade Team | NFL 1970s All-Decade Team | 1974 NFL Defensive Rookie of the Year | 1976 PFWA Defensive Player of the Year | NFL Defensive Player of the Year (1976) | 1983 NEA NFL Defensive Player of the Year | AFC Defensive Player of the Year (1976) | 20/20 Club | Pittsburgh Steelers #58 retired | Ranked #29 on NFL.com's Top 100 Players of All Time | Pro Football Hall of Fame inductee (1990)

AP Photo/Rusty Kennedy

HEIGHT 6'2"
WEIGHT 205
BORN June 11, 1956
COLLEGE University of Notre Dame
TEAMS San Francisco 49ers, 1979–1992
Kansas City Chiefs, 1993–1994
POSITION Quarterback

Like a golfer who performs at the top of his game for the majors, Joe Montana was at his best when he took the field for a Super Bowl. Time and again, on his way to four rings and three MVP titles with the San Francisco 49ers, Montana unveiled a new level of clutch when the most was on the line.

"There have been, and will be, much better arms and legs and much better bodies on quarterbacks in the NFL," former teammate Randy Cross told ESPN.com. "But if you have to win a game or score a touchdown or win a championship, the only guy to get is Joe Montana."

JOE MONTANA

TDS	G	COMP	ATT	PCT	YDS
273	192	2,929	4,600	63.2	40,551
	INT	SCK	RTG	YDS/G	
	139	313	92.3	211.2	

NICKNAMES

JOE COOL
COMEBACK KID

NOTED FOR HIS ABILITY TO REMAIN CALM UNDER PRESSURE, MONTANA HELPED HIS TEAMS TO 31 FOURTH-QUARTER COME-FROM-BEHIND WINS.

SUPER BOWL APPEARANCES

XVI, XIX, XXIII, XXIV

4-time Super Bowl champion (XVI, XIX, XXIII, XXIV) | 3-time Super Bowl MVP (XVI, XIX, XXIV) | 8-time Pro Bowl (1981, 1983, 1984, 1985, 1987, 1989, 1990, 1993) | 3-time AP First-Team All-Pro (1987, 1989, 1990) | 2-time NFL MVP (1989, 1990) | 2-time AP Second-Team All-Pro (1981, 1984) | 1989 NFL Offensive Player of the Year | 4-time NFC champion (1981, 1984, 1988, 1989) | PFW NFL Comeback Player of the Year (1986) | UPI NFC Player of the Year (1989) | 1989 Sportsman/Athlete of the Year | 1990 Sportsman/Athlete of the Year | 1977 NCAA Division I national champion | Cotton Bowl Classic MVP (1979) | NFL 1980s All-Decade Team | NFL 75th Anniversary All-Time Team | San Francisco 49ers #16 retired | Pro Football Hall of Fame inductee (2000)

AP Photo/Greg Trott

HEIGHT	6'2"
WEIGHT	200
BORN	October 13, 1962
COLLEGE	Mississippi Valley State
TEAMS	San Francisco 49ers, 1985–2000
	Oakland Raiders, 2001–2004
	Seattle Seahawks, 2004
	Denver Broncos, 2005*
	*Off-season and/or practice squad member only
POSITION	Wide Receiver

The brightest spot in the annals of Jerry Rice's brilliant Super Bowl career was Super Bowl XXIII, the 49ers' dramatic comeback effort against the Cincinnati Bengals. He pulled in 11 passes for 215 yards that day (both Super Bowl records) to form one half, with Joe Montana, of the most powerful offensive duo ever to take a Super Bowl field. It was his sole MVP award, but just one key piece of his Super Bowl footprint.

"I was always in search of that perfect game, and I never got it," he said at his Hall of Fame ceremony. "Even if I caught 10 of 12 passes, or two of three touchdowns in the Super Bowl, I would dwell on the one pass I dropped. I played for 20 years and I still believe in my heart I could play today. I played that long because I love this game of football. I loved everything about it, especially the fans. The stadium was my stage, and I was there every Sunday to put on a performance for the fans."

JERRY RICE

SUPER BOWL APPEARANCES
XXIII, XXIV, XXIX, XXXVII

NICKNAME

TDS	G	REC	YDS	AVG
197	303	1,549	22,895	14.8
	LNG	YDS/G	FUM	
	96	75.6	27	

WORLD

Rated #1 Greatest Player of All Time on the Top 100: NFL's Greatest Players | 3-time Super Bowl champion (XXIII, XXIV, XXIX) | Super Bowl MVP (XXIII) | 3-time NFC champion (1988, 1989, 1994) | AFC champion (2002) | 10-time AP First-Team All-Pro (1986, 1987, 1988, 1989, 1990, 1992, 1993, 1994, 1995, 1996) | 2-time AP Second-Team All-Pro (1991, 2002) | 13-time Pro Bowl (1986, 1987, 1988, 1989, 1990, 1991, 1992, 1993, 1994, 1995, 1996, 1998, 2002) | Pro Bowl MVP (1995) | 2-time AP NFL Offensive Player of the Year (1987, 1993) | 2-time NFC Offensive Player of the Year (1986, 1987) | PFWA MVP (1988) | UPI NFC Player of the Year (1988) | UPI NFC Rookie of the Year (1985) | Bert Bell Award (1987) | NFL 75th Anniversary All-Time Team | NFL 1980s All-Decade Team | NFL 1990s All-Decade Team | San Francisco 49ers #80 retired | College Football Hall of Fame inductee (2006) | Pro Football Hall of Fame inductee (2010) | NFL's All-Time Leader in Receptions | NFL's All-Time Leader in Receiving Yards NFL's All-Time Leader in Receiving Touchdowns

HEIGHT	6'5"
WEIGHT	265
BORN	December 13, 1960
COLLEGE	Tennessee State University
TEAMS	Chicago Bears, 1983–1993
	San Francisco 49ers, 1994–1995
	Chicago Bears, 1995–1996
	Indianapolis Colts, 1996–1997
	Philadelphia Eagles, 1997
POSITION	Defensive End

One of the most prolific tacklers on that team's vaunted defensive unit, Dent notched 17.5 sacks in 1984, just his second season with the Bears after arriving as an eighth-round draft pick out of Tennessee State. The next year, he picked up 17 more sacks, a Super Bowl ring, and an MVP trophy, recording three tackles, 1.5 sacks, and two forced fumbles while rendering New England's offensive efforts wholly ineffective.

RICHARD DENT

SCK	G	TCKL	AST	SFTY
	203	671	6	1
137.5	FF	INT		
	37	8		

NICKNAME

THE COLONEL

DENT WAS A FEATURED SOLOIST OF THE "SHUFFLING CREW" IN THE "SUPER BOWL SHUFFLE" VIDEO IN 1985.

SUPER BOWL APPEARANCES

XX, XXIX

AP Photo/NFL Photos

4-time Pro Bowl selection (1984, 1985, 1990, 1993) | 4-time All-Pro selection (1984, 1985, 1988, 1990)
2-time Super Bowl champion (XX, XXIX) | Super Bowl XX MVP | 100 Sacks Club | Pro Football Hall of Fame inductee (2011)

HEIGHT	6'5"
WEIGHT	255
BORN	January 6, 1964
COLLEGE	James Madison University
TEAMS	San Francisco 49ers, 1986–1991
	Dallas Cowboys, 1992–1996
	San Francisco 49ers, 1998–1999
POSITIONS	Defensive End, Linebacker

With a half century of Super Bowls in the book, only one man had won rings at 10 percent of them. Other players have competed in more Super Bowls than former San Francisco and Dallas defender Charles Haley, but no other individual has come away a winner five times.

An intense competitor known for brash, outspoken behavior during his playing career, Haley told the campus newspaper at his alma mater, James Madison University, that he was driven through his career by the ultimate prize: a chance to hold the Lombardi Trophy.

CHARLES HALEY

SCK	G	TCKL	AST	SFTY
100.5	169	485	13	1
	FF	INT		
	26	9		

NICKNAME

LAST NAKED WARRIOR

HALEY IS THE ONLY PLAYER IN NFL HISTORY WITH FIVE SUPER BOWL RINGS.

SUPER BOWL APPEARANCES

XXIII, XXIV, XXVII, XXVIII, XXX

2-time UPI NFC Defensive Player of the Year (1990, 1994) | 5-time Pro Bowl selection (1988, 1990, 1991, 1994, 1995) | 2-time All-Pro selection (1990, 1994)
5-time Super Bowl champion (XXIII, XXIV, XXVII, XXVIII, XXX) | 100 Sacks Club | Dallas Cowboys Ring of Honor | Pro Football Hall of Fame inductee (2015)

AP Photo/Greg Trott

"I'M GOING TO DISNEY WORLD!"

When Phil Simms became the first Super Bowl MVP to shout, "I'm going to Disney World!" after his New York Giants won Super Bowl XXI, he won more than just a trip to the Magic Kingdom. The now-iconic commercial, launched with Simms in 1987 and filmed with a new star player every year but one since, came with a $75,000 payday. The Disney commercial (some players visit Disney World and other Disneyland), has aired after every Super Bowl except in 2005, but the player at its center isn't always the MVP. After Super Bowl XLIX, for instance, Patriots quarterback Tom Brady won the MVP award, but defensive back Malcolm Butler, who saved the game for New England with an end-zone interception, was the one who got to hang out with Mickey Mouse.

HINESWARD

MALCOLM**SMITH**

AP Photo/John Raoux

JEROME**BETTIS**

AP Photo/John R...

TOM**BRADY**

Walt Disney World
WELCOMES
TOM BRADY
SUPER BOWL MVP

AP Photo/Peter Cosgrove

KURT**WARNER**

AP Photo/Marc Serota

HEIGHT   6'4"
WEIGHT   220
BORN   November 21, 1966
COLLEGE   University of California, Los Angeles
TEAM   Dallas Cowboys, 1989–2000
POSITION   Quarterback

8

When Aikman was immortalized in the Hall of Fame, former Cowboys offensive coordinator Norv Turner told the crowd about an interviewer who asked him which starting quarterback he would choose, out of any in the past or present in the NFL, for a crucial game.

"It was really a very easy question for me to answer," Turner said. "I told them I'd choose Troy. The interviewer politely asked me why, and I said, 'Because I want to win.' I further explained my answer. 'Troy was consistently the most accurate passer I've ever seen. What fans saw on Sundays, his teammates saw every day of the week.'"

TROY AIKMAN

TDS
165

G	COMP	ATT	PCT	YDS
165	2,898	4,715	61.5	32,942

INT	SCK	RTG	YDS/G	
141	259	81.6	199.6	

NICKNAMES

ROY
GODFATHER

KNOWN FOR STICKING
OUT HIS TONGUE WHEN
HE THROWS THE FOOTBALL.

SUPER BOWL APPEARANCES
XXVII, XXVIII, XXX

Consensus All-American (1988) | **Davey O'Brien Award (1989)** | 6-time Pro Bowl (1991, 1992, 1993, 1994, 1995, 1996) | *Sporting News* **First-Team All-Pro (1993)** | 2-time UPI Second-Team All-NFC (1994, 1995) | **3-time Super Bowl champion (XXVII, XXVIII, XXX)** | Super Bowl MVP (XXVII) 3-time NFC champion (1992, 1993, 1995) | **Walter Payton Man of the Year (1996)** | Dallas Cowboys Ring of Honor inductee (2005) | Pro Football Hall of Fame inductee (2006) | **College Football Hall of Fame inductee (2008)** | NCAA Silver Anniversary Award (2014) | Dallas Cowboys all-time career leader (career wins, pass attempts, pass completions, interceptions)

AP Photo/Tom DiPace

HEIGHT	5'9"
WEIGHT	210
BORN	May 15, 1969
COLLEGE	University of Florida
TEAMS	Dallas Cowboys, 1990–2002
	Arizona Cardinals, 2003–2004
POSITION	Running Back

22

22

There is much to say about Emmitt Smith, but a good starting point is 1993, the brightest point in an almost blinding career. In that one season, Smith won the NFL rushing crown, the NFL Most Valuable Player, the Super Bowl title, and the Super Bowl MVP award. No other pro player has ever been so decorated in such a short period of time.

"He's done everything possible that a running back could do," said former Cowboys safety Darren Woodson. "He's broken every record, he was a leader on and off the field, and the city of Dallas recognizes how special he was. Not only that, but the people of Phoenix started realizing how important he was to that team."

EMMITT SMITH

YDS	G	ATT	TDS	YDS/A	LNG
18,355	226	4,409	164	4.2	75
	YDS/G	FUM			
	81.2	61			

OFFENSIVE TEAM NICKNAME

THE TRIPLETS
(SMITH / AIKMAN / IRVIN)

SMITH WON THE THIRD SEASON OF *DANCING WITH THE STARS* IN 2006.

SUPER BOWL APPEARANCES

XXVII, XXVIII, XXX

8-time Pro Bowl (1990, 1991, 1992, 1993, 1994, 1995, 1998, 1999) | **4-time First-Team All-Pro (1992, 1993, 1994, 1995)** | Second-Team All-Pro (1991) | 4-time First-Team All-NFC (1992, 1993, 1994, 1995) | 2-time Second-Team All-NFC (1991, 1996) | **4-time NFL rushing leader (1991, 1992, 1993, 1995)** | 3-time Super Bowl champion (XXVII, XXVIII, XXX) | **Super Bowl MVP (XXVIII)** | 3-time NFC champion (1992, 1993, 1995) | **NFL 1990s All-Decade Team** | NFL Offensive Rookie of the Year (1990) | **NFL MVP (1992)** | NFL MVP (1993) | **NFL/NFC Offensive Player of the Year (1993)** | Dallas Cowboys Ring of Honor | **Pro Football Hall of Fame inductee (2010)**

AP Photo/Paul Spinelli

HEIGHT	6'3"
WEIGHT	215
BORN	June 28, 1960
COLLEGE	Stanford University
TEAM	Denver Broncos, 1983–1998
POSITION	Quarterback

7

By the time his 16-year career had concluded, Elway and the Denver Broncos had claimed two Super Bowl titles and an MVP award. But before he could claim a share of the Lombardi Trophy, he brought his Broncos to three Super Bowls—and lost all three.

It took Elway eight long years to get back, but when the Broncos faced the Green Bay Packers in Super Bowl XXXII, he finally tasted victory, with a 31-24 win powered by running back Terrell Davis. "Finally, after three Super Bowl failures, Elway's magnificent career is whole," wrote Rich Cimini of the *New York Daily News*. "At last, he has a Super Bowl legacy to stand on."

JOHN ELWAY

TDS
300

G	COMP	ATT	PCT	YDS
234	4,123	7,250	56.9	51,475
INT	SCK	RTG	YDS/G	
226	516	79.9	220.0	

NICKNAME

THE GENERAL

ELWAY IS THE OLDEST QUARTERBACK TO WIN A SUPER BOWL, WINNING HIS LAST AT THE AGE OF 38.

SUPER BOWL APPEARANCES

XXI, XXII, XXVI, XXXII, XXXIII

2-time Super Bowl champion (XXXII, XXXIII) | Super Bowl MVP (XXXIII) | 5-time AFC champion (1986, 1987, 1989, 1997, 1998) | 9-time Pro Bowl selection (1986, 1987, 1989, 1991, 1993, 1994, 1996, 1997, 1998) | 3-time AP Second-Team All-Pro (1987, 1993, 1996) | 4-time PFW First-Team All-AFC (1987, 1993, 1996, 1997) | AP NFL MVP (1987) | 2-time UPI AFC Offensive Player of the Year (1987, 1993) | Walter Payton NFL Man of the Year (1992) | Walter Camp Man of the Year (2009) | NFL 1990s All-Decade Team | Denver Broncos Ring of Fame | Denver Broncos #7 retired | Colorado Sports Hall of Fame | Pro Football Hall of Fame inductee (2004) | Denver Broncos all-time career leader (career wins, pass attempts, pass completions, passing yards, passing touchdowns, interceptions)

AP Photo/David Durochik

HEIGHT 5'11"

WEIGHT 210

BORN October 28, 1972

COLLEGE University of Georgia

TEAM Denver Broncos, 1995–2001

POSITION Running Back

Davis had only four healthy seasons in the NFL, but his accolades in that short span made up for his lack of longevity. At his peak, before knee problems truncated his career, Davis gained 2,008 yards and 21 touchdowns in the 1998 season alone, and he was twice named the league's Offensive Player of the Year.

Super Bowl XXXII marked the Broncos' vindication after four losses in the big game, and Davis came up big, becoming the first player to rush for three touchdowns in the Super Bowl and claiming the MVP award. "He reminded me of Jim Brown," Broncos running back Derek Loville said after the game.

TERRELL DAVIS

YDS	G	ATT	TDS	YDS/A	LNG
7,607	78	1,605	60	4.6	71
	YDS/G	FUM			
	97.5	20			

NICKNAME

T.D.

IN 2008, DAVIS ANALYZED BARACK OBAMA'S SPEECH ACCEPTING THE DEMOCRATIC PRESIDENTIAL NOMINATION ON AN EPISODE OF *THE COLBERT REPORT*.

SUPER BOWL APPEARANCES

XXXII, XXXIII

3-time Pro Bowl (1996, 1997, 1998) | 3-time First-Team All-Pro (1996, 1997, 1998) | 2-time Super Bowl champion (XXXII, XXXIII) | 2-time NFL Offensive Player of the Year (1996, 1998) | NFL MVP (AP, PFWA, SN, 1998) | UPI AFC Player of the Year (1996) | Super Bowl MVP (XXXII) | 3-time AFC rushing leader (1996, 1997, 1998) | NFL 1990s All-Decade Team | Single-Season 2,000 Rushing Yards Club | Denver Broncos 50th Anniversary Team | Denver Broncos all-time career leader (rushing attempts, rushing yards, rushing touchdowns)

HEIGHT	6'4"
WEIGHT	225
BORN	August 3, 1977
COLLEGE	University of Michigan
TEAM	New England Patriots, 2000–present
POSITION	Quarterback

In the modern era of the Super Bowl, no player has made as bold a mark on the big game as New England Patriots quarterback Tom Brady. Despite two difficult defeats to the New York Giants in Super Bowls XLII and XLVI, Brady returned to form in Super Bowl XLIX by commanding a late fourth-quarter drive that snatched victory from the Seattle Seahawks.

The win propelled Brady to new prominence in the Super Bowl record books. He shares the mark for most Super Bowl MVP awards (3) with Joe Montana and broke the record for most pass completions (37) and career Super Bowl touchdowns (13). He also became one of only three quarterbacks (with Montana and Terry Bradshaw) to claim four rings.

TOM BRADY

NICKNAME

TOM TERRIFIC

TDS	G	COMP	ATT	PCT	YDS
392	209	4,551	7,168	63.5	53,258
	INT	SCK	RTG	YDS/G	
	143	364	95.9	254.8	

BRADY HOLDS THE RECORD FOR THE MOST TOUCHDOWN PASSES IN A REGULAR SEASON WITH A TOTAL OF 50.

SUPER BOWL APPEARANCES

XXXVI, XXXVIII, XXXIX, XLII, XLVI, XLIX

4-time Super Bowl champion (XXXVI, XXXVIII, XXXIX, XLIX) | **3-time Super Bowl MVP (XXXVI, XXXVIII, XLIX)** | 6-time AFC champion (2001, 2003, 2004, 2007, 2011, 2014) | **2-time NFL MVP (2007, 2010)** | 2-time First-Team All-Pro (2007, 2010) | **Second-Team All-Pro (2005)** | 10-time Pro Bowl (2001, 2004, 2005, 2007, 2009, 2010, 2011, 2012, 2013, 2014) | **3-time NFL passing touchdowns leader (2002, 2007, 2010)** | 2-time NFL passing yards leader (2005, 2007) | *Sports Illustrated* Sportsman of the Year (2005) | *Sporting News* Sportsman of the Year (2004, 2007) | AP Male Athlete of the Year (2007) | **2-time NFL Offensive Player of the Year (2007, 2010)** | 3-time AFC Offensive Player of the Year (2007, 2010, 2011) | AP NFL Comeback Player of the Year (2009) | **PFWA NFL Comeback Player of the Year (2009)** | New England Patriots all-time leader (passing touchdowns, passing yards, pass completions, pass attempts, career wins) | NFL 2000s All-Decade Team

AP Photo/ Robert E. Klein

HEIGHT	6'0"
WEIGHT	209
BORN	December 28, 1972
COLLEGE	South Dakota State University
TEAMS	New England Patriots, 1996–2005 Indianapolis Colts, 2006–present
POSITION	Placekicker

4

4

Only four Super Bowls have been decided by a field goal, and two of those came from the foot of the same man—Adam Vinatieri. As the only kicker to win four Super Bowl rings and, as of 2015, the oldest active player in the NFL, Vinatieri has come to embody consistency and perseverance in a profession not characterized by either.

"It's very comforting to know if the game does come down to it, you're sending a guy out there that has kicked two game-winners for Super Bowl rings," Colts coach Chuck Pagano said of Vinatieri.

ADAM VINATIERI

NICKNAME

AUTOMATIC ADAM
MR. CLUTCH

ATT	G	FG
	303	478
571	FG%	XP%
	83.7	98.6

VINATIERI IS THE FIRST KICKER EVER TO WIN FOUR SUPER BOWL RINGS.

SUPER BOWL APPEARANCES

XXXI, XXXVI, XXXVIII, XXXIX, XLI

AP Photo/Tom DiPace

3-time Pro Bowl (2002, 2004, 2014) | **3-time First-Team All-Pro (2002, 2004, 2014)** | 2-time Golden Toe Award (2002, 2004) | **4-time Super Bowl champion (XXXVI, XXXVIII, XXXIX, XLI)** | 6-time AFC champion (1996, 2001, 2003, 2004, 2006, 2009) | **NFL Alumni Special Teams Player of the Year (2004)** | New England Patriots All-1990s Team | **New England Patriots All-2000s Team** | New England Patriots 50th Anniversary Team | **NFL 2000s All-Decade Team**

HEIGHT 6'4"
WEIGHT 218
BORN January 3, 1981
COLLEGE University of Mississippi
TEAM New York Giants, 2000–present
POSITION Quarterback

Other quarterbacks have more rings, and plenty have appeared in more Super Bowls. But no other signal caller has pulled out two comebacks like the ones directed by Eli Manning in Super Bowls XLII and XLVI.

In two Super Bowls with the Giants, Manning pulled out clutch performances punctuated by peerless catches, and his rewards both times were MVP trophies. He might be the younger brother in the long shadow of Peyton, but Eli is the Manning with the superior Super Bowl credentials.

ELI MANNING

NICKNAME

EASY

TDS	G	COMP	ATT	PCT	YDS
259	169	3,308	5,609	59.0	39,755
	INT	SCK	RTG	YDS/G	
	185	280	82.4	235.2	

MANNING WAS NAMED MOST VALUABLE PLAYER IN EACH SUPER BOWL, BECOMING ONE OF FIVE QUARTERBACKS IN HISTORY TO HAVE BEEN GIVEN THIS HONOR TWICE.

SUPER BOWL APPEARANCES

XLII, XLVI

2-time Super Bowl champion (XLII, XLVI) | 2-time Super Bowl MVP (XLII, XLVI) | 3-time Pro Bowl (2008, 2011, 2012) | 2-time NFC champion (2007, 2011) | *Sporting News* Sportsman of the Year (2008) | Johnny Unitas Golden Arm Award (2003) | Maxwell Award (2003) | NFL season record for fourth-quarter touchdown passes (15) | NFL season record for game-winning drives (8) | Most road wins in a single regular season and postseason by a starting quarterback (10) | Most passing yards in a single postseason (1,219) | New York Giants all-time leader (pass attempts, pass completions, passing touchdowns, passing yards) | New York Giants 80th Anniversary Team (2005)

AP Photo/Paul Sancya

HEIGHT 6'1"
WEIGHT 240
BORN May 15, 1975
COLLEGE Miami (FL)
TEAM Baltimore Ravens, 1996–2012
POSITION Middle Linebacker

52

Ray Lewis's two Super Bowls were a dozen years apart, and his presence on the field was so intimidating in the first one that he became just the sixth defensive player to earn the MVP award. But the second ring, clinched by a goal-line stand with Lewis as the heart of the defense, created a more compelling story because it became his last game after an unparalleled 17-year career.

"How could it end any other way than that?" Lewis told ESPN.com after Super Bowl XLVII. "And now I get to ride into the sunset with my second ring."

RAY LEWIS

TCKL	G	INT	AST
1,562	**228**	**31**	**493**
	SCK	SFTY	FF
	41.5	**1**	**19**

NICKNAME

MUFASA

LEWIS WAS THE FEATURED ATHLETE ON THE COVER OF THE MADDEN NFL 2005 VIDEO GAME.

SUPER BOWL APPEARANCES

XXXV, XLVII

2-time Super Bowl champion (XXXV, XLVII) | Super Bowl XXXV MVP | 13-time Pro Bowl (1997, 1998, 1999, 2000, 2001, 2003, 2004, 2006, 2007, 2008, 2009, 2010, 2011) | 7-time First-Team All-Pro (1999, 2000, 2001, 2003, 2004, 2008, 2009) | 3-time Second-Team All-Pro (1997, 1998, 2010) | 2-time AP NFL Defensive Player of the Year (2000, 2003) | 2-time AFC champion (2000, 2012) | 3-time AFC Defensive Player of the Year (2000, 2001, 2003) | 2-time NFL Alumni Linebacker of the Year (1999, 2003) | NFL 2000s All-Decade Team | Baltimore Ravens all-time career leader in tackles

AP Photo/Greg Trott

"THAT'S THE BIGGEST GAP IN SPORTS. THE DIFFERENCE BETWEEN THE WINNER AND THE LOSER OF THE SUPER BOWL."

John Madden

CHAPTER 8: STAR COACHES

VINCE LOMBARDI

CAREER AS COACH / ADMINISTRATOR

NEW YORK GIANTS	1954–1958	Offensive Coordinator
GREEN BAY PACKERS	1959–1967	Head Coach
GREEN BAY PACKERS	1968	General Manager
WASHINGTON REDSKINS	1969	Head Coach

AP Photo

In the decades that would follow Vince Lombardi's adoption of the Super Bowl as his team's personal playground, coaches would come along who would win three, even four, of the trophies that bear his name.

Lombardi won only two, which in some accountings would put him as a runner-up when considering the greatest Super Bowl coaches in the game's first half century. But he also took three NFL Championships in the years before the Super Bowl was established, and his footprint on the foundation of America's most epic sporting event is undeniable.

The image of Lombardi has become larger-than-life over the decades, a man immortalized in maxims and eponymous awards, so that his complexities as a man and as a coach have faded into the power of the myth. Lombardi was indeed a football genius and a visionary, a master motivator who advanced the game, even if he was prone to profane tirades and a lack of encouragement for the players in his locker room.

He came to the NFL from assistant coaching stints at Army and Fordham University when he accepted the offensive coordinator position with the New York Giants. Coaching side by side with defensive coordinator Tom Landry, Lombardi developed a reputation for obsessive attention to detail and innovative schemes that succeeded in putting points on the board.

In his first head coaching season, 1959 with the Green Bay Packers, Lombardi was named NFL Coach of the Year. Riding the force of his famed "power sweep" running play, his Packers won the NFL Championships in 1961, 1962, and 1965, and when the commissioners of the NFL and the AFL hatched the plan for the first world championship game in 1967, the Packers punched their ticket with a 12-2 record.

Lombardi led the Packers to victory in that first Super Bowl, 35-10 over the Kansas City Chiefs, and then reinforced his status as the greatest coach in the game the next year with a 33-14 victory over the Oakland Raiders. His team's average margin of victory in the two Super Bowls was 22 points, and if he had not made the decision to step away from the head coaching position after that season, he might have won another one.

Certainly, with such an emphatic claim to its first two Super Bowl titles, Lombardi left his mark on the game's record books. But he also influenced the spirit of the championship with a laser focus on excellence that made him a model to hundreds of coaches who would search for ways to motivate their teams in the years after he left his mark. The man who liked to remind his teams that "perfection is not attainable, but if we chase perfection, we can catch excellence" helped instill that excellence in the game of football at large and in its final postseason showdown.

AP Photo/NFL Photo/Vernon Biever

SUPER BOWL TITLES

2

REGULAR-SEASON RECORD

96-34-6

POSTSEASON RECORD

9-1

COMPOSITE RECORD

105-35-6

NFL COACH OF THE YEAR	1959 1961
WESTERN CONFERENCE TITLES	6
NFL CHAMPIONSHIPS (PRE-SUPER BOWL)	3

CHUCK NOLL

CAREER AS COACH / ADMINISTRATOR

SAN DIEGO CHARGERS	1960–1961	Defensive Line
SAN DIEGO CHARGERS	1962–1965	Defensive Coordinator Defensive Backfield
BALTIMORE COLTS	1966–1968	Defensive Coordinator Defensive Backfield
PITTSBURGH STEELERS	1969–1991	Head Coach

When Chuck Noll retired from coaching the Pittsburgh Steelers in 1991, the Pro Football Hall of Fame had not yet instituted a five-year waiting period between retirement and nomination. Fewer than two years later, Noll was enshrined—a legend who won more Super Bowls than any other coach and oversaw the deliberate construction of the Steelers dynasty of the 1970s.

Noll's fundamentals-first, businesslike approach to coaching football was illustrated vividly when he accepted the job with the Steelers in 1969. Up until that point, the team that is now considered one of the giants in NFL history had never won any kind of title and had recorded five consecutive losing seasons.

At the press conference where he was introduced, the media pressed him about the mess he was inheriting. "We'll change history," Noll said. "Losing has nothing to do with geography."

The quiet, steady Noll understood that history was rarely changed overnight, so he installed his system with the players already in the Steelers locker room and worked steadily to reinforce the team from both inside and outside. In the first two drafts after he took the job, he selected Joe Greene and Terry Bradshaw, two of nine Hall of Famers who came to the Steelers between 1969 and 1974 and comprised the backbone of the team that would soon take the Super Bowl by force.

With Noll's background as a defensive genius paired with his innovative defensive coordinator Bud Carson, the Steel Curtain started frustrating offenses on a regular basis, first shining on the world's biggest football stage in Super Bowl IX, with a 16-6 victory over the Minnesota Vikings. Noll, never one for flash or chatty media interviews, would nonetheless become a fixture during Super Bowl week for the next decade by winning three more rings in Super Bowls X, XIII, and XIV.

In the era before free agency, Noll stayed with the same team for 22 years and built a living monument to the game with players who shared his loyalty to the franchise. When he retired, he characteristically faded into the background, never writing a book or taking an endorsement deal. He avoided the spotlight, but his death at the age of 82 in 2014 made a media splash nonetheless.

"One of the lessons I learned from him was that you've never arrived, that you never get to the point where you are the best that you can be," wide receiver John Stallworth, who played on all four Super Bowl title teams, told ESPN.com's Scott Brown after his coach's death. "You could always get better at something. Don't just settle for where you are. I think I carry that more than anything. You can always be better."

SUPER BOWL TITLES

4

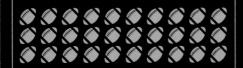

REGULAR-SEASON RECORD

193-148-1

POSTSEASON RECORD

16-8

COMPOSITE RECORD

209-156-1

UPI AFC COACH
OF THE YEAR — 1972

MAXWELL
FOOTBALL CLUB
NFL COACH OF
THE YEAR — 1989

AFC
CHAMPIONSHIPS — 4

BILL WALSH

CAREER AS COACH / ADMINISTRATOR

OAKLAND RAIDERS	1966	Running Backs Coach
CONTINENTAL FOOTBALL LEAGUE	1967	Coach
CINCINNATI BENGALS	1968–1975	Assistant Coach
SAN DIEGO CHARGERS	1976	Offensive Coordinator
STANFORD	1977–1978	Head Coach
SAN FRANCISCO 49ERS	1979–1988	Head Coach
STANFORD	1992–1994	Head Coach
SAN FRANCISCO 49ERS	1999–2001	Vice President and General Manager
SAN FRANCISCO 49ERS	2002–2004	Consultant

AP Photo/Paul Spinelli

Bill Walsh was calling the plays as the offensive coordinator for the Cincinnati Bengals in the early '70s under NFL legend Paul Brown, the team's head coach and general manager. Walsh was biding his time until he could run a team of his own and fully unleash his innovative offensive philosophy.

When Brown retired in 1975 and named a different assistant, Bill Johnson, to the top job, a wounded Walsh returned home to the West Coast. It would be four more years, after a year as a coordinator with the Chargers and two as the head coach at Stanford, before he would finally be at the helm of an NFL team.

Despite the amount of mental preparation Walsh had put in as he awaited his dream job, his first two San Francisco 49ers teams went 2-14 and 6-10. In that second season, 1980, the 49ers' fortunes were slowly starting to turn on the arm of an undersized quarterback named Joe Montana who was the perfect field general for Walsh's highly scripted, precise scheme.

Al Saunders, a longtime offensive coordinator for a host of NFL teams and a lifelong friend of Walsh, was witness to the offensive revolution that rippled through the game when Walsh started succeeding with principles such as scripted plays; obsessive attention to detail on every snap; short, methodical gains; and precise timing. "Bill approached football as an intellectual game; a game of strategy and execution," Saunders told Ron Jaworski in *The Games That Changed the Game*. "He saw it as an art form, a thing of beauty, something to be choreographed with everything working in harmony."

Walsh didn't even know whether the 49ers brass would keep him around long enough to see the fulfillment of the program he was assembling, but it was a good thing they were patient. In his third season in San Francisco, he led his team to its first Super Bowl appearance in Super Bowl XVI, and they displayed the West Coast offense on its biggest stage yet, defeating Walsh's old employer, the Bengals, 26-21.

Montana and Walsh were just getting started, especially since that first championship squad didn't even include future Montana targets Roger Craig and Jerry Rice. The 49ers next made it to the big game three years later in Super Bowl XIX, played in Walsh's old workplace at Stanford Stadium, and they took down Miami 38-16.

Their third and final title together, and the one that legitimized San Francisco's claim as the Super Bowl team of the '80s, was four years later in Super Bowl XXIII. With that 20-16 victory over the Bengals, Walsh proved his excellence as a master strategist and a motivator, but his true legacy is played out today in stadiums all over the country.

"When you look at today's precision offenses, like those of the Colts and the Saints, you are witnessing skilled, cerebral quarterbacks who understand and live by Walsh's principles," Jaworski wrote in his book. "Peyton Manning and Drew Brees honor the memory of Bill Walsh every time they put the ball in flight."

AP Photo/Atkins

SUPER BOWL TITLES
3

REGULAR-SEASON RECORD
92-59-1

POSTSEASON RECORD
10-4

COMPOSITE RECORD
102-63-1

NFL COACH OF THE YEAR   1981 1984

NFC CHAMPIONSHIPS   3

JOE GIBBS

CAREER AS COACH / ADMINISTRATOR

SAN DIEGO STATE UNIVERSITY	1964–1966	Offensive Line Coach
FLORIDA STATE UNIVERSITY	1967–1968	Offensive Line Coach
UNIVERSITY OF SOUTHERN CALIFORNIA	1969–1970	Offensive Line Coach
UNIVERSITY OF ARKANSAS	1971–1972	Running Backs Coach
ST. LOUIS CARDINALS	1973–1977	Running Backs Coach
TAMPA BAY BUCCANEERS	1978	Offensive Coordinator
SAN DIEGO CHARGERS	1979–1980	Offensive Coordinator
WASHINGTON REDSKINS	1981–1992	Head Coach
WASHINGTON REDSKINS	2004–2007	Head Coach
WASHINGTON REDSKINS	2007–present	President, Special Adviser

He had been inducted into the Pro Football Hall of Fame eight years earlier, and his NASCAR team had won two championships. Joe Gibbs was settled in North Carolina with his family and his three Super Bowl rings, and there was no reason to believe that would change.

Until Washington Redskins owner Daniel Snyder came calling one more time and Gibbs finally admitted how much he would like to return to the sidelines. For four seasons, from 2004 to 2008, he was the Redskins' head coach again, a stint fueled by nothing more than the love of the game and its players.

That second chapter in Gibbs's football coaching career didn't result in any Super Bowl titles, but his accomplishment of winning three in nine years during the first stay in the nation's capital was more than enough to secure his place on the Mount Rushmore of Super Bowl coaches.

A student of the game who learned under offensive mastermind Don Coryell in San Diego, Gibbs was a coach who inspired tremendous loyalty and toughness from his players while crafting such efficient and effective game plans that he won each of his three Super Bowls with a different quarterback.

In just Gibbs's second year as the Washington head coach, his squad made the franchise's second trip to the Super Bowl and secured its first trophy by outplaying the Miami Dolphins to the tune of a 27-17 triumph in Super Bowl XVII. Even as his defense didn't allow a single Miami pass completion in the second half, Gibbs celebrated with humility. "The truly great people in this profession are great for

years and years," he said. "Let's see how I am in 10 years."

The football world took that challenge and watched Gibbs do it again in Super Bowl XXII, which the Redskins took easily from the Broncos in a 42-10 rout. His third ring came four years later in Super Bowl XXVI, a 37-24 victory over the Buffalo Bills. A little more than a year after winning that trophy, he cited the need to spend more time with his family when resigning from the Redskins in an emotional news conference.

Gibbs might not have added to his list of Super Bowl wins when he returned to the team unexpectedly a decade later, but he won the hearts of fans with his loyalty and his continued efforts to win, even in an NFL that was different from the one he had left a decade earlier.

"I give him all the credit for putting us in a great position for the future," Snyder said at Gibbs's second retirement press conference.

SUPER BOWL TITLES
3

REGULAR-SEASON RECORD
124-60

POSTSEASON RECORD
16-5

COMPOSITE RECORD
140-65

NFL COACH   1982
OF THE YEAR   1983

NFC
CHAMPIONSHIPS   **4**

BILL BELICHICK

CAREER AS COACH / ADMINISTRATOR

BALTIMORE COLTS	1975	Special Assistant
DETROIT LIONS	1976	Assist Special Teams Coach
DETROIT LIONS	1977	Wide Receivers Coach Tight Ends Coach
DENVER BRONCOS	1978	Assistant Special Teams Coach Defensive Assistant
NEW YORK GIANTS	1979	Special Teams Coach Defensive Assistant
NEW YORK GIANTS	1980–1984	Linebackers Coach Special Teams Coach
NEW YORK GIANTS	1985–1990	Defensive Coordinator
CLEVELAND BROWNS	1991–1995	Head Coach
NEW ENGLAND PATRIOTS	1996	Assistant Head Coach Secondary Coach
NEW YORK JETS	1997–1999	Assistant Coach Defensive Backs Coach
NEW ENGLAND PATRIOTS	2000–present	Head Coach

Since unrestricted free agency began in 1993, Bill Belichick is the only coach who has won more than three Super Bowl titles. It would be an impressive feat regardless—especially after his Patriots claimed their fourth ring in 2015—but even more so in an era in which players have the freedom to shop themselves around and parity is the order of the day.

And as one of only two coaches to have won four Super Bowl championships, Belichick stands out in another way. His first three championships with the New England Patriots were collected in just four years, in Super Bowls XXXVI, XXXVIII, and XXXIX. The winningest active coach as of 2014, Belichick's winning percentage of .657 at that point ranked him third among all coaches in the league's history. He also ranks first in Super Bowl appearances by head or assistant coaches, with nine total appearances in his career.

After 15 years as a journeyman defensive assistant with seven different franchises, Belichick was introduced as the head coach of the Patriots in 2000, and he asserted himself quickly by flipping his new team's record from 5-11 in his first season to 11-5 in his second and then winning key games all the way to the Patriots' first Super Bowl as 14-point underdogs. They knocked off the favored Rams 20-17 to give New England its first-ever title.

Two years later, the Patriots won 12 straight games through a difficult schedule en route to a 14-2 regular-season record and a return to the Super Bowl against the Carolina Panthers, this time with New England as the favorites. In a tense game full of missteps on both sides, Belichick and his Patriots squeaked by for a 32-29 victory. It was a journey that gave Belichick a new level of respect in pro football.

"Around the league, teams were examining Bill Belichick and his system with fresh eyes, looking beyond his reputation as a defensive mastermind to the method behind his personnel decisions, his draft strategy, his symbiotic partnership with personnel director Scott Pioli, the series of crisis and responses that made the Patriots one of the most compelling stories in recent memory," wrote Michael MacCambridge in *America's Game*.

The third Patriots Super Bowl victory, just one year after the Panthers game, was another hard-fought battle, this time a 24-21 result over the Philadelphia Eagles. Besides the trophy, Belichick's squad also tied a record for most consecutive playoff wins that day, with nine, and the following season they would break the record. Through that remarkable streak, those in the know credited Belichick's coaching acumen with establishing a concentrated dynasty.

"Belichick never leaves anything undone," Eagles defensive coordinator Jim Johnson said after the game. "People credited [Patriots offensive coordinator] Charlie Weis for doing a great job and [defensive coordinator] Romeo Crennel, but I always felt you see his hand in everything."

SUPER BOWL TITLES
4

REGULAR-SEASON RECORD
211-109

POSTSEASON RECORD
22-9

COMPOSITE RECORD
232-118

NFL COACH OF THE YEAR
2003
2007
2010

AFC CHAMPIONSHIPS **6**

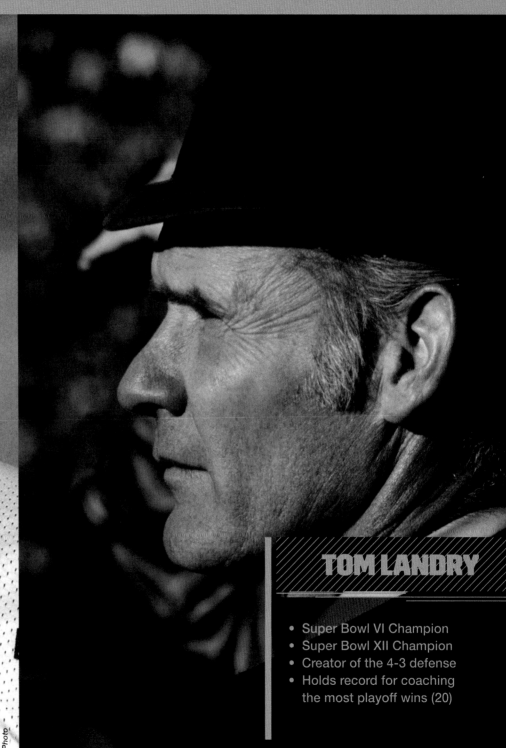

DON SHULA

- Super Bowl VII Champion
- Super Bowl VIII Champion
- Six-time NFL Coach of the Year
- Led the Dolphins to the NFL's only undefeated season (1972)

TOM LANDRY

- Super Bowl VI Champion
- Super Bowl XII Champion
- Creator of the 4-3 defense
- Holds record for coaching the most playoff wins (20)

AP Photo

AP Photo/Greg Trott

BILL PARCELLS

- Super Bowl XXI Champion
- Super Bowl XXV Champion
- Only coach to lead four different teams to the playoffs
- Has worked for six teams as either coach or executive

Winning more than one Super Bowl is a seismic accomplishment, and three coaches (in addition to Vince Lombardi, who won three championships before the Super Bowl began) have notched two Super Bowl titles in their career.

DON SHULA

CAREER AS COACH / ADMINISTRATOR		
DETROIT LIONS	1960–1962	Defensive Coordinator
BALTIMORE COLTS	1963–1969	Head Coach
MIAMI DOLPHINS	1970–1995	Head Coach

TOM LANDRY

CAREER AS COACH / ADMINISTRATOR		
NEW YORK GIANTS	1954–1959	Defensive Coordinator
DALLAS COWBOYS	1960–1988	Head Coach

BILL PARCELLS

CAREER AS COACH / ADMINISTRATOR		
NEW YORK GIANTS	1979–1980	Defensive Coordinator
NEW ENGLAND PATRIOTS	1980–1981	Linebacker Coach
NEW YORK GIANTS	1981–1982	Defensive Coordinator Linebacker Coach
NEW YORK GIANTS	1983–1990	Head Coach
NEW ENGLAND PATRIOTS	1993–1996	Head Coach
NEW YORK JETS	1997–1999	Head Coach
DALLAS COWBOYS	2003–2006	Head Coach
NEW YORK JETS	1997–2000	General Manager
MIAMI DOLPHINS	2008–2010	Executive Vice President of Football Operations
CLEVELAND BROWNS	2014–present	Courtesy Consultant

GATORADE®
BATH

Super Bowl XXI was the first to feature players giving the winning head coach a postgame Gatorade shower. The New York Giants had actually started dousing head coach Bill Parcells earlier in the season, with Jim Burt starting the tradition and Harry Carson sustaining it. After the Super Bowl victory over the Denver Broncos, Carson slipped on a yellow security jacket to sneak over to Parcells with a full cooler and catch him unawares. Even though a few coaches have managed to stay dry after their team's triumph, the shower of water or Gatorade has become closely linked with the Big Game—so much so that a common Super Bowl prop bet involves betting on the color of the Gatorade that will come down on the victorious coach's head.

AP Photo/ Jack Dempsey

AP Photo/David Longstreath

AP Photo/David J. Phillip

AP Photo/Lynne Sladky

AP Photo/Bill Waugh

AP Photo/David J. Phillip

AP Photo/Eric Draper

AP Photo/Chris O'Meara

AP Photo/David J. Phillip, File

AP Photo/David J. Phillip

AP Photo/Matt York

AP Photo/David J. Phillip

AP Photo/David J. Phillip

"THE GAME IS THE ULTIMATE SIGNIFICANCE TO ME BECAUSE IT IS SO IMPORTANT TO A LOT OF PEOPLE. IT HAS LEFT A MARK ON OUR CULTURE TO BE VOTED AS ONE OF THE BEST TO EVER PLAY."

Barry Sanders

CHAPTER 9: BEST PLAYERS WHO NEVER WON A SUPER BOWL

ATT: Attempts // AVG: Average // AST: Assists // COMP: Completions // FF: Forced Fumbles // FG: Field Goals // FG%: Field Goal Percentages // FUM: Fumbles // FR: Fumbles Recovered
G: Games // INT: Interceptions // LNG: Longest // PCT: Percentages // REC: Receptions // RTG: Ratings // SFTY: Safeties // SCK: Sacks // TDS: Touchdowns // TCKL: Tackles // XP: Extra Points
YDS: Yards // YDS/A: Yards per Attempt // YDS/G: Yards per Game

FRAN TARKENTON

Does a quarterback have to win a Super Bowl ring to be in the conversation for "best of all time"? Fran Tarkenton has a pointed opinion on that topic.

"I feel like I can outplay any of the quarterbacks that ever played," Tarkenton told the *St. Paul Pioneer Press* in 2013. "Go look at my record. Go look at my record in that era and what I did, the results that I got from passing and rushing. … In my mind, I played better than anybody that has ever played the position."

Tarkenton's pronouncements about his place in history are up for debate, but there is no doubt that his 0-3 record in the Super Bowl has diminished his legacy. When he retired in 1978 after 17 seasons in the league, Tarkenton held the records in all four major passing categories: completions, attempts, passing yards, and touchdowns.

From his four touchdown passes in his very first game as a Viking to his nine Pro Bowl touchdowns, Tarkenton accomplished almost everything that defines a big-time quarterback—except win the big one. And that shortcoming still eats at him, even decades later. "I've not forgotten," he said. "Every day and every night, it pisses me off."

AP Photo/NFL

	HEIGHT	6'0"
	WEIGHT	190
	BORN	February 3, 1940
	COLLEGE	University of Georgia
	TEAMS	Minnesota Vikings, 1961–1966
		New York Giants, 1967–1971
		Minnesota Vikings, 1972–1978
	POSITION	Quarterback

G	COMP	ATT	PCT	INT
246	3,686	6,467	57	266

TDS
342

YDS	SCK	RTG	YDS/G
47,003	274	80.4	191.1

NICKNAMES

THE MAD SCRAMBLER

FRANTIC FRAN / SCRAMBLIN' FRAN / SIR FRANCES

9-time Pro Bowl selection (1964, 1966, 1967, 1968, 1969, 1970, 1974, 1975, 1976) | AP First-Team All-Pro (1975) | AP Second-Team All-Pro (1973) | 1975 NFL MVP | 3-time NFC champion (1973, 1974, 1976) | AP NFL Offensive Player of the Year (1975) | UPI NFC Player of the Year (1975) | Pro Bowl MVP (1964) | Minnesota Vikings #10 retired | Minnesota Vikings Ring of Honor | Minnesota Vikings 25th Anniversary Team | Minnesota Vikings 40th Anniversary Team 50 Greatest Vikings | Pro Football Hall of Fame inductee (1986) | College Football Hall of Fame inductee (1987)

AP Photo

DICK BUTKUS

HEIGHT	6'3"
WEIGHT	245
BORN	December 9, 1942
COLLEGE	University of Illinois at Urbana–Champaign
TEAM	Chicago Bears, 1965–1973
POSITION	Middle Linebacker

AP Photo/Kevin T.

G	TCKL	AST	SCK
119	N/A	N/A	
SFTY	**FF**	**INT**	N/A*
1	N/A	22	

*SACKS AND FORCE FUMBLES WERE NOT KEPT AS OFFICIAL STATISTICS UNTIL 1982. THE NFL DID NOT RECORD TACKLES UNTIL 2001, ALTHOUGH SOME TEAMS KEPT THEIR OWN TALLIES BEFORE THAT YEAR.

NICKNAMES

THE ROBOT OF DESTRUCTION

THE MAESTRO OF MAYHEM / THE ENFORCER / THE ANIMAL

8-time Pro Bowl selection (1965, 1966, 1967, 1968, 1969, 1970, 1971, 1972) | 6-time First-Team All-Pro selection (1965, 1967, 1968, 1969, 1970, 1972) | 2-time Second-Team All-Pro selection (1966, 1971) | 2-time NEA NFL Defensive Player of the Year (1969, 1970) | NFL 75th Anniversary All-Time Team | NFL 1960s All-Decade Team | NFL 1970s All-Decade Team | Chicago Bears #51 retired | Illinois Fighting Illini #50 retired | College Football Hall of Fame inductee (1978) | Pro Football Hall of Fame inductee (1979) | Rated #10 NFL Player of All Time by NFL.com

The Chicago Bears are known for bruising linebackers, but every defender to line up at the position in the past 40 years has played in the shadow of Dick Butkus. His career, shortened to only eight seasons by a serious knee injury, is the stuff of legend even without a Super Bowl win among his accolades.

"There will never be another Butkus," said former Bears defensive lineman Dan Hampton. "He defined the position, changed the public's perception of the NFL. There's Ray Lewis, but Butkus will always be Butkus."

Opponents feared Butkus, the middle linebacker who made the Pro Bowl in every one of his seasons and developed a reputation as one of the most ferocious, intense individuals ever to deliver a tackle. His wife reportedly said that he was "born angry," and Butkus wasn't afraid to channel all of those emotions into hard-hitting, smashmouth football.

A bad knee (made worse by the full-speed approach to the game) necessitated his retirement at the age of 31, and Butkus was elected into the Pro Football Hall of Fame in 1979, the first year he was eligible. Few players have electrified their team and helped mold the understanding of a position like Butkus.

Pro Football Hall of Fame via AP Images

ALAN PAGE

It's a genuine challenge to find an area where Alan Page hasn't excelled. From 14 seasons as one of the best defensive tackles ever to take the field to a postfootball career in law and jurisprudence that made him the first black justice of the Minnesota Supreme Court, the lack of a Super Bowl ring hardly seems consequential.

Page, who played for the Minnesota Vikings from 1967 to 1978 and the Chicago Bears from 1978 to 1981, became a starter during the fourth game of his rookie season and started every game thereafter. He was selected as the NFL Defensive Player of the Year in 1971 and 1973, named the league's Most Valuable Player in 1971, and chosen for nine straight Pro Bowls.

During his career in Minnesota, Page also made it to Super Bowls IV, VIII, IX, and XII, but the Vikings never prevailed to win a title. His most productive Super Bowl was his last. In his team's 32-14 loss to the Raiders in Super Bowl XI, Page was responsible for 10 solo tackles, one assist, and a sack. He harbored no regrets about his football career, especially because his most impressive accomplishments came when he traded a helmet for a judge's robe.

"We shouldn't put down athletics, because that teaches children the value of teamwork and disciplined effort," he said at his 1988 Pro Football Hall of Fame induction. "But we are doing no favor to the young men of Los Angeles and Miami and Chicago if we let them believe a game will set them free."

AP Photo/Vernon Biever

HEIGHT	6'4"	
WEIGHT	245	
BORN	August 7, 1945	
COLLEGE	Notre Dame University	
TEAMS	Minnesota Vikings, 1967–1981 Chicago Bears, 1978–1981	
POSITION	Defensive Tackle	

G	TCKL	AST
218	N/A	N/A
SFTY	FF	INT
3	N/A	2

SCK
N/A*

*SACKS AND FORCE FUMBLES WERE NOT KEPT AS OFFICIAL STATISTICS UNTIL 1982. THE NFL DID NOT RECORD TACKLES UNTIL 2001, ALTHOUGH SOME TEAMS KEPT THEIR OWN TALLIES BEFORE THAT YEAR.

NICKNAME

TEDDY BEAR

1-time NFL champion (1969) | 3-time NFC champion (1973, 1974, 1976) | 9-time Pro Bowl selection (1969, 1970, 1971, 1972, 1973, 1974, 1975, 1976, 1977) | 6-time First-Team All-Pro selection (1969, 1970, 1971, 1973, 1974, 1975) | 3-time Second-Team All-Pro selection (1968, 1972, 1976) | 11-time First-Team All-Conference selection (1968, 1969, 1970, 1971, 1972, 1973, 1974, 1975, 1976, 1977, 1980) | NFL 1970s All-Decade Team | 1970 NFC Defensive Player of the Year | 1971 NFL MVP | 1971 AP NFL Defensive Player of the Year | 1971 UPI NFC Player of the Year | 1971 NFC Defensive Player of the Year | 1973 NEA NFL Defensive Player of the Year | Minnesota Vikings 25th Anniversary Team | Minnesota Vikings 40th Anniversary Team | Minnesota Vikings #88 retired, Ring of Honor | 50 Greatest Vikings

DAN MARINO

HEIGHT	6'4"
WEIGHT	228
BORN	September 15, 1961
COLLEGE	University of Pittsburgh
TEAM	Miami Dolphins, 1983–1999
POSITION	Quarterback

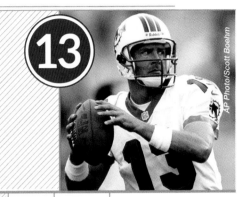

AP Photo/Scott Boehm

G	COMP	ATT	PCT	INT
242	4,967	8,358	57	252

YDS	SCK	RTG	YDS/G
61,361	270	86.5	253.6

TDS

420

NICKNAME

DAN THE MAN

9-time Pro Bowl (1983, 1984, 1985, 1986, 1987, 1991, 1992, 1994, 1995) I 3-time First-Team All-Pro (1984, 1985, 1986) I 3-time Second-Team All-Pro (1983, 1994, 1995) I NFL Rookie of the Year (1983) AFC champion (1984) I NFL MVP (1984) I NFL Offensive Player of the Year (1984) I 2-time UPI AFC Player of the Year (1984, 1994) I PFWA Comeback Player of the Year (1994) I Walter Payton Man of the Year (1998) I 12-time Miami Dolphins MVP (1983–1992, 1994–1995) I First to throw for 5,000 yards in single season (1984) I First to throw for 40 touchdowns in single season (1984, 1986) Pittsburgh Panthers #13 retired I Miami Dolphins #13 retired I Holds 31 Miami Dolphins records Holds numerous NFL records I College Football Hall of Fame (2002) I Pro Football Hall of Fame (2005) I Rated #25 NFL Player of All Time by NFL.com as of 2009 season

He was the sixth quarterback taken in the 1983 draft, but by his second season with the Miami Dolphins, Dan Marino had changed the way the NFL viewed the passing game.

By the time that 1984 season was over, he had passed for 5,084 yards, becoming the first quarterback to ever surpass 5,000 yards in a year. He also set a single-season record for touchdowns, with 48; claimed the NFL Most Valuable Player award; and brought the Dolphins to Super Bowl XIX against the San Francisco 49ers.

Despite Marino's charmed regular-season performance, Joe Montana and the 49ers owned the day and defeated the Dolphins 38-16 in the Super Bowl that ultimately represented Marino's only shot at a ring. Despite nine Pro Bowl appearances, six seasons of 4,000 yards or more, and the ownership of every NFL passing record upon his retirement in 1999, Marino never played in another Super Bowl.

"The last thing in the world you thought was that because Miami lost that Super Bowl that Dan would never get one," broadcaster Jim Lampley told *Sports Illustrated*. "That was the last thing that entered your mind. With the talent they had, that coaching staff, it was only a matter of how many."

AP Photo/Tom DiPace

THERE'S ALWAYS NEXT YEAR

Long-suffering. Frustrated. Futile. Those are words with which fans of four NFL franchises are all too familiar, especially every year when the Super Bowl rolls around and their favorite team is sitting home—again. The Detroit Lions fans win the dubious prize for staying faithful through the longest stretch of ineffectualness, followed closely by the Cleveland Browns fans (who score bonus points because their team was once taken from them in the middle of the night). Relatively speaking, the Jacksonville Jaguars are mere teenagers and the Houston Texans children in this quest, even if earlier fans of the Houston Oilers logged their own decades of near-misses and dashed hopes. Every September, those hopes ignite anew, and fans of these four teams know that when their Super Sunday finally does come they will set the bar for celebration at a new high.

AP Photo/Ed Andrieski

CLEVELAND BROWNS

FOUNDED	1945 (first franchise)
	1999 (second franchise)
BEST PLAYERS	Jim Brown, Otto Graham, Marion Motley, and Paul Warfield
OVERALL RECORD	505-442-13
PLAYOFF APPEARANCES	36
PLAYOFF RECORD	16-20
QUOTE	"Cleveland Browns fans, I'd argue, are the most loyal fan base to a team and an ownership that absolutely does not deserve them in all of sports," Will Leitch, Sports on Earth

AP Photo/Tony Avelar

WE'RE IN!

AP Photo/Rick Osentoski

DETROIT LIONS

FOUNDED	1934
BEST PLAYERS	Calvin Johnson, Bobby Layne, Barry Sanders, Joe Schmidt, and Doak Walker
OVERALL RECORD	528-625-32
PLAYOFF APPEARANCES	19
PLAYOFF RECORD	7-12
QUOTE	"I don't think the team is far off," Hall of Fame tailback Barry Sanders said on radio row before Super Bowl XLIX. "If they can come back and build on what we did this year? Hey, look, the Lions could be in Santa Clara (for Super Bowl 50) next year."

AP Photo/Bill Haber, File

AP Photo/James D Smith

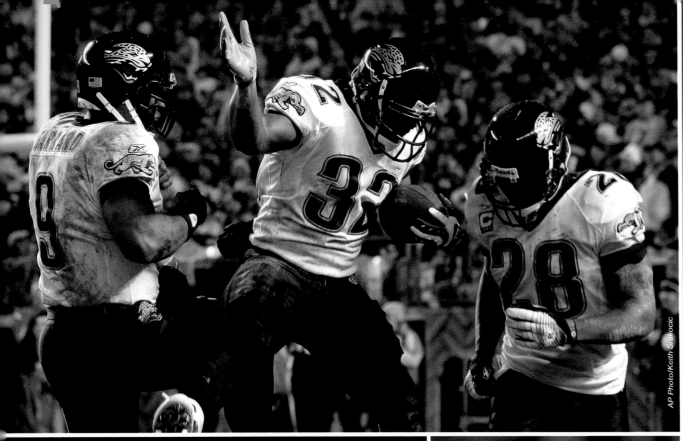

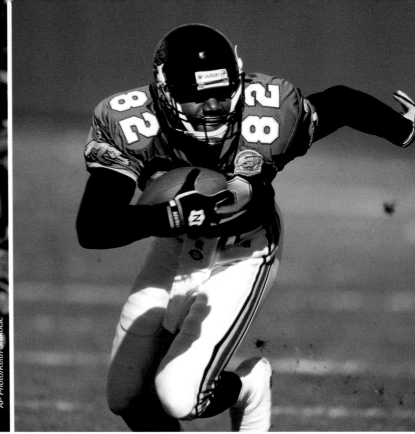

JACKSONVILLE JAGUARS

FOUNDED	1995
BEST PLAYERS	Tony Boselli, Mark Brunell, Kennan McCardell, Jimmy Smith, and Fred Taylor
OVERALL RECORD	147-173-0
PLAYOFF APPEARANCES	11
PLAYOFF RECORD	5-6
QUOTE	"It turns out sometimes you can't market the impossible … Not enough people live in Jacksonville to support a big NFL franchise through thick and thin," said Dan Wetzel of Yahoo Sports.

HOUSTON TEXANS

FOUNDED	2002
BEST PLAYERS	Arian Foster, Andre Johnson, Matt Schaub, and JJ Watts
OVERALL RECORD	88-120-0
PLAYOFF APPEARANCES	4
PLAYOFF RECORD	2-2
QUOTE	"I think that's a great goal to work towards," team CEO Bob McNair said of the prospect of the Texans competing in Super Bowl LII, which will be played in the Texans' home stadium. "It's never been done before. I'd love to see that happen."

BRUCE MATTHEWS

Bruce Matthews played in more games than any other lineman in NFL history, so it's ironic that none of those 296 games was a Super Bowl victory. Matthews was the NFL's Iron Man from 1983 to 2001 with the Houston Oilers and the Tennessee Titans, making a record 14 Pro Bowls and setting a new standard for excellence on the offensive line.

He was the starting left guard for his one Super Bowl appearance—the Super Bowl XXXIV loss to the St. Louis Rams that was decided by 1 yard when the Titans were stopped just short of the tying touchdown. A year later, he retired with his extraordinary streak of nearly 300 games without an injury, and in 2007 he was enshrined in the Pro Football Hall of Fame.

Matthews is part of a legendary football family. His father, Clay Sr.; his brother Clay Jr.; and his nephew Clay III have all made their marks on the NFL, and his sons Kevin Matthews (Carolina Panthers) and Jake Matthews (Atlanta Falcons) are now carrying on their dad's tradition of toughness and perseverance.

"I think he's the kind of guy that could have played in any era," his former teammate and coach Mike Munchak said at Matthews's Hall of Fame ceremony. "For 19 years, he was as good as anyone that's ever played the game."

AP Photo/Houston Chronicle/Howard Castleberry

	HEIGHT	6'5"
	WEIGHT	305
	BORN	August 8, 1961
	COLLEGE	University of Southern California
	TEAMS	Houston Oilers, 1983–2010 Tennessee Titans, 2011–2013
	POSITION	Offensive Guard

G	FUM	FR
296	5	10

NICKNAME

STRANGELY, BRUCE MATTHEWS NEVER HAD A NICKNAME.

Hall of Fame inductee | 14-time Pro Bowl selection (1988, 1989, 1990, 1991, 1992, 1993, 1994, 1995, 1996, 1997, 1998, 1999, 2000, 2001) | 10-time All-Pro selection (1988, 1989, 1990, 1991, 1992, 1993, 1996, 1998, 1999, 2000) | AFC champion (1999) | Bart Starr Man of the Year Award (2000) | NFL Alumni Offensive Lineman of the Year (2000) | NFL 1990s All-Decade Team Tennessee Titans #74 retired | All-time NFL record for games played by an offensive lineman (296) | Morris Trophy (1982)

AP Photo/NFL Photos/Kevin Terrell

ERIC DICKERSON

HEIGHT	6'3"
WEIGHT	220
BORN	September 2, 1960
COLLEGE	Southern Methodist University
TEAMS	Los Angeles Rams, 1983–1987
	Indianapolis Colts, 1987–1991
	Los Angeles Raiders, 1992
	Atlanta Falcons, 1993
POSITION	Running Back

29 29 29 29

AP Photo/Bill Janscha

G	ATT	TDS	YDS/A	YDS
146	2,996	90	4.4	13,259

LNG	YDS/G	FUM
85	90.8	78

NICKNAME

MR. FOURTH QUARTER

6-time Pro Bowl selection (1983, 1984, 1986, 1987, 1988, 1989) | 5-time AP First-Team All-Pro (1983, 1984, 1986, 1987, 1988) | 4-time NFL rushing champion (1983, 1984, 1986, 1988) | 1983 NFL/NFC Rookie of the Year | 1983 NFL Offensive Rookie of the Year | 1983 NFL MVP | 1986 NFL Offensive Player of the Year (AP) | 3-time UPI NFC Offensive Player of the Year (1983, 1984, 1986) | NFL 1980s All-Decade Team | St. Louis Rams #29 retired | Pro Football Hall of Fame inductee (1999) | Indianapolis Colts Ring of Honor inductee | Seventh-leading rusher of all time

Eric Dickerson played in the backfield for four different NFL teams, but he never got closer to the Super Bowl than a single NFC Championship Game, which his Los Angeles Rams team lost in a blowout.

It was 1985, and the Chicago Bears defense that later dominated the New England Patriots in Super Bowl XX limited Dickerson to 46 yards on the ground en route to a 24-0 victory. But despite a less than stellar postseason résumé, Dickerson assembled a career studded with highlight moments.

In 1984, his second season with the Rams, Dickerson passed O.J. Simpson as the all-time rushing leader in the NFL, finishing the year with 2,105 yards. In three of his first four seasons, Dickerson compiled more than 1,800 yards on the ground. Three times—twice with the Rams and once with the Colts—he was the NFL's rushing leader. Opposing defenses simply didn't have an answer for him.

"If you were blind," former Rams head coach John Robinson once said of Dickerson, "he could run right by you, and you wouldn't know it unless you felt the wind. He's unique that way. He's the smoothest runner I've ever seen."

After leaving the Rams for stints with the Colts, Raiders, and Falcons, Dickerson retired in 1993 after 11 seasons in the league. He was elected to the Hall of Fame in 1999, his first year of eligibility.

AP Photo/Al Golub

BRUCE SMITH

The Buffalo Bills of the 1990s wouldn't have made it to four straight Super Bowls without an abundance of talent. But of all of the players on those rosters, none owns a more indelible legacy than defensive end Bruce Smith.

As a starting point, Smith sacked opposing quarterbacks 200 times in his 19-year career, making him the all-time sack leader, with no active NFL player even in shouting distance (the closest is the Bears' Jared Allen, with 134). He was named to two NFL All-Decade Teams, for the 1980s and the 1990s, and he was selected for 11 Pro Bowls.

At Smith's 2009 Hall of Fame induction, his former Bills defensive coordinator Ted Cottrell recalled that Raiders head coach Art Shell consistently tried to contain Smith by putting two, or even three, offensive linemen on him for every snap. Even with those tactics, opposing teams found it nearly impossible to stop Smith from getting to their quarterbacks and stopping their running backs.

For Smith and the rest of his Bills teammates, the four Super Bowl losses will always sting. And when his 15 exemplary years in Buffalo and four in Washington were honored by selection into the Hall of Fame, Smith considered the tribute a salve for those defeats.

"This kind of takes away some of the pain from those Super Bowls," he said.

AP Photo/Kevin Higley, File

Four Seam Images via AP Images

HEIGHT	6'4"	
WEIGHT	265	
BORN	June 18, 1963	
COLLEGE	Virginia Tech	
TEAMS	Buffalo Bills, 1985–1999	
	Washington Redskins, 2000–2003	
POSITION	Defensive End	

G	TCKL	AST	SACK
279	1,075	149	200

SFTY	FF	INT	
2	0	28	

NICKNAME

BOO

11-time Pro Bowl selection (1987, 1988, 1989, 1990, 1992, 1993, 1994, 1995, 1996, 1997, 1998)

9-time First-Team All-Pro selection (1987, 1988, 1990, 1992, 1993, 1994, 1995, 1996, 1997) | 2-time Second-Team All-Pro selection (1989, 1998) | **4-time AFC champion (1990, 1991, 1992, 1993)** NFL 1980s All-Decade Team | **NFL 1990s All-Decade Team** | 2-time AP Defensive Player of the Year (1990, 1996) | **3-time PFWA Defensive Player of the Year (1990, 1993, 1996)** | 2-time NEA Defensive Player of the Year (1990, 1993) | **4-time UPI AFC Defensive Player of the Year (1987, 1988, 1990, 1996)** | Pro Bowl MVP (1987) | **Buffalo Bills Wall of Fame** | 2-time First-Team All-America (1983, 1984) | **1984 Outland Trophy** | Hall of Fame inductee

BARRY SANDERS

HEIGHT	5'8"	
WEIGHT	200	
BORN	July 16, 1968	
COLLEGE	Oklahoma State University–Stillwater	
TEAM	Detroit Lions, 1989–1998	
POSITION	Running Back	

AP Photo/Scott Boehm

G	ATT	TDS	YDS/A
153	3,062	99	5.0

LNG	YDS/G	FUM
85	99.8	41

YDS
15,269

NICKNAMES

B-TRAIN / BARREE

Heisman Trophy (1988) | Unanimous All-American (1988) | 10-time Pro Bowl (1989, 1990, 1991, 1992, 1993, 1994, 1995, 1996, 1997, 1998) | 6-time First-Team All-Pro (1989, 1990, 1991, 1994, 1995, 1997) | 4-time Second-Team All-Pro (1992, 1993, 1996, 1998) | 4-time NFL rushing champion (1990, 1994, 1996, 1997) | NFL MVP (1991) | NFL MVP (1997) | 2-time AP NFL Offensive Player of the Year (1994, 1997) | NFL Alumni Running Back of the Year (1997) | 2-time NFC rushing leader (1996, 1997) | NFL Offensive Rookie of the Year (1989) | Single-Season 2,000 Rushing Yards Club 10,000 Rushing Yards Club | NFL 1990s All-Decade Team | NFL record most consecutive 100-yard games (14) | NFL record most 1,500-yard seasons (5) | Holds 10 Detroit Lions team records Detroit Lions #20 retired | Third-leading rusher in NFL history | Rated #1 Most Elusive Running Back of All Time by NFL.com | Rated #17 NFL Player of All Time by NFL.com | Pro Football Hall of Fame inductee (2004)

His career had no gradual buildup, no slump. He just ran the ball like no one ever has for 10 years and retired at the top of his game. Even without a Super Bowl appearance, Barry Sanders is undeniably one of the most elusive running backs ever to play in the NFL.

Sanders, who played for the Detroit Lions from 1989 to 1998, topped 1,000 yards in every one of his 10 campaigns, and when he walked away at the age of 31, he was just 1,457 yards short of surpassing Walter Payton's all-time rushing record. All told, he rushed for 15,269 yards and 99 touchdowns in his career.

"No matter what year—you can say 1920 and you can say 2012—he will still be the best running back in the NFL any given time," former New England running back Curtis Martin said in an NFL Network documentary, *About Sanders*.

Fifteen years after his retirement, Sanders still held the record for most games with 100 or more rushing yards in a season and the most consecutive 100-yard rushing games (he accomplished that feat 14 times in 1997). His place in football history is guaranteed even if he never had the chance to shine on football's grandest stage.

AP Photo/Phil Meyers

TONY GONZALEZ

When bestowing superstar status on a player, it helps to find one who reinvented his position and who broke records and broke the mold at the same time. For the position of tight end in the NFL, Tony Gonzalez is that pioneer.

When Gonzalez retired in 2013 after 17 seasons with the Chiefs and the Falcons, he owned the records for receptions by a tight end (1,325), receiving yards, (15,127), receiving touchdowns (111), and 100-yard receiving games (30). He made the Pro Bowl 14 times, more than any other player except Bruce Smith and Merlin Olsen, who tied his mark. Selection for the Hall of Fame when he is eligible in 2019 is a foregone conclusion.

"Tony Gonzalez is an All-Pro's pro," Falcons receiver Roddy White told *USA Today* in 2011. "He's a Hall of Famer already. It's not just catching balls. He does everything right. He's very consistent. He stays after practice, catching balls and comes in early and does the weight room thing. He doesn't slack in any area of his game."

Six months after he called it quits, Gonzalez was still fielding calls from teams hoping to lure him back to the gridiron, but as he transitioned into a broadcasting career, he assured the media that he was finished. Even without a Super Bowl ring, his place in the history of the game is unparalleled.

AP Photo/Paul Spinelli

AP Photo/G. Newman Lowrance

HEIGHT	6'5"
WEIGHT	247
BORN	February 27, 1976
COLLEGE	University of California–Berkeley
TEAMS	Kansas City Chiefs, 1997–2008 Atlanta Falcons, 2009–2013
POSITION	Defensive End

G	REC	YDS	AVG	TDS
270	1,325	15,127	11.4	111

LNG	YDS/G	FUM		
73	56.0	6		

NICKNAME

GONZO

14-time Pro Bowl (1999, 2000, 2001, 2002, 2003, 2004, 2005, 2006, 2007, 2008, 2010, 2011, 2012, 2013) | 10-time All-Pro (1999, 2000, 2001, 2002, 2003, 2004, 2006, 2007, 2008, 2012) | 2-time NFL Alumni Tight End of the Year (2000, 2003) | First tight end to ever catch 1,000 passes | Pro Bowl all-time receptions leader (48) | Tied most Pro Bowl appearances by any player | NFL 2000s All-Decade Team | Consensus All-American (1996)

JUNIOR SEAU

HEIGHT	6'3"
WEIGHT	250
BORN	January 19, 1969
COLLEGE	University of Southern California
TEAMS	San Diego Chargers, 1990–2002
	Miami Dolphins, 2003–2005
	New England Patriots, 2006–2009
POSITION	Linebacker

AP Photo/Mary Schwalm

G	TCKL	AST
268	1,522	324
SFTY	FF	INT
0	11	18

SCK
56.5

NICKNAME

TASMANIAN DEVIL

12-time Pro Bowl (1991, 1992, 1993, 1994, 1995, 1996, 1997, 1998, 1999, 2000, 2001, 2002) | 8-time First-Team All-Pro (1991, 1992, 1993, 1994, 1995, 1996,1998, 2000) | 2-time Second-Team All-Pro (1997, 1999) | NFL Defensive Player of the Year (1992) | AFC Player of the Year (1994) | 2-time AFC Defensive Player of the Year (1992, 1998) | 4-time NFL Alumni NFL Linebacker of the Year (1992, 1993, 1994, 2000) | 3-time NFLPA AFC Linebacker of the Year (1992, 1993, 1994) | Walter Payton Man of the Year (1994) | NFL 1990s All-Decade Team | 2-time AFC champion (1994, 2007) | San Diego Chargers #55 retired | San Diego Chargers Hall of Fame | San Diego Chargers 50th Anniversary Team | San Diego Chargers 40th Anniversary Team | Pro Football Hall of Fame inductee (2015)

Three teams, 20 seasons, 1,522 tackles, and countless opponents who felt the aftereffects of his hits long after the clock had expired. Junior Seau was one of the most ferocious and effective linebackers ever to play the game, but despite two Super Bowl appearances, he never came away with a ring.

Seau came close with two teams: the San Diego Chargers in Super Bowl XXIX and the New England Patriots in Super Bowl XLII. He played in 12 Pro Bowls and was the NFL Defensive Player of the Year in 1992, but Seau's stellar career is overshadowed by his tragic death by suicide in May 2012. Speculation was rampant that Seau's suicide was linked to repetitive brain injuries during his two decades in the NFL, and in 2013 his family sued the league.

"He never really needed an award to solidify how good he was," his son Tyler Seau told the Associated Press when his father's Hall of Fame election was announced in 2015. "This kind of stuff was more for his family, for his mom, his dad, his brothers. Just to make them proud, make his family proud. For him, he knew what work he put in. So he knew where he was and where he stood amongst these men."

AP Photo by Tom DiPace

PART 3

THE SE

ETTING

SUPER BOWL
XLVII

SUPER BOWL XLVII
NOLA

Mercedes-Benz Superdome

SUPER BOWL

Jeff Lewis Photography

"WE WILL BEAT ANY OTHER CITY, ANY DAY, PUTTING ON AN EVENT."

Mitch Landrieu, mayor of New Orleans

CHAPTER 10: HOST CITIES

MIAMI

SUPER BOWLS HOSTED: II, III, V, X, XIII, XXIII, XXIX, XXXIII, XLI, XLIV

AP Photo/Patrick Semansky

Photo/Joe Tetta Images/AP Images

AP Photo/Lynne Sladky

Comedian Lenny Bruce once cracked, "Miami is where neon goes to die." It's airbrushed, glitzy, and humid, peppered with palm trees, imported sports cars, and tiny designer dogs. And it shares a key distinction with New Orleans as one of the cities to host more of the first 50 Super Bowls than any other.

For those who like their Super Bowl cities to reflect the personalities of the typical NFL fan, Miami doesn't quite fit. But for those who want to get away from it all and enjoy the best football in America in the midst of the decadence of a sunny party city, Miami has fit the bill perfectly—from Super Bowls II to XLIV.

The first five world championships played against a Miami backdrop unfolded in the Orange Bowl, the home of the Dolphins

from 1966 to 1986. The legendary venue, which was demolished in 2008, had a capacity of 80,010 when it was selected as the site for Super Bowl II in 1967. When Joe Robbie Stadium was opened in 1987, the Miami Super Bowls moved there, starting in 1989 with Super Bowl XXIII.

The Orange Bowl, which also played host to college football's longest home winning streak when the University of Miami notched 58 straight home games between 1985 and 1994, had a few distinctive features during its time as a favorite Super Bowl venue, including a water tank on the east end that was home to a live dolphin named Flipper. It also had political significance as the backdrop for President John F. Kennedy's Cuban Missile Crisis speech in 1962.

The history in Joe Robbie Stadium isn't quite as rich, perhaps because it had seven different names between its opening and 2014. Technically, two Super Bowls were played in Joe Robbie, one in Pro Player Stadium, one in Dolphin Stadium, and one in Sun Life Stadium, even if all were contested on the same piece of ground. The arena has fallen out of favor with the NFL in later years, especially after heavy rain in 2007. The NFL has hinted that the Super Bowl won't return until significant renovations, including a roof to protect fans from the elements, are made there.

Miami was home to some of the most memorable Super Bowl moments—on the field and off—in the history of the big game. Joe Namath walking off the field

and pointing skyward after his Jets' improbable comeback in 1969 and Joe Montana's 92-yard drive with 34 seconds remaining to best the Bengals 20-16 twenty years later are two of the most epic. The game's evolution and the mushrooming of the Super Bowl from a meaningful football game to a weeklong celebration of excess have both advanced along a time line with frequent and meaningful stops at the southern end of the Sunshine State.

AP Photo

AP Photo/Patrick Semansky

Jeff Lewis Photography

NEW ORLEANS

SUPER BOWLS HOSTED IV, VI, IX, XII, XV, XX, XXIV, XXXI, XXXVI, XLVII

City officials in New Orleans were scrambling in late 1974, when it became evident that the Superdome was not going to be finished in time for Super Bowl IX. Two previous championships had been played at Tulane Stadium, but the last one, in 1972, featured temperatures in the 30s, and the NFL had pinned their selection of the Big Easy on the hulking, modern new dome that had been under construction since 1971.

There is no record of how the NFL handled the news that their premier game would in fact be held at Tulane again (the Superdome finally opened in August of 1975). But despite that early misstep, the New Orleans dome holds a key distinction as the site of the most Super Bowls in American history.

Miami has hosted as many Super Bowls as New Orleans, with 10 each, but the Miami games were split evenly between two venues. The structure now known as the Mercedes-Benz Superdome has welcomed the big game eight times— through a power outage in 2013; a touchdown by the Fridge in 1986; a Desmond Howard punt return for a touchdown in 1997; and the biggest blowout in Super Bowl history, the San Francisco 49ers' 55-10 trouncing of the Denver Broncos in 1990.

The Superdome, the largest fixed dome structure, with a maximum football capacity of 76,468, has been the site of countless sports highlights and one notable news lowlight in its four decades. Its two uninterrupted tenants since its opening are the annual Sugar Bowl and as the regular–season home of the New

Orleans Saints. The darkest chapter in the structure's—and its city's—history was the aftermath of Hurricane Katrina in 2005. The building sustained extensive damage and became a last-resort refuge for 40,000 people driven from their homes by the surging floodwaters.

Despite speculation that the dome would be razed after Katrina, the city and the state of Louisiana rallied behind the iconic venue, and $330 million was poured into its renovation. In the ultimate symbol of the Superdome's resurgence, Super Bowl XLVII came to town in 2013 to make the tenth staging of the legendary game.

That Super Bowl was not without a dome-related story line, as the lights went out in half of the building at the beginning of the second half. The outage, which interrupted TV and radio coverage,

knocked out the air conditioning and Internet services, and left fans sitting in semidarkness and singing songs to pass the time, lasted for 33 minutes. Despite Beyoncé's high-octane halftime show featuring a barrage of special effects, her concert was not linked to the incident.

No one who has ever vacationed in New Orleans needs to speculate on its appeal to Super Bowl organizers. The city is a study in excess, a nonstop party that provides a fitting backdrop to the nation's most overhyped sporting event. One sports blogger, Amy K. Nelson from SB Nation, expressed a popular sentiment in 2013 when she proposed New Orleans as the game's permanent home, writing, "I know of no other city in which the combined debauchery and city grid could provide the best people-watching and communal experience."

LOS ANGELES

SUPER BOWLS HOSTED I, VII, XI, XIV, XVII, XXI, XXVII

AP Photo/NFL Photos

It's the birthplace of the Super Bowl and the site of some of its great moments, and if not for one unfortunate issue, Los Angeles might have surpassed Miami and New Orleans as the preeminent city of the big game. The barrier, of course, to the City of Angels' continuing association with the Super Bowl is the lack of NFL football in the nation's second-largest city.

For seven Super Bowl Sundays, Los Angeles was a prime destination for football fans that featured sunny January days in the 70s and memorable games such as Super Bowl I, with a runaway performance by Vince Lombardi's Packers; Super Bowl VII and its culmination of the Miami Dolphins' perfect season; and Super Bowl XIV, which featured 103,985 in the Rose Bowl for a mark that still stands as the highest attendance in the game's history.

The first two Tinseltown Super Bowls were played in the Los Angeles Coliseum, a venerable structure that has hosted two Summer Olympics and still serves as the home venue for the USC Trojans. Starting with Super Bowl XI in 1977, the game moved to the Rose Bowl, and five Super Bowls have been played in the giant horseshoe-shaped stadium whose tenants include its eponymous college bowl game; the UCLA Bruins football team; and, in past years, the L.A. Galaxy and the 1994 World Cup.

The last Super Bowl to be contested in the Rose Bowl was in 1993, a 52-17 Dallas Cowboys annihilation of the Buffalo Bills in Super Bowl XXVII. Two years after that game, the city that had been home to two NFL franchises found itself with none after the Rams were wooed to St. Louis and the Raiders returned to Oakland.

Since the NFL favors host cities with a strong commitment to the NFL (which is often demonstrated by new stadium construction), a city with no pro football and two stadiums dating back to the early 1920s is not even on its radar.

Despite those deficiencies, Los Angeles received some serious consideration as a candidate to host Super Bowl 50, a historical nod to bringing the game back to the place where it all started. NFL Commissioner Roger Goodell first mentioned the possibility of bringing the Golden Super Bowl to L.A. in 2009, when the city was entertaining two proposals to build new stadiums, Farmers Field and Los Angeles Stadium.

Even though plans are under way for the construction of both venues, firm construction schedules were not in

place in time to suit the NFL, and the fiftieth Super Bowl was awarded to San Francisco and its state-of-the-art Levi's Stadium, which opened in 2014. So the Super Bowl will return to the state of its birth, but, once more, sunny L.A. was left out in the cold and left to ponder its relationship with the league that once counted it as a favorite destination.

MARILYN MONROE

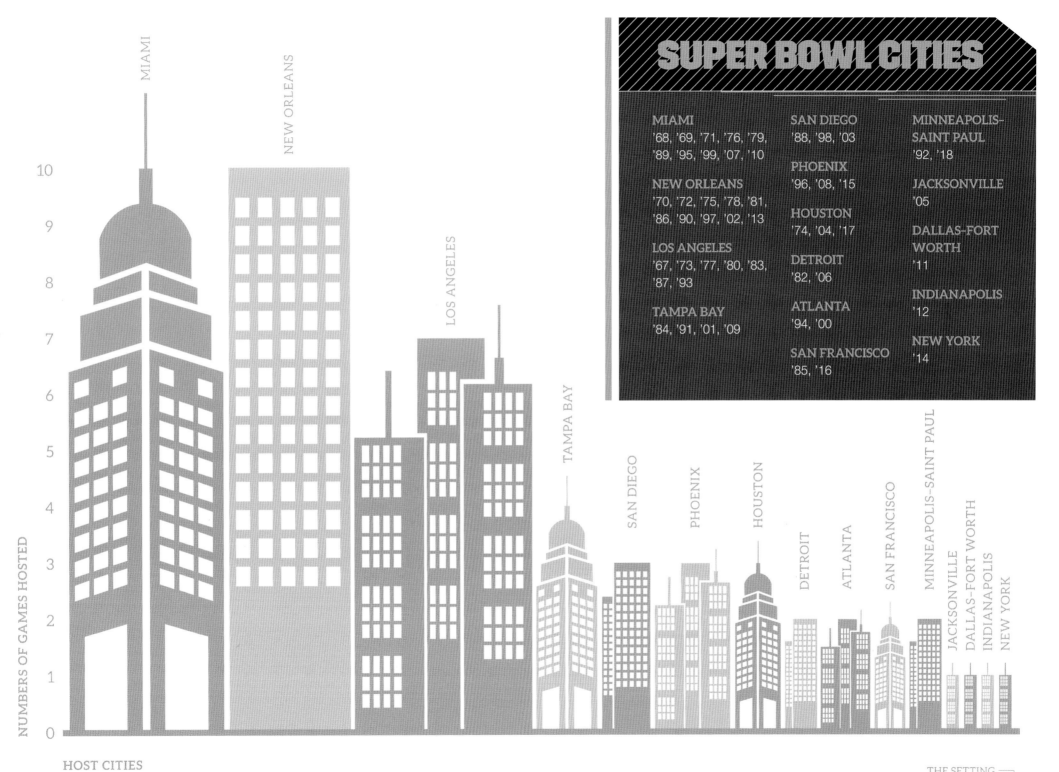

NUMBERS OF GAMES HOSTED

10

9

8

7

6

5

4

3

2

1

0

MIAMI

NEW ORLEANS

LOS ANGELES

TAMPA BAY

SAN DIEGO

PHOENIX

HOUSTON

DETROIT

ATLANTA

SAN FRANCISCO

MINNEAPOLIS–SAINT PAUL

JACKSONVILLE

DALLAS–FORT WORTH

INDIANAPOLIS

NEW YORK

HOST CITIES

SUPER BOWL CITIES

MIAMI
'68, '69, '71, '76, '79,
'89, '95, '99, '07, '10

NEW ORLEANS
'70, '72, '75, '78, '81,
'86, '90, '97, '02, '13

LOS ANGELES
'67, '73, '77, '80, '83,
'87, '93

TAMPA BAY
'84, '91, '01, '09

SAN DIEGO
'88, '98, '03

PHOENIX
'96, '08, '15

HOUSTON
'74, '04, '17

DETROIT
'82, '06

ATLANTA
'94, '00

SAN FRANCISCO
'85, '16

**MINNEAPOLIS–
SAINT PAUL**
'92, '18

JACKSONVILLE
'05

**DALLAS–FORT
WORTH**
'11

INDIANAPOLIS
'12

NEW YORK
'14

HOW TO TAILGATE

KISS THE COOK

BBQ

SITE SELECTION

Left, Work continues on the new Minnesota stadium in Minneapolis.
AP Photo/The Star Tribune, Elizabeth Flores

Top, Construction of the Lucas Oil Stadium in Indianapolis is shown in this aerial view taken in 2006. *AP Photo/The Indianapolis Star, WTHR, Charlie Nye*

Above, NFL football's Super Bowl XLVI sign on Monument Circle in Indianapolis. *AP Photo/Paul Sancya, File*

Minnesota Vikings owners Zygi Wilf (*left*) and Mark Wilf (*center*) attend an April 2014 press conference along with Minneapolis bid committee cochair Marilyn Carson Nelson (*right*) after Minneapolis was selected as the host for the 2018 Super Bowl at the NFL's spring meeting. *AP Photo/Paul Sancya, File*

By Super Bowl 50, the NFL had created a long list of requirements for its host cities, including necessities such as free use of 35,000 parking spaces for game day; a climate-controlled, domed stadium in areas whose average temperatures fall below 50 degrees; and access to three golf courses and two bowling venues. But in the early days of football's world championship game, it was enough to have a big stadium and plenty of sunshine.

The protocol for selecting a Super Bowl site has evolved and—like everything else attendant to the game—grown considerably more complicated over the decades. In the first few decades, when cities such as Miami, New Orleans, and Los Angeles hosted the majority of the games, the league owners looked primarily for warm cities that would be attractive as party spots and vacation destinations.

In the twenty-first century, as the selection procedure evolved from a closed-door vote to an elaborate bid process, a wider range of cities has played host to the sporting event that not only puts the media spotlight on a city but also infuses some $600 million into that area's economy. It has become a coveted prize, and it's not reserved just for warm-weather regions located near beaches anymore.

All but three of the first 20 Super Bowls were played in one of three cities: Miami, Los Angeles, or New Orleans. Since 1988, a total of 14 different cities has played host to the festivities. The variety of hosts, in more recent years, has included Minneapolis–Saint Paul in 1992, Jacksonville in 2005, and Indianapolis in 2012. The bidding process today takes place about four years before the game, and a glimpse into Indianapolis's surprising

winning campaign provides a peek into the changing priorities of the NFL in regard to the host city.

"The NFL's Super Bowl is usually gussied up in glitz, glamour, and bombast," wrote John Branch in a 2012 *New York Times* article. "The annual road show of indulgence thrives on a cocktail of outsize scale, self-promotion and ego. Indianapolis, a useful antonym for glitz, glamour and bombast, has a reputation for homespun subtlety."

Ultimately, the Indianapolis committee won over the selection panel with eagerness and the kind of down-to-earth values that are scarce in Miami and L.A. For instance, the official bid was delivered to NFL officials by a class of Indianapolis eighth graders. A well-known downtown steakhouse sent its famous shrimp cocktail to the committee members.

Granted a chance to be a Super Bowl city, Indianapolis responded by constructing an elaborate Super Bowl village, complete with a zip line that stood seven stories above downtown and stretched out for two blocks. Music, games, and other activities created a constant bustle in the downtown area under the giant letters— XLVI—erected at Monument Circle.

Ultimately, an innovative bid, a new stadium, and a successful NFL franchise gave Indianapolis a golden opportunity to earn the designation "Super Bowl city" and to prove that even if your name is Miami or New Orleans, you're going to have to work for it from this point on. In fact, in the race to stage the 2018 game, New Orleans lost its first-ever bid—to Minneapolis.

ECONOMIC IMPACT

AP Photo/Bryan Anderson

THE REAL COST
OF THE SUPER BOWL
EXPERIENCE

JUST THE ESSENTIALS*

Ticket/Average Price:	$4,600
Face Value:	$1,900
Most Expensive:	$7,000
Suite:	$726,000
Flight	$328
3-Day Car Rental	$213
2-Night Hotel Stay	$596
Food	$450
Jersey	$150

*Average cost for Super Bowl XLIX attendance

TOTAL: $6,337

SUPER BOWL XLIX:

Seattle
Seahawks

New England
Patriots

University of Phoenix Stadium
Phoenix, AZ

HOURS WORKED TO PURCHASE ONE SUPER BOWL XLIX TICKET

NATIONAL AVERAGE
Average Salary: $25.12 per hour
Hours Worked: 183 (23 days)

BOSTON
Average Salary: $35.05 per hour
Hours Worked: 131 (16 days)

SEATTLE
Average Salary: $32.60 per hour
Hours Worked: 141 (18 days)

PHOENIX
Average Salary: $24.93 per hour
Hours Worked: 185 (24 days)

▶ **FACT:** An estimated 1.5 million Americans will make the decision to call in "sick" Monday, and another 4.4 million people are expected to show up late for work, according to researchers.

It might be frigid in Minneapolis in January, but city leaders put together a successful bid to host the 2018 Super Bowl nonetheless. Concerns about cold weather can evidently be allayed by plans to build a $1-billion state-of-the-art stadium to host the game and develop a fan-friendly Super Bowl boulevard along a mile of downtown streets.

Clearly, those projects, as well as the bid process itself, are pricey for Minneapolis. But civic leaders who lead the charge to bring the Super Bowl to their cities are driven by the prospect of the staggering economic impact they will experience when hordes of people come to town for the world's biggest sporting spectacle. The NFL has been known to estimate an economic boon of $600 million or more for cities that are willing to take the plunge.

But in truth, projections in the area of economic impact can vary widely from reality, and many experts question whether bringing the football circus to town really injects life into the local economy. The true effect of hosting the Super Bowl can't be measured in a simple formula, distorted as it is by the nature of spending, the preexisting tourism traffic in the host city, and the displacement of tourists who choose not to come because the Super Bowl is in town.

Philip Porter, a professor of economics at the University of South Florida, has spent three decades analyzing the data from

Super Bowl host cities, and every year he is called upon by the media to present his findings—that despite the great financial lengths to which a city goes to host the game, the event has a negligible impact on boosting profits for local businesses and service providers.

Through his studies of a variety of Super Bowl cities in the past 30 years, Porter has tallied the taxable sales in counties that have hosted multiple Super Bowls, and his findings were surprising. For Hillsborough County, which includes Tampa, Super Bowl XXV in 1991 yielded $720.2 million in sales, less than the average January figure of $734.6 million. Ten years later, Tampa welcomed the game again, and this time the month including the game saw $1.44 billion in taxable sales, just a bit higher than the average January figure of $1.39 billion.

The key, Porter believes, is to trade estimates and projections for measurable data and to determine how much money is really poured into a local economy. Because the NFL is such a colossal business venture in and of itself, it sets up scores of temporary retail centers and fan experiences in the host city, thus effectively funneling money from the fans directly back to the league and leaving little profit behind.

Another economist who has studied the contrasting interpretations of the Super Bowl's impact explains the phenomenon

of Super Bowl spending this way: "Imagine an airplane landing at an airport and everyone gets out and gives each other a million bucks, then gets back on the plane. That's $200 million in economic activity, but it's not any benefit to the local economy."

Accounting for displacement is key, experts say, because most cities big enough to accommodate a Super Bowl stay fairly busy with tourism or convention traffic year-round. Of course, northern destinations such as Indianapolis and Minneapolis are more likely to receive a boost in the winter months, whereas cities such as Miami and Tampa are generally flush with visitors in the winter whether the Super Bowl is nearby or not.

In an effort to determine the actual impression left by Indianapolis's highly sought-after Super Bowl in 2012, the Indianapolis Super Bowl Committee commissioned an independent data analysis firm, Rockport Analytics, to study every economic aspect of the Super Bowl and its footprint on the city's retail, service, and hospitality industries. Among the findings:

- The gross spending total economic impact of Super Bowl XLVI for Indianapolis was estimated at $324 million, a figure that fell to a still-impressive $278 million when the effect of displacement was considered.

- About 116,000 visitors came to Indianapolis for Super Bowl XLVI and its related events. Of those, 68,500 attended the game as fans, and the rest were visitors without tickets, nonresident credentialed support staff, media personnel, and team members and support staff from the Giants and Patriots.

- Those nonresidents drawn to town by the big game stayed an average of slightly more than four days, and they spent more than $264 million locally during the 10-day period studied, averaging to about $571 per person, per day during that time frame.

- Retail and shopping were the source of the largest percentage of those expenditures, receiving 24 percent, followed closely by hotels, restaurants and bars, and rental car and other transportation services.

The truth about the Super Bowl and its actual bearing on a city's economy might be subject to smokescreens and complex variables, but the nation's cities are still keen to become the next setting of the ultimate convergence of competition, entertainment, and glitz.

Minneapolis officials jumped up and down, danced, and high-fived when they received word that the NFL owners had accepted their bid from a highly competitive group containing former host cities New Orleans

A Seattle Seahawks fan watches action against the New England Patriots during the second half of Super Bowl XLIX. *AP Photo/David Goldman*

and Indianapolis. The exposure, the hordes of visitors, and the influx of the nation's hottest athletes and celebrities prove irresistible to city officials, no matter what studies by economists might say.

"I'M JUST HERE SO I WON'T GET FINED."

Marshawn Lynch

CHAPTER 11: SIDESHOWS

SIDESHOWS

You can party like a rock star or a supermodel during Super Bowl week—but you'd better either know a VIP or be willing to part with some big bucks. It's probably a good thing that admission to the most elite parties is hard to obtain, because if anyone tried to hit all of the exclusive soirees, he or she might be too exhausted to take in the game on Sunday. If you're looking to raise eyebrows on your trip to the Super Bowl host city, you can brag about having entrée to one of these red-carpet affairs:

THE MADDEN BOWL

This party, usually held on the Friday before the Super Bowl, is the domain of some of the top players in the NFL and their VIP guests. It is a private gathering, but those who have been on the inside report musical guests such as Busta Rhymes and Run-D.M.C. providing the atmosphere for the main event and a Madden NFL video game tournament featuring professional football stars. At the party in New York before Super Bowl XLVIII, Carolina Panthers quarterback Cam Newton and Philadelphia Eagles running back LaSean McCoy prevailed to compete in the finals, and McCoy's Madden skills made him the champion.

LEATHER AND LACES

If you would rather mingle with supermodels than jocks, this is the party for you. Tickets range from $950 for an individual to $30,000 for a private cabana, and runway stars such as Kim Kardashian, Bar Refaeli, and Brooklyn Decker have hosted the two-night party. All of that perfection brings other VIPs as well. Past attendees have included Charlie Sheen, Kid Rock, and Hugh Jackman.

BUD LIGHT SUPER BOWL WEEK

Every winter Bud Light throws subtlety to the wind and sponsors an entire week of upscale parties before the Super Bowl, booking musical headliners such as Foo Fighters, Stevie Wonder, and Lil Wayne. The parties are private, unless you win a pass through a Bud Light promotion, and they are known for their exotic venues, including the 2014 gala held aboard a brand-new cruise ship docked on the Hudson River in New York.

TASTE OF THE NFL PARTY WITH A PURPOSE

An ideal destination for foodies and those who want their Super Bowl frivolities to make a difference, this annual party features chefs from every NFL city who prepare their signature dishes with sous chef assistance from NFL players. A portion of the proceeds for the pricey tickets, which range from $700 to $9,000, helps food banks across America battle hunger.

LeSean McCoy holding a trophy after winning the Madden Bowl video game tournament. *AP Photo*

Opposite page, Ludacris performs at the 2015 Maxim Super Bowl Party.

Top, Brian Kelley (*left*) and Tyler Hubbard from Florida Georgia Line perform at EA SPORTS Madden Bowl 2015.
Donald Traill/Invision for EA SPORTS/AP Images

DITKA AND JAWS CIGARS WITH THE STARS

This gathering has the feel of a traveling upscale man cave and offers the chance to smoke stogies with hosts Mike Ditka and Ron Jaworski and sports broadcasting notables such as Mike Tirico, Jon Gruden, and Mike Golic. The night's highlights include premium cigars, single-malt scotch, heavy appetizers, and a genuine red-carpet entrance. Tickets are available at levels ranging from $500 (for an individual) to $15,000 (for the Touchdown Partner package, offering a host of perks and 50 tickets to the event).

ESPN THE PARTY

This private party strives to be the biggest ticket in town, with 1,200 guests from the top echelons of sports and entertainment. Featured performers at the 2014 event in New York were Robin Thicke and Kendrick Lamar, and the guest list featured Evander Holyfield, Tim Tebow, CC Sabathia, and Nicole "Snooki" Polizzi, among others.

PLAYBOY PARTY

It's everything you would expect from a party sponsored by Hugh Hefner and his bunnies: Playboy models in full rabbit regalia, music by the likes of Nelly and Snoop Dogg, gambling tables with Playboy merchandise for the winners. "We always throw one of the best Super Bowl parties," one Bunny told *Newark Star-Ledger* columnist Peter Genovese, who managed to swing an invite to the 2014 bash. "People are going to talk about it for another three weeks."

Paul Bruinooge/Patrick McMullan
Sipa USA/Sipa via AP Images

TV COVERAGE

AP Photo/David Stluka

Consider these two facts: it is virtually impossible for an average American sports fan to score tickets to the Super Bowl and almost one-fourth of TV purchases nationwide are made just prior to the big game. It's a combination that means there is little room for error when it comes to Super Bowl television coverage.

From the broadcast team to the graphics to the camera angle choices during the halftime show, producers and crews tasked with presenting the Super Bowl to 111 million-plus viewers must be every bit as much on top of their game as the starting quarterbacks for the two teams along the line of scrimmage.

Since 2006, the rights to broadcast the Super Bowl have rotated annually between Fox, CBS, and NBC, each of which pays the NFL more than $1 billion a year for the right to show NFL regular-season and playoff games on its network. It's an expense the networks consider worthwhile because of the sport's unprecedented popularity, illustrated by the fact that every Super Bowl broadcast topples the one from the previous year as the most-watched TV show in history.

And even if it doesn't dominate the ratings everywhere across the globe, the Super Bowl has a respectable presence in a surprising number of foreign countries. Super Bowl XLVI was beamed to football fans in 180 different nations and in 30 different languages.

Such a hefty investment means those networks will leave little to chance when the Super Bowl rolls around each winter, dispatching their best people to the host city to convey every detail of the game before and after kickoff. More than a hundred different play-by-play announcers and analysts have worked in Super Bowl booths, with many more contributing reports from the sideline. While many of the big names in sports broadcasting have called Super Bowls, many consider the team of John Madden and Pat Summerall

the best team to ever occupy a Super Bowl booth.

"Besides Madden's unique personality and ability to relate to millions of viewers as if he was speaking with them individually, much of their success was about well-defined roles," Bob Raissman of the *New York Daily News* wrote of the two, who covered eight Super Bowls together. "Unlike many of his peers Summerall rarely stepped on Madden's tongue while straying into analyst territory."

With so many details to consider, it's a wonder that the Super Bowl hasn't been the stage for more wholesale technical difficulties. But problems—at least the kind that would be evident to viewers—are exceedingly rare in Super Bowl broadcasting. One challenging moment, which was no fault of the network, came in New Orleans at Super Bowl XLVII.

Due to a malfunction of a device installed at the SuperDome specifically to prevent a blackout from occurring, all power was lost in the arena for more than 30 minutes that year. The CBS team was able to

keep broadcasting through the hiatus because of backup power sources, but media critics weighing in after the game panned their handling of the surprising circumstances.

"CBS provided us with zero information on what was actually going on, what the NFL was saying, what the coaches felt, what the referees had been advised, hell, what a couple of fans were thinking as they sat in darkness," wrote Will Leitch of Sports on Earth. "It was just Tasker, to Wilcots, to Brown, to Sharpe to Sharpe to Sharpe, all of them yammering on aimlessly as the seconds ticked by on the highest-rated television program of the year."

The blackout might have been annoying for viewers, but it was small potatoes in the glitch department compared to what happened to a Comcast telecast of Super Bowl XLIII in Tucson. For 37 seconds, instead of tracking the latest plays in the Steelers-Cardinals matchup, Comcast customers in the Tucson area saw pornographic footage. The incident led to the eventual arrest of a former Comcast employee and prompted the company to issue $10 credits to 80,000 subscribers after the Super Bowl.

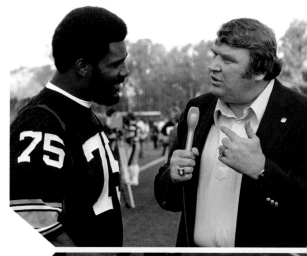

Bottom left, CBS announcer Pat Summerall (*left*) with NFL Commissioner Pete Rozelle at Super Bowl X between the Pittsburgh Steelers and the Dallas Cowboys. The Steelers defeated the Cowboys 21-7. *AP Photo/NFL Photos*

Top right, Former Oakland Raiders head coach John Madden (*right*) interviews Pittsburgh Steelers All-Pro defensive man "Mean Joe" Greene for a CBS program about Super Bowl XIV. *AP Photo*

Bottom right, San Francisco 49ers quarterback Colin Kaepernick (7) talks to head coach Jim Harbaugh during the Super Bowl XLVII blackout. *AP Photo/Scott Boehm*

Journalism is an honorable pursuit, practiced by professionals dedicated to uncovering truth and enlightening the public—except at the Super Bowl, where authentic journalists are smothered by the circus that substitutes for media coverage. More than 6,300 media representatives were credentialed for Super Bowl XLVIII, and the number grows each year.

Consider Media Day, an event so grand that it has a sponsor (Gatorade) and allows fans to buy $30 tickets just to sit in the stands and witness it. Actual working sportswriters are there, trying desperately to find an angle that hasn't already been prepackaged and disseminated dozens of times. But as they approach athletes and coaches, those reporters compete with hundreds of "journalists" who seem to have been inserted into the Media Day throng to magnify the spectacle.

In recent years, the characters who have managed to secure credentials for Media Day have included the TV Azteca personality who wore a wedding dress and proposed to New England quarterback Tom Brady, a Danish TV reporter dressed as the children's storybook character Waldo who hid in the crowd while one of his crew members asked players to find him, children tasked with getting a cute kid's angle on the big game, and a host of semifamous actors and comedians working for a seemingly endless array of entertainment outlets.

"Among the reporters were musician/actress Mandy Moore and comedian Anthony Anderson, who represented an annoying trend of giving press passes to B- and C-List celebrities and sending them in for a wild and crazy take on the game," wrote ESPN.com columnist Jim Caple in a 2003 column after Super Bowl XXXVII Media Day. "I don't get the point. This is the equivalent of the Raiders sending backup quarterback Marques Tuiasasopo to the Academy Awards and having him pester Meryl Streep with questions while she walks up the red carpet."

For those who aren't satisfied with just one day of outlandishness and preening, there's Radio Row, set up during all of Super Bowl week in a large hotel ballroom somewhere near the stadium and featuring tables of radio and television personalities packed cheek to jowl and interviewing the grab bag of notables from sports and entertainment whose publicists have scheduled appearances. More often than not, these celebrities are plugging a product or promoting an upcoming movie or show. Occasionally, football is discussed. It is a spectacle described by SB Nation in 2014 as "the soul-sucking marriage of sports media and brand awareness."

If you look carefully—if your eyes can focus amid the South American reporters wearing rhinestone-studded evening gowns and the reality TV stars shilling beauty products on Radio Row—tucked amid the absurd and the inexplicable are working sportswriters,

men and women who have been covering NFL teams for years and are desperately trying to produce compelling, noteworthy stories for their readers, viewers, and listeners.

It's no easy task, even if papers such as *The Boston Globe* have been known to send up to 30 reporters to the game when their home team is playing. Bona fide journalists chronicling the Super Bowl work 12-hour days, contend with limited player availability, and struggle to mine fresh content from the most overexposed media event on the planet. But in the end, it's still an unmatched opportunity for any reporter, *The Boston Globe* reporter Shalise Manza-Young told Peter King with mmqb.com, and even through the chaos the players and coaches at the center of the firestorm are happier than usual to dole out sound bites.

"Even Bill Belichick is happy Super Bowl week," Manza-Young said, "which is rare to see for those of us who cover him week-in and week-out."

One of the credentialed "reporters" at the Super Bowl XLIX Media Day was Barrel Boy, a portly man wearing a cowboy hat and a barrel emblazoned with the name of KNIX, the Phoenix radio station he represented. As Barrel Boy roamed the floor at the US Airways Center in search of a big scoop, the following exchange took place with Patriots cornerback Darrelle Revis:

Barrel Boy: "Do you know why McDonald's doesn't sell hot dogs?"

Revis: "Why are you wearing a barrel?"

Such hard-hitting journalism is commonplace at the event that has become an archetype of the Super Bowl's age of excess. For $28.50, fans can buy tickets and sit in the stands to watch

reporters become the story as athletes field overtures such as wedding proposals and invitations to try salsa dancing.

Presumably, wading through the fray are a few actual reporters trying to get legitimate quotes from athletes, but they are obscured by the brass bands, garish costumes, caricature artists, and general bedlam that has come to define this multiring circus.

"It's a decadent, outlandish side show that seems to get weirder and weirder every year," wrote Mashable.com's Sam Laird in 2015. "And bless it for that."

Even if the stunts associated with Media Day have multiplied in direct proportion to the game's growth as a national phenomenon, a pair of former Los Angeles

Rams players actually kicked off the madcap aspect of the event way back in 1975. As recounted by Grantland.com reporter Bryan Curtis, *Sport* magazine dispatched Lance Retzel and Fred Dryer to cover Super Bowl IX, hoping that the players would lend a unique perspective.

Retzel and Dryer had the unique part of their assignment down cold. Before they left Southern California, they visited a costume shop and rented outfits that transformed them into a pair of reporters from the 1920s. Then they slipped into their new identities (they called themselves "Scoops" and "Cubby") and stirred things up a little at an event that was, in that era, little more than an extended press conference.

"We ran down the hall into a ballroom where all the players, all the Steelers, were," Dryer said in the Grantland piece. "We went right up to Terry Bradshaw. We were the first guys to get to him. We asked him, 'Is it true that hat size is indicative of IQ, and if so, what is your hat size?'"

Recalled Retzel: "The entire press plan, the entire public relations plan, got tossed into the toilet the moment we went in there."

Journalism school graduates are in consensus about this: Media Day is a terrible representation of the fourth estate. But as entertainment goes, the Tuesday before the big game is a garish, wonderful example of the uniquely American spectacle that is the Super Bowl.

A SAMPLING OF ECCENTRIC SUPER BOWL MEDIA DAY QUESTIONS:

Q "WHO IS YOUR FAVORITE TEENAGE MUTANT NINJA TURTLE?"

A "DEFINITELY RAFAEL. HE'S SARCASTIC, FUNNY, AND AGGRESSIVE."
—Seattle Seahawks linebacker Bobby Wagner

Q "TELL ME, WHY DO THEY CALL YOU BOOMER?"
—From a Japanese reporter to San Francisco 49ers quarterback Joe Montana

Q "DO YOU BELIEVE IN VOODOO, AND CAN I HAVE A LOCK OF YOUR HAIR?"
—To St. Louis Rams quarterback Kurt Warner

Q "IS THIS A MUST-WIN GAME?"
—To Seattle Seahawks head coach Pete Carroll

Q "WHAT ARE YOU GOING TO WEAR TO THE GAME ON SUNDAY?"
—From MTV's Julie Brown to Dallas Cowboys running back Emmitt Smith

Q "DO YOU WATCH *REAL HOUSEWIVES OF NEW JERSEY*?"
—To Denver Broncos quarterback Peyton Manning

#knixcountry #barrelboy
KNIX 102.5

AP Photo/Paul Spinelli

Q "WHAT IS YOUR RELATIONSHIP WITH THE FOOTBALL?"

A "I'D SAY IT'S STRICTLY PLATONIC."
—Tennessee Titans defensive back Joe Salave'a

THE TWELFTH
MAN

PLAYERS BEHAVING BADLY

No single sporting event is bigger than the Super Bowl, so everything in the game's orbit is overblown as well. Giant media presence. Extravagant halftime shows. Overpriced commercials. An above-average tendency for professional athletes to behave idiotically.

Sports stars making the news for misbehavior off the field is certainly not a novelty, but something about Super Bowl week seems to elevate the folly. Whether it's the nerves of the upcoming game, the temptations of the Super Bowl festivities in cities often known for their nightlife, or the feeling of invincibility for a player at the top of his game, the list of players who made the worst decision of their lives on the brink of the biggest game of their lives is jarringly long.

MAX MCGEE

For proof that player waywardness is as old as the Super Bowl itself, look no further than McGee, the Packers wide receiver who stayed under the covers fully clothed during Vince Lombardi's bed check before Super Bowl I and then went out carousing in Beverly Hills with a group of stewardesses. At 34, McGee rarely played and didn't think his night out would have any bearing on the game the next day, but when Boyd Dowler went down with an injury early in the game, McGee went in and proceeded to catch seven passes for 138 yards and two touchdowns.

JOE NAMATH

As if guaranteeing and delivering an unlikely victory in Super Bowl III weren't enough, Namath was legendary for his raucous nights on the eves of big games. *New York* magazine's Jimmy Breslin spent a night on the town with Namath a few months after the quarterback led the Jets to the Super Bowl victory over the Colts and asked him how he prepared for the game. Namath's response: "I went out and got a bottle and grabbed this girl and brought her back to the hotel in Fort Lauderdale, and we had a good time the whole night."

AP Photo

THOMAS HENDERSON

The linebacker known as "Hollywood" had such impressive speed that the Cowboys used him to run reverses on kickoff returns, but by Super Bowl XIII his fast lifestyle had started to catch up with him. In his 1987 autobiography Henderson admitted that he snorted cocaine out of a Vicks inhaler on the sideline throughout the game against the Pittsburgh Steelers. After recovering from his addiction, Henderson has devoted his life to telling his story to others struggling with drugs, saying, "I'm the opposite of the guy who played in Super Bowl XIII."

STANLEY WILSON

Perhaps no pre–Super Bowl incident had as much bearing on its team's Super Bowl performance as the relapse of Stanley Wilson on the eve of Super Bowl XXIII. Wilson had already served two NFL-mandated suspensions for cocaine use, and when he was late to a team meeting, a Cincinnati Bengals assistant went to his hotel room and found him in a drug-fueled stupor. Not only was Wilson barred from playing the next day but he was also banned from the league for life, and Bengals head coach Sam Wyche has always maintained that his presence in the backfield could have been a game changer in Cincinnati's 20-16 loss to San Francisco.

EUGENE ROBINSON

He was a pillar of the defense for the Atlanta Falcons and such a model citizen that the Christian group Athletes in Action presented him the Bart Starr Award for "high moral character" the day before Super Bowl XXXIII. That night, Eugene Robinson was arrested for soliciting oral sex from an undercover cop posing as a prostitute. The drama surrounding the event kept players and coaches up half the night; head coach Dan Reeves opted to play Robinson the next day, and the Falcons fell to the Denver Broncos 34-19.

JIM MCMAHON

The Big Easy was the epicenter for even more revelry in the days leading up to Super Bowl XX, and most of it seemed to swirl around the Chicago Bears' unpredictable quarterback. According to Michael Wenreb's book *Bigger Than the Game: Bo, Boz, the Punky QB, and How the '80s Created the Modern Athlete*, McMahon hit the French Quarter streets every night, sampling the bars and even stopping to relieve himself in a doorway on Chartres Street. But McMahon's biggest controversy came on something he didn't even do—a false report of a radio interview he supposedly gave in which he made disparaging statements about the citizens of New Orleans. Two dozen women protested outside McMahon's hotel, carrying rolls of toilet paper and signs that said, "McMahon, put your headband over your mouth."

JOHN MATUSZAK

The Raiders defensive end was known as one of the baddest boys in the NFL, so it might not have been wise to send him to New Orleans for Super Bowl XV. Matuszak famously offered to chaperone his younger players in the French Quarter, saying, "I'm going to see that there's no funny business. I've had enough parties for 20 people's lifetimes. I'll keep our young fellows out of trouble." The next night, Matuszak was spotted rolling in from Bourbon Street at 3 a.m.

AP Photo /Brian Horton

AP Photo/John Swart

SUPER BOWL RINGS

SUPER BOWL I, 1967
GREEN BAY PACKERS

AP Photo/NFL Photos

Custom rings have been created for the winning teams of every Super Bowl. The first, awarded to the Green Bay Packers after their 35-10 victory over the Kansas City Chiefs, was yellow gold with a round diamond and an engraving that read, "Green Bay Packers World Champions 1966," since the game had not yet been officially dubbed the Super Bowl.

SUPER BOWL II, 1968
GREEN BAY PACKERS
AP Photo/NFL Photos

SUPER BOWL III, 1969
NEW YORK JETS
AP Photo/NFL Photos

SUPER BOWL IV, 1970
KANSAS CITY CHIEFS
AP Photo/NFL Photos

SUPER BOWL V, 1971
BALTIMORE COLTS
AP Photo/NFL Photos

SUPER BOWL VI, 1972
DALLAS COYBOYS
AP Photo/NFL Photos

SUPER BOWL VII, 1973
MIAMI DOLPHINS
AP Photo/NFL Photos

SUPER BOWL VIII, 1974
MIAMI DOLPHINS
AP Photo/NFL Photos

SUPER BOWL IX, 1975
PITTSBURGH STEELERS
AP Photo/NFL Photos

SUPER BOWL X, 1976
PITTSBURGH STEELERS
AP Photo/NFL Photos

SUPER BOWL XI, 1977
OAKLAND RAIDERS
AP Photo/NFL Photos

SUPER BOWL XII, 1978
DALLAS COWBOYS
AP Photo/NFL Photos

SUPER BOWL XIII, 1979
PITTSBURGH STEELERS
AP Photo/NFL Photos

SUPER BOWL XIV, 1980
PITTSBURGH STEELERS

AP Photo/NFL Photos

SUPER BOWL XV, 1981
OAKLAND RAIDERS

AP Photo/NFL Photos

SUPER BOWL XVI, 1982
SAN FRANCISCO 49ERS

AP Photo/NFL Photos

SUPER BOWL XVII, 1983
WASHINGTON REDSKINS

AP Photo/NFL Photos

SUPER BOWL XVIII, 1984
LOS ANGELES RAIDERS

AP Photo/NFL Photos

SUPER BOWL XIX, 1985
SAN FRANCISCO 49ERS

AP Photo/NFL Photos

SUPER BOWL XX, 1986
CHICAGO BEARS

AP Photo/NFL Photos

The largest Super Bowl ring ever made for a player was a size 23, crafted for William "The Refrigerator" Perry after Super Bowl XX. The average man wears a ring between a size 10 and 12. Perry later sold his ring, but a 10-year-old boy who had bought the ring out of his savings account later returned it to Perry. "He said Perry lost the ring through hard times, and that he only had one ring," the boy's mother said.

SUPER BOWL XXI, 1987
NEW YORK GIANTS

AP Photo/NFL Photos

SUPER BOWL XXII, 1988
WASHINGTON REDSKINS

AP Photo/NFL Photos

SUPER BOWL XXIII, 1989
SAN FRANCISCO 49ERS

AP Photo/NFL Photos

SUPER BOWL XXIV, 1990
SAN FRANCISCO 49ERS

AP Photo/Paul Spinelli

SUPER BOWL XXV, 1991
NEW YORK GIANTS

AP Photo/NFL Photos

SUPER BOWL XXVI, 1992
WASHINGTON REDSKINS

AP Photo/NFL Photos

SUPER BOWL XXVII, 1993
DALLAS COWBOYS

AP Photo/NFL Photos

SUPER BOWL XXVIII, 1994
DALLAS COWBOYS

AP Photo/NFL Photos

**SUPER BOWL XXIX, 1995
SAN FRANCISCO 49ERS**

AP Photo/Michael Burr

**SUPER BOWL XXX, 1996
DALLAS COWBOYS**

AP Photo/NFL Photos

**SUPER BOWL XXXI, 1997
GREEN BAY PACKERS**

AP Photo/NFL Photos

**SUPER BOWL XXXII, 1998
DENVER BRONCOS**

AP Photo/NFL Photos

**SUPER BOWL XXXIII, 1999
DENVER BRONCOS**

AP Photo/NFL Photos

**SUPER BOWL XXXIV, 2000
ST. LOUIS RAMS**

AP Photo/NFL Photos

SUPER BOWL XXXVIII, 2004
NEW ENGLAND PATRIOTS

AP Photo/NFL Photos

In 2005 Patriots owner Robert Kraft was visiting Russian President Vladimir Putin when he showed the ring to Putin. Kraft did not intend to give the ring to Putin, but the Russian took it anyway and displayed it in the Kremlin library. Kraft, who didn't go public with the story until 2014, said that someone in the White House asked him to let Putin keep the ring. "I took out the ring and showed it to [Putin], and he put it on and he goes, 'I can kill someone with this ring,'" Kraft said about the incident. "I put my hand out and he put it in his pocket, and three KGB guys got around him and walked out."

**SUPER BOWL XXXV, 2001
BALTIMORE RAVENS**

AP Photo/NFL Photos

**SUPER BOWL XXXVI, 2002
NEW ENGLAND PATRIOTS**

AP Photo/Michael Burr

**SUPER BOWL XXXVII, 2003
TAMPA BAY BUCCANEERS**

AP Photo/NFL Photos

SUPER BOWL XXXIX, 2005
NEW ENGLAND PATRIOTS

AP Photo/NFL Photos

The heaviest Super Bowl ring was awarded to the New England Patriots after they prevailed over the Philadelphia Eagles in Super Bowl XXXIX. The ring weighed 110 grams, or roughly the weight of an iPhone.

SUPER BOWL XL, 2006 PITTSBURGH STEELERS

(On ring finger)

SUPER BOWL XLIII, 2009 PITTSBURGH STEELERS

(On middle finger)

If a team has won multiple Super Bowls, its ring will typically contain diamonds signifying each previous Super Bowl victory.

AP Photo/Ed Rieker

MAKING THE RINGS

Every year jewelry companies submit bids to produce the rings for the Super Bowl, and the winning team selects the manufacturers. Jostens has produced 30 rings, and Balfour and Tiffany's have also each been selected to make the prizes. The NFL covers up to $5,000 each for rings, and teams that want to reward more people or spring for pricier hardware must cover the extra costs themselves. Besides players and coaches, team support staff, cheerleaders, and other key personnel might receive rings at the discretion of the team owner. The New York Giants' victory in Super Bowl XLII came a year after Ernie Accorsi's retirement from nine years as the team's general manager. But virtually every player on that championship team, including MVP Eli Manning, had been acquired or drafted by Accorsi, so owner John Mara made sure his former GM received a ring. "He deserves as much credit for this as anyone," Mara told The *New York Times*.

SUPER BOWL XLII, 2008 NEW YORK GIANTS

AP Photo/Julie DeCrow, File

SUPER BOWL XLI, 2007 INDIANAPOLIS COLTS

AP Photo/The Indianapolis Star, Kelly Wilkinson

SUPER BOWL XLIV, 2010 NEW ORLEANS SAINTS

AP Photo/Patrick Semansky

SUPER BOWL XLV, 2011 GREEN BAY PACKERS

AP Photo/Mike Roemer

The Packers became the first team to receive platinum rings when they won Super Bowl XLV.

SUPER BOWL XLVI, 2012 NEW YORK GIANTS

AP Photo/John Minchillo

SUPER BOWL XLVII, 2013 BALTIMORE RAVENS

AP Photo/Patrick Semansky

SUPER BOWL XLVIII, 2014 SEATTLE SEAHAWKS

AP Photo/Elaine Thompson

THE LOMBARDI TROPHY

FACTS ABOUT PROFESSIONAL FOOTBALL'S MOST COVETED PRIZE:

The trophy, which features a regulation-sized football created entirely out of sterling silver, takes Tiffany's silversmiths nearly four months to complete. It is crafted at a Tiffany's workshop in New Jersey.

The first four trophies were inscribed with the words "World Professional Football Championship." The statue was renamed the Lombardi Trophy in 1970 after the death of legendary Packers coach Vince Lombardi.

AP Photo/NFL Photo/Vernon Biever

Following the ceremony on the field in which the winning team's owner is presented with the trophy, it is taken back to Tiffany's for the name of the winning team to be hand engraved on its surface.

AP Photos/David Drapkin

VINCE LOMBARDI TROPHY

NFL

HEIGHT	WEIGHT
22 in.	**7 lbs.**

After the New York Jets were awarded the trophy following their triumph in Super Bowl III, they reportedly left it behind at the Orange Bowl in Miami.

AP Photo/NFL Photos

AP Photo/Seth Wenig

"I THINK MIAMI, NEW ORLEANS, SAN DIEGO, ALL THOSE WARM-WEATHER CITIES ARE THE BEST CITIES FOR A GAME OF THAT MAGNITUDE."

Don Shula

CHAPTER 12: FROM THE SIDELINES

THE GAME BALL

For an accountant it's tax season; for retail employees it's Black Friday; and for the workers in the Ada, Ohio, Wilson football factory, it's the three days following the AFC and NFC Championship Games.

From Sunday to Tuesday—when the balls must be shipped UPS to the two competing teams—the 130 employees at the Ada plant work around the clock to produce 120 custom game balls, stamped with the Super Bowl logo, the names of the two teams, and the game's location. For those workers, this is a labor of love fueled by their company's 75-year relationship with the NFL and the anticipation of seeing their handiwork in the world's biggest football game.

The NFL, representing that quintessentially American sport, is aptly the only league whose championship balls are manufactured in the United States. The baseballs for the World Series hail from Costa Rica, and a factory in China produces the basketballs that are used for the NBA Finals. The small Midwestern town of Ada—population 5,500—watches every Super Bowl with a keen eye on the ball and a sense of pride in the vital role its residents play in the festivities.

"The people at church come up and talk to me about it all the time," Wilson lockstitch sewer Glenn Hanson told The New York Times in 2008. "They ask, 'Are those your balls that they're using?' He answers, 'Yeah, I probably sewed them.' And they get a pretty big thrill out of it."

Of the 120 Super Bowl balls that are handcrafted in the Ada factory each January, 54 are designated as practice balls for use by the teams when they arrive in the host city, and 54 are reserved as game balls. The remaining 20 are special kicker balls, used only in the kicking game and distinguishable from the other 108 by the K stamped on each ball and their delivery method—the kicker balls are sent separately to the official NFL hotel one week before the game.

After the game, Wilson sells pigskins that actually saw action in the Super Bowl for $139. (Official replica Super Bowl balls are also available for a fraction of that price.) And just in case a collector is concerned that his or her prized football did not actually touch Super Bowl turf, Wilson adds a DNA dye to the laces on game day, after the officials inspect the balls, to certify those 54 as genuine.

The laces of the 120 balls designated for the Super Bowl are marked with a special dye, visible only under a special light, to certify their authenticity.

In just three days, the Super Bowl balls are crafted in Wilson's Ada, Ohio, factory and custom stamped in two places—with the official logo for the upcoming Super Bowl on one side and the names of the teams and the game's location on the other. *AP Photo/David Stluka*

The inscription "The Duke" on every NFL football is in homage to Wellington Mara, the longtime Giants owner, whose father, Tim, named him after the Duke of Wellington.

Glenn Hanson sews together the full ball in the process of making the official game balls for NFL Super Bowl XLIV at the Wilson Sporting Goods football factory in Ada, Ohio. *AP Photo/Amy Sancetta*

Of course, the value of a Super Bowl ball is elevated considerably if a star from that particular game puts his autograph on it. An authentic ball from Super Bowl XLVI autographed by Giants quarterback and MVP Eli Manning was priced at $700 on eBay three years after the game, and balls signed by Russell Wilson of the Seahawks and Aaron Rodgers of the Packers after they led their teams to Super Bowl victory went for prices ranging from $500 to $600.

Wilson produces balls for every NFL game throughout the season and the playoffs, and some features of the balls are consistent for every type of game. All NFL game balls have 16 lace holes and one lace threaded through them; all are made with a single cowhide, usually from a cow hailing from Kansas or Nebraska; and all are stamped with the moniker "the Duke."

"The Duke" designation is homage to longtime Giants owner Wellington Mara, whose father, Tim, along with Bears owner George Halas, first endorsed Wilson as the official football distributor for the NFL. Halas recommended that Wellington "the Duke" Mara (the nickname came from Giants players when he was a boy) be honored on the balls, and Wilson complied starting in 1941. "The Duke" balls were discontinued in 1969, but when Mara died in 2005, Wilson resurrected the emblem on all NFL balls in his memory.

The Super Bowl logo is the main element that sets balls apart physically when the big game rolls around, but the policies regarding the Super Bowl balls are also a little different from those for a typical game. For one thing, according to NFL rules, only 36 balls are required to be presented for inspection prior to a regular game, as opposed to the 54 for the Super Bowl. As for the kickers' balls, the league typically requires only eight for outdoor stadiums and six for indoor venues.

One little-known rule is consistent for any game: in the case of adverse field conditions, the center for the offensive team can deem a ball too slippery or messy to hold and request a new playable ball. The rationale for this policy, it would seem, is that the center is the player who can assess the ball with the most regularity. With the preponderance of Super Bowls played in domed stadiums, centers get scant opportunities to request new game balls in Super Bowls, but it could happen, and Wilson's supply of 54 balls virtually assures that a new pigskin would be available.

As Wilson puts it on the company's website, "We have had a ball at every Super Bowl."

THE WEATHER

WHEN THE ELEMENTS BECAME THE STORY

Only 16 of the 49 Super Bowls in history were played in stadiums with domed or retractable roofs—which means that two-thirds of the time, the sporting event whose every detail is meticulously planned is saddled with a colossal X factor.

Of course, the vast majority of those outdoor games were contested in climates with mild weather year-round. But rain, wind, and even anomalous cold can and have happened, and the show—and the game—must go on.

Groundskeeper George Toma, under cover, and his son Chip Toma (*right*) examine the turf on the playing field at the Rose Bowl. Heavy rains pelted much of Southern California, but the bad weather was not expected to interfere with Super Bowl XVII. *AP Photo*

AP Photo

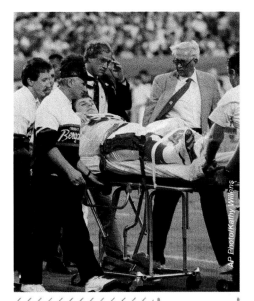

AP Photo/Kathy Willens

AP Photo/Julie Jacobson

AP Photo/Charlie Riedel

39°F
4°C

76°F
24°C

67°F
19°C

52°F
11°C

SUPER BOWL VI

New Orleans has hosted more Super Bowls than any other city but Miami, but after the second championship played there, it was no wonder that the NFL threatened to stay away permanently if the city didn't construct a dome. Super Bowl VI between the Dallas Cowboys and the Miami Dolphins was the coldest outdoor Super Bowl on record, with temperatures at game time recorded at 39 degrees in Tulane Stadium.

SUPER BOWL XXIII

Not cold or rain but wind was the natural variable at this game in Miami's Joe Robbie Stadium. The wind blew steadily throughout the game at 15–20 mph, with gusts recorded at 25 mph and up. The 49ers compensated for the strange conditions with a 20-16 victory, despite a field goal by Bengals kicker Jim Breech that was essentially blown through the goal posts by the stiff wind. However, the weather wasn't the most serious environmental factor hindering the two teams that day. Due to an error by the grounds-keeping crew, the field's suction system had been left on and sucked every bit of moisture out of the playing surface, leaving it as hard as concrete and contributing to several broken bones.

SUPER BOWL XLI

If this game between the Indianapolis Colts and the Chicago Bears had kicked off in the afternoon, like the early Super Bowls did, they might have enjoyed a few dry moments. As it was, nearly an inch of rain fell unrelentingly from afternoon through midnight or later at Dolphins Stadium in Miami and soaked the game and its spectators from start to finish. Each team had trouble holding onto the ball in the conditions, with a total of six turnovers in the first half. Surprisingly, the Colts prevailed 29-17 even though they play their home games in a perfectly dry dome.

SUPER BOWL XLV

The first Super Bowl played in the Dallas–Fort Worth area proved that a dome isn't always enough to keep out the elements. A rare ice storm slammed north Texas a week before the game, followed by five inches of snow three days later. It was a double whammy that created a transportation nightmare and even caused several serious injuries to passersby when huge slabs of ice fell from Cowboys Stadium and hit people walking by on the outdoor plaza. *Sports Illustrated* writer Peter King surveyed Interstate 30, rendered useless by the thick snow, and tweeted, "This is officially a debacle."

UP IN THE
AIR

THUNDERBIRDS
SUPER BOWL XLIX

BLUE**ANGELS**
SUPER BOWL XLIII

AP Photo/Scott Boehm

GOODYEAR**BLIMP**
SUPER BOWL VIII

AP Photo/NFL Photos

BLUE**ANGELS**
SUPER BOWL XXXII

AP Photo/Brian Diggs

GOODYEAR**BLIMP**
SUPER BOWL XXVII

AP Photo/Reed Saxon

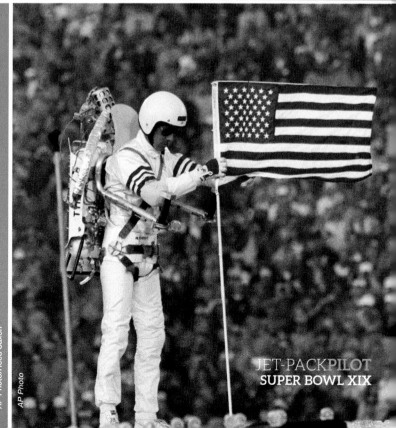

JET-PACK**PILOT**
SUPER BOWL XIX

AP Photo

CHEERLEADERS

THE TOP OF THE PYRAMID

- Not all NFL teams have cheerleaders. Pittsburgh, Green Bay, Cleveland, Detroit, Chicago, and the New York Giants do not sponsor cheerleading teams.

- During Super Bowl XLV between the Pittsburgh Steelers and the Green Bay Packers, neither team brought cheerleaders, making it the first such game since Super Bowl II.

- Cheerleaders on the winning Super Bowl team also receive Super Bowl rings at the discretion of the team owner.

- During broadcast NFL games, cheerleaders are on TV for only about three seconds.

- The *Boston Herald* reported in 2004 that Michelle Ebrecht, who cheered for the Patriots from 1998 to 2003, had lost her ring commemorating New England's 20-17 victory over St. Louis at a local nightclub, and she turned to the media in hopes that the ring might be found and recovered.

" For me, it's valuable because there's only one first," Ebrecht said, referring to the first of the Patriots' Super Bowl wins in that decade. "It's something we [cheerleaders] treasured for all the time and work we put in. "

- The league allows NFL teams to bring 32 cheerleaders to perform at the Super Bowl.

- In Super Bowl XLVI between the Giants and the Patriots, the New England cheerleaders performed alone, which isn't totally uncommon.

Ric Tapia/TapiaPhoto

In 1967 Larry Jacobson decided he wanted to take in the first NFL-AFL Championship, soon to be known as the Super Bowl. He got a round-trip flight from San Francisco to Los Angeles for he and his date, bought two tickets to the game, and ate dinner while they were there. All in all, the day cost Jacobson less than $100.

For Jacobson, who has attended every Super Bowl, one of the most drastic trends over the decades has been the skyrocketing cost of tickets, from $12 for that first championship (a price many considered exorbitant) to the going rate of $2,500 per ticket today through secondary vendors and well into five figures from scalpers.

According to a 2011 analysis of ticket prices by The Dallas Morning News, the tickets stayed at $12 until Super Bowl IV, when they jumped to $15 for the next five years. In Super Bowl IX fans shelled out $20, and the next jump in face value was the most drastic—to $30 at Super Bowl XII. That price lasted for three years, until another $10 price hike brought the tickets to $40 for admission to Super Bowl XV.

As the popularity of the game mushroomed, so did the value of the tickets, and those wanting to attend Super Bowl XVIII had to shell out $60. The trend of a $15 or $20 increase in face value every few years continued steadily until Super Bowl XXX, when tickets took a one-year leap from $200 to $275. The next big jump, from XXXIX to XL, was from $550 to $650, with face value creeping past $1,000 for most tickets by 2014.

Tickets under $1,000 do still exist, but if you want one, you have to be extremely lucky. Only 1 percent of all Super Bowl tickets are actually sold at face value to fans, and those are distributed through a lottery. For Super Bowl XLVIII, 30,000 fans entered, and 1,000 winners were selected.

If they don't score admission through a Super Bowl sponsor or a team connection, most of the fans who make the trip to the game buy either through a ticketing website such as Ticketmaster or StubHub, which offered tickets from $2,500 and up for Super Bowl XLIX in Arizona, or from scalpers in the host city.

Approximately 75 percent of the tickets for each Super Bowl are divided between the 32 NFL teams, with 35 percent of those going to the two competing teams and 6 percent to the host team, according to a 2014 New York Times article. Whatever is left is generally kept by the NFL to give out to corporate sponsors and other dignitaries.

Despite NFL efforts to curtail scalping in recent years, stories abound of resold tickets going for close to $20,000. Starting with Super Bowl XLVIII, the league started giving tickets to the fans who won tickets through the two teams at the stadium on game day after they had passed through security. Fans received their tickets and went to their seats, but they were not permitted to go outside the Meadowlands—a concerted effort to prevent scalping.

NFL owners have pushed to increase the face value of the best seats in the Super Bowl venue, a league representative told The Wall Street Journal in 2013, to allow the league to capture some of the profit currently going to third-party agents.

"We are looking to close the gap between the face value of the ticket and the true value of a ticket to what has become the premier sports and entertainment event," NFL spokesman Brian McCarthy said.

Two tickets for Super Bowl XLIV. The total cost of admission was $900 each, or $1,800 for the pair.
AP Photo/David J. Phillip

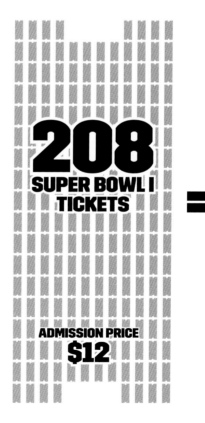

208
SUPER BOWL I TICKETS

ADMISSION PRICE
$12

=

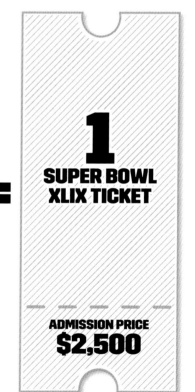

1
SUPER BOWL XLIX TICKET

ADMISSION PRICE
$2,500

PART 4

THE

"IF POLITICIANS HAVE ELECTION DAY AND HOLLYWOOD HAS THE OSCARS, ADVERTISING HAS THE SUPER BOWL."

Jerry Femina, advertising executive

CHAPTER 13: THE COMMERCIALS

THE
COMMERCIALS

Top left, Master Lock's iconic "Marksman" commercial aired during the Super Bowl from 1974 to 1983. Master Lock

Many discussions of Super Bowl advertising begin with Apple's groundbreaking "1984" ad that evoked George Orwell's futuristic book and aired the same year as its title. But the Super Bowl was played for 17 years before Apple took to the game's airwaves. What did football fans watch between the plays in the early years? The answer to that question reveals much about the seismic growth of both the advertising industry and the Super Bowl as a cultural lightning rod.

Even though the games in the late 1960s were broadcast to TV viewers, the commercials themselves didn't start to make news until the early '70s, and, appropriately, the star of the first Super Bowl upset was also featured in its earliest memorable ad. Joe Namath led his New York Jets to a stunning victory over the

Baltimore Colts in Super Bowl III and instantly became the most sought-after celebrity for endorsements of that era. His 1973 Noxzema shaving cream ad alongside a still-unknown Farrah Fawcett was silly and more than a little risqué for the time.

The next Super Bowl commercial frequently mentioned as a conversation piece in the 1970s was first aired during Super Bowl VII, the same one that featured Broadway Joe and his shaving cream. The product in the spotlight was the Master Lock padlock, and what the spot lacked in production style it made up for in authenticity, showing an actual field test of a man shooting a bullet through the center of a Master Lock—which stayed locked despite the hole in the center. Four decades later *The Christian Science*

Monitor ranked it as one of the top five Super Bowl ads ever.

But the early commercial with the most cultural staying power, contrary to popular belief, did not premier at the Super Bowl. The world first saw Pittsburgh Steelers defensive lineman Mean Joe Greene accept a Coke from an adorable little boy and then toss him his jersey with the famous line, "Hey, kid, catch!" in October of 1979, but the spot saw its largest audience when it aired a few months later during the Super Bowl XIV telecast.

Probably the only commercial ever to spawn a TV movie, a 1981 special called *The Steeler and the Pittsburgh Kid*, it has also been copied and spoofed frequently through the decades. In addition, it presented

a new side to one of the toughest pillars of Pittsburgh's legendary Steel Curtain defense. "I was suddenly approachable," Greene said at a presentation at the Coca-Cola headquarters in 2014. "Little kids were no longer afraid of me, and older people—both women and men—would come up and offer me a Coke."

Below, Former Pittsburgh Steeler and star of Coca-Cola's 1979 television commercial, "Mean" Joe Greene. *AP Photo*

TOP SUPER BOWL
COMMERCIALS
OF THE PAST 25 YEARS

To some extent, Super Bowl ads are in the eye of the beholder, and like modern art, everyone has a different interpretation of what works. But starting in 1989, *USA Today* developed its Ad Meter, a survey that recruits volunteers to vote on their favorite Super Bowl spots in real time using a handheld meter. Since 2013, online Facebook votes have also been included in the tally. Presenting the Ad Meter champions over the past quarter century:

1989, AMERICAN EXPRESS

Jon Lovitz and Dana Carvey take competing credit cards to the big game.

1990, NIKE

A montage of a series of iconic announcers narrating some of the most unforgettable sports moments of the era, with a featured cameo by Harry Caray.

1991, DIET PEPSI

Ray Charles is the star of this catchy musical production featuring the jingle "You've Got the Right One, Baby."

1992, NIKE

Michael Jordan and Bugs Bunny (aka Hare Jordan) battle a team of martians in space. The ad inspired the 1996 movie *Space Jam*.

1993, McDONALD'S

His Airness makes his second appearance at the top in this shooting battle between Jordan and Larry Bird for a Big Mac. "Over the expressway, over the river, off the billboard, through the window, off the wall, nothing but net."

1994, PEPSI

Two chimps are the subjects of a scientific study, with one drinking Coke and the other drinking Pepsi. The Pepsi chimp is found six weeks later cruising to the beach in a Jeep full of beautiful women.

1995, PEPSI

A boy at the beach, trying to get the last drops from his Pepsi bottle, sucks through the straw so hard that he sucks himself into the bottle, prompting his little sister to exclaim, "Mom, he's done it again!"

Opposite page, Andy Samberg, Akiva Schaffer, and Jorma Taccone, (*left to right*), of The Lonely Island, check out the competition's videos on the set of a promotional shoot for Doritos "Crash the Super Bowl," Sunday, in New York. *Diane Bondareff/AP Images for Doritos.*

Top left, Roughly 10 million people tuning in to the Super Bowl are mainly watching for the commercials. So much so that "Super Bowl Commercial Watching Parties" have been continuing to trend.

1996, PEPSI

While Hank Williams's "Your Cheatin' Heart" plays in the background, a Coca-Cola delivery man is captured on security camera stealthily pulling a can of Pepsi out of the next cooler, only to trigger an avalanche of Pepsi cans.

1997, PEPSI

Five grizzly bears in a small California town perform a choreographed dance to a Pepsi song inspired by the Village People's "YMCA." An old man looks out the window and remarks, "Heaven help us if they ever learn the Macarena."

1998, PEPSI

Skysurfer Troy Hartman and a goose try to outdo each other's feats and then share a Pepsi in midflight.

1999, BUDWEISER

The first Clydesdale ad to win *USA Today*'s top honors features two Dalmatians from the same litter, separated as puppies, who pass each other on the road as one rides on a Clydesdale-drawn beer truck and one on a fire engine.

2000, BUDWEISER

A canine actor named Rex is trying to whip up some tears but is unable to. The director suggests he think about his worst day, which was the memory of him attempting, and failing, to chase a Budweiser truck.

2001, BUD LIGHT

Comedian Cedric the Entertainer kills the mood on a romantic date when he dances with a bottle of Bud Light and it explodes all over the woman.

2002, BUD LIGHT

A man has an unfortunate encounter with satin sheets after his wife lures him to bed with the promise of cold Bud Light.

2003, BUDWEISER

A zebra watches and rewatches an instant replay during a snowy game between teams of Clydesdales.

2004, BUD LIGHT

Two guys with dogs try to outdo each other by showing how their dogs can fetch bottles of Bud Light.

2005, BUD LIGHT

A skydiving instructor tries to entice his fearful rookie jumper out of the hatch with a six-pack of Bud Light, but it's the pilot who jumps out after it instead.

2006, BUD LIGHT

One man's plan to keep his friends away from his Bud Light by installing a revolving wall backfires when the residents of the apartment next door encounter a "magic fridge."

2007, BUDWEISER

Animals are back in this spot, with a beachful of crabs hijacking and then bowing down to a cooler full of Bud Light.

2008, BUDWEISER

A Clydesdale rejected from the hitch team is whipped into shape by a Dalmatian friend in this *Rocky*-inspired ad.

2009, DORITOS

Frito-Lay proved that Madison Avenue doesn't have a market on creativity with this ad, the first fan-generated commercial from the "Crash the Super Bowl" contest to take honors. In it, a man convinces his coworkers that a snow globe is a crystal ball that will bring free Doritos.

2010, SNICKERS

The first celebrity ad to win the Ad Meter poll in nearly a decade, this commercial puts Betty White in the middle of a pickup football game.

2011, TIE, BUD LIGHT

A man housesitting for a group of intelligent dogs puts them to work serving at his party and then cleans up after them as they play poker together afterward.

2011, TIE, DORITOS

A man taunts his girlfriend's pug through a plate glass window with a bag of Doritos, but the pug has the last word.

2012, DORITOS

The third "Crash the Super Bowl" ad to reign supreme in the poll features a dog bribing his owner with Doritos after the man witnesses the dog burying his wife's cat. The ad reportedly cost the creator just $20 to produce.

2013, BUDWEISER

This tearjerker follows the friendship of a horse trainer and a Clydesdale and their heartfelt reunion in a parade.

2014, BUDWEISER

Continuing the reign of sweet Clydesdales spots, in this commercial, a puppy forms a strong bond with a Clydesdale that grows despite their owner's efforts to keep them apart.

2015, BUDWEISER

The latest entry in the heartrending combination of Clydesdales and puppies depicts a group of horses helping to protect a lost puppy from a threatening wolf and then escort him home to his frantic owner.

THE RISING COST
OF SUPER BOWL ADVERTISING

In a nice bit of numeric symmetry, Super Bowl 50 might be the first big game for which 30-second advertising spots cost $5 million. It's a number so exorbitant that the average viewer watching those commercials can't get his or her mind around what the figure even means, but consumer and advertising experts differ on whether companies are getting their money's worth.

A commonly quoted statistic—and one that is guaranteed to make executives salivate—is that more than 100 million people see a Super Bowl advertisement. Ever since the 2010 telecast surpassed the 1983 series finale of *M*A*S*H** as the most watched show in history, every Super Bowl since that year has topped the previous ones in number of viewers. And in an age of on-demand television, it is one of the few big TV events left that must be viewed live.

Most of the Americans who settle in to watch the Super Bowl in their living room or at a party are more likely to run for snacks or beer during the game itself than during the commercials. Certainly, the general buzz that envelops the game centers on commercials in equal parts with the halftime show and the football game itself. But do the commercials really move people to open their wallets?

In 2014, *Advertising Age* reported on a study by the research firm Communicas revealing that only one in five Super Bowl ad viewers decides to make a purchase on the basis of the commercial. The researchers also found that brand recognition from Super Bowl commercials is lower than that associated with other high-profile advertising events because creative expectations are so high. In other words, you might enjoy an ad, but you aren't really sure what it's selling.

But despite the lack of a clear correlation between ads and sales, observers point out that a company with a Super Bowl commercial moves the needle in more ways than just consumer behavior. It's more difficult to measure the impact of creating a buzz around a brand name from a popular commercial, especially when the ripples from that ad include pre–Super Bowl publicity and ongoing social media effects.

$42,000
1967 30-SECOND
TV COMMERCIAL

"What event can better tie-in and harness the power of digital and social media?" wrote advertising executive Rob Siltanen in a 2014 piece on Forbes.com. "And what other event better allows your brand and products to be talked about for weeks leading up to the event, during the event, and for weeks, months, and even years after the event?"

Buying a spot during the Super Bowl broadcast can also be a way for an upstart company to serve notice that it is in the market to stay and ready to play in the big leagues. Few people had heard of the job-search website Monster.com before its iconic 1999 ad featuring kids discussing what they wanted to be when they grew up. A decade later, the company was bringing in some $900 million in revenue annually. In 2013, a commercial for the unique SodaStream carbonated-beverage creator represented the company's commitment to competing in the soft drink market.

"It's really a statement that we are playing serious," CEO Daniel Birnbaum told *AdAge* magazine. "It has opened doors for us."

The Monument to Joe Louis as seen in Detroit was featured in one of the most talked-about Super Bowl ads, Chrysler's "Born on Fire." The two-minute ad was unusual for its length, airing during a broadcast in which a 30-second spot costs $3 million. *AP Photo/Carlos Osorio*

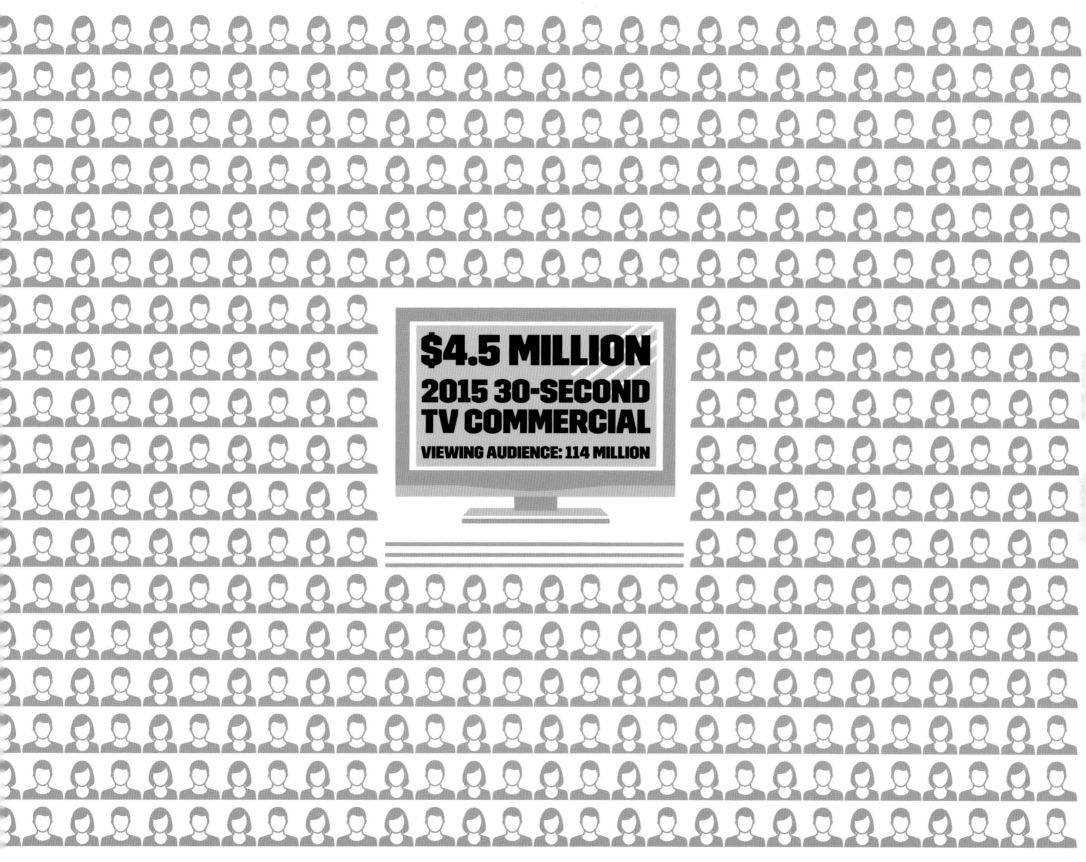

$4.5 MILLION
2015 30-SECOND
TV COMMERCIAL
VIEWING AUDIENCE: 114 MILLION

There was a time in the not-so-distant past when Super Bowl spots were a closely guarded secret, to be revealed in a quick 30 seconds during the broadcast. As everything about media has been transformed by the Internet age, the secrets are now out.

A company's objective in spending $4 million or more on a Super Bowl commercial has changed, from unveiling a surprise hit to creating the largest possible media footprint. And many companies believe that the way to do that is to unveil their ad before the big game even arrives.

In 2011, Volkswagen's popular ad "The Force," featuring a young boy clad as Darth Vader using the force to control his dad's car, was released on YouTube five days before the Super Bowl, and in that time it attracted 20 million views,

according to *Fortune* magazine. The ad was a sensation, and the following year more than half of the Super Bowl spots were released ahead of game day.

"I think you're going to find that, come the game, people will be like 'Shush, shush, stop—here comes the Taco Bell ad; you have to see this," Taco Bell CEO Greg Creed said on *CBS This Morning* in an interview about the trend.

Some advertisers are moving beyond the sneak peek to lengthier "behind-the-scenes" pieces, such as Honda's online video that was essentially a longer version of Matthew Broderick's updated *Ferris Bueller's Day Off* spot in 2012, while other companies have released films about the making of Super Bowl ads or clever promotions such as Newcastle's "non-commercial" with Anna Kendrick, "Behind

the Scenes of the Mega Huge Football Game Ad Newcastle Brown Ale Almost Made," which generated more than three million YouTube views.

Even if companies don't let the cat completely out of the bag before the Super Bowl, many are leaning on social media for advance buzz and audience participation. One pioneer in this area is Doritos, whose "Crash the Super Bowl" contest, created in 2006, allows viewers to create their own ads and then vote for the favorite, which then airs on Super Sunday. Billed as the largest online video contest in the world, the 2012 competition brought in more than 6,000 original submissions.

Other brands create different types of viewer participation, such as Anheuser-Busch's 2010 campaign that allowed customers to choose their favorite Super

Bowl ad on Facebook (an ad featuring the Clydesdales, which the beer company had originally cut from its package, was the winner) and the 2013 Coca-Cola promotion in which fans voted for which group—cowboys, showgirls, or motorcyclists—should reach the oasis first in their Super Bowl ad concept. Voters in that campaign could chime in using Facebook, Twitter, Instagram, or Tumblr.

"It's not just a commercial you're creating," Greg DiNoto, the chief creative officer of Deutsch NY, told CBS News. "You're creating the center of a whole communications effort that's going to last beyond the Super Bowl."

Top left, Many brands release their Super Bowl commercials early online, so fans get to enjoy the spots well ahead of the actual airing of the game.

COMPANIES MADE OR BROKEN
BY SUPER BOWL COMMERCIALS

Economists and executives can argue about the cost-benefit ratio of Super Bowl commercials and whether they truly move the needle for consumers, but some companies have been undeniably affected by their decision to wade into the deep, rushing river of Super Bowl advertising. Some were changed for the good with higher profiles and more favorable bottom lines, while others went into free fall after their ads bombed. Here are five brands that were either made or broken on Super Bowl Sunday:

APPLE

The only national broadcast of Apple's iconic "1984" ad was during Super Bowl XVIII, but the dystopian scene reminiscent of George Orwell's classic book and the intrusion of a runner throwing a hammer at the screen depicting Big Brother was seminal for the young, virtually unknown technology company. In the 90 days after the spot aired, Apple sold 90 percent more units than expected of the product the ad introduced—a new computer called Macintosh.

Steve Jobs, chairman of the board of Apple Computer, leans on the new "Macintosh" personal computer. *AP Photo/Paul Sakuma, File*

GODADDY

In a 2005 column about upcoming Super Bowl advertising, ESPN.com's Darren Rovell made reference to GoDaddy's impending commercial in Super Bowl XXXIX, and he explained that the website, "which sells Web domain names, can benefit from the massive audience that watches the Super Bowl." The fact that a national sports business writer had to explain GoDaddy to his readers goes a long way to illustrate the impact of Super Bowl advertising on the company. In just a few short years—and with the help of a few raunchy ads that have drawn pregame media attention—GoDaddy has become one of the companies you keep an eye on at Super Bowl time, just to see what it'll do next. More importantly, in the six years after that initial Super Bowl ad, its share of the domain name market swelled from 16 percent to more than 50 percent.

MONSTER.COM

So little known was this job-hunting website in 1999 that even an average Super Bowl ad would have boosted its profile, but instead Monster.com burst onto the scene with one of the most talked-about commercials of the past 15 years. With kids earnestly speaking lines such as, "I want to climb my way up to middle management" and "I want to have a brown nose," the spot helped turn Monster.com into a company with annual revenues of $900 million and instant name recognition. On the Monday after the Super Bowl, résumés posted on the site jumped from the average 1,500 to 8,500.

JUST FOR FEET

In one of the most dramatically unhappy endings for a Super Bowl advertising story, this company's Super Bowl XXXIII commercial, according to Business Insider, "virtually killed the company on the spot." The spot featured a group of white men in a Humvee pursuing a barefoot Kenyan runner on the Sahara, giving him drugged water and leaving him passed out. When he awakes, he sees running shoes on his feet and cries out, "Nooooo!" Widely panned as ineffective and racist, the ad prompted Just for Feet to file a lawsuit against its ad agency and then drop the suit before filing for Chapter 11 just months after the Super Bowl ad.

ANHEUSER-BUSCH

The antithesis of a start-up, Anheuser-Busch has been brewing beer since 1852 but has established itself as a titan of modern Super Bowl advertising. Thirteen of the top 17 ads since 1999, as measured by the *USA Today* Ad Meter, have been commercials for either Budweiser or Bud Light, and the Clydesdales have become the most anticipated recurring characters in the breaks between football action. For Super Bowl XLIX the company used the Super Bowl to introduce new packaging for their "Up for Whatever" ad campaign— bottles printed with a variety of messages proclaiming Bud Light as the perfect beer for a variety of scenarios.

In this photo, altered with an Instagram filter, a detail view of the Super Bowl XLIX logo is seen on a Bud Light bottle. *AP Photo/Aaron M. Sprecher*

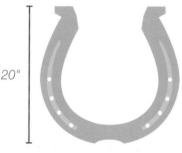

5.5"

Light Horse

20"

Clydesdale

Super Bowl viewers traditionally love animals, and creative teams have been known to feature everything from chimps to pigeons to badgers in their commercials. But only one type of animal is so closely tied to the big game that its potential exclusion from the broadcast prompted a public outcry.

In 2010, Anheuser-Busch announced that even though a Budweiser Clydesdale ad had been produced, it had not made the cut for its Super Bowl slate. But late in the planning process, due in part to pushback from Clydesdale fans, the company reconsidered. Through Facebook, Anheuser-Busch asked fans to vote for

the ad that would fill its final, fourth-quarter slot; the Clydesdale ad took 70 percent of the votes and ended up on the air.

Since that hiccup, the brewery has embraced the public's emotional connection with the horses and produced spots that have earned both widespread acclaim and tender moments sandwiched between ridiculous celebrities and talking babies. The two Clydesdale commercials that aired in 2014, "Puppy Love" and "Hero's Welcome," were both nominated for Emmys in the Outstanding Commercial category.

The 2014 offerings featured a Clydesdale's ongoing bond with a puppy he befriended

on the farm where both animals grew up and poignant footage of a soldier's return home from Afghanistan. For the "Hero's Welcome" commercial, the advertising agency filmed Lt. Chuck Nadd's return to his hometown of Winter Park, Florida, and the parade—complete with a full team of Clydesdales pulling the Budweiser wagon —that was held in his honor. The ad concludes, "Every Soldier Deserves a Hero's Welcome," and it had Super Bowl viewers unexpectedly diving for a tissue before the Seahawks and Broncos could line up for the next play.

With poignant tributes honoring the military and promoting patriotism—another iconic

Clydesdale horseshoes measure more than 20 inches from end to end and weigh about five pounds—more than twice as long and five times as heavy as the shoes worn by light horses.

Trainer Robin Wiltshire (*right*) cracks a whip as a Clydesdale canters down a turn-of-the-century New York streetscape at Warner Bros. studios in Burbank, California, during the filming of a Budweiser beer commercial to be aired during the 2009 Super Bowl. *AP Photo/Damian Dovarganes/File*

Above, The iconic clydesdales displayed on the nation's largest brewery. *AP Photo/James A. Finley*

Opposite page, Berry Farrell of the Anheuser-Busch Clydesdale breeding farm leads a mother Clydesdale and her baby at Grant's farm near St. Louis, Mo. *AP Photo/ James A. Finley*

Springs Ranch in Boonville, Missouri. Not just any Clydesdale can make the cut to pull an Anheuser-Busch wagon or appear in an iconic Super Bowl commercial; featured horses must have a bay coat with four white legs, a white blaze, and a black mane and tail. They must be geldings, be at least four years old, stand 72 inches at the shoulder, and weigh between 1,800 and 2,300 pounds.

In a genre where superstars, flashy setups, and bawdy humor often win the day, Clydesdale commercials are consistently sweet, even reverent, and their themes of patriotism and friendship seem to steady the chaos that often characterizes Super Bowl ad offerings. Americans take notice, perennially voting the commercials as their favorites, and in a 2013 ranking of the best Super Bowl ads of the century, Peter Hartlaub of msnbc.com named the 9/11 Clydesdale tribute, entitled "Respect," as number one, because of both its meaning and its lasting legacy in the world of advertising.

"Somber and patriotic advertising became more common after the Budweiser 'Respect' ad," Hartlaub wrote. "Along with the classic 1980 Coca-Cola commercial with Mean Joe Greene, this Super Bowl commercial has been getting buzz in recent years as the greatest of all time."

Even though Anheuser-Busch seems to have a firm grasp on the Clydesdales' importance in the Super Bowl advertising canon, the company doesn't hitch its marketing plan to just one wagon. As the Super Bowl's highest-spending advertiser, shelling out about $149 million in advertising time for the big game between 2009 and 2013, the brewery has also used the valuable spots to unveil new products, feature celebrities such as Arnold Schwarzenegger to promote Bud Light, and introduce Rex the Wonder Dog in an ad that was the top-rated spot in 2000. But through the madcap plotlines and the glitz, the Clydesdales trot on.

Clydesdale moment showed the horses kneeling before the New York City skyline in a Super Bowl ad after the September 11 attacks—it's no wonder that the Clydesdales have earned a permanent place in American football and advertising lore. But the distinctive horses' association with Anheuser-Busch actually goes back nearly 50 years earlier than their first starring role in a Super Bowl commercial.

The first convergence of the distinctive horses and the venerable brewery was in 1933, when the Twenty-First Amendment to the Constitution ended the nationwide

practice of prohibition. August Busch Jr., the son of the company's CEO, wanted to celebrate the occasion, so he surprised his father by arranging for a team of six Clydesdales to pull a wagon loaded with Anheuser-Busch beer down the St. Louis street in front of the brewery.

In 1940, Anheuser-Busch started breeding Clydesdales, a unique breed of draft horse originally developed in Scotland in the nineteenth century. The brewery's herd has grown to about 200 Clydesdales, with the horses stabled primarily at the Budweiser Clydesdale Stables in St. Louis and Warm

The Budweiser Dalmatian mascot stands on the back section of the world famous Clydesdale hitch. *Cheryl Senter/AP Images*

"I PREDICT ONE OF THESE TWO TEAMS WILL WIN THE SUPER BOWL."

Gilbert Gottfried

CHAPTER 14: FUN AND GAMES

LAS VEGAS GAMBLING

Hope springs eternal for sports gamblers, so many will choose to ignore this statistic: the Las Vegas oddsmakers have won the day in 22 of the past 24 Super Bowls. Favorites are 33-15 straight up and 26-18-2 against the spread, and even when the underdogs prevail, they cover the spread about three-fourths of the time.

There are exceptions, of course, such as the Giants' 16-0 upset of the Patriots in 2008 (even then the sportsbooks lost only $2.6 million), but the history of Super Bowl wagers tilts the playing field sharply toward the bookies.

Of course, past trends have done nothing to stem the financial flood pouring into Vegas each year as the Super Bowl approaches. Every Super Bowl yields a new record for the amount of money wagered, with a combined $119.4 million in 2014 dwarfing the previous record of $98.9 million set in 2013. And when the Seattle Seahawks dismantled the favored Denver Broncos 43-8 in 2014, that Super Bowl set another gambling record—the sportsbooks raked in an unprecedented $19.7 million from their betting clients.

Betting lines and point spreads inspire intense study among bettors, but they aren't the only reason the Super Bowl is the most wagered-upon sporting event in the world. Part of the event's appeal, for oddsmakers and their clients alike, is the breadth of proposition bets, or prop bets, that make everything from the MVP selection, to the coin toss, to the national anthem an opportunity to cash in.

Wagering on games has been around as long as the games themselves, but prop bets are believed to date back to 1986, to Super Bowl XX and an unforgettable player named William "Refrigerator" Perry. At 6 foot 2 and 300-plus pounds, Perry was already a well-known member of the Chicago Bears juggernaut during his 1985 rookie season, even if defensive coordinator Buddy Ryan refused to play him for part of the season and head coach Mike Ditka made the surprising decision to put him in at fullback in certain short-yardage situations. When the Bears made the Super Bowl, the Vegas bookmakers decided to capitalize on Perry's popularity by posting odds as to whether he would score a touchdown in the big game against New England.

The Fridge's odds fluctuated in the two weeks before the Super Bowl, going as high as 75 to 1 and—as the unusual bet attracted the attention of the media and bets poured in—ending up at 2 to 1 on game day. Late in a game that had long been decided in Chicago's favor, the Bears were on the 1-yard line and Ditka put Perry in at fullback. Perry got the ball and barreled in for a touchdown that was meaningless on the scoreboard but momentous for the Las Vegas bookmakers, who seized on the novelty of small bets that could make every part of the game—on and off the field—potentially profitable.

When the first sportsbooks were formed in Vegas in the mid-'70s, the large casinos widely ignored sports betting. Sports wagers were assessed higher taxes than typical casino gambling, and bookies did

not consider them lucrative enough to be worthwhile. But a convergence of events elevated Super Bowl betting from bush league to the marquee: a Nevada legislator successfully lobbied for a drastic reduction in the sports gambling tax; bookmakers started seeking unique, smaller bets that would appeal to casual vacationers at the casinos; and Caesar's Palace started to throw extravagant Super Bowl parties, inviting ex-players and ex-coaches from the NFL and drawing crowds of football fans to the city each winter.

The Fridge wager is believed to be the first highly publicized prop bet in the sports world, but the managers of the sportsbooks got the first inkling of prop bets and their lucrative nature in 1980, when the season finale of *Dallas* asked one question that gripped the nation: Who shot J.R.? Sonny Reizner, who ran the Hole in the Wall casino, saw a golden opportunity and posted odds on which character pulled the trigger. Reizner ultimately had to pull the plug on the bet when the Nevada Gaming Board argued that Vegas couldn't wager on something that was written in a television script.

But the interest in the "Who Shot J.R.?" bet proved to Reizner and others that the betting public would put their dollars down on anything that interested them enough, and William "Refrigerator" Perry was one

of the most interesting athletes of the mid-'80s playing in the most-watched game in sports. Prop bets were born, and today they increase in number and variety every year.

Most of the action put down for the Super Bowl now goes toward the growing number of prop bets, and with such a dizzying array of specialized bets, the casinos are bound to come out ahead when all is said and done. But there are a few proposition bets that are notorious long shots, bets that can be quite expensive for the sportsbooks if bettors are willing to reach for long odds. The longest shot in 2014, with a payout of $999,900 on a $100 bet, would

$119.4 MILLION IN BETS WERE PLACED ON SUPER BOWL XLVIII

have cashed in if either the Broncos or the Seahawks had scored only four points, or two safeties. Other extravagant odds are attached to the unlikely chance that a total of seven points or less would be scored in the game or that no touchdowns would be scored by either team.

But for bettors who don't want to take a crazy gamble but still enjoy playing steep odds, a proposition bet on the likelihood of either a two-point conversion or a safety hits a good middle ground. A safety at any time during the game has paid off at least 6:1 in three of the past five Super Bowls, but the odds were 10 times higher than

that on the wager that a safety would be the first score of the game—a prop bet that made a number of people richer in 2014 when Broncos running back Knowshon Moreno fell on the ball in his own end zone to prevent a Seahawks defensive touchdown.

Chicago Bears defensive tackle William "The Fridge" Perry. *AP Photo/Al Golub*

When a New York woman was fed up with her husband's excessive spending on Super Bowl pools run out of his favorite bar, she wrote a poignant complaint to the NY State Liquor Authority, venting, "My husband spends all his money on these pools and not on our children."

The pools in question, run in a traditional Super Bowl "box" format, promised upward of $200,000 for the winner, and the proprietor of the Talk of the Town Tavern in Staten Island was reportedly keeping 10 percent off the top when wagers were placed, according to the *New York Post*.

It was that practice, along with the unusually lucrative pot, that got the attention of law enforcement after the wife lodged her complaint, and in December 2013 SLA investigators stormed in during the establishment's Christmas Eve party and mandated an end to the Super Bowl pools by citing a state law that prohibits gambling in any business where alcoholic beverages are served.

The *Post* reported that another bar in the Bronx had quietly run a Super Bowl box pool for years with a prize of $500,000—the target of anyone willing to put up $5,000 for each square in the pool. Super Bowl competitions with such meteoric stakes are generally not publicized, both because of the risk of a legal crackdown and because individuals willing to pony up $5,000 are usually attracted not through typical avenues but by word of mouth in serious gambling circles.

High-stakes pools such as the illegal ones operated in Staten Island are certainly available if you know where to look and you want to swim in the deep water, but for sports fans looking to make a casual wager, the best environment is often the workplace. When the Super Bowl rolls around each winter, many employers consider a slight loss of productivity an acceptable trade-off for the fun, usually friendly competition that comes from a Super Bowl office pool.

Variations abound, but the most common type of office contest is the Super Bowl box pool, which usually features 100 boxes on a sheet of paper with the names of the two competing teams on the vertical and horizontal axes. Players put in a certain amount of money to sign their name in one or more boxes, and then the pool administrator draws numbers 0 through 9 to correspond to each row and column. Prizes are awarded if the final digit of each team's final score lines up with the box a pool player has selected. For smaller offices or Super Bowl parties, the grid can be drawn with 25 squares, with two numbers selected for each square instead of one.

Linn Energy is a Houston-based oil and gas company with more than 1,800 employees, and informal pools celebrating everything from college football to March Madness to the Super Bowl are commonplace within the firm, said Mark Cahill, Linn's vice president for marketing. Because the Super Bowl is a one-day event, as opposed to seasons

Liz Rogers (*center*) and her friend Caitlin O'Connor (*left*) celebrate as the Broncos complete a pass, while watching the first half of Super Bowl XLVIII against the Seahawks inside Jackson's, a sports bar and grill in Denver. *AP Photo/Brennan Linsley*

that enable Fantasy Football or other ongoing workplace rivalries, it calls for a simpler structure, and Linn annually puts out a typical box pool where those putting money into the pool are randomly assigned squares on the grid. But at Super Bowl time, like the other opportunities for friendly wagers in a work setting, the mini-rivalries created by office pools serve a larger corporate purpose.

"I think the challenge in this world is to make connections, with your employees and with your teams, and anything you can do to strengthen your connections with your teams is going to help," Cahill said.

Other popular office Super Bowl diversions are proposition bet wager sheets, which take guesses on the outcome of a certain

number of side bets for that year's game, from the result of the coin toss, to the first player to score, to the topic of the first commercial. In some offices or groups of friends, players simply guess the score or margin of victory, and the pool goes to whoever comes the closest.

Other sporting events, notably, the NCAA Basketball Tournament in March, inspire considerable side betting in places of business, and some offices even organize pools for cultural events such as the Academy Awards. But a 2013 study conducted by the Society for Human Resource Management found that the Super Bowl is the event that inspires the most homegrown office pools, with 39 percent of the respondents reporting such diversions in their workplace. (March

Madness was the second-most popular office pool event, with 36 percent.)

Official tolerance—or encouragement—of Super Bowl office pools varies widely from workplace to workplace, but the SHRM study revealed that 81 percent of the companies polled have no written or unwritten policy forbidding office wagering games, and the vast majority of the 355 human resources professionals who participated in the study said that they believed office pools have a positive effect on relationships between employees, team building, and employee engagement.

Based on the past 49 Super Bowls, the three most profitable numbers to have in your squares are 0, 7, and 3.

AP Photo/David J. Phillip

PROPOSITION BETS

FIRST SCORE
First player to score or the jersey number of the first player to score.

FIRST TYPE OF SCORE
One of the prop bet areas that has harmed sportsbooks most lately is the safety, because the payout odds for safety are fairly steep. In 2014 the game opened with a safety, a rarity that gave gamblers a 60:1 payout.

PLAYER BEHAVIOR
Bets have been placed on whether certain players would taunt others or cry during the national anthem.

TURNOVERS
First quarterback to throw an interception/first receiver to drop a pass.

OVERTIME
Whether a game will go into overtime.

TOTAL NUMBER OF POINTS SCORED
Two of the longest-odds bets, both of which have never happened, are one team scoring exactly four points or the total scores of both teams equaling seven points or less.

GATORADE
The color of the Gatorade used to shower the winning coach.

AP Photo/Patrick Semansky

AP Photo/Michael Conroy

THE WEATHER
Whether it will rain or snow during the game or whether the stadium will experience a power outage.

THE LENGTH OF THE NATIONAL ANTHEM
The longest version of America's least singable song came from Alicia Keys in 2013. She stretched it out to 2:36, setting the anthem over/under for the following year at 2:30.

AP Photo/David J. Phillip

ATTIRE OF THE HALFTIME PERFORMERS
A few examples: Will someone experience a wardrobe malfunction? Will one of the Red Hot Chili Peppers perform shirtless? What type of hat will Bruno Mars wear?

THE COIN TOSS
Through 2015, tails had a slight edge over heads in the pregame coin toss, with the score standing at tails 25, heads 24.

AP Photo/Greg Trott

MVP OF THE GAME
When linebacker Malcolm Smith won the MVP trophy in 2014, his name had not even been listed on the betting sheet, so those who put money on "the field" received a payout.

AP Photo/Todd Rosenberg

THE GROWING PHENOMENON OF
SUPER BOWL PARTIES

As appealing as one's own couch can be on game day, when the nation's biggest football game rolls around, more than one-fourth of Americans will venture out to a Super Bowl party, and the social side of Super Sunday becomes more of a phenomenon every year.

A 2015 study by the National Retail Federation revealed that of the 184 million people estimated to watch Super Bowl XLIX on TV, 25.9 percent planned to catch the action at a party. An additional 13 million, or 7 percent, would watch the game at a restaurant or bar. And where there are parties, there is spending, and Super Bowl parties do their fair share to contribute to the American economy. The typical game viewer surveyed spent an average of $77.88 on food, decorations, or other Super Bowl accouterments, with the total spending linked to the big game exceeding $14 million.

Whether party guests are avid football fans—the ones planted on the couch with a prime view of the action—or the people at every party more interested in proximity to the guacamole than the game, the Super Bowl party has become entrenched in American tradition.

NFL Chief Marketing Officer Mark Waller has called professional football "America's last great campfire," and on Super Bowl Sunday campers are gathered around the warm glow of large-screen televisions, often newly purchased. Of the viewers polled in the NRF study, 8.8 percent planned to buy a new TV to get the crispest and most authentic view of the Super Bowl possible.

Even through lean economic seasons and scandals in the NFL, everything that touches the Super Bowl is on an upward curve, so it's no surprise that new parties crop up every year. And as the halftime show and the commercials have sought to edge touchdowns and tackles out of the spotlight in the past two decades, non-sports fans have plenty of motivation to show up at a party—even if they never actually know the score of the game.

In an era when the Super Bowl XLVIII halftime performance drew four million more viewers than the game itself, parties in every corner of the nation reach their apex when the players jog into the locker room for the midgame break. But that wasn't always the case. Thirty years ago, a Pennsylvania dietician named Mary Pinto addressed the problem of Super Bowl gluttony in an Associated Press article, proving simultaneously that in 1985 big game parties were on America's radar and the halftime show was not.

In the story, Pinto suggested an ideal solution for Super Bowl partygoers who were worried about consuming too many calories during the game: taking a brisk walk or a jog during halftime. "Most of the halftime show is just a replay of the first half anyway," she said. "Why watch when you can run around the block? If you don't, you might just end up with a bigger end zone."

According to a *Time* magazine study, 26 percent of Americans will attend Super Bowl parties, and 18 percent will host one.

13 MILLION
PEOPLE EXPECTED TO TRAVEL TO LOCAL BAR

43 MILLION
PEOPLE PLAN TO HOST SUPER BOWL PARTIES

$14 MILLION
TOTAL SPENT ON FOOD, DECORATIONS, AND OTHER SUPER BOWL ACCOUTERMENTS

For a January 2014 segment on *Good Morning America*, employees of the website Buzzfeed built a colossal snack spread platform called the "Snackadium" on the show's outdoor set, using hot dogs and hamburgers as a foundation and 16 metal office supply bins to hold everything from cold cuts to candy. "If you think that constructing a field goal post out of beef jerky isn't just as physically demanding as playing in the Super Bowl, then you're wrong," Buzzfeed food editor Emily Fleischaker told *GMA* host Josh Elliott.

The Buzzfeed snack arena, complete with a field of guacamole and bean dip end zones, is just one of many snack stadium iterations available as the centerpiece for any neighborhood Super Bowl party with an industrious host. Party planners might well spend days constructing their snackadium and filling it with every manner of party food, but the growing trend indicates that hosts would consider it time

well spent if the edible stadium properly highlights the most important element of any Super Bowl party: the food.

The snackadium is a fitting symbol for the nation's second-largest food consumption day after Thanksgiving, especially since it is designed to hold a vast array of party food selections. But despite the increase of football-themed dishes and presentation fueled by websites such as Pinterest, a few tried-and-true classic dishes still make up the core of most Super Bowl Sunday spreads.

Chips and dip, chicken wings, pizza, beer, and soda are considered the compulsory staples, and in recent years some astounding statistics have backed up the hunch that America's diet on that one Sunday evening could constitute a public health crisis.

Friends have been gathering and snacking on Super Bowl Sunday for decades, but

if consumption figures are any indication, the number and scope of parties are on the rise nationwide. And according to Jan DeLyser of the California Avocado Commission, the Super Bowl might be partly responsible for their fruit's massive surge in popularity as a party food in the past decade.

As early as the 1970s, the Avocado Commission conducted marketing campaigns to connect guacamole and other avocado-based products with the Super Bowl, DeLyser said, and the two have become more intertwined each year. In 2004, Americans consumed 32.4 million pounds of avocado on Super Bowl Sunday. Just a decade later in 2004, the nation's total avocado consumption was 99.1 million pounds. In recent years, the Fourth of July has surpassed the Super Bowl as the top avocado holiday, DeLyser said, but the Super Bowl set the pace in those early years.

All of those avocados, wings, and pizza can get pricey for a Super Bowl party host, especially for those who throw subtlety to the wind and construct a snackadium. But the grocery store hauls of most party hosts don't even approach the price tag of the party offered by the Old Homestead Steakhouse in New York City.

For a hefty $150,000, a football fan with a taste for the extravagant can offer 20 friends the game spread of a lifetime: made to order to the host's specifications, but with menu options such as Porterhouse steaks, lobster, and Dom Perignon champagne. The host chooses the menu, party time, and location, and Old Homestead provides the best of everything.

"It's over-the-top expensive, excessive and extraordinary—but so is the Super Bowl," Old Homestead co-owner Marc Sherry told the *New York Daily News*.

GAME-DAY GRUB

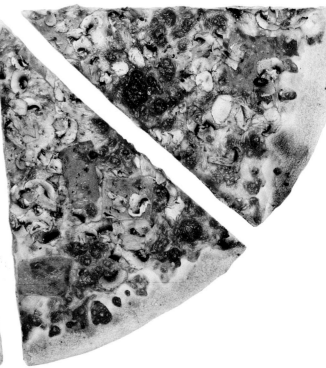

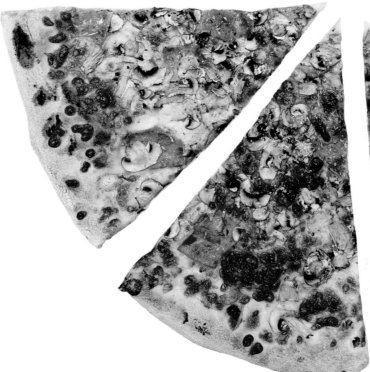

Careful studies of Super Bowl consumption reveal that Americans eat:

80 MILLION

avocados, mostly in the form of guacamole, enough to fill a football field 12 feet deep. (*Men's Health*)

11 MILLION SLICES

of pizza. Twice as many pizzas as any other day of the year, according to several major chains. (*Domino's*)

FOOT-LONG FACT

The classic game-day submarine sandwich, monikered "sub" because it resembles an actual submarine vessel, is also known regionally in the United States as a "hero," "grinder," "hoagie," and "po' boy."

8 MILLION POUNDS
of popcorn (*Shape*)

1.25 BILLION
portions of chicken wings,
enough to put 572 wings on
every seat in all 32 NFL stadiums
(*American Chicken Council*)

11 MILLION POUNDS
of tortilla and potato chips (*Shape*)

$2.37 MILLION
spent on soda (*Shape*)

20% INCREASE
in antacid sales the Monday after the
big game (*Huffington Post/Poo-Pourri*)

" I WANT YOU TO STEP BACK FROM THE GUACAMOLE DIP. I WANT YOU TO PUT THE CHICKEN FINGERS DOWN AND TURN YOUR TELEVISION ALL THE WAY UP!"

Bruce Springsteen

CHAPTER 15: LIVE ENTERTAINMENT

AP Photo / Jim Mahoney

American sports were already inextricably linked with "The Star-Spangled Banner" when the Super Bowl started—it was first sung at a national sporting event at a 1918 World Series game between the Red Sox and the Cubs—and from Super Bowl I on, the song has been performed by pop stars, country singers, marching bands, singing groups, and one renowned opera singer.

Far more understated than the halftime show for obvious reasons of patriotism, the national anthem has still, over the years, borne the distinct personalities of the artists delivering it. And through the years, host stadiums have become increasingly compelled to plan some accompaniment to the anthem, such as the giant flag stretched out on the field and the fireworks that highlighted opera star Renée Fleming's rendition in 2014.

Singer Idina Menzel performs the national anthem prior to Super Bowl XLIX between the New England Patriots and Seattle Seahawks.
AP Photo/Perry Knotts

SUPER BOWL IV

1970

AL HIRT

SUPER BOWL XXV

1991

WHITNEY HOUSTON

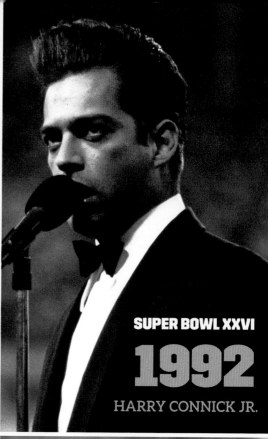

SUPER BOWL XXVI

1992

HARRY CONNICK JR.

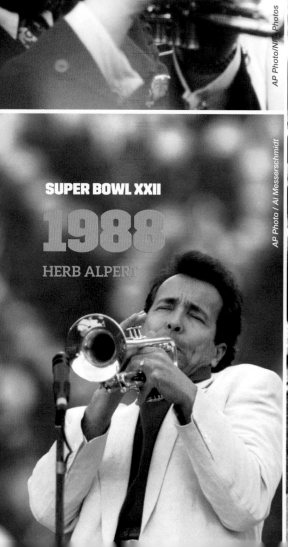

SUPER BOWL XXII

1988

HERB ALPERT

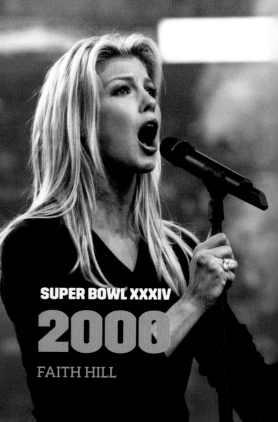

SUPER BOWL XXXIV

2000

FAITH HILL

SUPER BOWL XL

2006

ARETHA FRANKLIN

AP Photo/David Drapkin

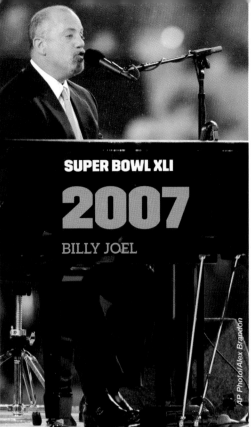

SUPER BOWL XLI

2007

BILLY JOEL

AP Photo/Alex Brandon

SUPER BOWL XLIV

2010

CARRIE UNDERWOOD

AP Photo/David J. Phillip

For television viewers, camera crews know that a requisite part of experiencing America's song is watching football stars moved to tears as they absorb the song, the stadium, the moment—sometimes singing along, sometimes just soaking it all in. The Super Bowl as an event is rife with excess, but to see those men's faces is to boil it down to the essence of the game and the players who are seeing the realization of a dream.

Instrumental accompaniment has ranged from nonexistent in a cappella versions to full orchestras, but the anthem stands or fails on the ability of the vocalist to command a huge stadium with a big song. The high points, through five decades of renditions, have ranged from jazz trumpeter Al Hirt's unique performance in Super Bowl IV to Whitney Houston's soul-rending version at Super Bowl XXV, stirring a nation galvanized by the Persian Gulf War. Rolling Stone called it "one of the most stunning moments in American sports history."

Houston's national anthem was so treasured that it made two different appearances on the Billboard Top 20 charts: once in 1991 after that Super Bowl and again a decade later after the 9/11 attacks. Faith Hill's spare, beautiful interpretation of the song at Super Bowl XXXIV has shown up on the national country charts several times since she performed it in Atlanta.

Of course, there have been national anthem misadventures through the decades, too, such as when pop diva Christina Aguilera flubbed the lyrics at XLV and country star Garth Brooks walked out of the stadium 45 minutes before he was scheduled to sing at Super Bowl XXVII because of a dispute with NBC over the airing of his new music video. (The network and Brooks reached a détente just in the nick of time but not before the Super Bowl staff spotted Jon Bon Jovi in the stands and asked him to be on standby.)

Since the Brooks controversy, the NFL has recommended that artists prerecord their anthems, and singers such as Jennifer Hudson were known to have lip-synched their renditions of the song. As former Super Bowl music director Ricky Minor said in *The Making of the Super Bowl: The Inside Story of the World's Greatest Sporting Event*, prerecording is encouraged because there is no stage more massive—and no setting in which a miscue would receive more negative attention.

"That's the right way to do it," Minor said. "There's too many variables to go live. I would never recommend any artist go live, because the slightest glitch would devastate the performance."

HALFTIME SHOWS

The first halftime show ever presented during a pro football game, in 1922, featured dog tricks, a Wild West demonstration, and an appearance by the legendary Jim Thorpe. When the first Super Bowl was played 45 years later, entertainment was a requisite part of the football experience, but the halftime show of today's big game bears little resemblance to those that broke up the action in the early years.

From marching bands to showcases for pop icons, with detours into campiness, patriotism, and even a touch of scandal, the Super Bowl halftime performance has traveled the same trajectory as everything else that touches America's greatest sporting event—every year flashier, more high-tech, and more extravagant.

SUPER BOWL I

1967

UNIVERSITY OF ARIZONA
SYMPHONIC MARCHING
BAND // GRAMBLING STATE
UNIVERSITY MARCHING BAND
AL HIRT // ANAHEIM HIGH
SCHOOL DRILL TEAM AND
FLAG GIRLS

SUPER BOWL II

1968

GRAMBLING STATE
UNIVERSITY MARCHING
BAND

SUPER BOWL III

1969

"AMERICA THANKS"

FLORIDA A&M UNIVERSITY
MARCHING BAND // MIAMI-
AREA HIGH SCHOOL
MARCHING BANDS

At Super Bowl III the narrator
quoted Martin Luther King Jr.,
who had been assassinated
the previous year.

GRAMBLING
STATE
MARCHING BAND

SUPER BOWL IV

1970

CAROL CHANNING
SOUTHERN
UNIVERSITY
MARCHING BAND

AP Photo

SUPER BOWL V

1971

UP WITH PEOPLE
SOUTHEAST MISSOURI
STATE MARCHING BAND

SUPER BOWL VI

1972

"SALUTE TO LOUIS
ARMSTRONG"

ELLA FITZGERALD
CAROL CHANNING
AL HIRT // U.S. MARINE
CORPS DRILL TEAM

Ella Fitzgerald led a tribute
to another jazz legend, Louis
Armstrong, who had died the
year before.

AP Photo/NFL Photos

SUPER BOWL VII

1973

"HAPPINESS IS"

UNIVERSITY OF MICHIGAN
MARCHING BAND
WOODY HERMAN
ANDY WILLIAMS

AP Photo/NFL Photos

SUPER BOWL VIII

1974

"A MUSICAL AMERICA"

UNIVERSITY OF TEXAS
LONGHORN BAND
JUDY MALLETT (MISS
TEXAS 1973) ON FIDDLE

THE EVENTS

300

SUPER BOWL IX

1975

"TRIBUTE TO DUKE
ELLINGTON"

MERCER ELLINGTON
GRAMBLING STATE
UNIVERSITY MARCHING
BAND

AP Photo/NFL Photos

SUPER BOWL X

1976

"200 YEARS AND
JUST A BABY"

UP WITH PEOPLE

SUPER BOWL X
WAS THE FIRST
TO BRING IN A
CONCERT-QUALITY
SOUND SYSTEM
FOR THE HALFTIME
PERFORMANCE

SUPER BOWL XI

1977

"IT'S A SMALL WORLD"

LOS ANGELES UNIFIED ALL-
CITY BAND // AUDIENCE
CARD STUNT

"SUPER BOWL XIII CARNIVAL"

KEN HAMILTON
VARIOUS CARIBBEAN BANDS

Few early halftime shows illustrate the early chaos of football's premier entertainment act more vividly than the Caribbean Carnival of Super Bowl XIII. At the midway point of the game between the Steelers and the Cowboys, an actor named Ken Hamilton hosted a tour of Caribbean nations, all set on a massive blue tarp featuring painted versions of various islands. Fans were taken on a tour of the Caribbean courtesy of a rolling boat-float captained by Hamilton.

Jim Steeg, who oversaw 26 halftime performances over the years, could later take credit for such marvels as Michael Jackson at Super Bowl XXVII and U2 at Super Bowl XXXVI, but the Caribbean cruise was his first and most mishap-riddled show. First, the musicians booked to represent Haiti didn't show up, and then the engine on the float died "somewhere around Puerto Rico," as Steeg recalled to ESPN.com in 2007. And in the coup de grace, the float got hung on the goalpost as it tried to exit the field, holding up the second half by eight minutes and infuriating Pittsburgh head coach Chuck Noll.

SUPER BOWL XII

1978

"FROM PARIS TO THE PARIS OF AMERICA"

TYLER APACHE BELLES DRILL TEAM AND APACHE BAND // PETE FOUNTAIN AL HIRT

The halftime show at Super Bowl XII featured two Frisbee-catching dogs.

AP Photo/Scott Boehm

SUPER BOWL XIV

1980

"A SALUTE TO THE BIG BAND ERA"

UP WITH PEOPLE
GRAMBLING STATE UNIVERSITY MARCHING BAND

AP Photo/NFL Photos

SUPER BOWL XV

1981

"A MARDI GRAS FESTIVAL"

SOUTHERN UNIVERSITY
MARCHING BAND
HELEN O'CONNELL

SUPER BOWL XVI

1982

"A SALUTE TO THE
'60s AND MOTOWN"

UP WITH PEOPLE

SUPER BOWL XVII

1983

"KALEIDO-SUPER-SCOPE"

LOS ANGELES SUPER
DRILL TEAM

SUPER BOWL XVIII

1984

"SUPER BOWL XVIII'S
SALUTE TO THE
SUPERSTARS OF THE
SILVER SCREEN"

UNIVERSITY OF
FLORIDA MARCHING
BAND // FLORIDA STATE
UNIVERSITY MARCHING
BAND

SUPER BOWL XIX

1985

"A WORLD OF
CHILDREN'S DREAMS"

TOPS IN BLUE

SUPER BOWL XX

1986

"BEAT OF THE
FUTURE"

UP WITH PEOPLE

Up With People's halftime
performance at Super Bowl
XX was the first to use a large
wooden stage—it stretched
from one 32-yard line to
the other—that had to be
assembled on the field.

SUPER BOWL XXI

1987

"SALUTE TO HOLLYWOOD'S
100TH ANNIVERSARY"

GEORGE BURNS // MICKEY
ROONEY // GRAMBLING
STATE UNIVERSITY
MARCHING BAND // USC
MARCHING BAND
DISNEY CHARACTERS
SOUTHERN CALIFORNIA-
AREA HIGH SCHOOL DRILL
TEAMS AND DANCERS

Super Bowl XXI was a tribute
to a century of Hollywood,
featuring a variety of
performers and costumed
Disney characters.

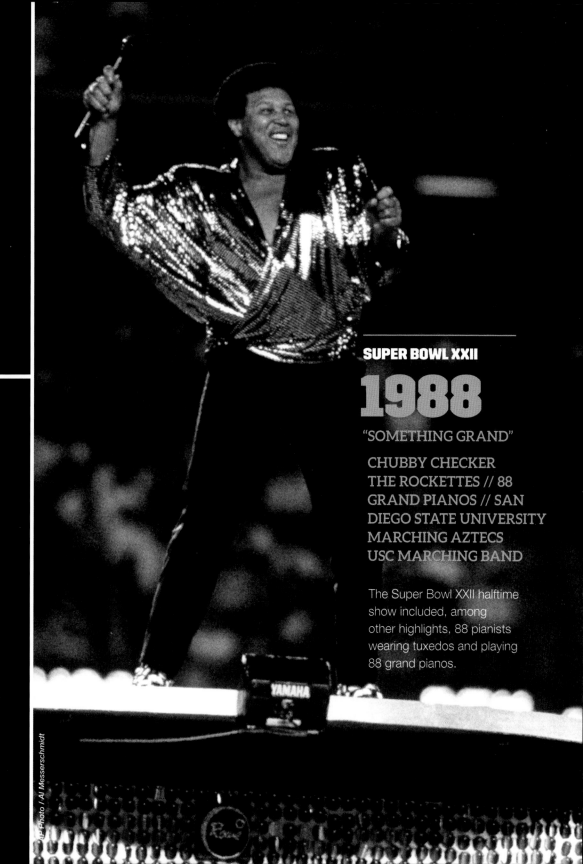

AP Photo / Al Messerschmidt

SUPER BOWL XXII

1988

"SOMETHING GRAND"

CHUBBY CHECKER
THE ROCKETTES // 88
GRAND PIANOS // SAN
DIEGO STATE UNIVERSITY
MARCHING AZTECS
USC MARCHING BAND

The Super Bowl XXII halftime
show included, among
other highlights, 88 pianists
wearing tuxedos and playing
88 grand pianos.

1989

"BE BOP BAMBOOZLED"

ELVIS PRESTO // SOUTH
FLORIDA-AREA DANCERS
AND PERFORMERS

It is alternately considered one of the strangest halftime shows in Super Bowl history and an extravaganza that helped turn the tide from glorified marching band performance to full-scale production. The Super Bowl XXIII spectacle featured a Solid Gold dancer named Alex Cole playing the part of "Elvis Presto," 3D glasses for everyone in Joe Robbie Stadium, and a stunt known as the world's largest card trick, featuring replicas of playing cards underneath every seat.

Known as "Be-Bop Bamboozled," the show was campy and outrageous, but its sheer over-the-top nature set the pace for what would become must-watch halftime entertainment. The producer of the event, Dan Witkowski, was an unknown who won the NFL over with his plans for an ambitious extravaganza that is, for better or worse, remembered vividly decades later. "Would we do it the same now? Of course not," Witkowski told popdust.com in 2011. "But it was just a fluffy thing."

AP Photo / Al Messerschmidt

SUPER BOWL XXIV

1990

"SALUTE TO
NEW ORLEANS"

PETE FOUNTAIN // DOUG
KERSHAW // IRMA
THOMAS // NICHOLLS
STATE UNIVERSITY
MARCHING BAND
SOUTHERN UNIVERSITY
MARCHING BAND
USL MARCHING BAND

SUPER BOWL XXV

1991

"A SMALL WORLD
SALUTE TO 25 YEARS
OF THE SUPER BOWL"

NEW KIDS ON THE BLOCK
DISNEY CHARACTERS
WARREN MOON // 2,000
LOCAL CHILDREN
AUDIENCE CARD STUNT

SUPER BOWL XXVI

1992

"WINTER MAGIC"

GLORIA ESTEFAN
OLYMPIC FIGURE SKATERS
BRIAN BOITANO AND
DOROTHY HAMILL

Figure skating at the Super
Bowl—this unusual act
featured skaters Brian
Boitano and Dorothy Hamill
opening the Super Bowl XXVI
halftime show.

Fox aired a live episode of
"In Living Color" during
halftime in an effort to attract
viewers to their network.
The public relations ploy
worked—Super Bowl ratings
went down 10 points
during halftime.

1993

"HEAL THE WORLD"

MICHAEL JACKSON

The show that lit up halftime at Super Bowl XXVII is still the gold standard of halftime performances—the first time a superstar shined brightly enough to fill all of the spaces of the nation's most massive sporting event. The star was, of course, Michael Jackson, and the King of Pop reigned powerfully at the Rose Bowl, mixing his signature dance moves with his peerless style—the white glove, the gold military-style jacket, the black fedora pulled down low.

As Jackson commanded the field through numbers such as "Billie Jean" and "Black or White," viewers who had ignored the football action preceding the show started to tune in—and Super Bowl XXVII was later revealed as the first big game to see a spike in ratings during halftime. As quickly as Jackson could moonwalk, TV executives understood the power of the halftime performance to broaden the reach of the Super Sunday phenomenon.

AP Photo/Rusty Kennedy

SUPER BOWL XXIX

1995

"INDIANA JONES AND THE TEMPLE OF THE FORBIDDEN EYE"

PATTI LABELLE
INDIANA JONES AND MARION RAVENWOOD
TEDDY PENDERGRASS
TONY BENNETT
ARTURO SANDOVAL
MIAMI SOUND MACHINE

SUPER BOWL XXVIII

1994

"ROCKIN' COUNTRY SUNDAY"

CLINT BLACK // TANYA TUCKER
TRAVIS TRITT // THE JUDDS

SUPER BOWL XXX

1996

"TAKE ME HIGHER: A CELEBRATION OF 30 YEARS OF THE SUPER BOWL"

DIANA ROSS

To make a dramatic exit from her Super Bowl XXX performance, Diana Ross was removed from the field by a helicopter.

AP Photo / Al Messerschmidt

AP Photo/Kevin Reece

AP Photo/Elaine Thompson

AP Photo/Mark Duncan

SUPER BOWL XXXI

1997

"BLUES BROTHERS BASH"

THE BLUES BROTHERS
(Dan Aykroyd, John Goodman,
James Belushi)
JAMES BROWN // ZZ TOP
CATHERINE CRIER

SUPER BOWL XXXII

1998

"A TRIBUTE TO MOTOWN'S 40TH ANNIVERSARY"

BOYZ II MEN // SMOKEY ROBINSON
MARTHA REEVES // THE TEMPTATIONS
QUEEN LATIFAH // GRAMBLING STATE
UNIVERSITY MARCHING BAND

SUPER BOWL XXXIII

1999

"CELEBRATION OF SOUL, SALSA, AND SWING"

GLORIA ESTEFAN // STEVIE WONDER
BIG BAD VOODOO DADDY
SAVION GLOVER

THE EVENTS

SUPER BOWL XXXIV

2000

"A TAPESTRY OF NATIONS"

PHIL COLLINS
TINA TURNER
CHRISTINA AGUILERA
ENRIQUE IGLESIAS
TONI BRAXTON

FEATURING
80-person choir
Edward James Olmos (narrator)

AP Photo / Al Messerschmidt

AP Photo / Al Messerschmidt

AP Photo/Donna McWilliam

AP Photo/Amy Sancetta

AP Photo / Al Messerschmidt

SUPER BOWL XXXV

2001

"THE KINGS OF ROCK AND POP"

AEROSMITH // 'N SYNC
BRITNEY SPEARS
MARY J. BLIGE // NELLY

SUPER BOWL XXXVI

2002

U2

Fewer than five months before the Rams and the Patriots took the field in Super Bowl XXXVI, thousands of Americans perished in the 9/11 attacks. The Super Bowl that followed the nation's most profound loss naturally included some tributes—a stirring Budweiser ad and Mariah Carey's powerful rendition of the national anthem among them. But the most memorable acknowledgment of the victims came at halftime, in a show featuring a rock band from Ireland.

U2 wasn't originally scheduled to headline halftime that year, but after agreeing to perform, Janet Jackson pulled out of the show because she wasn't comfortable with the role in wake of the 9/11 attacks. What resulted when Bono and company took the field was therapeutic and moving—as U2 performed, the names of each of the tragedy's 2,977 victims scrolled slowly across a mammoth screen hung at midfield. As the *Boston Globe's* Dan Shaughnessy wrote, "U2's Super Bowl halftime performance—with names of the deceased from 9/11 scrolling while they played 'Where the Streets Have No Name,' was the greatest halftime show in the history of sporting events. Hands down."

AP Photo/Tony Gutierrez

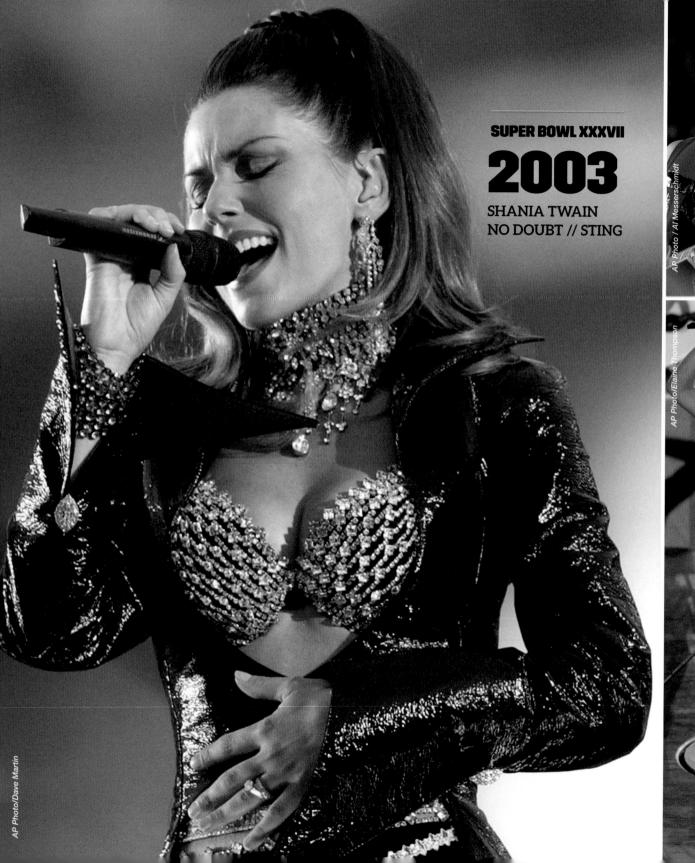

AP Photo/Dave Martin

2003

SHANIA TWAIN
NO DOUBT // STING

AP Photo / Al Messerschmidt

AP Photo/Elaine Thompson

SUPER BOWL XXXVIII
2004
JANET JACKSON // P. DIDDY // NELLY
KID ROCK // JUSTIN TIMBERLAKE

AP Photo/Elise Amendola

AP Photo/David Phillip

Janet Jackson declined to perform at the post-9/11 halftime, but when she appeared as the headliner two years later, she became part of Super Bowl lore in the world's most notorious case of indecent exposure. In just a few seconds, as Justin Timberlake reached for her jacket as he sang the words, "Gonna have you naked at the end of this song," Jackson was exposed to hundreds of millions of TV viewers for 9/16 of a second, a new phrase was coined in America and the halftime performances of the future were immediately put on high alert.

So pivotal was the event that became immortalized as the "wardrobe malfunction" that the network airing the Super Bowl instituted a five-second delay for the halftime broadcast. To help ward off any future embarrassing incidents, the NFL also dipped into its aging rocker file for the next six Super Bowls, with featured performers including Mick Jagger, Paul McCartney, and the Who. The snafu even led to the launch of the ubiquitous video-sharing website YouTube, whose founders were inspired by their fruitless search for videos of the incident in the days following the Super Bowl.

© ZUMA Press, Inc./Alamy

AP Photo/Amy Sancetta

2005

PAUL MCCARTNEY

Paul McCartney represented the first older rock legend to take the stage, booked as a safe act after the wardrobe catastrophe of the year before.

Jeff Lewis Photography

SUPER BOWL XL

2006
THE ROLLING STONES

AP Photo/Jeff Roberson

AP Photo/David J. Phillip

AP Photo/Carlos Osorio

2007

PRINCE

FEATURING:
Florida A&M University Marching
100 Band

As *Rolling Stone* proclaimed in its ranking of top halftime shows, "No one is cooler than Prince. It's a scientific fact." And when he brought that inimitable coolness to the massive stage of the Super Bowl XLI halftime show, the artist currently known as Prince turned in a performance as cutting-edge as anyone at the top of the charts in 2007. With an electric mix of his own hits such as "Baby, I'm a Star" and "Let's Go Crazy" with classic covers of songs such as "All Along the Watchtower" and "Proud Mary," Prince set a new standard for what halftime star power looks like nearly 15 years after Michael Jackson first stole the show.

To cap off what was already an epic concert, Prince sang his iconic "Purple Rain" as showers fell around him in Sun Life Stadium. "The heavy rain made the smoke and lights seem mysterious, instead of merely ridiculous. And there was a sneaky thrill in watching Prince steal the field from guys three times his size, if only for a few moments," wrote Kelefa Sanneh in a *New York Times* review.

AP Photo/Kevork Djansezian

AP Photo/Mark Humphrey

AP Photo/Winslow Townson, file

AP Photo/Amy Sancetta

AP Photo/Charlie Krupa

AP Photo/Paul Spinelli

SUPER BOWL XLV

2011

THE BLACK EYED PEAS
USHER // SLASH

FEATURING:
Dallas/Ft. Worth-area
high school drill teams
and dancers

© ZUMA Press, Inc. / Alamy

AP Photo/Chris O'Meara

SUPER BOWL XLVI

2012

MADONNA // NICKI MINAJ
M.I.A. // LMFAO //CEE LO GREEN

FEATURING:
Andy Lewis
Avon High School Drumline
Center Grove High School Drumline
Cirque Du Soleil
Fishers High School Drumline
Franklin Central High School Drumline
Southern University Dancing Dolls
200-person choir of Indianapolis locals

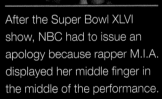

After the Super Bowl XLVI
show, NBC had to issue an
apology because rapper M.I.A.
displayed her middle finger in
the middle of the performance.

Photo by Frank Micelotta/Invsion/AP

AP Photo/Paul Sancya

AP Photo/Ben Liebenberg

SUPER BOWL XLVII

2013

BEYONCÉ
DESTINY'S CHILD

Beyonce's reunion with
Destiny's Child, which
featured a dozen dancers
and a flaming stage,
was considered a top
performance.

Jeff Lewis Photography

2014

BRUNO MARS
RED HOT CHILI PEPPERS

Bruno Mars's performance attracted 115.3 million viewers—4 million more than the game itself.

AP Photo/Todd Rosenberg

AP Photo/Ben Margot

AP Photo/Paul Sancya

2015

**KATY PERRY
LENNY KRAVITZ
MISSY ELLIOTT**

FEATURING:
Arizona State University
Sun Devil Marching Band

As the NFL made its decision about the halftime entertainment for Super Bowl XLIX, the league reportedly asked some of the performers who were in contention to contribute a portion of their post–Super Bowl income back to the NFL. When Katy Perry was announced as the headliner, she told ESPN that she would not agree to the "pay to play" proposal.

Jeff Lewis Photography

Jeff Lewis Photography

AP Photo/Ben Margot

AP Photo/David J. Phillip

CONCLUSION

It was 1990, and the nation was preparing to celebrate the first landmark anniversary of the Super Bowl—the twenty-fifth. In the introduction for a book lauding the first quarter century of the game, Pete Rozelle, who had just retired the year before as the NFL commissioner, marveled at the scope of the spectacle he had helped create.

"For Super Bowl XXV, ABC is getting $850,000 for one 30-second commercial!" Rozelle wrote in *The Super Bowl: Celebrating a Quarter-Century of America's Greatest Game*. "I don't care what kind of financial numbers you're used to, that's a staggering amount."

We can only surmise how professional football's greatest early visionary would react to the news that 30-second spots for the fiftieth game will cost advertisers about $5 million or the fact that twice as many Americans today tune in to watch the NFL draft in April as the final game for the world's most popular sporting event, the World Cup.

The Super Bowl is already gargantuan by any measure you wish to apply: ticket prices, the cost of airing commercials, social media reach, TV viewership, or the star power of the halftime performers. What started as an idea for an exciting football game between competing leagues became the athletic flashpoint for a nation, and the meteoric rise of all things touching the Super Bowl shows no sign of slowing.

In the late '70s, NFL commissioner Rozelle hired a mild-mannered 33-year-old Indiana native as the league's director of special events. Jim Steeg always shunned the spotlight, but in his 26 years in that position, the so-called Super Bowl Czar did more than perhaps anyone else to add voltage and transform the big game into a colossal happening.

Steeg is credited with, among other things, bringing the first big-name singer to the microphone for the national anthem when he invited Diana Ross in 1981, installing the first giant TV screen in a stadium in 1983, orchestrating Michael Jackson's historic halftime show in 1993, and helping select U2 as the ideal artist to take the Super Bowl stage just months after 9/11.

In 2007 Steeg left the NFL for a position with the San Diego Chargers, but the event he and Rozelle helped transform from a mere championship game into an engrossing phenomenon shows no signs of hitting a plateau. Like a snowball that triggered an avalanche, the Super Bowl is still barreling downhill, pulling in more fans, more dollars, and more hype every time the NFL's two top teams meet with more than a half century of history behind them.

SUPER BOWL MASTER CHART

GAMES	DATE	WINNING TEAM	LOSING TEAM	SCORE	SITE	NATIONAL ANTHEM	HALFTIME HEADLINER
Super Bowl I	1/15/1967	Green Bay Packers	Kansas City Chiefs	35-10	Memorial Coliseum, Los Angeles	University of Arizona Band	University of Arizona Band
Super Bowl II	1/14/1968	Green Bay Packers	Oakland Raiders	33-14	Orange Bowl, Miami	Grambling State Band	Grambling State Band
Super Bowl III	1/12/1969	New York Jets	Baltimore Colts	16-7	Orange Bowl, Miami	Lloyd Geisler	Florida A&M Band
Super Bowl IV	1/11/1970	Kansas City Chiefs	Minnesota Vikings	23-7	Tulane Stadium, New Orleans	Al Hirt	Carol Channing
Super Bowl V	1/17/1971	Baltimore Colts	Dallas Cowboys	16-13	Orange Bowl, Miami	Tommy Loy	Up With People
Super Bowl VI	1/16/1972	Dallas Cowboys	Miami Dolphins	24-3	Tulane Stadium, New Orleans	U.S. Air Force Chorale	Ella Fitzgerald
Super Bowl VII	1/14/1973	Miami Dolphins	Washington Redskins	14-7	Memorial Coliseum, Los Angeles	Little Angels Choir	University of Michigan Band
Super Bowl VIII	1/13/1974	Miami Dolphins	Minnesota Vikings	24-7	Rice Stadium, Houston	Charley Pride	University of Texas Band
Super Bowl IX	1/12/1975	Pittsburgh Steelers	Minnesota Vikings	16-6	Tulane Stadium, New Orleans	Grambling State Band	Mercer Ellington
Super Bowl X	1/18/1976	Pittsburgh Steelers	Dallas Cowboys	21-17	Orange Bowl, Miami	Tom Sullivan	Up With People
Super Bowl XI	1/9/1977	Oakland Raiders	Minnesota Vikings	32-14	Rose Bowl, Pasadena	Vikki Carr, "America the Beautiful"	Los Angeles Unified Band
Super Bowl XII	1/15/1978	Dallas Cowboys	Denver Broncos	27-10	Superdome, New Orleans	Phyllis Kelly	Tyler Apache Belles Drill Team
Super Bowl XIII	1/21/1979	Pittsburgh Steelers	Dallas Cowboys	35-31	Orange Bowl, Miami	The Colgate Thirteen	Ken Hamilton
Super Bowl XIV	1/20/1980	Pittsburgh Steelers	Los Angeles Rams	31-19	Rose Bowl, Pasadena	Cheryl Ladd	Up With People
Super Bowl XV	1/25/1981	Oakland Raiders	Philadelphia Eagles	27-10	Superdome, New Orleans	Helen O'Connell	Southern University Band
Super Bowl XVI	1/24/1982	San Francisco 49ers	Cincinnati Bengals	26-21	Silverdome, Pontiac, MI	Diana Ross	Up With People
Super Bowl XVII	1/30/1983	Washington Redskins	Miami Dolphins	27-17	Rose Bowl, Pasadena	Leslie Easterbrook	Los Angeles Super Drill Team
Super Bowl XVIII	1/22/1984	Los Angeles Raiders	Washington Redskins	38-9	Tampa Stadium, Tampa	Barry Manilow	Florida and Florida State Bands
Super Bowl XIX	1/20/1985	San Francisco 49ers	Miami Dolphins	38-16	Stanford Stadium, Stanford, CA	San Francisco Chorus	Tops in Blue
Super Bowl XX	1/26/1986	Chicago Bears	New England Patriots	46-10	Superdome, New Orleans	Wynton Marsalis	Up With People
Super Bowl XXI	1/25/1987	New York Giants	Denver Broncos	39-20	Rose Bowl, Pasadena	Neil Diamond	George Burns, Mickey Rooney
Super Bowl XXII	1/31/1988	Washington Redskins	Denver Broncos	42-10	Jack Murphy Stadium, San Diego	Herb Alpert	Chubby Checker
Super Bowl XXIII	1/22/1989	San Francisco 49ers	Cincinnati Bengals	20-16	Joe Robbie Stadium, Miami	Billy Joel	Elvis Presto
Super Bowl XXIV	1/28/1990	San Francisco 49ers	Denver Broncos	55-10	Superdome, New Orleans	Aaron Neville	Pete Fountain
Super Bowl XXV	1/27/1991	New York Giants	Buffalo Bills	20-19	Tampa Stadium, Tampa	Whitney Houston	New Kids on the Block

GAMES	DATE	WINNING TEAM	LOSING TEAM	SCORE	SITE	NATIONAL ANTHEM	HALFTIME HEADLINER
Super Bowl XXVI	1/26/1992	Washington Redskins	Buffalo Bills	37-24	Metrodome, Minneapolis	Harry Connick Jr.	Gloria Estefan
Super Bowl XXVII	1/31/1993	Dallas Cowboys	Buffalo Bills	52-17	Rose Bowl, Pasadena	Garth Brooks	Michael Jackson
Super Bowl XXVIII	1/30/1994	Dallas Cowboys	Buffalo Bills	30-13	Georgia Dome, Atlanta	Natalie Cole	Clint Black
Super Bowl XXIX	1/29/1995	San Francisco 49ers	San Diego Chargers	49-26	Joe Robbie Stadium, Miami	Kathie Lee Gifford	Patti LaBelle
Super Bowl XXX	1/28/1996	Dallas Cowboys	Pittsburgh Steelers	27-17	Sun Devil Stadium, Tempe, AZ	Vanessa Williams	Diana Ross
Super Bowl XXXI	1/26/1997	Green Bay Packers	New England Patriots	35-21	Superdome, New Orleans	Luther Vandross	The Blues Brothers
Super Bowl XXXII	1/25/1998	Denver Broncos	Green Bay Packers	31-24	Qualcomm Stadium, San Diego	Jewel	Boyz II Men
Super Bowl XXXIII	1/31/1999	Denver Broncos	Atlanta Falcons	34-19	Pro Player Stadium, Miami	Cher	Gloria Estefan
Super Bowl XXXIV	1/30/2000	St. Louis Rams	Tennessee Titans	23-16	Georgia Dome, Atlanta	Faith Hill	Tina Turner
Super Bowl XXXV	1/28/2001	Baltimore Ravens	New York Giants	34-7	Raymond James Stadium, Tampa	Backstreet Boys	Aerosmith
Super Bowl XXXVI	2/3/2002	New England Patriots	St. Louis Rams	20-17	Superdome, New Orleans	Mariah Carey	U2
Super Bowl XXXVII	1/26/2003	Tampa Bay Buccaneers	Oakland Raiders	48-21	Qualcomm Stadium, San Diego	Dixie Chicks	Shania Twain
Super Bowl XXXVIII	2/1/2004	New England Patriots	Carolina Panthers	32-29	Reliant Stadium, Houston	Beyoncé	Janet Jackson
Super Bowl XXXIX	2/6/2005	New England Patriots	Philadelphia Eagles	24-21	Alltel Stadium, Jacksonville, FL	U.S. military combined choirs	Paul McCartney
Super Bowl XL	2/5/2006	Pittsburgh Steelers	Seattle Seahawks	21-10	Ford Field, Detroit	Aaron Neville, Aretha Franklin	The Rolling Stones
Super Bowl XLI	2/4/2007	Indianapolis Colts	Chicago Bears	29-17	Dolphin Stadium, Miami	Billy Joel	Prince
Super Bowl XLII	2/3/2008	New York Giants	New England Patriots	17-14	University of Phoenix Stadium	Jordin Sparks	Tom Petty
Super Bowl XLIII	2/1/2009	Pittsburgh Steelers	Arizona Cardinals	27-23	Raymond James Stadium, Tampa	Jennifer Hudson	Bruce Springsteen
Super Bowl XLIV	2/7/2010	New Orleans Saints	Indianapolis Colts	31-17	Sun Life Stadium, Miami	Carrie Underwood	The Who
Super Bowl XLV	2/6/2011	Green Bay Packers	Pittsburgh Steelers	31-25	Cowboys Stadium, Arlington, TX	Christina Aguilera	The Black Eyed Peas
Super Bowl XLVI	2/5/2012	New York Giants	New England Patriots	21-17	Lucas Oil Stadium, Indianapolis	Kelly Clarkson	Madonna
Super Bowl XLVII	2/3/2013	Baltimore Ravens	San Francisco 49ers	34-31	Superdome, New Orleans	Alicia Keys	Beyoncé
Super Bowl XLVIII	2/2/2014	Seattle Seahawks	Denver Broncos	43-8	Metlife Stadium, East Rutherford, NJ	Renée Fleming	Bruno Mars
Super Bowl XLIX	2/1/2015	New England Patriots	Seattle Seahawks	28-24	University of Phoenix Stadium	Idina Menzel	Katy Perry

BIBLIOGRAPHY

Freeman, Mike. *Undefeated: Inside the 1972 Miami Dolphins' Perfect Season*. New York: HarperCollins, 2012.

Jaworski, Ron. *The Games That Changed the Game: The Evolution of the NFL in Seven Sundays*. New York: Random House, 2010.

Lodato, Francis R., and Raymond M. *But We Were 17 and 0*. Lake Worth, FL: Q Pub, 1986.

MacCambridge, Michael. *America's Game*. New York: Random House, 2004.

McGinn, Bob. *The Ultimate Super Bowl Book*. 2nd ed. Minneapolis, MN: MVP Books, 2012.

Pearlman, Jeff. *Boys Will Be Boys*. New York: Harper Perennial, 2009.

Pomerantz, Gary. *Their Life's Work: The Brotherhood of the 1970s Pittsburgh Steelers, Then and Now*. New York: Simon and Schuster, 2013.

Wiebusch, John, ed. *The Super Bowl: Celebrating a Quarter-Century of America's Greatest Game*. New York: Simon and Schuster, 1990.

Online sources are available for review at www.SuperBowl50Book.com.

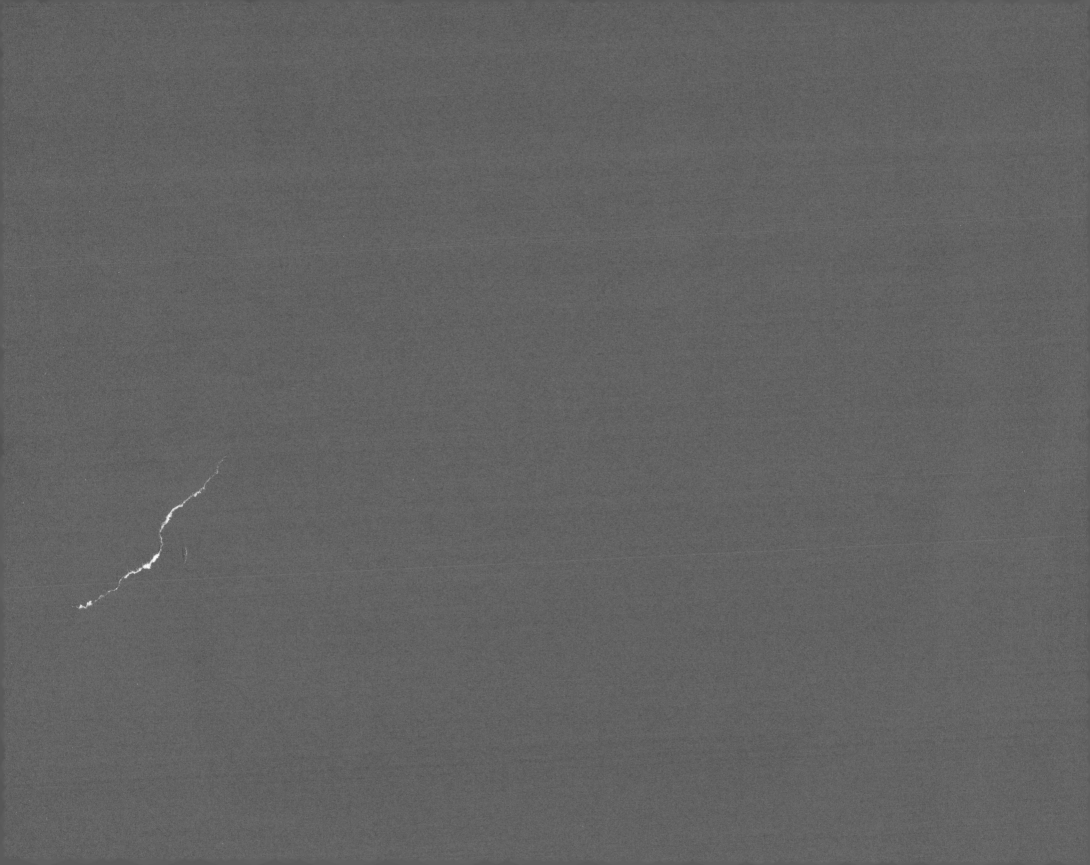